How Words Mean

For Edith
Thank you for *my* English words.

How Words Mean

Lexical concepts, cognitive models,
and meaning construction

VYVYAN EVANS

OXFORD
UNIVERSITY PRESS

OXFORD

UNIVERSITY PRESS

Great Clarendon Street, Oxford OX2 6DP

Oxford University Press is a department of the University of Oxford.
It furthers the University's objective of excellence in research, scholarship,
and education by publishing worldwide in

Oxford New York

Auckland   Cape Town Dar es Salaam   Hong Kong   Karachi
Kuala Lumpur Madrid Melbourne Mexico City   Nairobi
New Delhi Shanghai Taipei Toronto
With offices in
Argentina Austria Brazil Chile Czech Republic France Greece
Guatemala Hungary Italy Japan South Korea Poland Portugal
Singapore Switzerland Thailand Turkey Ukraine Vietnam

Published in the United States
by Oxford University Press Inc., New York

ISBN 978-0-19-923467-7

Printed in the United Kingdom by
Lightning Source UK Ltd., Milton Keynes

Contents

Words

OUT of us all
That make rhymes,
Will you choose
Sometimes—
As the winds use
A crack in the wall
Or a drain,
Their joy or their pain
To whistle through—
Choose me,
You English words?

I know you:
You are light as dreams,
Tough as oak,
Precious as gold,
As poppies and corn,
Or an old cloak;
Sweet as our birds
to the ear,
As the burnet rose
In the heat
Of Midsummer:
Strange as the races
Of dead and unborn:
Strange and sweet
Equally,
And familiar,
To the eye,
As the dearest faces
That a man knows,
And as lost homes are:
But though older far
Than oldest yew,
As our hills are, old,
Worn new
Again and again:

Young as our streams
After rain:
And as dear
As the earth which you prove
That we love.

Make me content
With some sweetness
From Wales,
Whose nightingales
Have no wings,
From Wiltshire and Kent
And Herefordshire,
And the villages there,
From the names, and the things
No less.
Let me sometimes dance
With you,
Or climb,
Or stand perchance
In ecstasy,
Fixed and free
In a rhyme,
As poets do.

Edward Thomas

Acknowledgements

LCCM Theory has been under development since May 2005. Since that time the research which has culminated in the present work has benefitted from discussions with a number of colleagues to whom I am indebted. For their feedback on many aspects of the ideas presented in the following pages I am particularly grateful to Daniel Casasanto, Paul Chilton, Alan Cienki, Peter Harder, George Lakoff, Chris Sinha, Andrea Tyler, and Jörg Zinken. For reading and commenting on various chapters I am extremely indebted to Daniel Casasanto, Peter Harder, and three anonymous readers for Oxford University Press. I also gratefully acknowledge the assistance of Laura Michaelis who provided leads and advice on certain aspects of Construction Grammar. I am grateful for the insight and wisdom of all of the above, and ask for their forbearance where I have chosen to ignore aspects of their excellent advice. No doubt the present work would be less prone to error than it otherwise is had I adopted all of the many sound suggestions that have been put to me. In addition, I owe a special thank you to Stéphanie Pourcel, both for her feedback on many of the issues and ideas presented here, and for her indefatigable support in all else. I am also grateful to two of my graduate students: Kyle Jasmin and Andrea Morgado de Matos. Both Kyle and Andrea have engaged with LCCM Theory in their own research, forcing me to rethink some significant details, making the work richer and sounder than it might otherwise have been. I also gratefully acknowledge the faith and support of John Davey, my editor at Oxford University Press. Finally, with immense gratitude, I acknowledge the support and love of my mother, Edith, who first taught me how words mean. This book is dedicated to her.

Preface

What is the subject matter of this book?

This book represents a contemporary treatment of word meaning and how words are combined in service of situated meaning in language understanding. That is, I am concerned with the areas that are traditionally referred to as *lexical semantics* and *compositional semantics*. I use the term *meaning construction* to refer to the phenomenon (or rather phenomena) I address in the following pages. The problem that the book seeks to address concerns how to account for the inherent variation in meaning exhibited by words, as is evident in their use in different contexts. That is, I am concerned with how words mean.

This problem comes in a number of forms, as illustrated below:

(1) a. He decided to declare his undying love for her
     b. He told the customs officer he had nothing to declare
     c. The Prime Minister, Neville Chamberlain, was obliged to declare war on Germany following the Nazi invasion of Poland

(2) a. France is a region of outstanding natural beauty
     b. France is a pivotal country in the European Union

(3) a. France defeated New Zealand in the 2007 Rugby World Cup
     b. The ham sandwich has wandering hands

(4) a. My boss is a pussycat
     b. The time for a decision has arrived

In the examples in (1), the form *declare* appears to have a distinct meaning in each example; in (1a), the meaning of *declare* relates to a forthright assertion of a particular fact or belief. In (1b) *declare* relates to a legal requirement to make a formal statement as to whether dutiable goods are being transported across an international border crossing. The use of *declare* in (1c) relates to a specific sort of speech act, which brings about a change in a given legal state (in this case bringing about a state of war between two nation states), which can only be performed by a person holding a particular officially sanctioned position in a given institution (in this case the head of the British government, officially appointed by the British monarch). The distinct meanings associated with *declare* are usually deemed, by linguists, to constitute conventional *senses* or *sense units*, which are stored in long-term semantic memory, typically referred to as the *mental lexicon*. That is, the different semantic contributions of *declare* in each example are held to be the result of (at least) three distinct meanings of *declare*, which are stored in memory.

In the examples in (2), the form *France* also appears to have a distinct meaning in each example. For instance, in (2a) *France* refers to a particular geographic region identified as France. In (2b) France relates to a particular political entity, a nation state which has political and economic influence of a particular sort. Yet, linguists ordinarily view variation of meaning of this sort as having a different status vis-à-vis the *declare* examples in (1). That is, France is not held to exhibit two distinct senses. Rather, the perspective often taken assumes that context serves to fill in, in some way, the precise semantic details, thereby allowing the language user to interpret the referent of *France* in each example.

The examples in (3) relate to the phenomenon known as *metonymy*, which makes use of a particular salient meaning associated with the form in order to identify a related referent. For instance, in (3a) *France* relates not to a geographical region or political nation state (as in (2)), but rather to a team of fifteen rugby players who represent France in the game of rugby. Similarly, in (3b) the *ham sandwich* relates to a customer who ordered a ham sandwich, in the context of an imaginary dialogue between two waitresses in a café. While some linguists have taken the view that metonymy is a function of inferencing strategies, guided by the context of use, as with the examples of France in (2), others, notably cognitive linguists, have assumed that metonymy is a conceptual phenomenon, and hence non-linguistic cognitive principles license given metonymic instances of words (see Kövecses and Radden 1998). Put another way, from this latter perspective, the variation in word meaning apparent in (3) is of a distinct kind from the nature of variation in word meaning apparent in (2), and, for that matter, in (1).

Finally, the examples in (4) have been variously referred to as *metaphor*. In (4a) the referent of *my boss* is being conceptualized in terms of some aspect of what it is to be a pussycat: presumably, qualities relating to relative docility. In (4b) *time* has motion ascribed to it: *arrived*. Yet, *time* does not relate to an entity that can literally arrive, in the same way, for instance, that other entities, such as people, can. Some scholars, working primarily on examples of the sort illustrated in (4a), involving the predicate nominative (or "is a") construction, have claimed that metaphor constitutes a form of comparison (e.g., Gentner, Bowdle, Wolff, and Boronat 2001). Others have argued that it involves a form of categorization (e.g., Carston 2002; Glucksberg 2003). Still others, notably Lakoff and Johnson (1980, 1999), who have primarily examined data of the type exemplified by (4b) understand metaphor to involve systematic correspondences between structured domains of experience, for instance, Time and Space. These are thought of as being the province not of language, but rather, underlying conceptual correspondences or mappings, known as *conceptual metaphors*.

The challenge that data such as the above raises for the analyst is as follows. On the face of it, and intuitively, word meanings appear to be relatively stable. After all, for language to be effective in facilitating communication, words must have associated with them relatively stable semantic units, established by convention, and hence widely known throughout a given linguistic community. However, words are *protean* in nature. That is, and as illustrated above, they can shift meanings in different contexts of use. The challenge then, in accounting for meaning construction in a theory of language understanding, is to be able to model the nature of the linguistic knowledge that language users must have access to, while being able to account for the way word meanings shift in varying contexts of use.

The received view in linguistics, and philosophy of language, has attempted to reconcile this challenge by distinguishing between two kinds of meaning: a context-independent, "timeless" meaning associated with words, and a context-dependent meaning. That is, words contain context-independent meanings which can be interpreted in context-dependent ways by virtue of the application of various principles of interpretation, e.g., the Gricean maxims. For a contemporary account of this "neo-Gricean" perspective, see Levinson (2000). This general perspective, which Recanati (2004) refers to as *literalism*, enshrines as axiomatic a principled distinction between semantics and pragmatics. The position that I develop in this book, one which is in keeping with much recent research discussed in the pages which follow, takes the view that the distinction between semantics and pragmatics is not principled. Rather, it is artificial.

My approach to accounting for the inherent variation in word meaning is to posit a principled separation between the linguistic system—the linguistic knowledge that words encode—and the conceptual system—the non-linguistic knowledge that words facilitate access to. This distinction I model in terms of the theoretical constructs of the *lexical concept* and the *cognitive model*. These two constructs are central to the theory developed in these pages. Hence, I refer to the approach as the *Theory of Lexical Concepts and Cognitive Models* (or *LCCM Theory* for short). Briefly, a lexical concept is a bundle of varying sorts of knowledge—described in detail in Chapters 6 and 7—which are specialized for being encoded in language. In contrast, cognitive models constitute a body of coherent and structured non-linguistic knowledge—described in detail in Chapters 9 and 10. Cognitive models consist of "recorded" perceptual and subjective states including information derived from sensory-motor perception, proprioception, and introspective states, including emotions, the visceral sense, cognitive states, and so forth. In addition, to be able to produce rehearsals of perceptual and subjective states, albeit in attenuated form, the perceptual symbols can be combined providing novel conceptualizations. The re-enactments of perceptual and subjective states and the novel conceptualizations are referred to as *simulations*.

Hence, cognitive models provide a level of non-linguistic knowledge which is specialized for being accessed via lexical concepts.

The LCCM approach works as follows. Words encode a core content, the lexical concept, which relates to highly schematic information: *linguistic content*. This represents the core information associated with a given word. In addition, words facilitate access to a large body of non-linguistic content: *conceptual content*. This is achieved by virtue of a lexical concept facilitating access to a body of cognitive models, which I refer to as a word's *semantic potential*. Not all of the cognitive models to which a word facilitates access are activated in any given utterance. Hence, the variability in word meaning arises from the partial activation of the semantic potential to which a word facilitates access.

In presenting LCCM Theory, I develop a unified account of the range of phenomena presented in examples (1) to (4) above. That is, I treat the phenomena above, while distinct, as being continuous and hence being explainable in terms of a common set of representational and compositional mechanisms. This does not mean, however, that I provide identical explanations for each of the phenomena I address, as we shall see.

Finally, LCCM Theory is an attempt to develop a cognitive linguistics account of lexical representation and meaning construction. One impulse in cognitive linguistics has been to develop accounts of meaning construction which privilege non-linguistic processes. This is true both of Conceptual Metaphor Theory (Lakoff and Johnson 1980, 1999) and Conceptual Blending Theory (Fauconnier and Turner 2002), for example. Indeed, these approaches remain important in the present work. Any linguistically centred account of language understanding, such as LCCM Theory, must interface with these, as discussed later in the book. Nevertheless, my main concern is to integrate and build on many of the important advances in terms of research on linguistic semantics and grammar evident in cognitive linguistics, and to incorporate these with recent advances in philosophy and cognitive psychology, which have provided fresh impetus for an "empiricist" approach to knowledge representation (e.g., Barsalou 1999, 2008; Prinz 2002; see also Gallagher 2006; Johnson 2007).

Who is the book for?

The book has been written with a number of different readers in mind. This inevitably brings with it a number of challenges, in terms of coverage, accessibility, and so on. Firstly, the book attempts to cater for general linguists who may not be familiar with cognitive linguistics. I have attempted to situate LCCM Theory, as an account of lexical semantics and compositionality, in terms of the core assumptions and approaches of cognitive linguistics. I have included discussion of many of the background assumptions, and have attempted to situate the theory presented here in terms of how it reacts to received approaches in cognitive linguistics (both to semantics and pragmatics, but also to grammar), and in terms of the relevant cognitive linguistics approaches upon which it builds. Accordingly, I hope that the book will provide a useful way of approaching some of the seminal work that has been developed over the last couple of decades in cognitive linguistics, as well as current trends and new directions.

The second reader I have in mind is the cognitive scientist. One of the potential pitfalls that a linguist faces in attempting to provide an account of meaning construction is to provide an account that is psychologically plausible. My aim in the present work has been to develop such an account, one that is firmly grounded in some of the most recent work on knowledge representation available. Hence, my account of cognitive models, for instance, employs, by way of illustration, the recent work on *perceptual symbol systems* associated with the pioneering work of Lawrence Barsalou and his various collaborators. While the flavour of that work is empiricist, it is highly plausible, given our current knowledge of the brain, based on research in cognitive neuroscience, and is, in outline, consonant with the approach to embodied cognition prevalent in cognitive linguistics. As such, I hope to provide the cognitive scientist with an account of lexical representation and semantic composition which sits with what is, at present, the best developed simulation account of knowledge representation available. Such an account, I hope, will show what linguists can do for cognitive psychology and cognitive science more generally, and provide a programmatic framework that can both further theoretical development and provide a basis for future experimental work.

The third reader is the cognitive linguist. As discussed below, one of my aims has been to provide a joined-up account of linguistic semantics. This necessitates drawing upon significant, and often complementary, cognitive linguistic theories that address semantics and grammar, while developing an account which is orthogonal to, and hence complementary to, cognitive linguistic approaches which are not primarily concerned with (accounting for) language. In so doing, I attempt to unify some of the diverse strands of research in cognitive linguistics, as well as presenting an account which appropriately emphasizes the significance of language in meaning construction processes, by taking seriously its semantic complexity.

The final reader I have in mind is the educated lay reader. Such a reader will be interested in language and how it interfaces with the mind, and the role of language in contributing to meaning construction. These are central issues in developing an account of how words mean.

Vyvyan Evans
www.vyvevans.net
January 2009

List of Figures

List of Tables

Abbreviations

Note that definitions of technical terms can be found in the Glossary on p. 339.

CR	cognitive representation
CS	Conceptual System
E	event
F	figure
ICM	Idealized Cognitive Model
LASS	Language and Situated Simulation
LCCM	Lexical Concepts and Cognitive Models
LM	landmark
LS	linguistic system
NP	noun phrase
NTL	Neural Theory of Language
OBJ	Object
Obl	Oblique
P	preposition
PP	perspective point
PSS	Perceptual Symbol Systems
RO	reference object
RP	reference point
S	Sentence
SEL	Sense Enumerative Lexicon
SFoR	spatial frame of reference
SUBJ	Subject
TFoRs	temporal frames of reference
TNS	tense
TR	trajector
V	Verb
VP	verb phrase

Part I

Introduction

The four chapters that make up Part I lay the foundations for the development of LCCM Theory in the remainder of the book. Chapter 1 addresses the inherent variation in word meaning in situated contexts of use, the central problem addressed in the book. Also reviewed—and rejected—is the standard account of meaning in linguistic semantics, referred to as *literalism*. Chapter 2 introduces the theoretical starting points and assumptions upon which LCCM Theory rests. Chapter 3 introduces the perspective provided by cognitive linguistics, and shows how this informs the development of LCCM Theory. Chapter 4 provides an informal introduction to the account of word meaning provided by LCCM Theory.

1

Words and meaning

[M]eaning is the "holy grail" not only of linguistics, but also of philosophy, psychology, and neuroscience...Understanding how we mean and how we think is a vital issue for our intuitive sense of ourselves as human beings. For most people, meaning is intuitively the central issue in the study of language—far more important than understanding details of word order or morphology.

Ray Jackendoff, *Foundations of Language* (2002: 267)

Providing an account of the nature of meaning and meaning construction processes is, as observed in the quotation above, the Holy Grail of linguistics as well as a range of related disciplines in the humanities and the social and cognitive sciences. In this book I am concerned with word meaning, and the role of words in meaning construction: how words mean. This is fundamental to an account of the role of language in giving rise to meaning. Nevertheless, accounting for the role of words in meaning construction has proved to be both controversial and problematic for much of the relatively short history of linguistics as a discipline, as well as for research on language within philosophy, and, indeed, for work more generally in cognitive science.

The specific problem that I address in this book is this: how do we account for the inherent variation of word meaning in language use? That is, the meaning associated with any given word form appears to vary each time it is used, in terms of the conceptualization that it, in part, gives rise to. To illustrate, consider the following examples focusing on the form *France*:

(1) a. France is a country of outstanding natural beauty
     b. France is one of the leading nations in the European Union
     c. France beat New Zealand in the 2007 Rugby World Cup
     d. France voted against the EU constitution in the 2005 referendum

In these examples the meaning associated with *France* varies across each instance of use. In the first example, *France* relates to a specific geographical landmass coincident with the borders of mainland France. In the second example, *France* relates to the political nation state, encompassing its political infrastructure, political and economic influence, and its citizens, including those in French overseas territories. In the example in (1c) *France* relates to the team of fifteen rugby players, drawn from the pool of rugby players of French citizenship, who represented the French nation in the 2007 Rugby World Cup. In the final example, *France* relates to the French electorate, and specifically that part of the electorate which voted against proceeding with ratification of a proposed EU constitution in a national referendum in 2005.

These examples illustrate that a word form such as *France* appears to be protean in nature: its meaning is flexible, in part dependent upon the **context** of its use. This notion of context must include, at the very least, all of the following, discussed in more detail later in the chapter: (i) the other words that make up the utterance itself, (ii) the background knowledge shared by the speaker and hearer, (iii) the physical venue and temporal setting of the utterance, and (iv) the communicative intention of the speaker, as recognized and interpreted by the hearer, in service of facilitating the interactional goal(s).

My task in this book is to provide a theoretical account of the flexibility associated with word meaning in language use. To do so, we will need to examine and develop an account of a number of issues. Firstly, I will develop an account of **semantic structure**, which is to say, the nature of much of the linguistic knowledge associated with words.[1] This must include an account of the knowledge of **usage patterns** associated with words, including what counts as an appropriate **context of use**, given the notion of the components of context just sketched, and elaborated on below. Secondly, I will develop an account of **conceptual structure**. This relates to the non-linguistic knowledge representations that words tap into and can draw upon in situated language use. Together, an account of semantic structure and conceptual structure constitutes an account of what I refer to as **semantic representation**. Thirdly, I develop an account of the linguistic processes that facilitate **composition**, giving rise to distinct conceptualizations associated with a word such as *France* as illustrated in the examples above. Finally, I attempt to do all this while bearing in mind that meaning construction constitutes a form of **joint action** (Clark 1996), in service of situated communicative goals. Hence, the approach I take to lexical and compositional semantics must be thoroughly grounded in a **usage-based** perspective (Langacker 2000). The tack I take, in presenting an account of the issues just outlined, is to develop and introduce a new—or at least a differently nuanced—theory of lexical representation and meaning construction. This is termed the **Theory of Lexical Concepts and Cognitive Models** (LCCM Theory). I begin the presentation of this new approach in the next chapter.

However, we must first examine the received view of word meaning that has emerged in contemporary linguistics, and consider problems that arise for it. This will allow us to move towards a new account of lexical representation, and **compositionality**—how words are composed in service of situated meaning construction. This is our task in the present chapter.

---

[1] I will specify the nature of semantic structure assumed by LCCM Theory in Part II of the book.

The received view of word meaning

The standard account of word meaning, at least in the dominant Anglo-American tradition, I refer to as **literalism**; in this I am following Recanati (2004). In fact, literalism is less an account of word meaning, being more an account of the nature of linguistic semantics in general, of which word meaning is clearly a central aspect. Literalism is also less an account associated with any individual scholar. Nevertheless, it is probably fair to claim, as Recanati does, that it represents the dominant position in modern linguistics with respect to the nature of word meaning, **sentence meaning**, and **speaker meaning**. In particular, literalism takes as axiomatic the principled division of labour between **semantics**—the context-independent aspects of meaning—and **pragmatics**—the context-dependent aspects of meaning. In this section I first present the perspective provided by literalism, before going on to argue, in subsequent sections, why a new perspective on word meaning, and the role of words in meaning construction, is required.

Literalism views sentence meaning as a consequence of adding or composing smaller units of meaning, together with the grammatical configurations in which they appear. In other words, accounting for linguistic meaning, from this perspective, assumes that the "ingredients" of language are words and rules, with rules serving to conjoin "atomic" meaning elements encoded by words. On this view, a descriptively adequate account of linguistic semantics should provide an observationally accurate account of these "elements of meaning" (associated with words or a single word), and the "rules of combination" (resulting in a sentence).

Identification of the elements of meaning is often referred to as **componential analysis**. This approach seeks to work out how to represent the meanings of words, or more precisely, what are termed **lexemes**—the meaning that is held to underlie a series of related forms, for example, *sing, sang, sung, singing*, and so forth, which are assumed to all have the same meaning, SING. The essential insight of this approach is that word meanings are made up of atomic elements or components. Typically, lexical items are thought of as being tagged with syntactic, morphological, and semantic features.

An early such componential-style analysis was that developed by Katz and colleagues (Katz and Fodor 1963; Katz and Postal 1964; Katz 1972). In this account, word meanings consist of semantic markers and distinguishers. Semantic markers comprise the information shared by words, while distinguishers constitute the idiosyncratic information specific to a given word meaning. For instance, based on Katz and Postal (1964), the polysemous senses for the word *bachelor* can be represented as in (2), where the semantic markers are given in parentheses and the semantic distinguishers are given in square brackets.

(2) a. (human) (male) [who has never married]
     b. (human) (male) [young knight serving under the colours of another]

    c. (human) [recipient of the lowest academic degree]
    d. (non-human) (male) [young fur seal without a mate]

More recent and more sophisticated componential analyses of word meaning are provided by Anna Wierzbicka (e.g., 1996) in her **Natural Semantic Metalanguage** (NSM) account of word meaning, and Ray Jackendoff (1983, 1990) in his theory of **Conceptual Semantics**. Nevertheless, it is important to point out that neither Wierzbicka nor Jackendoff endorse all aspects of literalism. In particular, they do not take the view that compositional (i.e., sentence level) semantics patterns after reference, nor that sentence meaning should be truth evaluable (see the discussion below).

However, the hallmark of componential accounts, and the view of word meaning adopted under literalism, is that word meanings are assumed to be relatively fixed and stable. Put another way, the semantic primitives which make up a given word meaning can be identified independently of context.

Once identified, word meanings are integrated, by applying the rules of the grammar, in order to provide sentence meaning. Literalism, then, assumes that the contribution of language to meaning construction is essentially additive in nature, positing grammatical principles which ensure that the semantic units which result are unable to change or delete the meanings of the units which are conjoined to form a larger semantic unit or expression. This restriction serves to make a larger expression, for instance a sentence, **monotonic** with respect to its component parts, where the term "monotonic" has to do with the view that the component parts retain their original meanings in the larger expression (e.g., Cann 1993). Thus, the individual word meanings do not alter their meaning in the larger semantic units of which they form part.

Once composition has occurred, this gives rise to sentence meaning. Under literalism, sentence meaning, technically known as a **proposition**, is **truth evaluable**—although this issue is potentially problematic.[2] That is, a sentence—a well-formed grammatical string of words—is held to "carry" a meaning which patterns after reference: the conventional assignment of a worldly entity and state of affairs to the complex linguistic expression resulting from composition of the individual elements in forming a sentence. The meaning associated with the sentence constitutes the proposition, that is, the sentence meaning. Thus, in the following example sentence:

---

[2] A number of scholars working in the Pragmatic tradition (e.g., Bach 1997; Carston 2002; Recanati 2004) have observed that it is often (or usually) the case that the linguistic form uttered by an interlocutor underdetermines the sentence meaning. That is, utterances are often not propositional, but have to be completed by what has been termed **pragmatic intrusion**, such that inferential processes are required in order to render the utterance propositional and hence truth evaluable. Carston, for instance, refers to the notion that linguistic meaning underdetermines sentence meaning (i.e., the proposition expressed) as the **Underdeterminacy thesis**. For instance, while the following example from Carston (2002: 17): *On the top shelf*, relates to a specific location, as Carston notes, "[W]hat is meant by a speaker...is something sentence-shaped (propositional), presumably quite obvious in the context [for example, 'the item you are looking for is on the top shelf']."

(3) Brighton is 50 miles south of London

the proposition "carried" by the sentence can be evaluated as being true or false with respect to the state of affairs which holds in the world. In this case, the proposition expressed by (3): that Brighton is 50 miles from London, is true.

Thus far, we have been addressing the first half of literalism: the study of semantics. According to literalism, word meanings and the resulting sentence meaning, is context-independent. However, the full meaning of a sentence, what is referred to as speaker meaning, may also depend on context. This aspect of meaning falls under the purview of the sub-branch of linguistics known as pragmatics.

The distinction between sentence meaning and speaker meaning was introduced by the British philosopher Paul Grice (e.g., 1989). Grice distinguished between what a sentence means, its literal meaning, and what a sentence implicates, by virtue of the context in which it is deployed, and the speaker's communicative intention in deploying it in the particular context of use. The latter sort of meaning is what Grice referred to as speaker meaning. According to literalism then, there is a principled distinction between semantics, which is concerned with literal or sentence meaning, and pragmatics, which is concerned with context-based speaker meaning: what is implicated.

To illustrate, let's reconsider the sentence in (3). The literal meaning of this sentence relates to a state of affairs in the world referenced by the proposition expressed by this sentence. However, the proposition expressed is independent of any given context of use. To illustrate, now consider (3) as part of an exchange between two interlocutors in (4) who are driving to Brighton, are just north of London, and whose petrol gauge is hovering just above empty.

(4) A: Do you think we can make it to Brighton without filling up?
     B: Brighton is 50 miles south of London

According to literalism, the sentence expressed by B means what it does: Brighton is 50 miles south of London, which is truth evaluable independent of any given context because it can be assessed by virtue of a context-independent state of affairs: in the world, Brighton really is 50 miles south of London.

However, in the context associated with the exchange in (4), it means more than this. This is because the use of this sentence in this context implicates something in addition to the literal meaning expressed by the sentence. The implicature associated with the sentence uttered by B is that the travellers cannot reach Brighton unless they first obtain more petrol for their car. Thus, the speaker meaning is a consequence of interpreting the communicative intention of the speaker in deploying the sentence meaning in a given context. A somewhat simplified overview of the main elements of literalism are presented in Figure 1.1.

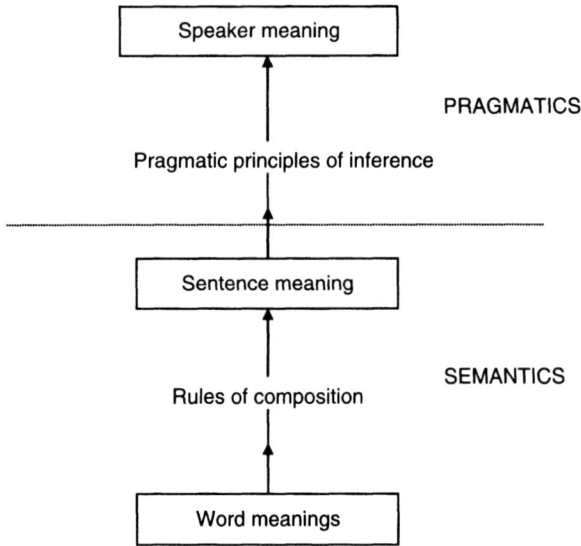

FIGURE 1.1. An overview of literalism

In sum, and from the perspective of literalism, word meanings involve relatively fixed and context-independent atoms of meaning. These atoms are concatenated, given the rules of the grammar, and then interpreted, by virtue of principles of language use. The context-independent atoms of meaning associated with words contribute to sentence meaning, and speaker meaning relates to the use to which sentences are put (including the context-independent word meanings which constitute them), which speaker meaning builds upon.

Problems with the received view

Literalism as an approach to meaning construction suffers from a fatal problem: the principled separation between context-independent (sentence) meaning and context-dependent (speaker) meaning. Put another way, the difficulty at the heart of literalism is the principled division of labour that it posits between semantics and pragmatics. In terms of the approach to word meaning adopted by literalism, words are assumed, apart from a number of notable exceptions such as **indexicals** (for instance *he*, or *here*), to have meanings tied to them which are context-independent. This follows as word meaning falls under the purview of semantics (rather than pragmatics).

However, a by now large number of scholars have argued that the principled separation of context-independent and context-dependent meaning (the semantics/pragmatics distinction) is illusory.[3] From this it follows that the position that word meanings are context-independent is potentially problematic. For instance, in the Pragmatics tradition, researchers have shown that the meaning of a given word, and hence the truth conditions of the sentence to which the word contributes, is typically (perhaps always) a function of context/background knowledge (see in particular Carston 2002; Searle e.g., 1983; Recanati 2004).

By way of illustration, consider the following examples of *open* based on those discussed by Searle (1983):

(5)   a. John opened the window
      b. John opened his mouth
      c. John opened the book
      d. John opened his briefcase
      e. John opened the curtains
      f. The carpenter opened the wall
      g. The surgeon opened the wound
      h. The sapper opened the dam

As Searle observes, in examples such as these the meaning of *open* is a function of what he refers to as the "background", which is to say our knowledge of the sorts of ways in which entities and objects of different kinds are opened. Crucially, the different ways in which we can open things is a function of our **encyclopaedic knowledge**, which is to say knowing about and experience with the very different sorts of operations involved. For instance, opening a wound involves, for instance, the skilled use of a scalpel on flesh, to create an aperture of a certain size and shape for a particular purpose, such as to clean the wound and/or remove potentially damaged or diseased tissue. The opening of a wall involves different sorts of tools, typically carpentry tools of a particular kind, which are applied to a wall, made typically of wood, and resulting in an aperture of a certain size and shape for a very different sort of purpose: for instance to create or insert a doorway. Both of these operations differ from opening a mouth, which involves muscle gestures on a pre-existing aperture, or opening curtains, which doesn't involve an aperture at all, both of which serve very different functions. Finally, opening a dam by a sapper involves knowledge relating to warfare—a sapper is a military explosives expert—and destroying the dam in question as part of a military action. Thus, understanding what *open* means in (5h) involves knowledge of a very different sort of event, agents, and purposes.

---

[3] For a flavour of the range and nature of the problems that have been raised for a principled separation between context-independent and context-dependent dimensions of meaning, see, for example, the approaches to language and situated communication highlighted by the following: Carston 2002; Clark 1996; Coulson 2000; Croft 2000; Evans 2004*a*; Fauconnier 1987; Lakoff 1987; Langacker 1987; Recanati 2004; Sperber and Wilson 1995; Sweetser 1999; Tyler and Evans 2003).

In addition, in each of these examples the sort of encyclopaedic knowledge involved is a function of the utterance context in which the word is embedded. Thus, not only is the meaning of the word a function of quite distinct sorts of encyclopaedic knowledge, the sort of encyclopaedic knowledge to which the word provides access is a function of the context in which the word is embedded. That is, the linguistic context in part serves to narrow the sort of encyclopaedic knowledge to which *open* relates in each example. Thus, and as Searle observes, the semantic contribution that *open* makes to the truth conditions of sentences, such as these, varies, being a function of the sentential context in which it is embedded.

While the examples above relate to literal sentences, the context dependence of *open* is even more marked if we consider uses that are, intuitively, more figurative in nature. Consider the following indicative set of examples:

(6) a. The discussant opened the conversation
     b. John opened a bank account
     c. John opened the meeting
     d. John opened a dialogue
     e. The Germans opened hostilities against the Allies in 1940
     f. The skies opened
     g. He opened his mind to a new way of thinking
     h. He finally opened up to her

The meaning of *open* in each of these examples relates to distinct sorts of actions, events, and situations. In the first example, opening a meeting requires a designated authority: a meeting "chair", who, in declaring the meeting open, performs a specific speech act, thus facilitating the meeting process. In opening a dialogue, two (or more) interlocutors begin and continue a conversation that can take place face-to-face, electronically via email, on the telephone, or via the exchange of letters. To open such an exchange relates to the initiation of the exchange. To open a bank account involves completing certain formalities such as an interview with a bank official, financial checks, and the filling in of paperwork. In contrast, to open hostilities, as in the example in (6e), concerns the initial actions involved in warfare. Thus, each of these uses of *open* relates to very different forms of initiations, involving different sorts of events, procedures, and agents. In contrast, in the example in (6f), the usage of *open* relates to a sudden and heavy downpour of rain, while the last two examples relate to flexibility of thinking and emotional responses and/or being more expansive in terms of spoken, physical, or emotional interactions.

What examples such as those in (5) and (6) illustrate is the following. Firstly, a word such as *open* provides access to an impressively diverse array of encyclopaedic knowledge involving distinct scenarios, actions, events, and agents. As we have just seen, things that can be "opened" include an array of different sorts of physical entities and abstract events—which is related to Searle's notion of "background".[4] Understanding the examples in (5) and (6) involves complex and detailed knowledge about the sorts of scenarios that *open* relates to in each example and, thus, the specific way in which *open* applies in each case. After all, opening a mouth involves a very different form of opening than when a carpenter opens a wall, or when a sapper opens, and thus destroys, a dam. Hence, the meaning of *open* in each example is, in part, a function of tapping into the encyclopaedic knowledge, in order to determine the specific meaning of *open* in each example. Put another way, it is the scenario that *open* relates to that, in part, determines the nature of the meaning associated with *open* in each case.

Secondly, in each case it appears to be the sentential context, which is to say the other words in the sentence, which serve to direct the sort of encyclopaedic knowledge that *open* provides access to. That is, while *open* has a large body of knowledge, in the sense of a sophisticated range of scenarios and events that it can be applied to, what I will refer to as its **semantic potential**, the sentential context serves to guide and narrow the specific sorts of knowledge that a given instance of *open* actually relates to. In sum, the meaning of *open* appears to be a function of (i) (sentential) context which guides the (ii) encyclopaedic knowledge to which *open* relates in a given instance of use.

While the general problem in literalism is the strict separation between context-independent meaning (semantics), and context-dependent meaning (pragmatics), this gives rise to two problems for the resulting view of word meaning. Under literalism, word meaning falls under the purview of semantics. We saw in the previous section that under literalism word meanings are held to be: (i) stable and relatively circumscribed knowledge units, and (ii) context-independent. Hence, word meanings, which while susceptible to contextual interpretation (at least if meaning is understood in referential terms as in a possible world semantics), are held to constitute circumscribed knowledge units which are stored and can be deployed independently of other sorts of knowledge. Words meanings are thus separable from other kinds of knowledge such as the kind of representation(s) I have referred to as encyclopaedic knowledge. They are conceived as constituting fixed and relatively stable bundles of semantic elements, additionally tagged with syntactic and morphological features.

As we have just seen with our discussion of *open*, word meanings do appear to relate to and draw upon a potentially large body of knowledge, which following other scholars (e.g., Haiman 1980; Langacker 1987) I have been

---

[4] While encyclopaedic knowledge, in the sense that I use it here, and as developed in cognitive linguistics (see the discussion in Chapter 3), is arguably related to Searle's notion of "background" it is not quite the same. For Searle, background has to do with what we might think of as knowledge which constitutes entrenched, non-representational practice. What I take from Searle is the idea that word meaning is always contextualized with respect to knowledge which, in (large) part, determines the linguistic meaning.

referring to as encyclopaedic in nature. Moreover, the meaning of *open* only ever appears in given contexts of use, even when these are the minimal contexts of use deployed by the linguist: a numbered "linguistic example" set off and embedded in the running text of technical articles published in academic journals.[5] In other words, word meaning emerges from a large semantic potential which is narrowed by the sentential (and extra-linguistic) context in which it is embedded. As such, word meaning appears to be guided by and a function of context: words, I suggest, do not mean independently of context. Thus, the fundamental problem with literalism is that it attempts to artificially divorce (word) meaning from (situated meaning in) context of use. More precisely, literalism lives in something of a fool's paradise. It holds that language users retain an idealized, timeless meaning for *open* which they neatly keep apart from the situated meanings of *open* which arise from its use in examples such as in (5) and (6). The mistake that literalism makes, then, is in being reductionist and simplistic about meaning.

An additional challenge: figurative language

As we have just seen in our discussion of *open,* the protean nature of word meaning relates both to literal and figurative uses. A challenge for any theory of **lexical representation**—which is to say, the mental representations associated with words, consonant with the protean nature of word meaning discussed in this chapter—is to provide an account of literal and figurative language. Under literalism, these are treated as radically different sorts of language. It is often assumed, from this perspective, that figurative language involves the "defective" use of literal language, as argued, for instance, by Searle ([1979] 1993). On this view, the use of figurative language arises from the context-dependent interpretation of literal language, and thus involves principles of pragmatic inference being applied once the context-independent sentence meaning has been derived. Put another way, figurative language is a function of language use, and thus falls under the purview of pragmatics, rather than semantics proper.

The difficulty for what we might refer to as the **literalism perspective on figurative language**, is as follows. This perspective predicts that understanding a literal sentence should be faster than understanding a figurative expression: we must first understand what the sentence means before we can interpret what the speaker intends us to infer by using the sentence in a non-literal way. However, as has been shown, based on investigations of psycholinguistic processing, language users often appear to be equally as efficient in computing the meaning of figurative language utterances as they are non-figurative ones (Gibbs 1994; Glucksberg 2001, 2003; see also Giora 1997, 2003).

---

[5] See similar arguments made by scholars including Clark (1983); Coulson (2000); Evans (2006); Fauconnier (1997); Langacker (1987); Sweetser (1999); Tyler and Evans (2003).

The challenge, then, that awaits an account of lexical representation and the role of words in meaning construction is to work out the difference, if any, between the role and function of literal and figurative word use in meaning-construction processes. To illustrate the nature of the challenge, let's consider the following example:

(7)   John's boss is a pussycat

Presumably this utterance doesn't mean that John's boss is a pussycat, in the sense of a four-legged organism, with a tail and pointy ears that utters "miaow." Rather, the meanings associated with the phrases *John's boss* and *pussycat* have to be integrated with the **predicate nominative construction**, which ordinarily carries a class-inclusion meaning.[6] Informally, this construction has the following syntax: "SUBJECT is an NP," and means, again informally: "The subject is a type of the entity specified." To illustrate, consider the following:

(8)   John's boss is a pianist

The meaning that a language user would ordinarily derive, for an example such as this, would be that John's boss is included in the category of those who play the piano and thus constitutes a pianist, and that this situation persists through time. But, the same construction does not provide a class-inclusion reading for the previous example in (7). The challenge then, for our account of the variation in word meaning, is to be able to provide an explanation as to why (7) means something other than what it literally says, while (8) means what it does literally appear to say.

The nature of context

I suggested above that the fundamental problem with literalism is that it attempts to artificially divorce meaning from context of use. Before proceeding with an attempt to identify the ingredients of a theory of word meaning and meaning construction, we must first get an initial sense of the different sorts of context which serve to narrow the meaning of a word. Accordingly, we will begin to see that the notion of context is a complex and multifaceted phenomenon crucial for language use and language understanding. Accordingly, the notion of context is fundamental to the development of LCCM Theory that I begin to sketch in the next chapter, and develop in detail in the

---

[6] The nominative predicative construction involves the copular or "linking" verb *be* which combines with a nominal, e.g., "a pianist." The nominal functions as the essential part of the clausal predicate: "is a pianist." Langacker (1991a) in his analysis of the nominative predicate construction argues that *be* encodes the "continuation through time of a stable situation characterized only as a stative relation" (*ibid.* 65).

rest of the book.[7] Hence, the account of word meaning provided is diametrically opposed to that offered by literalism.

As the approach I take is usage-based, I use the term **utterance**, rather than sentence, in discussing word meaning. This reflects my assumption that it is only by taking account of language in use that we can hope to fully understand the nature of word meaning. It also follows from the position that sentences, as understood in linguistic theory, are artificial theoretical constructs, abstracted from actual **usage events**, which is to say, utterances. I will have more to say about the distinction between sentences and utterances in Chapter 4.

Utterance context

As we saw with the examples relating to *France* and *open* above, the utterance elements which occur in a given utterance contribute, in part, to determining the meaning of the word. That is, and as suggested above, the utterance provides a context which assists in narrowing the meaning of the word in question. To illustrate, consider the following examples:

(9)   a. On May 1st my grandfather expired
      b. On May 1st my driving licence expired

The meaning of *expired* in each example is a function of the utterance in which it is embedded. In the first example, *expired* relates to an event involving death, while in the second, *expired* relates to expiry of the term for which an individual's right to drive on the public highway was sanctioned or "licensed."

Now consider another example involving a verb. This involves the following well-known context-dependent alternation associated with the verb *bake*:

(10) a. Fred baked the potato
      b. Fred baked the cake

While the example in (10a) relates to a change-of-state reading, the example in (10b) relates to a creation reading. That is, in (10b) the meaning of *bake* can be paraphrased by "made" or "created", while the meaning of *bake* in (10a) cannot be paraphrased in this way. The shift in meaning associated with *bake* appears to be a function of the object associated with *bake*: potato versus cake, and thus the specific consequence(s) that baking has for particular entities designated. While a potato is rendered edible by virtue of baking, as its interior becomes soft and it is thus easier to consume, an "uncooked cake" is not in fact normally thought of as a cake, but as a "potential cake." While the process of baking does not affect the existential status of a potato, but

---

[7] By incorporating the notion of context into the theory, the approach I take is fundamentally concerned with language in use, and thus, as already observed, is usage-based in nature.

rather affects its state, a cake only in fact exists once it has been baked, as baking is one of the requisite stages involved in making a cake.

My final example of the role of utterance context in contributing to the meaning of a given word relates to what Schmid (2000) terms "shell nouns." According to Schmid, "Shell nouns make up an open-ended functionally-defined class of abstract nouns that have, to varying degrees, the potential for being used as conceptual shells for complex, proposition-like, pieces of information" (*ibid.* 4). Common examples of shell nouns include: *case, chance, fact, idea, news, point, problem, position, reason, report, situation, thing.* The significance of shell nouns for the present discussion is that the semantic value of the shell noun is normally determined by the utterance context. Moreover, the shell noun itself serves to characterize and encapsulate the idea whose meaning it simultaneously takes on. Thus, the meaning associated with the shell noun is, paradoxically, both a function of and a contributor to the utterance context in which it is embedded. To illustrate, consider the following example drawn from Schmid (2000):

(11) The Government's **aim** is to make GPs more financially accountable, in charge of their own budgets, as well as to extend the choice of the patient

In the example in (11) the shell noun is in bold. The idea the shell noun relates to is underlined. The shell noun, the noun phrase in which it occurs, and the idea it relates to, which here is mediated by the copula *is*, are collectively termed the "shell-content-complex."

According to Schmid, the meaning of the shell-content-complex in examples such as this are a function of the specific combination of the shell noun and the idea it relates to. That is, the shell-like function of the shell noun is not an inalienable property of the noun itself, but rather derives from the way it is used. In this example, the speaker presents a particular idea ("to make GPs more financially accountable, in charge of their own budgets, as well as to extend the choice of the patient") as an "aim". This provides a particular characterization for the idea. Moreover, by providing this characterization, the shell noun also serves to **encapsulate** the various components and complex ideas contained in the idea as a single, relatively stable, albeit temporary, concept. It does so by casting "this complex piece of information into one single noun phrase" (*ibid.* 7). Evidence for this unity comes from the next sentence presented in (12):

(12) **The Government's aim** is to make GPs more financially accountable, in charge of their own budgets, as well as to extend the choice of the patient. Under **this new scheme**, family doctors are required to produce annual reports for their patients...

Here we see that once the complex idea has been encapsulated, it can be glossed with a different characterization as signalled by the shell noun phrase *this new scheme*, marked in (12) in bold. In essence, the content associated with shell nouns comes from the ideas, that is, the utterance context, they relate to. Yet, the ideas receive their characterization, and even their construal as a single unified idea, from their participation in a shell-content-complex.

Manner of utterance

The manner of the utterance can provide a context which serves, in part, to determine the meaning of a particular word. For instance, whether a particular word receives stress or emphasis of some kind can contribute to the meaning of the word. Consider the following by way of illustration.

(13)   a. Look at that blàckbird
        b. Look at that black bìrd

The compound *blackbird* receives primary stress on the adjective *black*. In contrast, a bird that happens to be black, but is not a blackbird, receives primary stress on *bird*, as in the second example. Here, stress serves as a type of **contextualization cue**, serving to determine, in part, the semantic contribution of *black* to the utterance.[8]

Extra-linguistic context

The time, venue, or medium (e.g., spoken or written), or the genre of the medium (e.g., newspaper report versus spoken lecture) of an utterance can contribute to the meaning of given words, and thus provide a context. In this case, the context is extra-linguistic as it constitutes the "location," broadly construed, in which the utterance occurs. To illustrate, consider the following utterance:

(14)   "I watched the young lady approach the bar."

The meaning of *bar* in this utterance is determined, in part, by the kind of venue to which the utterance relates. For instance, if uttered in a court of law, the notion of bar would refer to the raised platform at which the judge sits. If said in a public house, it would refer to the area at which alcohol is ordered and purchased.

Consider another example of extra-linguistic context, this time employing the word *safe* in the context of a child playing on the beach. The examples are based on Sweetser (1999):

---

[8] The term "contextualization cue" was coined by Gumperz (1982). In borrowing the term here, I am using it in a slightly different way from that of Gumperz who applied it in the context of his work on code-switching.

(15) a. The child is safe
      b. The beach is safe
      c. The shovel is safe

In this context, the meaning of (15a) is that the child will not come to any harm. However, given the extra-linguistic context, (15b) does not mean that the beach will not come to harm. Instead, it means that the beach is an environment in which the risk of the child coming to harm is minimized. Similarly, (15c) does not mean that the shovel will not come to harm, but that it will not cause harm to the child using it to dig in the sand. These examples illustrate that there is no single fixed property that *safe* assigns to the words *child*, *beach*, and *shovel*. In order to understand the utterances we must interpret them, in part, with respect to a specific extra-linguistic context, a scenario, which holds. In this scenario, there is a child on a beach, employing a spade to dig in the sand. In order to successfully interpret these utterances we must also draw upon our encyclopaedic knowledge relating to children, beaches, and shovels, and the potential harm that shovels can cause if mis-used, for instance.

Encyclopaedic knowledge

Earlier in this chapter I noted that the utterance context serves to narrow that part of the encyclopaedic knowledge to which a word potentially provides access. What I have in mind by encyclopaedic knowledge has been referred to by a range of terms in the linguistics and cognitive science literature. These include the following: **background knowledge, common-sense knowledge, sociocultural knowledge,** and **real-world knowledge.** By encyclopaedic knowledge I have in mind the highly detailed, extensive, and structured knowledge we as humans appear to have access to in order to categorize the situations, events, and entities we encounter in our everyday lives and in the world, and the knowledge we draw upon in order to perform a range of other higher cognitive operations including conceptualization, inference, reason, choice, and the knowledge which language appears to rely upon. This kind of knowledge is primarily non-linguistic, or conceptual in nature, and appears to constitute a vast structured body of relational information which psychologists sometimes refer to as **frames** (e.g., Barsalou 1992, 1999; Barsalou *et al.* 1993). Although I will revise the notion of encyclopaedic knowledge as the book proceeds, the notion of encyclopaedic knowledge will be central to the theory of word meaning and compositional semantics developed in this book.

While speakers and hearers call upon encyclopaedic knowledge in using language, this knowledge thereby serves as a kind of context against which words receive and achieve meaning. For instance, the meaning of *France* in each of the examples in (1) above, draws upon a different body of knowledge. In the example in (1a) we draw upon our knowledge of the geographical landmass associated with France, while in (1b) we draw upon our knowledge of France as a political entity, a nation state.

Interactional norms as context

A particular sort of encyclopaedic knowledge which provides a salient form of context relates to interactional or behavioural norms. This notion is sometimes referred to as a **cultural script** or a **cultural routine**, or simply as a **script**, particularly as developed in the computational literature associated with the work of Schank and Abelson (1977). For instance, the following restaurant script is adapted from Schank and Kass (1988: 190):

(16) 1. Agent goes to restaurant
      2. Agent is seated
      3. Agent orders meal from waiter
      4. Waiter brings meal to agent
      5. Agent eats meal
      6. Agent gives money to restaurant
      7. Agent leaves restaurant

A cultural script such as this constitutes an interactional norm which provides the context against which words derive a particular meaning.[9] For instance, the meaning of the word *restaurant* is, in part, informed by knowledge relating to the script captured in (16).

Interactional goals as context

Another form of context which serves, in part, to determine the meaning of a given word constitutes the interactional goals of the interlocutors. According to Clark (1996), linguistic communication is a form of joint action, in which interlocutors negotiate, establish, and attempt to achieve interactional goals.[10] These goals, which can be explicitly signalled, or arise due to the extra-linguistic context or some aspect of encyclopaedic knowledge such as a cultural script, serve as the context against which the meaning of lexical items can be, in part, determined.

For instance, consider the following service encounter in a fast-food restaurant:

(17) Customer: [Waits at serving counter]
      Server: [Appears after a short delay after fetching another cus-
                 tomer's order] Hi!
      Customer: A double whopper meal please.

---

[9] Fillmore's (e.g., 1982) notion of a **semantic frame**, discussed in the next chapter, provides a related construct to that of script.

[10] These issues are discussed in more detail in Chapter 11.

Clark observes that in service encounters such as this one, interlocutors, through joint action, negotiate the accomplishment of communicative goals. In this example the server indicates their availability to take the customer's order by greeting the customer. That is, the customer takes the greeting, the utterance *Hi!*, as signalling an offer to receive the customer's order. Clearly, in order for *Hi!* to have this meaning, the server and customer must share an understanding as to the nature of the interaction and its objectives: the server is there to receive a food order (which is achieved by the greeting) and the customer wishes to place an order.

Discourse topic as context

The final kind of context I will mention relates to the notion of discourse topic. In general terms, interlocutors often appear to derive word meaning from what they take the discourse topic to be. For instance, consider the following utterance:

(18)   That hike is killing me

In the context of a conversation on a recent central bank base-rate increase, this mention of *hike* might relate to the financial pain involved in an increase in mortgage repayments. However, in the context of a discussion of a recent cross-country walk, the pain might be more physical in nature.

The point, then, of this discussion has been the following. Context is a complex and multifaceted phenomenon. Moreover, the meaning associated with a word in any given instance of use is, in part, a function of the particular sort of context, linguistic or otherwise, in which it is embedded, and of which it forms a part. Put another way, word meaning is protean, its semantic contribution sensitive to and dependent on the context which it, in part, gives rise to.

This bears on the discussion of the nature of word meaning under literalism in the following way: the precise semantic contribution of each word appears to be a function of the context in which it is embedded. Put another way, words do not have discrete, timeless (i.e., context-independent) meanings, contra the assumption under literalism.

A possible solution? Sense Enumerative Lexicons

If the fixed, componential view of word meaning offered by literalism fails, what then? A possible solution to the apparent variation in word meaning exhibited in language use might be to posit a vast number of distinct senses. For instance, rather than assuming that the range of meanings associated with, say, *open* in the examples above are somehow due to context and/or encyclopaedic knowledge, we might assume that *open* has exactly the same number of distinct meanings, technically known as **senses**, as the number of different sentences in which it appears, and that each of these are stored in long-term semantic memory.

Pustejovsky (1995) in his pioneering work on lexical semantics refers to approaches which posit a large number of distinct senses for given lexical items as **Sense Enumerative Lexicons** (or SELs for short). However, as Pustejovsky observes, even such accounts cannot predict the creative use of words in novel contexts. That is, even lexicons which assume a high degree of granularity fail on the score of descriptive adequacy in the face of the linguistic facts. Thus, word meaning in language use cannot be predicted from knowledge of the conventional range of uses to which words are put, even when one assumes a highly granular lexicon: one that posits a large number of distinct senses. This follows as the number of distinct word senses required, even for a single word, would need to be infinite, a position that, given memory constraints, is untenable, even allowing for the significant capabilities that language users have in terms of semantic memory.

To illustrate the foregoing, consider the lexical item *fast*, discussed by Pustejovsky. It is commonly assumed that this word has a number of **conventional senses**—mentally stored semantic units—associated with it. These include the following:

(19)   a fast car   [$fast_1$: to move quickly]

(20)   a fast typist   [$fast_2$: to perform some act quickly]

(21)   a fast decision [$fast_3$: to require little time for completion]

However, the definitions provided do not fully capture the "type"-semantics that these examples of *fast* are instances of. For instance, *fast* illustrated in (19) relates to an entity capable of moving quickly, whilst the type illustrated in (20) relates to entities capable of performing actions quickly, and so on. That is, each putatively conventional sense of *fast* has associated with it selectional restrictions, what I will refer to as **selectional tendencies**. The "to move quickly" sense, for instance, selects for members of the class of movable entities.

However, now consider the following example:

(22)   a fast driver

This usage of *fast* concerns not the actions of the driver. That is, it is not the actions of the driver which are performed quickly. Nor would this utterance normally refer to such actions, even if they were performed quickly. Rather, this expression refers to the speed at which cars controlled by the driver in question ordinarily proceed relative to some norm, such as the established speed limit for a particular road. In other words, this is an instance of $fast_1$ rather than $fast_2$. Yet, *fast*, in this example, relates to the vehicle driven by the driver, rather than, strictly, the driver. Thus, the combination of fast₁, with *driver*, produces a novel reading in which *fast* might be paraphrased as "to cause to move quickly".

Now consider the following example:

(23)   the fast lane (of the motorway)

Presumably this usage of *fast* also relates to fast₁. Yet, *the fast lane* is a venue for rapid locomotion rather than an entity capable of rapid locomotion. In other words, both the uses of *fast* in (22) and (23) while seemingly related to the meaning of *fast* in (21) have different semantic selectional tendencies, and somewhat novel meanings. We could posit that both (22) and (23) constitute distinct senses. However, we can continue finding novel uses of *fast*, for which we could produce a virtually infinite listing. Indeed, the same argument applies to sense 2 and 3 of *fast*.

In addition, a particular novel use can appear to feature nuances of different senses:

(24)   We need a fast garage for our car, as we leave the day after tomorrow

As Pustejovsky (1995) notes, this use of *fast* appears to be a "blend" of both fast₂ and fast₃: a garage which carries out repairs quickly and takes little time to do so.

What this discussion of *fast* reveals, then, is that all the examples we have considered, and might wish to consider, upon close analysis predicate in a slightly different way. In other words, each unique instance has a distinct utterance context, and is associated with a slightly different semantic value. Thus, we can conclude from this that, in principle, every instance of use of a word such as *fast* has a different meaning. To take a "Sense Enumerative" approach to word meaning would be to sanction an infinite proliferation of word senses stored in memory by language users. Such a position is psychologically untenable.

Words as contextual expressions

The observation with which this book proceeds, then, is that words are never meaningful independent of the utterance in which they are embedded, and the encyclopaedic knowledge and extra-linguistic context which guide how words embedded in an utterance should be interpreted. Indeed, evidence from the perspectives of social psychology, cognitive psychology, interactional sociolinguistics, cognitive linguistics, corpus linguistics, and computational linguistics reveals that the view that words constitute fixed, context-independent structures, and that meaning construction is appropriately modelled in terms of the straightforward approach to compositionality sketched above is untenable.

As observed by a large number of scholars, the meanings associated with words are flexible, open-ended, and highly sensitive to utterance context. Such scholars include, but are by no means limited to Allwood (2003), Carston (2002), Clark (1983, 1996), Coulson (2000), Croft (1993, 2000), Croft and Cruse (2004), Cruse (2002), Evans (2004a), Fauconnier (1997), Fauconnier and Turner (2002), Goffman (1981), Gumperz (1982), Harder (2009), Herskovits (1986), Lakoff (1987), Langacker (1987), Pustejovsky (1995), Sperber and Wilson (1995), Sweetser (1999), Dancygier and Sweetser (2005), and Tyler and Evans (2003). Indeed, as Croft (1993) observes, meaning construction appears to proceed by virtue of the meaning associated with a given word being interpreted once the meaning of the entire utterance has been established. That is, individual word meaning is determined by the encyclopaedic knowledge to which words provide access, as guided by context, rather than utterance meaning being a consequence of concatenating context-independent word meanings. As such I argue that words are **contextual expressions**. From this perspective, as utterance meaning is the result of assigning meaning to words in both linguistic and non-linguistic context, the end product is due to all three factors. Hence, meaning cannot be assigned unambiguously to words alone. Rather the semantic contribution associated with individual words emerges from the mélange: words *are* contextual expressions. From a usage-based perspective on language (e.g., Croft 2000; Langacker 2000; see Evans and Green 2006 for a review), this state of affairs is entirely natural, as I shall suggest in later chapters.

Accordingly, in this book I argue against the received view that words "carry" meaning. In point of fact, I will be arguing that meaning is not a property of words, or even language, per se. Rather my contention is that meaning arises as a function of the way in which words (and language) are deployed by language users in socioculturally, temporally, and physically contextualized **communicative events**, which is to say utterances, due to a complex battery of linguistic and non-linguistic processes, in service of the expression of situated communicative intentions.

Of course, to say that words do not "carry" meaning does not entail the claim that the semantic structure associated with linguistic units such as words is wholly indeterminate. This position, which may be associated with some usage-based approaches to language (e.g., Thompson 2002; Croft and Cruse 2004; see Harder 2009 for a description of the risk of ending up in the extreme position he calls "usage fundamentalism"), is hard to maintain. After all, as pointed out by Sweetser (1999), the very distinct readings typically derived from utterances of the following kind:

(25)   a. John ran up the stairs
       b. John ran down the stairs

have to do with the fact that lexical forms are associated with relatively well-established—in the sense of conventionalized—semantic representations. For instance, the fact that (25a) means something quite different from (25b) is a consequence of switching the particle *up* for *down*. As we shall begin to see in the next chapter, my claim is not that words do not have stable semantic representations associated with them. I argue that they do, and refer to these as **lexical concepts**. Rather, my claim is that these lexical concepts provide access to encyclopaedic knowledge—a semantic potential—which is constrained and determined by context. Thus, the semantic structure (lexical concept) that a word is conventionally associated with does not in fact equate with the word's meaning. Word meaning, from this perspective, is always a function of a situated interpretation: the context in which any word is embedded and to which it contributes.

A further problem: compositionality

In the foregoing we have considered the nature of word meaning. I suggested that the problem to be accounted for, the inherent variation of word meaning in language use, is, in part, a function of words providing access to encyclopaedic knowledge. This in turn is narrowed by context, effectively delimiting which part of the encyclopaedic knowledge—the semantic potential—available to any given word is activated in any given utterance.

Yet, providing such an account is not enough if we are to fully get to grips with the contribution of words to meaning construction. To do so, we must, in addition, be able to account for how utterance (i.e., sentence) meaning arises. Utterance meaning involves several, often many, linguistic units, each of which individually exhibits great variability (Goldberg 2006; see also Kay and Michaelis forthcoming). That is, one must also be able to account for the integration of lexical and constructional meanings: we require an account of semantic compositionality, one that is coherent with the observable facts of language, and, of course, one which is cognitively plausible.

One of the most sobering realizations for any cognitive scientist attempting to grapple with the role of language in meaning construction is that despite the apparent ease with which we construct and interpret utterances in our everyday lives, the nature of semantic composition is a deceptively complex process. Moreover, the details of this process are far from being fully understood. For instance, the way in which the meaning of even a "simple" sentence is constructed is incredibly complex.

To illustrate, consider the example of: *The cat jumped over the wall*, discussed by Tyler and Evans (2003). This utterance describes a jump undertaken by a cat. Figure 1.2 presents some diagrams which present possible trajectories of the jump.

While there are at least four possible trajectories associated with this utterance, the canonical interpretation is that the cat begins the jump on one side of

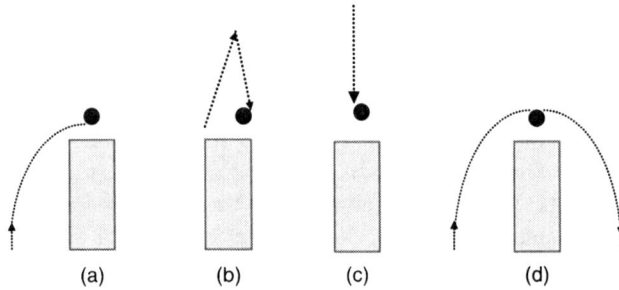

FIGURE 1.2. Possible trajectories for: *The cat jumped over the wall*

the wall, moves through an arc-like trajectory, and lands on the other side. Figure 1.2(d) best captures this interpretation. The issue to be accounted for is why it is that the reading typically derived relates to the trajectory diagrammed in 1.2(d) rather than one of the others. That is, what is it that excludes the trajectories represented in Figures 1.2(a–c)? After all, the utterance contains a number of words that have a range of interpretations. The behaviour described by *jump* has the potential to involve a variety of trajectory shapes. For instance, jumping from the ground to the table involves the trajectory represented in Figure 1.2(a). Jumping on a trampoline relates to the trajectory in 1.2(b). Bungee jumping involves the trajectory in 1.2(c). Finally, jumping over a puddle, hurdle, wall, etc., involves an arc-like trajectory as in 1.2(d). If the lexical item *jump* does not, in itself, specify an arc-like trajectory, but is vague with respect to its shape, then perhaps the preposition *over* is responsible.

Yet, *over* can also have several possible interpretations. It might be associated with an "across" interpretation: when we walk *over* a bridge (a horizontal trajectory). It can be associated with an "above" interpretation, as when an entity such as a hummingbird is *over* a flower (higher than but in close proximity to). Equally, *over* can have an "above" interpretation, as when a plane flies *over* a city: much higher and lacking close proximity. The point is that a word such as *over* can be used when different kinds or amounts of space are involved, and with a number of different trajectories/paths of motion. Hence, the received view that words are associated with fixed meanings, and that utterance meaning comes from concatenating the meanings of the individual words combined in a given utterance, underestimates the complexity involved in combining words, and the principles involved in their combination. An important aspect of the theory to be developed in this book relates to semantic composition, which is the subject of Part III.

Research issues to be addressed

The issues highlighted in this chapter relate to two issues central to my concerns in this book: the role of words in meaning construction, and the nature of semantic composition. My first objective, and the subject of Part II of this book, is to provide an account of lexical representation. As already noted above, I advance the perhaps controversial claim that words do not in fact have meaning, although this position is not without precedent, particularly in the psychology literature (e.g., Barsalou *et al.* 1993; Murphy 1991). On my account, meaning is a function of an utterance, rather than a given lexical representation associated with a word, or other symbolic (i.e., linguistic) unit. I make the case for words, and symbolic units in general, being associated with the construct of the lexical concept, a unit of semantic structure. A lexical concept is a conceptual representation specialized for being encoded in and externalized by language. This idea is developed in more detail later in the book, beginning with discussion in the next chapter. Additionally, an account of lexical representation would be incomplete without considering the level of conceptual structure to which lexical concepts provide access. This level is populated by what I will refer to as **cognitive models**, for reasons that will become apparent in later chapters.

Having developed an account of lexical representation, my second concern is to provide an account of the meaning-construction processes which make use of the semantic and conceptual levels of representation in service of situated utterance meaning. This issue, which I refer to as **semantic compositionality**, is the subject of Part III of the book. This involves an account of how lexical concepts are integrated in specific utterances: linguistically mediated usage events. The chapters in Part III address two key aspects of this process respectively, namely, the mechanisms of **lexical concept selection**, and **fusion**. Part IV of the book applies the theory of meaning construction developed to figurative language, arguing for a dynamic usage-based approach to figurative language understanding. One of the main claims to arise here is the position that language use often identified as constituting metaphor and metonymy arises from regular meaning-construction processes, which are, in principle, no different from those that give rise to non-figurative language. Thus, the present approach argues that figurative meaning derives from a meaning-construction process which marshals conventional linguistic resources (lexical concepts) together with the non-linguistic conceptual resources to which lexical concepts afford access. Thus, the position to be developed argues that there is continuity between literal and figurative language understanding. The treatment presented complements Conceptual Metaphor Theory (e.g., Lakoff and Johnson 1980, 1999), as I shall argue.

While on the face of it a new theory, LCCM Theory is, in fact, grounded in recent advances in the theoretical movement known as **cognitive linguistics**. As we shall see in Chapter 3, in certain respects it is not a new theory at all, but rather a synthesis of several extant approaches and theories that populate cognitive linguistics. However, the synthesis itself is genuinely novel, especially in so far as it serves to integrate cognitive linguistics approaches to grammatical organization, lexical semantics, semantic composition, and figurative language. In so doing, it attempts to unify the complementary and sometimes competing theories and approaches that abound in cognitive linguistics. Moreover, while the role of language in semantic composition is crucial to cognitive grammarians (e.g., Langacker 1987, 2008; Goldberg 1995, 2006), it has tended to be ignored (or at least downplayed) in contemporary accounts of meaning construction in cognitive linguistics (e.g., Fauconnier and Turner 2002). LCCM Theory also serves to restore, or at least redress, the centrality of language to semantic compositionality, whilst also recognizing the importance of non-linguistic processes in meaning construction, pointed to by Fauconnier and Turner, and indeed others, not least in the work of George Lakoff (see, for example, Lakoff 1993, 1996, 2006; Lakoff and Johnson 1980, 1999).

As we shall see, LCCM Theory takes its name from the two central constructs upon which it is built, the lexical concept and the cognitive model. The purpose of the next three chapters then, is to begin to sketch an account of LCCM Theory. The rest of the book will work out the details.

Summary

This chapter has argued that the received view of meaning in linguistics, what I refer to as literalism, is flawed in a number of respects. The distinction it posits between sentence meaning and speaker meaning makes a principled distinction between context-independent meaning (semantics) and context-dependent meaning (pragmatics). The consequence of this for word meaning is that word meanings are assumed to be stable and relatively delimited "atoms of meaning," which are context-independent. I have argued, on the contrary, that word meaning is inherently variable in language use. This is a function of both encyclopaedic knowledge and context of use. I have suggested that word meaning provides access to a sophisticated and structured body of non-linguistic encyclopaedic knowledge. This constitutes a word's semantic potential. The precise part of this semantic potential which is relevant in any given utterance is a function of context, which serves to narrow or constrain the semantic potential. Thus, word meaning is always, in part, a function of and determined by context. I have also argued that the notion of context is a complex and multifaceted phenomenon which includes linguistic as well as non-linguistic aspects of the communicative event. In addition I have argued that a Sense Enumerative Lexicon approach to word meaning is unable to capture the rampant variation in meaning exhibited by words in language use. I have also pointed to the problem for any theory of compositionality that arises by acknowledging such variation in word meaning. This follows as the meaning of any utterance is a function, in part, of the word meanings which comprise it, and yet, each of these word meanings varies on each occasion of use.

2

Towards a new account of word meaning

The purpose of this chapter is to outline the theoretical orientation that provides the foundation for the study of meaning construction presented in this book. This involves examining several recent advances in the study of language, and the way they interface with conceptual organization, all achieved in the context of cognitive linguistics. I begin, in the next section, by presenting, in the most general terms, the overarching assumptions which inform the approach I take. I then present five recent and significant developments that have emerged in language science, which inform the development of LCCM Theory. Following on from this, I discuss the principled distinction at the heart of LCCM Theory: the distinction between semantic structure, on the one hand, and conceptual structure on the other. This distinction, operationalized in terms of the distinct theoretical constructs: the lexical concept and the cognitive model, represents the hallmark of the Theory of Lexical Concepts and Cognitive Models—LCCM Theory for short. Moreover, this distinction is what, as we shall see in later chapters, makes the approach to encyclopaedic semantics developed here distinct from its forebears in cognitive linguistics.

Starting points

In this section I briefly review, from a very general perspective, my starting points for the study of meaning construction presented in this book. These can be summarized as follows:

- Meaning construction occurs at the interface between language, communication, and cognition and can only be fruitfully studied by virtue of an interdisciplinary effort. The sorts of research areas implicated include at least the following: cognitive linguistics (including cognitive stylistics and cognitive poetics), cognitive anthropology, discourse analysis and (interactional) sociolinguistics, gesture studies, developmental psychology, social psychology, neuropsychology, cognitive psychology, and (cognitive) neuroscience. Clearly, such an ambitious interdisciplinary endeavour is beyond the scope of the present work. Nevertheless, I attempt to integrate recent findings and theoretical frameworks from cognitive linguistics, and recent findings from cognitive psychology, in a way that presents a coherent starting position from which to begin to develop a more detailed view of meaning construction. My purpose is to create a psychologically plausible, programmatic framework which can feed into present and future work in the other areas of concern mentioned above. In particular, given recent advances in cognitive linguistics, discussed in more detail below, and in Chapter 3, part of the motivation behind the development of LCCM Theory is to present a "joined-up" cognitive linguistic theory of word meaning and meaning construction. In so doing, I aim to build upon recent advances, synthesizing a number of theoretical perspectives concerned with meaning as **conceptualization**,[1] and meaning as part of the study of grammar. This should provide a set of concrete ideas on how language contributes to meaning construction, and should facilitate empirical testing, both in terms of behavioural studies—those that ask human subjects to make judgements and perform activities of various sorts—and those that deploy brain-imaging techniques.

- Meaning construction is influenced by usage. This involves situated acts of language use and other non-verbal cues, such as gestures, in service of the expression of situated, goal-directed communicative intentions, in a particular physical setting and a cultural milieu, making use of various cognitive mechanisms and processes. I address some of these in this book.
- The study of the role and contribution of language to meaning construction is now a tractable problem, and the outstanding unifying challenge yet to be grappled by many of the social and cognitive sciences. Accordingly, the attempt to integrate and advance recent research findings that aim at a psychologically plausible model of the role of language in meaning construction processes is both timely and overdue.

Recent significant developments

LCCM Theory arises in the context of five significant developments which have emerged, in turn, in the context of cognitive linguistics. These relate to:

- Embodied cognition
- Lexical representation
- Encyclopaedic semantics
- The symbolic nature of grammar
- The interactional nature of situated language use

---

[1] I use the term conceptualization interchangeably with meaning construction.

In this section I introduce these developments.[2]

Embodied cognition

The thesis of **embodied cognition** is at the heart of much research within cognitive linguistics (Evans 2004a; Evans and Green 2006; Johnson 1987, 2007; Lakoff 1987; Tyler and Evans 2003), and has been influential in developments in cognitive psychology (in particular Barsalou 1999; Barsalou *et al.* 1993; Glenberg 1997).[3] This thesis—also referred to as **grounded cognition** (Barsalou 2008)—and first developed in cognitive linguistics by Lakoff and Johnson (e.g., 1980) holds that the human mind in general, and conceptual representation in particular, is **grounded** in bodily, neurological, and subjective states. That is, the range of **concepts** that populate the human **conceptual system**—the repository of concepts that form the basis of higher-level cognitive operations such as categorization, reason, choice, and so on—is a function of the species-specific nature of our bodies, and neuro-anatomical substructures, which have evolved to the particular ecological niche that we, as humans, inhabit. What this thesis means, in practical terms, is that cognitive function is not a consequence of a disembodied mind, which functions independently of body-based states (perceptual, motoric, cognitive, subjective, and so forth), a view enshrined in the mind/body dualism associated with seventeenth-century French philosopher René Descartes. Indeed, as observed by the neuropsychologist Antonio Damasio (1994): "...the mind derives from the entire organism as an ensemble...[and] depends on brain-body interactions" (*ibid.* 225–6). He continues:

> [T]he mind arises from activity in neural circuits, to be sure, but many of those circuits were shaped in evolution by functional requisites of the organism...a normal mind will happen only if those circuits contain basic representations of the organism, and if they continue monitoring the states of the organism in action. In brief, neural circuits represent the organism continuously, as it is perturbed by stimuli from the physical and sociocultural environments, and as it acts on those environments.
>
> (*ibid.* 226)

In essence, Damasio's argument is that the brain, which computes the mind, evolved in order to facilitate the survival of the body. In so doing, this gave rise to a mind which arises from a symbiotic brain–body interaction, what Mark Johnson refers to as: *The body in the mind.*[4]

---

[2] While each of the developments discussed here has precursors which antecede cognitive linguistics, the emergence of cognitive linguistics in the 1980s has provided them with a sharpened focus. For a review of historical antecedents of cognitive linguistics see Nerlich and Clarke (2007).

[3] For a recent book-length survey of experimental support for the embodied nature of cognition see Gibbs (2006). For related perspectives which posit that cognitive function and/or knowledge representation is grounded in multimodal states/mechanisms see Allport (1985), Barsalou (1999), Damasio (1989), Glenberg (1997), Martin (2001, 2007), and Thompson-Schill (2003). For important perspectives on the embodied nature of language see, for example, Glenberg and Kaschak (2002), Kaschak and Glenberg (2000), Vigliocco *et al.* (2009), and Zwaan (2004).

[4] *The body in the mind* is the title of Johnson's seminal 1987 book.

The notion of embodied cognition is fundamental to the account of semantic representation in LCCM Theory, as we shall see in Part II of the book. Both linguistic and conceptual representations are grounded in bodily and cognitive states, which emerge from the situated action of the human organism. In short, the two theoretical constructs at the heart of LCCM Theory: the lexical concept and the cognitive model, are, in slightly different ways, grounded in the states experienced by the body–brain coupling that gives rise to the embodied human mind.

Lexical representation

Recent work in **cognitive lexical semantics**—that branch of cognitive linguistics which is concerned with word meaning—as well as recent work in corpus linguistics, has begun to show that the nature of lexical representation is extremely complex. This complexity requires that we rethink the nature of the linguistic knowledge associated with words.[5] In this section I briefly mention three of the recent findings which relate to this complexity:

- Polysemy is conceptual in nature
- Words are associated with selectional tendencies
- Grammatical categories have a semantic basis

Since the seminal work of Claudia Brugman and George Lakoff (e.g., Brugman 1988; Brugman and Lakoff 1988; Lakoff 1987), it has become clear that part of the variation associated with word meaning is due to word forms being associated with distinct underlying conceptual representations: the phenomenon of **conceptual polysemy**. Polysemy occurs when a word form exhibits more than one distinct but related meaning conventionally associated with it. Brugman and Lakoff argued that these distinct but related meanings arise due to language users having a range of distinct but related meanings stored in their heads, in **semantic memory**, hence, "conceptual" polysemy: the polysemy which is exhibited is a function of underlying granularity in semantic memory. To illustrate, consider the following examples which all employ the verbal form *flying*:

(1) The plane/bird is flying (in the sky)   [SELF-PROPELLED AERODYNAMIC MOTION]

(2) The pilot is flying the plane (in the sky)   [OPERATION OF ENTITY CAPABLE OF AERODYNAMIC MOTION]

(3) The child is flying the kite (in the breeze)   [CONTROL OF LIGHTWEIGHT ENTITY]

---

[5] Many formal and computational approaches to word meaning traditionally assume that words comprise bundles of semantic, syntactic, and morphological features (see Pustejovsky 1995; Tyler and Evans 2003 for discussion, and Evans and Green 2006 for a review).

(4)   The flag is flying (in the   [SUSPENSION OF LIGHTWEIGHT
       breeze)   OBJECT]

For convenience I have glossed the semantic contribution of each of the instances of *flying*. The glosses appear in small capitals inside square brackets alongside the relevant examples. In (1) *flying* relates to the ability of an entity such as a bird to undergo self-propelled motion. In the example in (2) *flying* relates to the ability to operate an entity such that it can undergo aerodynamic motion. In (3) the meaning of *flying* has to do with the control of an entity such that it remains airborne, while in (4) *flying* relates to the suspension of a lightweight entity that is attached to another entity.

While these meanings are distinct, they are nevertheless intuitively related. After all, while the example in (1) might, for many people, represent the most typical instance of *flying*, what we might refer to, following Lakoff (1987) as the **central** (or **prototypical**) **sense,** the application of *flying* in (2) relates to the operation of an entity such that it undergoes aerodynamic motion close to that in (1). Similarly, the meaning of *flying* in (3) is close to that in (2) in that control is a salient aspect of the meaning. Finally, the meaning of *flying* in (4) is close to that in (3) in that the lightweight entity in question, while not under the control of an agent, is nevertheless attached to the ground, in the case of (4) due to a flagpole. In cognitive lexical semantics, it has been common to model polysemous senses in terms of a radiating lattice structure arranged with respect to a central sense or **prototype** (e.g., Lakoff 1987; Tyler and Evans 2001, 2003).[6]

The second recent finding relates to what, in the previous chapter, I referred to as selectional tendencies. Recent work in cognitive lexical semantics (e.g., Dąbrowska 2009; Evans 2004a, 2005, 2006) and in corpus linguistics (Atkins 1987; Gries and Divjak 2009) suggests that part of the linguistic knowledge associated with words includes the kinds and range of semantic arguments with which a word sense can co-occur and the grammatical constructions in which a particular word sense can appear. While any given usage of a word will have its own unique selectional requirements, in terms of, for instance, with which other words and grammatical constructions it will co-occur, general patterns ("tendencies") can be established, and form part of the conventional knowledge associated with a particular word sense. In Part II of the book I will characterize this notion in terms of what I refer to as a **lexical profile.**[7]

To illustrate, reconsider the distinct senses of *flying* exhibited above in (1) to (4). A salient grammatical feature for verbs is transitivity, which is to say whether they take a direct object or not. While a verb like *die* doesn't: *He died,* a verb such as *kick* does: *He kicked the ball.* One way of beginning to distinguish the lexical

---

[6] See Evans and Green (2006: ch. 10) for an overview.

[7] Other terms have been used to express a similar idea including "ID Tag" (Atkins 1987) and "behavioural profile" (Gries and Divjak 2009).

profiles of the four senses of *flying*, above, is to examine which of the senses are transitive (require a direct object) and which are intransitive (do not require a direct object). For instance, the senses associated with *flying* in (1) and (4) do not take a direct object, while those in (2) and (3) do.

Further distinctions can be made between the lexical profiles of the senses if we examine the semantic selectional tendencies associated with each. This concerns the semantic arguments with which a given sense can co-occur. For instance, the [SELF-PROPELLED AERODYNAMIC MOTION] sense of *flying* as in (1) only applies to entities that are capable of self-propelled aerodynamic motion. Entities that are not self-propelled, such as tennis balls, cannot be used in this sense (*the tennis ball is flying in the sky*).

The sense of *flying* in (2): [OPERATION OF ENTITY CAPABLE OF AERODYNAMIC MOTION] is restricted to the operation by an entity which can be construed as an agent, and, moreover, to entities that can undergo self-propelled aerodynamic motion. Further, the entity must be able to accommodate the agent and thereby serve as a means of transport. This explains why aeroplanes and hot air balloons are compatible with this sense, but entities unable to accommodate an agent are not. This is illustrated by example (5).

(5)   ??He was flying the sparrow across the English Channel

Nevertheless, entities which can be construed as being guided, or at least susceptible to being trained by a volitional agent, which nevertheless cannot accommodate an agent, are partially sanctioned by this lexical concept, as the following example illustrates:

(6)   He succeeded in flying the homing pigeon across the English Channel

In the case of [CONTROL OF LIGHTWEIGHT ENTITY] as evidenced by the use of *flying* in (3), this sense of *flying* appears to be restricted to entities that are capable of becoming airborne by turbulence, and can be controlled by an agent on the ground. This lexical concept appears to be specialized for objects such as kites and model/remote-controlled aeroplanes.

The final sense, glossed as [SUSPENSION OF LIGHTWEIGHT OBJECT], selects for entities that can be supported by virtue of air turbulence, but remain "connected to" the ground. This lexical concept applies to flags as well as hair and scarves, which can "fly" in the wind.

The third finding concerns the position that grammatical categories have a semantic basis. In particular, I am here concerned with **lexical classes** as semantic categories. Until relatively recently, particularly in the previously dominant tradition of formal linguistics associated with the work of Generative Grammar, it was assumed that lexical classes, e.g., nouns, verbs, adjectives, etc., were purely grammatical categories, determined on the basis of **distribution**—where in the sentence the form appears—and **morphology**—in particular, the kind of **inflection**, for instance, word-ending, associated with a form. For example, consider the following English sentence:

(7)   The boy kicked the boys

Here *boy* can be inflected with the plural marker -*s* and can appear either in subject or object position. On this basis, it counts as a noun. In contrast, the lexical form *kick* can be inflected with the past tense marker -*ed* and cannot appear in subject or object position. Thus, it counts as an instance of a verb.

More recently, work in cognitive approaches to grammar has argued that the morphological and distributional properties of lexical classes such as nouns and verbs are a reflex of semantic categories (e.g., Croft 2002; Langacker 1987; Wierzbicka 1988). In other words, what makes a word a noun or a verb is a function, not of abstract grammatical features reflecting the word's distribution in a sentence, but rather the semantic properties of the word itself. On this view, lexical class is an emergent property of word function.

For instance, Langacker (1987) argues what makes a given word a noun is that it describes what he refers to as a **thing**, which he operationalizes in terms of a **region** in some **domain**. For instance, while the lexical item *book* designates a physical artefact (a region), in the domain of physical space, the lexical item *team* designates a collection of individuals who interact cooperatively (a region) in the domain of physical space. On Langacker's view, some things can designate or **profile**—which is to say to conceptually highlight—regions in more than one domain. For instance, the noun *(a) flash* profiles a region in the domain of vision and time. With respect to vision, the region relates to the entire visual field. With respect to time, the region concerns a moment, and thus, a minimal unit of time.

In contrast, Langacker argues that (lexical items which count as) verbs profile a **relation**, rather than a thing. The difference is that a relation encodes an entity which has a temporal dimension, in the sense that it designates an entity which holds over time. For example, *(to) run* counts as a dynamic verb as it profiles an action which sequentially evolves, or changes, over time. Analogously, a stative verb, such as *(to) breathe*, profiles an event which persists and thus holds over time.

LCCM Theory incorporates all of the insights discussed here, developing a suitably sophisticated view of lexical representation. The relevant notions: the symbolic unit, and lexical concept, are developed in Part II of the book.

Encyclopaedic semantics

The third recent development relates to the nature of the knowledge to which words provide access. In recent years work in cognitive linguistics, inspired by research on knowledge representation in cognitive psychology, has argued that word meaning is a function of the vast repository of encyclopaedic knowledge to which it is connected. Two influential theories of encyclopaedic semantics have been put forward, by Langacker (e.g., 1987) and Fillmore (e.g., 1982, 1985).

The basic insight is that word meaning is always relativized with respect to a larger body of knowledge without which it could not be properly understood. This is variously referred to as **base** (Langacker) or **semantic frame** (Fillmore). To illustrate consider the word *diameter*. The meaning of this word is a function of that part of the circle which it designates. In other words, the meaning of *diameter* is a function of the base (or semantic frame), namely the entire circle with respect to which its meaning is derived. From this perspective, word meaning involves both a **profile**, what is designated, which constitutes a substructure in a larger structure, and namely a base (Langacker 1987). According to Langacker, word meaning is thus a function of **profile/base organization**, and as such cannot be separated from the larger knowledge units to which it affords access. Consider Figure 2.1 which depicts a circle. This base can provide numerous profiles, e.g., arc (Figure 2.1a), radius (Figure 2.1b), diameter (Figure 2.1c), circumference (Figure 2.1d), and so on. Crucially, each profile is understood with respect to the base: circle.

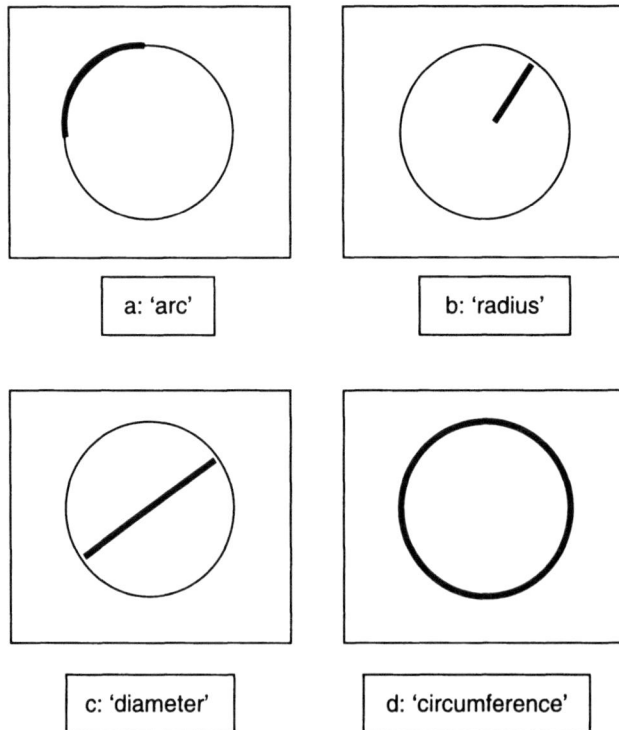

FIGURE 2.1. Different profiles derived from the same base

The encyclopaedic semantics perspective reveals that word meanings are related to larger (and more complex) knowledge structures. However, the approach taken in this book diverges from the received view of encyclopaedic semantics in cognitive linguistics, as developed by Langacker (1987), for instance. For Langacker, semantic structure is equated with conceptual structure: the knowledge base is part of the meaning of a word. Hence, there is no distinction between representations encoded by language and those that relate to the human conceptual system. The position developed in LCCM Theory is that the representations encoded by language are of a very different kind than those in the conceptual system. As the human conceptual system is continuous with the conceptual system of other primates (Barsalou 2005; Hurford 2007), and preceded, in evolutionary terms, the much later emergence of language (Deacon 1997; Donald 1991; Mithen 1996; Renfrew 2007; Tomasello 1999), then the meanings represented in the two systems are likely to be of distinct kinds.[8] This is enshrined in LCCM Theory in the separation between the two theoretical constructs that provide the theory with its name, the lexical concept and cognitive model.

The basis for this nuanced perspective on encyclopaedic semantics is the result of recent work in cognitive psychology. Recent theories of knowledge representation, such as the recent work on **frames**, has emphasized the relational nature of knowledge representation (see Barsalou 1991, 1992*a*, 1992*b*; Barsalou *et al.* 1993). More recent work has emphasized the role of **simulations**: rehearsals of body-based and cognitive states (Barsalou 1999, 2003, 2008; see also Glenberg and Kaschak 2002; Zwaan 2004). The notion of a frame *qua* large-scale, coherent mental representation, and the infinite set of simulations that it can give rise to, is an issue that I shall take up in detail in Chapters 9 and 10. As we shall see, these notions feed into the theoretical construct of the cognitive model. However, I discuss in slightly more detail below the way in which semantic representation is separated, in LCCM Theory, into distinct linguistic and conceptual representations.

The symbolic nature of grammar

The fourth significant development has emerged in the context of **cognitive approaches to grammar**. Here linguistic units—the entities which populate a language user's mental grammar—are treated as being inherently meaningful, in the same way, in principle, as words. That is, grammatical constructions "above" the level of the word, for instance, sentence-level patterns of syntax, have been found to have meaning conventionally associated with them. Hence, grammatical constructions, like words, are symbolic in nature.

This perspective, associated in particular with the theories of **Cognitive Grammar** (e.g., Langacker 1987, 1991*a*, 1991*b*, 1999, 2008) and **Cognitive Construction Grammar** (Goldberg 1995, 2006)—the two grammatical theories

---

[8] See the discussion in Chapter 9.

which have most influenced the development of LCCM Theory—holds that a grammatical unit such as the sentence string SUBJ V OBJ1 OBJ2, variously known as the **double object construction** and the **ditransitive construction** has a conventional meaning associated with it. Goldberg (e.g., 1995), who has studied the ditransitive construction in detail, argues that this construction exhibits polysemy in the same way as words. She shows that one of the meanings conventionally associated with ditransitive syntax is the following: X INTENDS Y TO RECEIVE Z. To illustrate consider the following example:

(8)   John baked Mary a cake

This sentence exemplifies the ditransitive construction, consisting of a subject, *John*, a verb, *bake*, and two objects: *Mary* and *a cake*. In terms of the schematic meaning held to be associated with the syntax exhibited in (8), X corresponds, in this example, to *John*, Y to *Mary* and Z to the *cake* in question. Thus, the meaning of the sentence can be paraphrased as follows: John intended Mary to receive the cake by virtue of baking it. However, the verb *bake* does not ordinarily have the 'intend Y to receive Z' semantics associated with it. That is, all things being equal, *bake* does not ordinarily have a meaning of transfer associated with it. Goldberg compellingly shows that it must be the construction itself which has this novel meaning associated with it, thus facilitating the intended transfer meaning associated with the act of baking a cake.

The consequence of adopting a symbolic approach to grammar is that grammar is no longer viewed as constituting an abstract set of rules which operate on words. Rather, the lexicon and grammar form a continuum, each consisting of bipolar **symbolic units** comprising a form and meaning: a **phonological pole** and a **semantic pole**, also known as the **lexicon-grammar continuum**, as depicted in Figure 2.2 (Croft 2002; Langacker 1987; Goldberg 1995). From this perspective, semantic composition becomes at once more complicated than the received view, and more straightforward. It is more straightforward in the sense that semantic composition in LCCM Theory involves **nested integration** of lexical concepts within larger lexical concepts.

For instance, the meaning of *bake*—to create an item such as a cake—must be integrated with the ditransitive construction: X INTENDS Y TO RECEIVE Z, such that *bake* implies 'X intends Y to receive Z' by virtue of baking.[9] However, this view of semantic composition is also more complex. The integration of lexical concepts—the semantic structures associated with symbolic units such as words and constructions—has to proceed in a way which is compatible with integration of the range of meanings associated with each of the lexical concepts in question. There are complex possibilities involved in the meaning of each lexical concept, each of which must be compatible with the lexical concepts which they are being integrated within: the

---

[9] The issue of "nested integration" is discussed in Part III of the book.

←——Open-class elements   Closed-class elements ——→

FIGURE 2.2. The lexicon-grammar continuum

phenomenon of nested integration just alluded to. For instance, *bake* must be integrated in the larger linguistic unit, the ditransitive construction, and the meaning of *bake* must be integrated in a way which is compatible with this larger unit.

One of the issues that Goldberg studies in detail in her pioneering work is that words, and larger, multi-word constructions, are integrated in such a way that the semantics of each fuse with the other providing a derived meaning which is more than the sum of the parts. For instance, Goldberg argues that both verbs and larger constructions have, as part of their meaning, slots for semantic arguments. These constitute part of the semantic frame—in the sense of Fillmore—associated with each construction, be it a verb or a larger linguistic unit such as the ditransitive construction. With respect to verbs, Goldberg refers to these semantic arguments as **participant roles**, while for sentence-level constructions, such as the ditransitive construction, she refers to such slots as **argument roles**. While the verb *bake* brings with it two participant roles: the baker and the object of baking, the ditransitive brings three: the agent, the object of transfer and the recipient. A consequence of **fusion** of the two sorts of constructions is that the more specific "baker" role of *bake* is fused with the agent slot of the ditransitive construction: the more specific role of "object of baking" is fused with the "object of transfer" role which comes from the ditransitive construction (see Figure 2.3). What motivates this is **semantic coherence**, which Goldberg formalizes in terms of what she calls the **Semantic Coherence Principle**.[10] In addition, the ditransitive construction adds a role not present in the *bake* semantic frame: that of intended recipient who is to receive the object of baking. The fusion of the ditransitive construction and the verb *bake* is illustrated in Figure 2.3.

The point is that semantic composition, from this perspective, is not due to language being constituted in terms of words and rules, with the rules being abstract conventions for combining "atoms" of meaning, the words. Rather, a language system consists of symbolic units—conventional symbolic assemblies of form and meaning—at all levels. Semantic composition is thus the result of integrating the semantic material associated with the various symbolic units, including sentence-level constructions.

We end up with an utterance such as: *John baked Mary a cake*, which provides meaning which is far more specific than the highly schematic

---

[10] This principle states that participant roles are matched with argument roles with which they overlap, such that one can be construed as an instance of another. For instance, general categorization principles enable us to determine that the Baker participant role of the verb *bake* overlaps sufficiently with the argument role Agent, of the ditransitive construction, because both share semantic properties such as Animacy, Intentionality, Causation, and so forth.

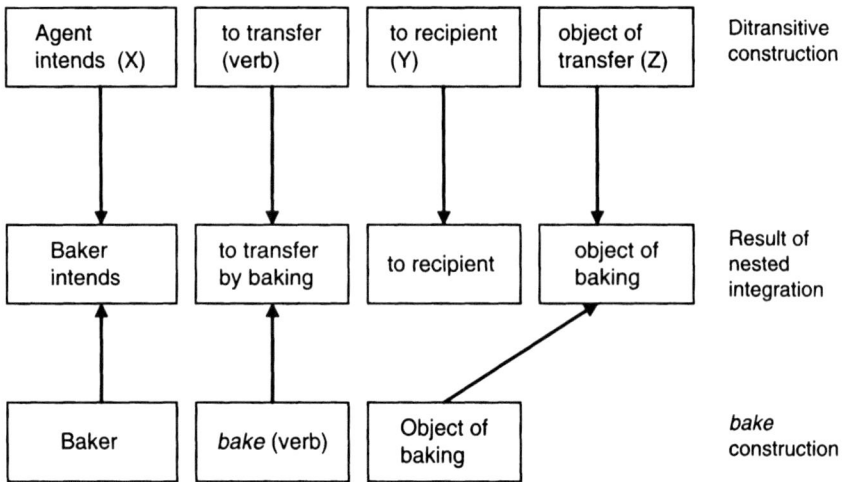

FIGURE 2.3. Fusion of the ditransitive and bake constructions

meaning of the ditransitive construction. This is due to the specific semantic frame associated with *bake*, which brings a particular activity and specific participant roles. Equally, the schematic semantic structure provided by the ditransitive construction serves to encode a particular scene, and frames the activity associated with *bake* within the context of this scene. Thus the activity encoded by *bake*, its semantic frame, is conceptualized in terms of an "intention to cause transfer" scenario, thus licensing the addition of the intended recipient role.

Intuitively, the symbolic perspective nicely captures the following insight. *Bake* is normally a two-place, i.e., a transitive, predicate. Canonically, it requires an agent and a patient: *John baked the cake*. The semantics of intended transfer are not, typically, a function of the verb *bake*. From this perspective, the approach sketched by Goldberg is compelling.

In more general terms, the symbolic perspective on grammar provided by scholars such as Goldberg, Langacker, and others is intuitively appealing. The insight is that one function of grammar is to encode scenes and scenarios relating to everyday experience. This is particularly clear in the work of Goldberg. Scenes and scenarios include agents performing actions, agents transferring objects to recipients, agents causing other entities to move from one location to another, and so on. Goldberg formalizes this observation in terms of the **scene-encoding hypothesis**. One of her basic observations is that sentence-level constructions serve to encode many of the typical scenes and scenarios we experience in our everyday lives. Such scenes involve several kinds of participants, and are encoded by sentence-level constructions. Table 2.1 illustrates some of the sentence-level constructions studied by Goldberg, and the scenes from experience they encode.

TABLE 2.1. Constructions and their corresponding scenes from experience
Key: Subj=subject, Obj=object, Obl=Oblique object (i.e., an object that forms part of a prepositional phrase), comp=complement

Construction	Form	Meaning	Example	Humanly relevant scene
Ditransitive	Subj V Obj1 Obj2	X CAUSES Y TO RECEIVE Z	*John sent Mary a love letter*	Agent gives an object to a recipient
Caused motion	Subj V Obj Obl	X CAUSES Y TO MOVE Z	*John sneezed the letter off the table*	Agent moves an object from one location to another
Resultative	Subj V Obj comp	X CAUSES Y TO BECOME Z	*The anaesthetist rendered the patient unconscious*	Agent acts on a patient causing them to undergo a change of state
Intransitive motion	Subj V Obl	X MOVES Y	*The wasp flew into the room*	Entity moves to a new location
Conative	Subj V at Obl	X DIRECTS ACTION AT Y	*John kicked at the rat*	Agent directs an action towards another entity

The usage-based nature of language

As we saw in the previous chapter, Grice (e.g., 1989) made a distinction between what a given sentence means and what its use means in a given context: the distinction between sentence meaning and speaker meaning.[11]

In modern linguistics, this distinction between sentence and speaker meaning is embodied in the disciplinary distinction between semantics and pragmatics, and informs the received view of the study of meaning: literalism. From the perspective of literalism, semantics—the study of sentence meaning—is normally considered to be primary, and prior to pragmatics—the study of speaker meaning. The supremacy of semantics is enshrined in **formal semantics**, the tradition which is directly descended from the logic-inspired work of the ideal language philosophers.

However, in seminal work, Herbert Clark (e.g., 1996) points out that in fact this perspective situates things the wrong way round. Clark argues that

---

[11] During the twentieth century the study of meaning in the analytic philosophy of language tradition was split into two camps. The first, the "ideal language philosophers" including Frege, Russell, Carnap, and Tarski, argued that the meaning of a sentence is comprised of its component parts, and meaning reflects reference. Thus, linguistic symbols could be assigned worldly entities absent a given context of use. The second group, the so-called "ordinary language philosophers", including Austin, Strawson, and the later Wittgenstein, argued that absent a specific context words cannot refer. Both groups were straddled by Paul Grice who offered a way of uniting both sets of concerns by distinguishing between sentence and speaker meaning, and arguing that both are required for a full account of meaning. See Recanati (2004) for a review of some of these concerns.

speaker meaning is logically prior to sentence meaning.[12] After all we can't talk about words and sentences having meaning without assuming a speaker and a hearer who are using the words and sentences in order to accomplish interactional goals. As Clark puts it: "Signals [i.e., words and sentences] aren't important merely because they mean things. They are important because they are used in discourse to accomplish the participants' goals" (*ibid.* xx). Put another way: "Words and sentences are types of signals, linguistic units abstracted away from any occasion on which they might be used, stripped of all relation to particular speakers, listeners, times and places. [Yet] ... utterances are the actions of producing words, sentences, and other things on particular occasions by particular speakers for particular purposes" (*ibid.* 128). Clark's point is that the conventions—the words and grammatical constructions—that linguists study under the guise of sentence meaning are, in fact, abstractions, derived from language in use, and hence are logically dependent on language use, that is, speaker meaning.

In cognitive linguistics, the most influential usage-based model of language is the theory of Cognitive Grammar developed by Langacker (e.g., 1987, 1991*a*, 2008). In Cognitive Grammar, the symbolic units that make up an individual language user's knowledge of the language system are derived from language use. This takes place by processes of **abstraction** and **schematization**. Abstraction is the process whereby structure emerges as the result of the generalization of patterns across instances of language use. For example, a speaker acquiring English will, as the result of frequent exposure, "discover" recurring words, phrases, and sentence-level constructions in the utterances they hear, together with the range of meanings associated with those symbolic units. Schematization is a special kind of abstraction, which results in representations that are much less detailed than the actual utterances that give rise to them. Schematization results in **schemas**. This is achieved by setting aside points of difference between actual structures, leaving just the points they have in common: a schema.

To illustrate, consider the examples in (9), focusing in particular on the meaning of the preposition *in*:

(9)   a. The kitten is in the box
      b. The flower is in the vase
      c. The crack is in the vase

These examples involve spatial scenes of slightly different kinds, where *in* reflects a spatial relationship between the **figure** (F) and the **reference object** (RO). In (9a) the F, *the kitten*, is fully enclosed by the RO, *the box*. However, in the other two examples, *in* does not prompt for quite the same kind of relationship. In (9b) the flower is not fully enclosed by the vase, since it partly

---

[12] Clark uses the term "signal meaning" to refer to sentence (and word) meaning.

protrudes from it. In (9c) *in* does not prompt for a relationship of enclosure in quite the same way: the crack is on the exterior of the vase, as opposed to the volumetric interior. As these examples illustrate, the specific spatio-geometric details associated with the enclosure meaning of *in* is not fixed, but is derived in part from the utterance context.

The schema that arises from these specific examples leaves aside the context-specific details. Rather, it gives rise to a highly abstract spatial relation involving enclosure: the commonality arising across each context of use. It is this commonality that establishes the schema for *in*. Moreover, the schema for *in* says very little about the nature of the F and RO, only that they must exist, and that they must have the basic properties that enable enclosure. Crucially, Cognitive Grammar assumes that the symbolic units which populate the mental grammar are nothing more than schemas, abstracted from language use. We shall begin to see, in Chapter 4, how LCCM Theory enshrines language use as fundamental to its account of meaning construction. Specifically, I argue that linguistically encoded semantic units, the lexical concepts, underspecify for their situated interpretation. A situated interpretation is, by definition, a function of language use.

Semantic structure versus conceptual structure

Cognitive linguists—for example Talmy (2000) and Langacker (1987)—have distinguished between two types of semantic knowledge: that which is rich and that which is schematic. This distinction is implicit in the work of Langacker and explicit in the work of Talmy. Talmy, for instance, distinguishes between schematic meaning associated with what he refers to as the **closed-class** or **grammatical subsystem**, and the rich meaning associated with the **open-class** or **lexical subsystem**. To illustrate, consider the following example:

(10)   A *popstar kissed* the *fans*

The forms in bold: **a**, **-ed**, **the**, and **-s** are associated with the grammatical subsystem. Their semantic contribution relates to whether the participants (*popstar/fans*) evoked by (10) can be easily identified by the hearer—the use of the indefinite article **a** versus the definite article **the**—that the event took place before now—the use of the past-tense marker **-ed**—and how many participants were involved—the presence or absence of the plural marker **-s**.

In contrast, the forms in italics: *popstar*, *kiss*, and *fan* are associated with the lexical subsystem. That is, their semantic contribution relates to the nature of the participants involved in the experiential complex, and the relationship holding between them, namely one involving a kiss. In other words, while the closed-class forms encode content relating to structural aspects of what we might refer to as the **experiential complex** evoked, the open-class forms give rise to detailed information concerning the nature of the participants, scenes involving the participants, and the states and relationships that hold.

The distinction in types of semantic representation is also present in Cognitive Grammar (e.g., Langacker 1987). As we saw above, Langacker argues that lexical classes such as nouns and verbs encode schematic meaning.[13] Another distinction claimed to hold between nouns and verbs has to do with whether there is a temporal dimension encoded. Langacker maintains that verbs (but not nouns) relate to time, and encode the evolution of a particular event or state through time.[14] A further schematic aspect of meaning has to do with whether a form encodes a schematic **trajector** (TR) and/or **landmark** (LM). For example, Langacker argues that relational lexical classes, such as prepositions, encode a highly schematic TR and LM as part of their semantic structure.[15] For instance, in terms of an expression such as: *under the sofa*, it is by virtue of *under* encoding a schematic LM that a noun phrase (NP) can be integrated with the preposition *under*, giving rise to the complex expression: *under the sofa*.[16]

In addition to schematic meanings of this sort, Langacker also assumes that words encode "rich" semantic content. As we saw earlier in the discussion of encyclopaedic semantics, this is conceived of in terms of a profile/base complex, in which a given form designates or profiles a given substructure within a base.

The distinction between schematic versus rich aspects of meaning can also be seen in Goldberg's work on Construction Grammar. Recall that Goldberg argues that sentence-level constructions, such as the ditransitive, have a highly schematic meaning associated with them, serving to encode argument roles. In contrast, individual words such as the verbs which populate these constructions, e.g., *bake*, are associated with rich frames and participant roles.

In this book I argue that the distinction between schematic versus rich meaning identified by Talmy, Langacker, and Goldberg actually reflects a distinction in types of meaning representation, and that the two distinct types of representation relate to distinct systems. Schematic meaning relates to representations that are specialized for being encoded by language. That is, such representations take a form that is highly schematic in nature, specialized for being encoded in the auditory (or signed) medium that is language. Representations of this sort are what I refer to as semantic structure. The

---

[13] The distinction between verbs and nouns concerns the nature of what is being profiled: a region in a domain, in the case of nouns, and the relations that hold between such regions, in the case of verbs.

[14] Langacker refers to this as **sequential scanning**. He distinguishes the way in which verbs encode time from the way time is encoded by other "relational" lexical classes, such as adjectives, adverbs, and prepositions (see Langacker 1987, 1991*b*, 1999, 2008; see Evans and Green 2006 for a review).

[15] Indeed, this notion is important for constituency in Cognitive Grammar.

[16] In Langacker's terms, the NP **elaborates** the **conceptually dependent** preposition *under*. I will discuss what it means to be conceptually dependent in more detail in Part II of the book. The issue of elaboration, in the sense of Langacker, will be discussed in more detail in Part III of the book.

theoretical construct I develop to model semantic structure is that of the lexical concept. In contrast, the rich representations are associated with the conceptual system, and are not directly encoded by language—although language facilitates access to this level. Representations of this sort are what I refer to as conceptual structure. The theoretical construct I develop to model conceptual structure is that of the cognitive model. Cognitive models involve a frame and simulations deriving from the frame. As briefly introduced, simulations are reactivations of sensory-motor, cognitive, and subjective states, based on, but not identical to the perceptual and subjective experiences that are stored in the conceptual system.

Part of my argument in this book is that semantic structure and conceptual structure form two distinct levels of representation, and do so because they inhere in two distinct representational systems: the **linguistic system** and the conceptual system. Following arguments presented by Barsalou *et al.* (forthcoming), I suggest that the linguistic system evolved, in part, by facilitating more effective control of the extant representations in the conceptual system.[17] That is, linguistic representations are specialized for providing a "scaffolding" to structure conceptual representations, thereby facilitating their use in communication. While the conceptual system evolved for action and perception, i.e., for non-linguistic purposes, the emergence of language facilitated the use of conceptual representations in linguistically mediated meaning construction, thereby providing cognitively modern humans with a significant evolutionary advantage. With the association of linguistic and conceptual representations, humans were able to engage in the advanced symbolic behaviours that led to the explosion of sophisticated ritual practice, material culture, art, and science around 50,000 years ago during the later Stone Age, the period that archeologists refer to as the Upper Paeleolithic (Mithen 1996; see also Renfrew 2007).

In essence, the argument I shall be making during the course of the book is that semantic structure and conceptual structure involve fundamentally distinct sorts of representations. Moreover, it is this distinctiveness that facilitates meaning construction. It is by virtue of semantic structure facilitating access to conceptual structure that words appear to be protean in nature. That is, what we might informally refer to as the "meaning shifting" properties, so to speak, associated with words is a symptom of there being two distinct types of representation implicated in meaning construction.

But to claim that there are two distinct representational systems involved in meaning construction is not to adopt a modular perspective (e.g., Fodor 1983). **Modularity** holds that the mind consists of domain-specific encapsulated modules, which work by virtue of one module working on the output of another. As we shall see, in LCCM Theory meaning arises by virtue of a dynamic exchange taking place between the linguistic and conceptual

---

[17] This is discussed in more detail in Chapter 9.

systems. Meaning construction involves a continual interplay involving distinct types of representations. The conceptual system must be consulted before other linguistic representations can be properly constructed and interpreted and vice versa. Thus, there is no place for strict modularity here. Yet, while I eschew modularity, I do claim, as we shall see, that the representational types in the two systems are wholly distinct. The schematic meaning representations, the lexical concepts, characteristic of the linguistic system are non-simulation providing. That is, lexical concepts do not encode or otherwise give rise, directly, to rehearsals of perceptual states. Yet, they can facilitate the activation of conceptual representations which do give rise to simulations. As we shall begin to see in more detail later in the book, the principled separation of semantic structure from conceptual structure calls for a revised approach to encyclopaedic semantics as adopted in cognitive linguistics. I address this issue in some detail in Part II of the book.

In order to summarize some of the key points developed in this section, I conclude with a brief reminder of some of the key terms and distinctions made. These are terms and distinctions that are central to LCCM Theory, which I shall be using throughout the rest of the book:

- The *linguistic system* consists of symbolic units.
- *Symbolic units* are made up of phonological forms and lexical concepts.
- The *conceptual system* consists of cognitive models.
- *Cognitive models* are constituted by frames and give rise to a potentially limitless set of simulations.[18]
- *Lexical representation* is made up of symbolic units and cognitive models, and is the primary substrate deployed in linguistically mediated meaning construction.
- *Semantic representation* is the semantic dimension of lexical representation and consists of the interaction between cognitive models and lexical concepts.
- *Semantic structure* relates to the content encoded by lexical concepts, and is the type of semantic unit encoded by the linguistic system.
- *Conceptual structure* relates to the content encoded by cognitive models, and is the form of representation encoded in the conceptual system.

In order to better illustrate these distinctions and how they intersect, Figure 2.4 provides a diagrammatic representation of lexical structure, the subject of Part II of the book. In Figure 2.4 the dashed line between the lexical concept in the linguistic system and the cognitive model—represented by the circle—in the conceptual system represents a path of access which associates the two. Figure 2.5 attempts to convey the nature of semantic representation in LCCM

---

[18] The notion of a cognitive model is based on Barsalou's (1999) notion of a **simulator**. The precise nature of a cognitive model, and its relationship with the construct of simulator, is discussed in Chapters 9 and especially 10.

LEXICAL REPRESENTATION

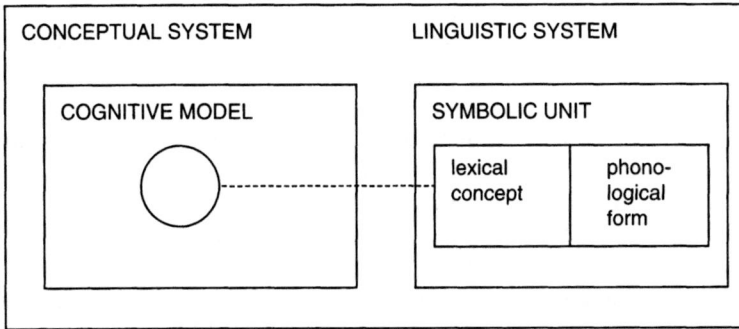

FIGURE 2.4. Lexical representation in LCCM Theory

LEXICAL REPRESENTATION

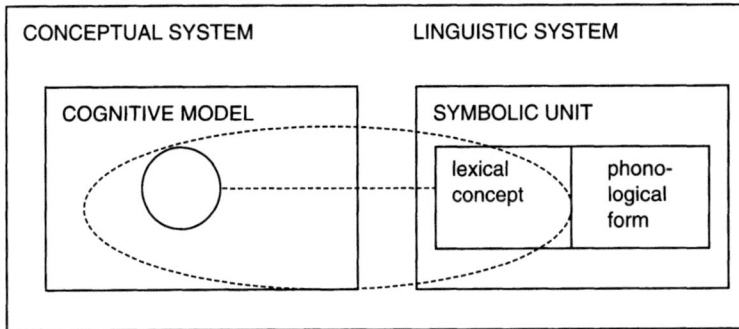

FIGURE 2.5. Semantic representation in LCCM Theory

Theory. Figure 2.5 is the same as Figure 2.4 except that it additionally features a dashed elipse encircling the lexical concept—in the linguistic system—and the cognitive model—in the conceptual system—the two types of representation which collectively comprise semantic representation.

Summary

In this chapter I have, in broad terms, outlined the starting points and guiding assumptions of the Theory of Lexical Concepts and Cognitive Models (LCCM Theory). The starting point for this study is the observation that word meaning is inherently variable or protean across situated instances of use. In attempting to address this issue, LCCM Theory arises from five recent developments in the language sciences. These relate to (i) the embodied nature of cognition, (ii) the view that lexical representation is more sophisticated than has previously been assumed, (iii) the view that lexical representations relate, in part, to non-linguistic knowledge structure, (iv) the view that the mental grammar consists of symbolic assemblies of form and meanings, rather than words and abstract rules which operate on words, and (v) the view that meaning construction arises in the context of language use, which is to say the situated and interactional nature of linguistically mediated communication between interlocutors. That is, meaning arises as a function of the expression of situated communicative intentions. I also discussed, in this chapter, the principled distinction at the heart of LCCM Theory, the presumption that the linguistic and conceptual systems consist of distinct types of representation: the lexical concept and the cognitive model. As we shall see, although distinct, these representational types interact and thereby give rise to the apparently protean nature of word meanings. In short, LCCM Theory assumes a principled distinction between semantic structure and conceptual structure.

3

Cognitive linguistics

As the present treatment of lexical representation and semantic composition is grounded in the perspective known as cognitive linguistics, this chapter briefly introduces the cognitive linguistics enterprise. Cognitive linguistics is arguably the most rapidly developing approach to the relationship between language, mind, and human sociocultural experience in the language sciences, and is increasingly influential in the interdisciplinary project known as cognitive science. In this chapter I present its guiding assumptions and also briefly review its two best-developed sub-branches: (i) cognitive semantics, and (ii) cognitive approaches to grammar. I do this in order to provide a context for the discussion at various points throughout the book. I then discuss the ways in which LCCM Theory builds upon and complements some of the specific (and most influential) theories that populate cognitive linguistics.

The cognitive linguistics enterprise

A number of the recent developments discussed in the previous chapter, upon which LCCM Theory is based, derive from cognitive linguistics. In particular, LCCM Theory takes as its starting point the core assumptions and primary commitments of the cognitive linguistics enterprise. Accordingly, in this section I briefly introduce the nature of the cognitive linguistics enterprise for those readers to whom it may be unfamiliar, before proceeding, in the following section, to identify how LCCM Theory relates to some of the specific theories that populate cognitive linguistics, theories which are antecedent, in the sense that these are theories that LCCM Theory builds upon and/or responds to.[1]

Cognitive linguistics is a modern school of linguistic thought and practice, concerned with investigating the relationship between human language, the mind, and sociophysical experience. It originally emerged in the 1970s and arose out of dissatisfaction with formal approaches to language, which were then dominant in linguistics and philosophy. While its origins were, in part, philosophical in nature, cognitive linguistics has always been strongly influenced by theories and findings from the other cognitive sciences as

---

[1] A comprehensive book-length introduction to cognitive linguistics is Evans and Green (2006).

they emerged during the 1960s and 1970s, particularly cognitive psychology. Nowhere is this clearer than in work relating to human categorization, particularly as adopted by Charles Fillmore in the 1970s (e.g., Fillmore 1975) and George Lakoff in the 1980s (e.g., Lakoff 1987). Also of importance have been earlier traditions such as Gestalt psychology, as applied to the structure of language by Leonard Talmy (e.g., 2000) and Ronald Langacker (e.g., 1987). Finally, the neural underpinnings of language and cognition have had long-standing influence on the character and content of cognitive linguistic theories, from early work on how visual biology constrains colour-term systems (Kay and McDaniel 1978) to more recent work under the rubric of the Neural Theory of Language (Feldman 2006; Gallese and Lakoff 2005). In recent years, cognitive linguistic theories have become sufficiently sophisticated and detailed to begin making predictions that are testable using the broad range of converging methods from the cognitive sciences.[2]

It is important to note that cognitive linguistics is best described as an "enterprise" precisely because it does not constitute a single closely articulated theory. Rather, it represents an approach that has a number of core commitments and guiding principles, which have led to a diverse range of complementary, overlapping (and sometimes competing) theories.

The cognitive linguistics enterprise is characterized by two fundamental commitments: the **Generalization Commitment** and the **Cognitive Commitment** (Lakoff 1990).

The Generalization Commitment represents a commitment to characterizing general principles that apply to all aspects of human language. This goal is just a special subcase of the standard commitment in science to seek the broadest generalizations possible. In contrast to the cognitive linguistics approach, other approaches to the study of language, such as literalism, often separate the language faculty into distinct areas such as semantics (word and sentence meaning), pragmatics (meaning in discourse context), morphology (word structure), syntax (sentence structure), and so on. As a consequence, there is often little basis for generalization across these aspects of language, or for the study of their interrelations.

Cognitive linguists acknowledge that it may often be useful to treat areas such as syntax, semantics, and morphology as being notionally distinct. However, given the Generalization Commitment, cognitive linguists do not start with the assumption that the "modules" or "subsystems" of language are organized in significantly distinct ways, or indeed that wholly distinct modules even exist. Thus, the Generalization Commitment represents a commitment to investigating how the various aspects of linguistic knowledge emerge from a common set of human cognitive abilities upon which they draw, rather than assuming that they are produced in encapsulated modules of the mind.

---

[2] See Gonzalez-Marquez *et al.* (2007) for introductory essays by leading researchers on empirical methods in cognitive linguistics.

The Generalization Commitment has concrete consequences for studies of language. Firstly, cognitive linguistic studies focus on what is common among aspects of language, seeking to re-use successful methods and explanations across these aspects. For instance, just as word meaning displays prototype effects[3]—there are better and worse examples of referents of given words, related in particular ways—so various studies have applied the same principles to the organization of morphology (e.g., Taylor 2003), syntax (e.g., Goldberg 1995), and phonology (e.g., Jaeger and Ohala 1984).

The second commitment is the Cognitive Commitment (Lakoff 1990). This represents a commitment to providing a characterization of the general principles for language that accord with what is known about human cognition from the other cognitive and brain sciences, particularly psychology, artificial intelligence, cognitive neuroscience, and philosophy. In other words, the Cognitive Commitment asserts that models of language and linguistic organization should reflect what is known about the human mind, rather than purely aesthetic dictates such as the use of particular kinds of formalisms or economy of representation, as in the case of formal approaches to linguistics.[4]

The Cognitive Commitment has a number of concrete ramifications. Firstly, linguistic theories cannot include structures or processes that violate known properties of the human cognitive system. For instance, if sequential derivation of syntactic structures violates time constraints provided by actual human language processing, then it must be jettisoned. Secondly, models that use known properties of human cognition to explain language phenomena are more parsimonious than those that are built from a priori simplicity metrics. For example, quite a lot is known about human categorization, and a theory that reduces word meaning to the same mechanisms responsible for categorization in other cognitive domains is simpler than one that hypothesizes a separate system for representing, for instance, lexical semantics. Finally, it is incumbent upon the cognitive linguistic researcher to find convergent evidence for the cognitive reality of components of any model or explanation—whether or not this research is conducted by the cognitive linguist.

Cognitive linguistics practice can be divided, approximately, into two main areas of research: **cognitive semantics** and **cognitive (approaches to) grammar** (see Figure 3.1).

The area of study known as cognitive semantics is concerned with investigating the relationship between experience, the conceptual system, and the semantic structure encoded by language. In specific terms, scholars working in cognitive semantics investigate **knowledge representation**—which I also refer to as conceptual structure—and meaning construction. Research in cognitive semantics employs language as the lens through which these cognitive phenomena can be investigated. Consequently, research in cognitive semantics tends to

---

[3] See Lakoff (1987) and Taylor (2003).
[4] See Croft (1998) for discussion of this.

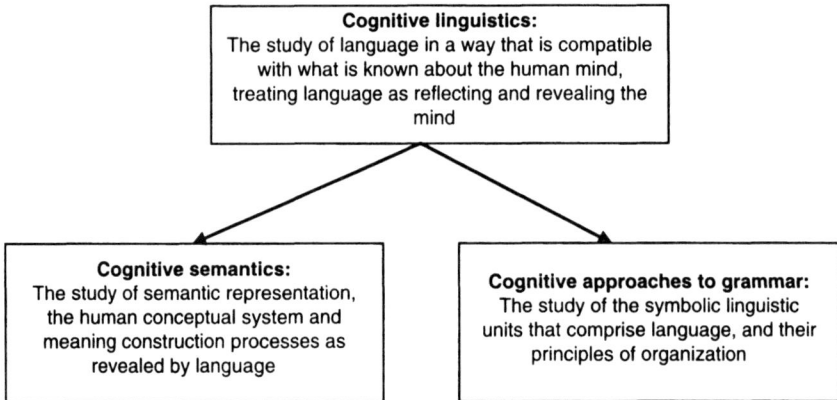

FIGURE 3.1. The study of meaning and grammar in cognitive linguistics

be interested in modelling the human mind just as much as it is concerned with investigating linguistic semantics, which is to say semantic structure.

In contrast, a cognitive approach to grammar is concerned with modelling the language system: the **mental grammar**, rather than the nature of mind per se. However, it does so by taking as its starting points the conclusions of work in cognitive semantics. This follows as meaning is central to cognitive approaches to grammar. Indeed, it is worth observing that the centrality of meaning for the study of grammar is another way in which cognitive approaches to grammar are fundamentally cognitive, as observed by Talmy (2000).

Although the study of cognitive semantics and cognitive approaches to grammar are occasionally separate in practice, this by no means implies that their domains of enquiry are anything but tightly linked—most work in cognitive linguistics finds it necessary to investigate both meaning and grammatical organization simultaneously.

As with research in cognitive semantics, cognitive approaches to grammar have also typically adopted one of two foci. Scholars such as Ronald Langacker (e.g., 1987, 1991a, 1991b, 1999, 2008) have emphasized the study of the cognitive principles that give rise to linguistic organization. In his theory of Cognitive Grammar, Langacker has attempted to delineate the principles that structure a grammar, and to relate these to aspects of general cognition.

The second avenue of investigation, pursued by researchers including Bergen and Chang (2005), Croft (2002), Fillmore and Kay (Fillmore et al. 1988; Kay and Fillmore 1999), Goldberg (1995, 2006), Lakoff (Lakoff and Thompson 1975; Lakoff 1987), and Michaelis and Lambrecht (1996), aims to provide a more descriptively and formally detailed account of the linguistic units that comprise a particular language. These researchers attempt to provide a broad-ranging inventory of the units of language, from morphemes to words, idioms, and phrasal patterns, and seek accounts of their structure, compositional possibilities, and relations. Researchers who have pursued this line of investigation are developing a set of theories that are collectively known as **construction grammars.** This general approach takes its name from the view in cognitive linguistics that the basic unit of language is the symbolic unit, as introduced above. Such symbolic units are also known, in construction grammars, as constructions.[5]

Antecedents of LCCM Theory

The approach to lexical representation and semantic compositionality to be presented in the rest of the book has feet in both cognitive semantics, and cognitive approaches to grammar. It constitutes a cognitive semantic theory as it is concerned with meaning-construction processes, figurative and non-figurative language and thought, and the relationship between semantic structure and conceptual structure. Thus, one of the goals of LCCM Theory is to provide a theoretical account of how language might interface with other aspects of cognitive structure and processing, and as such to provide a window on the human conceptual system.

However, and unlike some of the recent cognitive semantic theories of meaning construction, notably **Mental Spaces Theory** and **Conceptual Blending Theory**, LCCM Theory also constitutes a theory of language, which is to say linguistic organization and structure. That is, LCCM Theory is centrally concerned with some of the key aspects of linguistic knowledge, and the symbolic nature of language which, as I shall argue in detail later in the book, plays a key role in semantic compositionality. Indeed, compositionality is one of the hallmarks of the symbolic abilities available to human beings, of which language is an instance *par excellence.* In particular, the study of lexical concepts, one of the central concerns of the book, is a study in the nature of semantic structure, which represents a key aspect, perhaps the central aspect, of the study of the mental inventory of linguistic knowledge, i.e., the nature of grammar. From this perspective then, LCCM Theory constitutes a cognitive approach to grammar.

In order to draw out these points, I briefly discuss below some of the antecedent theories in cognitive linguistics, upon which LCCM Theory draws and/or builds in order to begin to give a sense of (i) its distinctive contribution, and (ii) how it attempts to synthesize sometimes divergent cognitive linguistic theories, in order to begin to move to a single "joined-up" cognitive linguistic theory. One goal is to provide a unified perspective, relating linguistic structure and organization on the one hand, and meaning construction on the other.

---

[5] See Goldberg (2006: ch. 10) for discussion of the different varieties of Construction Grammar.

Meaning construction

Within cognitive semantics there have been two significant attempts to address the role of language in meaning construction. These relate to Mental Spaces Theory, developed by Gilles Fauconnier (1994, 1997), and the more recent Conceptual Blending Theory, developed by Gilles Fauconnier and Mark Turner (2002; see also Coulson 2000), which builds upon Mental Spaces Theory.

Mental Spaces Theory represents an attempt to account for issues of reference in discourse which have proved problematic in the Anglo-American philosophy of language tradition. The novelty of Mental Spaces Theory is that it provides a way of modelling discourse in terms of **mental spaces**—distinct regions of conceptual space, giving rise to a **mental spaces lattice**. Thus, discourse is conceived as being partitioned across a network of mental spaces, which proliferate as we think and talk (see Figure 3.2).

The later development of Conceptual Blending Theory adopts aspects of the architecture of Mental Spaces Theory in order to model the creativity associated with meaning construction and the use of language in meaning construction as well as developing significant theoretical machinery of its own. However, what is common to both theories is that their primary focus concerns compositional mechanisms that operate at the conceptual rather than at the linguistic level. In other words, neither of these theories is primarily focused on the nature of or contribution of linguistic knowledge, including words, to meaning-construction processes—what Fauconnier refers to as **backstage cognition**. For instance, an important concern of both these theories is the importance of conceptual mechanisms and processes in meaning construction. By way of illustration, consider the following quotation:

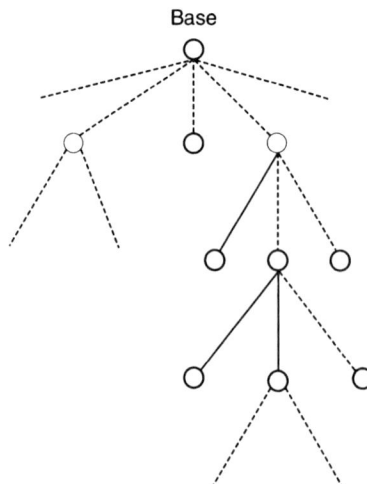

FIGURE 3.2. A lattice of mental spaces

Language, as we use it, is but the tip of the iceberg of cognitive construction. As discourse unfolds, much is going on behind the scenes: New domains appear, links are forged, abstract meanings operate, internal structure emerges and spreads, viewpoint and focus keep shifting. Everyday talk and commonsense reasoning are supported by invisible, highly abstract, mental creations, which ... [language] ... helps to guide, but does not by itself define.

(Fauconnier 1994: xxii–xxiii)

For Fauconnier, some of the most important, and therefore some of the most interesting, aspects of meaning construction lie "behind the scenes," not in language, but at the conceptual level. This level he refers to as "Level C" (Fauconnier 1997), the level at which meaning construction occurs. For both Mental Spaces Theory and Conceptual Blending Theory the role of language in meaning construction is reduced to that of providing relatively impoverished prompts which serve as minimal instructions for the far richer conceptualization processes which occur at Level C. Consider the following quotation from Mark Turner by way of illustration:

Expressions do not mean; they are prompts for us to construct meanings by working with processes we already know. In no sense is the meaning of [an] ... utterance "right there in the words." When we understand an utterance, we in no sense are understanding "just what the words say"; the words themselves say nothing independent of the richly detailed knowledge and powerful cognitive processes we bring to bear.

(Turner 1991: 206)

My point is not to deny the importance of conceptualization processes which occur "above" the level of language, and which are self-evidently essential for meaning construction, as both Fauconnier and Turner rightly observe. Nor do I deny that, in relative terms, linguistic units serve to prompt for rich conceptualization processes. Nevertheless, thus far in the development of contemporary approaches to meaning construction in cognitive linguistics, the role of words in meaning-construction processes has been underplayed. While the semantic values associated with linguistics units— what I refer to as lexical concepts—are impoverished with respect to the conceptual knowledge structures to which they afford access, and are also impoverished with respect to the conceptualizations to which they give rise, they nevertheless exhibit significant complexity and sophistication.

My purpose in this book is to explore some of this complexity, and the role it plays in interfacing with the conceptualization processes of backstage cognition, studied by scholars such as Coulson (e.g., 2000), Fauconnier, Turner, and others. Accordingly, LCCM Theory can be thought of as a theory of **frontstage cognition**. It represents an attempt to study the complexity of the semantic units (lexical concepts) associated with linguistic units such as words, and the central role they play in language understanding. Such a theory must, of course, mesh with a theory of backstage cognition. Thus, the theory to be developed attempts to remain consistent with what we now know about the nature of the conceptualization processes that give rise to meaning construction, and thus the general perspective provided by Mental Spaces Theory and Conceptual Blending Theory.

The division of labour that holds between frontstage and backstage theories of cognition can be delineated as follows. A theory of frontstage cognition (e.g., LCCM Theory) involves an account of the following:

- the relationship between lexical forms and semantic structure,
- the nature of the relationship holding between semantic structure (inhering in the linguistic system) and conceptual structure (inhering in the conceptual system),
- the principles of lexical composition that serve to integrate lexical concepts and facilitate the selective activation of conceptual structure, and
- the role of context, including the interactional and goal-directed nature of language in serving to convey situated communicative intentions.

Theories of backstage cognition (e.g., Conceptual Metaphor Theory, Mental Spaces Theory, and Conceptual Blending Theory) involve the following:

- the non-linguistic principles that facilitate conceptual integration of structure as prompted for by language,
- the integration of background non-linguistic knowledge structures, e.g., frames, in service of the construction of sophisticated and novel conceptual structures (what Fauconnier and Turner refer to as **pattern completion**),
- the dynamic construal of conceptualizations (what Fauconnier and Turner refer to variously as **elaboration** or **running the blend**)

The ultimate aim of both frontstage and backstage approaches to cognition is to achieve the following:

- a model of discourse meaning: a dynamic and temporary set of ideas, represented and partitioned in conceptual space, which is an emergent and evolving property of situated communication, and mediated, in part, by language.

The interaction between frontstage and backstage theories of cognition is summarized in Figure 3.3.

Lexical representation

One of the key aspects associated with an account of frontstage cognition relates to lexical representation, which is the subject of Part II of the book. As we saw in the previous chapter, lexical representation constitutes (i) the inventory of linguistic knowledge available to language users (symbolic

```
┌─────────────────────────────────────┐
│    A model of discourse meaning      │
└─────────────────────────────────────┘
                   ▲
                   │
┌─────────────────────────────────────┐
│  A model of backstage cognition: the │
│   processes and principles of        │
│  conceptualization prompted for by   │
│  processes of frontstage cognition   │
└─────────────────────────────────────┘
                   ▲
                   │
┌─────────────────────────────────────┐
│   A model of frontstage cognition: the │
│  nature of linguistic knowledge, context, │
│  lexical integration, and activation of non- │
│   linguistic knowledge, in service of │
│   prompting for processes of backstage │
│              cognition               │
└─────────────────────────────────────┘
```

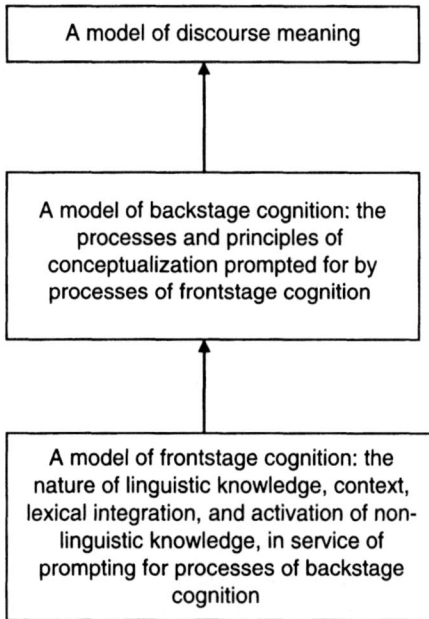

FIGURE 3.3. The interaction of frontstage and backstage approaches to cognition

units), and (ii) knowledge as to how this interfaces with non-linguistic knowledge in the conceptual system (cognitive models).

A key aspect of lexical representation is semantic structure, modelled in terms of lexical concepts—the subject of Chapters 6 and 7. The hallmark of many lexical concepts, and a key aspect of semantic structure, concerns knowledge of the other words and constructions with which a given lexical concept can co-occur. Indeed, in the discussion of *flying*, in examples (1) to (4) in the previous chapter, we saw that distinct lexical concepts associated with this form pattern in distinct ways in terms of their selectional tendencies—for example, the semantic arguments they co-occur with. As noted, I use the term lexical profile to refer to semantic structure of this sort. The approach to the lexical profile developed in LCCM Theory builds upon the earlier theory of **Principled Polysemy**, a cognitive linguistic theory of lexical representation, developed in two book-length treatments by Andrea Tyler and myself (Evans 2004*a*; Tyler and Evans 2003).

The earliest work on Principled Polysemy (e.g., Tyler and Evans 2001, 2003) focused on the lexical representations associated with spatial particles such as prepositions. Later work (e.g., Evans 2004*a*, 2005) was concerned with a different lexical class, namely nouns, and specifically the abstract noun *time*.

Principled Polysemy as a theory of lexical representation was, in large measure, responding to methodological problems associated with earlier work in cognitive lexical semantics, particularly the early pioneering work of Claudia Brugman and George Lakoff in their work on the English preposition *over* (Brugman and Lakoff 1988; Lakoff 1987). For instance, Dominiek Sandra (1998), a psycholinguist, challenged cognitive lexical semanticists to develop clear decision principles that make semantic network analyses objective and verifiable, and thus avoid what he referred to as the **polysemy fallacy**. The fallacy relates to the following fallacious reasoning: because a lexical item exhibits a novel meaning in context, each distinct semantic contribution is due to a distinct underlying sense stored in memory. According to Sandra this reasoning is fallacious as it does not follow that all or even many distinct instances associated with a lexical item provide evidence for distinct senses stored in semantic memory. Indeed, work by Brugman and Lakoff, which serves to proliferate the number of senses associated with *over*, for instance, can be criticized on similar grounds to models of lexical semantics that constitute Sense Enumerative Lexicons, discussed in Chapter 1. Indeed, this is the tack I will take in the next chapter, where I briefly review the model of word meaning proposed by Brugman, Lakoff, and others.

Tyler and I, in the earlier phase of research on Principled Polysemy addressing prepositions, sought to provide decision principles that would achieve two goals:

- they should serve to determine what counts as a distinct sense (i.e., a lexical concept—a term that was used for the first time in the context of Principled Polysemy in Evans 2004a), and thus should distinguish between senses stored in semantic memory, and context-dependent meanings constructed "online," and
- they should establish the prototypical or central sense associated with a particular semantic network. This point is important because cognitive semanticists have not always agreed about the central senses of semantic categories. For example, while Lakoff (1987) argued that the central sense for *over* is the ABOVE-ACROSS meaning, Kreitzer (1997) has argued more recently that it is an ABOVE meaning.

In our 2003 book *The Semantics of English Prepositions*, Tyler and I sought to provide decision principles that could be applied to the entire class of English prepositions. Here I will briefly outline the principles we proposed in that work for the first of these issues: how to determine what counts as distinct lexical concept associated with a given prepositional form.

We provided two criteria for determining whether a particular sense of a preposition counts as a distinct lexical concept:

i. For a sense to count as distinct, it must involve a meaning that is not purely spatial in nature, and/or a spatial configuration holding between

the Figure (F) and Reference Object (RO) that is distinct from the
other senses conventionally associated with that preposition; and

ii. There must also be instances of the sense that are context-independent:
instances in which the distinct sense could not be inferred from another
sense and the context in which it occurs.

To see how these criteria are applied, consider the utterances in (1) and (2):

(1)   The hummingbird is hovering over the flower

(2)   The helicopter is hovering over the city

In (1), *over* designates a spatial relation in which the F, *the hummingbird*, is
located higher than the RO, *the flower*. In (2), *over* also designates a spatial
relationship in which the F, *the helicopter*, is located higher than the RO.
In these examples, neither instance of *over* involves a non-spatial interpretation, and both senses encode the same spatial relation. According to
the first criterion, then, the two instances do not encode distinct senses, so
the second criterion does not apply. The sense of *over* that is represented in
both these examples is what Tyler and I called the ABOVE sense. Now
compare the example in (3) with (1) and (2).

(3)   John nailed a board over the hole in the ceiling

In (3), the spatial configuration between the F and RO is not consistent with
the ABOVE meaning in (1) and (2); in (3) the board is actually below the hole
in the ceiling. In addition, there is a non-spatial aspect to this sense: part
of the meaning associated with *over* in (3) relates to COVERING, because the RO
(*the hole*) is obscured from view by the F. This COVERING meaning is not
apparent in examples (1) and (2). The presence of this non-spatial aspect in
the sense of *over* in (3) meets the first assessment criterion, which means we can
now consider the second criterion. In doing so, we must establish whether the
COVERING meaning is context-independent or constructed "online."

Tyler and I argued that the meaning of *over* in (3) cannot be computed
online, and is therefore context-independent. In other words, the knowledge
that *over* in (3) has an ABOVE meaning does not allow us to infer a COVERING
meaning from the context supplied by (3). To elaborate this point, Tyler and
I provided a different example in which the COVERING meaning is derivable
from context. Consider example (4).

(4)   The tablecloth is over the table

In (4), the F (*the tablecloth*), is above—and in contact with—the RO (*the
table*). The interpretation that the table is covered or obscured by the table-

cloth can be inferred from the fact that the tablecloth is above the table, together with our encyclopaedic knowledge that tablecloths are larger than tables and the fact that we typically view tables from a vantage point higher than the top of the table. This means that the meaning of COVERING associated with *over* in (4) can be inferred from the ABOVE lexical concept exhibited, together with encyclopaedic knowledge. This type of inference is not possible in (3) because the spatial relation holding between the F and the RO is one that would normally be encoded by the expression *below—The board is below the hole in the ceiling—* given our typical vantage point in relation to ceilings. According to Tyler and Evans (2003) then, the COVERING meaning of *over* in (3) must therefore be stored as a distinct lexical concept associated with *over*.

The problem with the perspective provided by the model of Principled Polysemy, as just sketched, is that it is not always clear how one goes about determining whether a meaning is contributed by or independent of context. After all, as I observed in the opening chapter, any given instance of use of any word will always represent a distinct meaning given the context in which it is embedded. For instance, the meaning of *want* in the examples below is necessarily distinct in each example precisely because the desire being expressed relates to a different sort and thus is unique on each occasion of use:

(5) a. I want a cigarette
     b. I want a beer
     c. I want a hamburger
     d. I want a pizza

The point of the Principled Polysemy approach was to determine the sense units—i.e., lexical concepts—that words, *qua* lexical forms, have associated with them. Thus, the difficulty with the version of Principled Polysemy model developed by Tyler and Evans (2001, 2003) is that it could not in fact do this, as context necessarily enters into any given meaning. It sought to isolate meaning from context, which is, by definition, impossible.[6]

In a later version of Principled Polysemy (Evans 2004a, 2005) I developed criteria that reformulated the methodology for identifying distinct lexical concepts. The reformulation allowed for the critical role of context in contributing to word meaning by building the notion of context into the decision principles, rather than by attempting to exclude it. These criteria operationalized utterance context in terms of the semantic and grammatical selectional tendencies, which is to say, the range of semantic arguments and grammatical constructions with which broad classes of meaning types co-occur, as illustrated in the discussion of *flying* in Chapter 2. This later work improves the criteria for identifying distinct lexical concepts, and forms the basis for the

---

[6] See Evans (forthcoming) for a discussion of some of the drawbacks of Principled Polysemy as presented in Tyler and Evans (2003).

lexical concept identification procedure developed in LCCM Theory.[7] I report on this in Chapter 7, and address the issue of polysemy from the LCCM perspective in Chapter 8.

Figurative language

One of the major successes of cognitive linguistics has been to model the complexity and richness of the human imagination. Until relatively recently in linguistics and in cognitive science more generally, it was assumed either that the human imagination was peripheral to cognition or that it could not be systematically studied. The cognitive linguistics enterprise has provided an approach to studying human imagination, and has been influential in arguing that language reveals systematic processes at work in human imagination. Cognitive linguists have argued that such processes are central to the way we think.

The role of imagination in human thought has been approached, in cognitive linguistics, by way of positing relatively stable knowledge structures which are held to inhere in long-term memory. These knowledge structures are termed **conceptual metaphors** (Lakoff and Johnson 1980, 1999) and are claimed to have psychological reality, with reasonably robust empirical support (see Boroditsky 2000; Casasanto and Boroditsky 2008). In addition, conceptual metaphors are held to be manipulated by virtue of conceptual integration networks becoming established in service of backstage cognition as discussed above (see Fauconnier and Turner 1998, 2002; Grady 1997, 2005). The way in which these structures and processes have been studied has predominantly been to examine systematicities in figurative language, particularly in the study of conceptual metaphors. George Lakoff and Mark Johnson, the proponents of the study of conceptual metaphor and the architects of Conceptual Metaphor Theory, argue that figurative language is a consequence of the existence of a universal set of pre-linguistic **primary metaphors** (Lakoff and Johnson 1999; see also Grady 1997), and a language-specific set of **compound** (or **complex**) **metaphors**, both of which map structure from more concrete domains of conceptual structure, referred to as **source domains**, onto less easily apprehended aspects of conceptual structure, referred to as **target domains**. Together these knowledge structures are held to give rise both to the productive use of figurative language as well as to more creative aspects, such as poetic metaphor, for instance (see Lakoff and Turner 1989).

Despite the importance of Conceptual Metaphor Theory in terms of accounting for deeply ingrained systematicities in conceptual structure, it is

---

[7] I argue in Chapter 7 that the lexical profile of a lexical concept, which is to say knowledge relating to its selection tendencies, can be deployed in order to identify which lexical concept motivates a given instance of use in context. This provides a methodology for identifying distinct but semantically related lexical concepts associated with the same form.

not a theory about language, nor about figurative language understanding. Rather, Conceptual Metaphor Theory primarily provides an account of knowledge representation. Indeed, in spite of its success, it fails to adequately account for systematicities in language, for instance within a single language,[8] nor in terms of accounting for detailed differences in figurative expression that emerge cross-linguistically.[9] What is required, therefore, is a cognitive linguistic account of frontstage cognition: an account of how the symbolic resources in a specific language interface with the conceptual structure (i.e., conceptual metaphors) in service of situated figurative meaning construction. In Part IV of the book I argue that LCCM Theory is required in order to account for how figurative language (semantic structure) interfaces with conceptual metaphors (conceptual structure) in figurative language understanding. Thus, as with Conceptual Blending Theory, Conceptual Metaphor Theory remains an essential part of an overall account of meaning construction.

Grammar

The account of language provided by LCCM Theory additionally builds on recent advances in cognitive linguistics in other ways. By virtue of studying the "linguistic prompts"—in the sense of Fauconnier and Turner, discussed above—that contribute to meaning-construction processes, I am, necessarily, studying the nature of the contents of the mental grammar: the linguistic knowledge that language users must call upon in order to be able to deploy language in service of the situated expression of communicative intentions. Thus, in part, my object of study is language, rather than solely the conceptual system, in the sense defined in the previous chapters. In this, the present research effort can be classified as also constituting a cognitive approach to grammar.

Nevertheless, the objectives of LCCM Theory differ in two notable ways from other cognitive approaches to grammar, particularly Cognitive Grammar (Langacker, e.g., 2008), and Cognitive Construction Grammar (Goldberg, e.g., 2006). The first relates to the sharp distinction drawn in LCCM Theory between semantic structure and conceptual structure, as discussed in the previous chapter, and in more detail in Part II of the book. For instance, one criticism that has been levelled at Langacker's (1987, 1991a) Cognitive Grammar relates to the relationship between semantic structure and conceptual structure. Langacker argues that semantic structure as en-coded in language "is" conceptual structure. For instance, in Cognitive Grammar, semantic structure is, in large part, equated with non-linguistic or encyclopaedic knowledge. This is also true of the approach to lexical representation proposed by Alan Cruse, as reported in Croft and Cruse (2004). By way of illustration consider the following representative quotations from Langacker.

---

[8] See, for instance, Evans (2004a: ch. 5).
[9] See, for instance, Silva Sinha *et al.* (forthcoming).

[S]emantic units are characterized relative to cognitive domains, and any concept or knowledge system can function as a domain for this purpose... The meaning of an expression typically involves specifications in many cognitive domains.

(*ibid.* 1987: 63)

We can think of semantic space as the multifaceted field of conceptual potential within which thought and conceptualization unfold; a semantic structure can then be characterized as a location or a configuration in semantic space.

(*ibid.* 76)

The term conceptual structure will be applied indiscriminately to any such entity [i.e., thoughts, concepts, perceptions, images, and mental experience in general], whether linguistic or non-linguistic in nature. A semantic structure is then defined as a conceptual structure that functions as the semantic pole of a linguistic expression. Hence semantic structures are regarded as conceptualizations shaped for symbolic purposes according to the dictates of linguistic organization.

(*ibid.* 98)

What Langacker appears to have in mind is that the semantic material—informally the meaning, what he formally refers to as a **predication**—associated with a lexical form, i.e., a word, relates directly to the contents of conceptual structure. In principle, this conceptual structure relates to a diverse and sophisticated body of non-linguistic knowledge, what Langacker refers to as a **domain matrix**. Take, for instance, the word *uncle*. The meaning of *uncle*, on this view, is potentially a function of the vast body of encyclopaedic knowledge we have of what it means to be someone's uncle. In addition to the specific relationship holding between the child of uncle's sibling, this also includes detailed knowledge relating to marital relations, familial relations, the social status of uncles, the types of behaviours associated with uncles, as well as individual knowledge any given individual may have with respect to uncles they have known. Yet while this knowledge is encyclopaedic, it is for Langacker part of semantic structure, i.e., directly encoded by a lexical form. Langacker's argument is that there is no principled way of separating putative linguistic from non-linguistic semantic representation.

On the contrary, I argue in detail in Part II that there is a clear and principled distinction that can be made. I sketched the outlines of such a distinction in the previous chapter where I introduced arguments for distinguishing between the types of representations held in the linguistic and conceptual systems. Not only are there logical and some suggestive empirical reasons[10] to think that semantic structure and conceptual structure constitute distinct levels of representation, but separating out these two levels also greatly facilitates an account of the protean nature of word meaning, as we shall begin to see in the next chapter, and in more detail in Part III of the book.

---

[10] See the review in Barsalou *et al.* (forthcoming).

One way in which the present proposals can be interpreted is as a clarification on the nature of the interface between semantic structure and conceptual structure, and a corrective on the encyclopaedic semantics approach adopted in cognitive linguistics. In specific terms, LCCM Theory suggests that rather than the semantic representation encoded by language being equated with conceptual structure, semantic structure takes a distinct form. Specifically, semantic structure, unlike conceptual structure, is directly encoded in language, and takes a specialized and highly elaborate form: what I refer to as lexical concepts. While lexical concepts *are* concepts, they encode a highly schematic form of semantic representation, one that is specialized for being directly encoded in and externalized via language. In contrast, conceptual structure takes a qualitatively distinct form, which I model in terms of the theoretical construct of the cognitive model.

In other words, the encyclopaedic knowledge that Langacker equates with the semantic pole of linguistic expressions, is not, in LCCM Theory, what is meant by semantic structure. Rather, semantic structure relates to the range of purely linguistic information that lexical forms are conventionally associated with, which is detailed in Chapters 6 and 7.

In addition, lexical concepts provide **access sites** to conceptual structure. Langacker says something apparently similar, suggesting that words provide "points of access" to conceptual structure. However, he appears to mean something quite different. As noted, on Langacker's view word meanings relate directly to and thereby, in part, constitute encyclopaedic knowledge, *qua* conceptual structure. In LCCM Theory, lexical concepts (i.e., semantic structure) are quite distinct from the non-linguistic conceptual knowledge to which they potentially afford access, as we will see in detail in Part II of the book.

The second way in which LCCM Theory differs from other cognitive approaches to grammar can be approached with respect to **Cognitive Construction Grammar**: the version of Construction Grammar developed in the work of Adele Goldberg (1995, 2006). LCCM Theory adopts the position that lexical concepts are associated with all linguistic units. Lexical concepts are then fused, to produce **lexical conceptual units** which are then interpreted, which is to say they receive an **informational characterization** from the cognitive models to which they afford access. This view is consistent with the general position advocated in Cognitive Construction Grammar. As we saw in the previous chapter in discussing the symbolic basis of language, (sentence-level) constructions are held to have a semantic value independent of the words which instantiate them. That is, constructions have meaning in their own right. Moreover, constructions can be fused. For instance, the ditransitive construction involves a schematic meaning which can be fused with the meaning of the individual linguistic units which constitute it. This is similar to the position to be developed here. The main difference is in terms of focus and detail.

Cognitive Construction Grammar is primarily concerned with developing an account of the sorts of (grammatical) constructions that a language such as English has at its disposal. In particular, the focus has been on describing and providing a theoretical architecture to account for formal aspects of language, by studying which forms can co-occur, and the general semantic patterns associated with such forms. In contrast, LCCM Theory is primarily concerned not with a descriptive analysis of the forms that populate a given language. Rather, it is largely concerned with:

i. examining and describing the range of lexical concepts, *qua* semantic units, associated with a given language,
ii. the way these lexical concepts afford access to non-linguistic conceptual knowledge structures in service of deriving what I refer to as an informational characterization: that is, a situated interpretation, and
iii. the way in which these lexical concepts can combine in service of prompting for processes of meaning construction: that is, backstage cognition.

The approach taken here, to emphasize lexical concepts—the semantic pole of symbolic units, rather than the formal pole—stems from the view that the forms are primarily the "vehicles" for making semantic representations available for communicative (i.e., intersubjective) purposes. Indeed, to make this point explicit, I henceforth use the term **phonological vehicle** (or **vehicle** for short), to refer to a given lexical form. It is the semantic units themselves, the lexical concepts, whose ability to afford access to conceptual knowledge, and to be combined in a range of ways, that provide the essential component of the mental grammar deployed by language users in service of constructing meaning. Thus, the present approach to the study of grammar exhibits a difference in emphasis from that of Cognitive Construction Grammar, and indeed other versions of Construction Grammar, including the more formal constraint-based versions such as Sign-based Construction Grammar (Brenier and Michaelis 2005; Sag 2007).

Summary

In this chapter I have situated LCCM Theory in the larger cognitive linguistics enterprise of which it is a part. I began by introducing cognitive linguistics, and by briefly reviewing its primary commitments and guiding assumptions: notably the Generalization Commitment and the Cognitive Commitment. I argued that LCCM Theory represents a cognitive semantic theory, concerned as it is with the nature of meaning, meaning construction, and the relationship between literal and figurative language and thought. LCCM Theory is also a cognitive theory of grammar, as it focuses on the nature of the semantics of grammar, both in terms of lexical representation, and the way in which lexical representations are fused or composed, giving rise to larger units of language. I also considered the way in which LCCM Theory serves to build on antecedent theories in cognitive linguistics. In so doing, I suggested that LCCM Theory provides a frontstage theory of meaning construction, which must interface with an account of the so-called backstage processes involved. I also suggested that LCCM Theory serves as a corrective on previous approaches to the relationship between semantic structure and conceptual structure in cognitive linguistics, an issue addressed in further detail in Chapter 9. In particular, in this chapter I argued for a principled distinction between semantic structure: the semantic information encoded by language, and the non-linguistic conceptual knowledge to which language affords access.

4

Word meaning in LCCM Theory

I observed at the outset of the book that word meanings are protean in nature: words appear to exhibit (often significant) variation in their **semantic contribution** across utterances. As Jean Aitchison strikingly puts it: "Word meanings cannot be pinned down, as if they were dead insects. Instead, they flutter around elusively like live butterflies" (Aitchison 1994: 39–40). In this chapter I argue as follows: the key to developing an account of the protean nature of words, as exhibited in meaning construction, is to provide a descriptively adequate account of (i) the sorts of knowledge that words provide access to, and (ii) an account of how word meanings, and the knowledge structures to which they afford access, are integrated (or composed).

My main purpose in this chapter is to present a very general overview of the architecture of LCCM Theory, and in particular, the approach I will be adopting with respect to how words provide access to non-linguistic knowledge representations. In so doing, I present some of the key assumptions that underpin the theory. Accordingly, this chapter provides a highly informal introduction to the theoretical architecture, and the way the model serves to account for the role of words in language understanding. My overall aim, then, is to provide an accessible sketch of LCCM Theory, in order to ease the passage to the technical details of the theory which are presented in Parts II and III of the book.

The chapter begins, in the next section, by briefly reviewing some previous approaches to word meaning. I argue that the difficulty with these approaches, from the present perspective, is that (i) they fail to recognize that semantic representation must include semantic structure (linguistic knowledge) as well as conceptual structure (non-linguistic knowledge), and (ii) they are not usage-based in nature. I then sketch the perspective that underpins LCCM Theory, and examine, briefly, a recent approach to language understanding that, in certain respects, is consonant with the account of semantic representation presented in this book. This is the programmatic **Immersed Experiencer framework** developed by Zwaan (2004). In the subsequent section I turn to a discussion of the usage-based perspective that informs LCCM Theory, before employing the specific proposals developed there as a basis for introducing the outlines of the theory. Finally, I present an illustration of how LCCM Theory works in terms of accounting for the role of words in language understanding.

Previous approaches to word meaning

Until relatively recently, models of semantic representation typically failed to observe that word meaning is subject to the sort of variation in language use described in Chapter 1. Thus, prior to the 1980s, lexical semanticists often assumed that the semantic contribution of a word was a consequence of a stable and relatively rigid knowledge structure (Allwood 2003; Harder 2009). More recently, linguists have begun to attempt to provide theories of word meaning which are compatible with the variation in meaning observed. There have been at least three sorts of accounts that have been invoked by scholars who recognize that word meaning is protean in nature, and thus who take issue with the view of word meaning adopted under literalism. I will characterize these three approaches as follows:

    i. The **sense-enumerative perspective**. This involves positing a vast number of distinct senses associated with a given lexical form, which attempts to exhaust the possibilities that actually occur in language.
    ii. The **abstract underlying semantic representation perspective**. This sort of approach employs cognitive and/or linguistic "devices" (including context) that operate on relatively abstract (in the sense of under-specified) underlying semantic/lexical entries in order to generate surface interpretations of words.
    iii. The **semantics plus pragmatic principles perspective**. This approach assumes relatively stable underlying semantic/lexical entries (semantics) together with specific principles/rules of interpretation (pragmatics).

I briefly review each of these perspectives in slightly more detail, by focusing on a well-known exemplar.

The sense-enumerative approach posits a proliferation of distinct sense units associated with a given form, which are held to be stored in the mental lexicon. A well-known representative example is the study of the English preposition *over* by Brugman and Lakoff (1988; see also Lakoff 1987), briefly discussed in the previous chapter. Lakoff and Brugman, in their various publications on the topic, argue for a highly granular mental repository of sense units, positing a large number of distinct senses associated with the lexical form *over*. This approach Lakoff (1987) refers to as the **full-specification account**. The difficulties associated with this specific version of this general approach have been outlined in detail elsewhere.[1] However, as has

---

[1] See, for instance, Kreitzer (1997); Tyler and Evans (2003); Vandeloise (1990); and Evans and Green (2006: ch. 10) for a review.

been pointed out by Pustejovsky (1995) any sense-enumerative approach is unlikely to be able to fully predict the range of senses associated with even a single word. This follows as any given usage of an individual lexical item will always be unique, and thus provide a subtle context-dependent meaning distinction. In turn, this is the case as distinct instances of use often correlate with what I have referred to as distinct selectional tendencies in terms of collocational patterns.[2] For instance, even the expression *I want*, as exemplified in the utterances *I want a beer* versus *I want a cigarette*, involve different kinds of semantic arguments and thus two distinct semantic contributions of *want*. Informally, the sort of "want" involved is of a different kind in each case. The range of semantic arguments with which any lexical item can co-occur will always far outnumber even the most detailed full-specification or sense-enumerative accounts available. As part of the task of the lexical semanticist is to be able to account for the range of semantic arguments with which a form can be combined, adopting a sense-enumerative approach leads, in effect, to infinite polysemy. Some scholars, including Sandra (1998) and Sinha and Kuteva (1995), have roundly criticized this tendency, arguing that it amounts to a methodological failure.[3]

The second perspective proposes the following. Rather than expanding the number of distinct senses that must be stored in the lexicon, the lexical entry itself can be made more abstract and thus more flexible. This might include adding various semantic dimensions or "slots" to the lexical entry which can be differentially selected for based on the linguistic context which combines with the lexical entry in question, and the ways in which lexical entries are combined, or **coerced** into behaving. A well-known example of such an approach is that of Pustejovsky (1995). In his account, Pustejovsky argues for relatively abstract lexical **meta-entries**. Although abstract in nature, these meta-entries contain more potential for detail and thus far more flexibility than has traditionally been associated with lexical entries, particularly as advocated in computational and formal approaches to lexical semantics, with one or two notable exceptions (e.g., Sperber and Wilson 1995; Carston 2002). This is achieved by positing so-called **qualia roles** associated with any given meta-entry. These qualia roles, which have unspecified values in the underlying meta-entry, relate, at least for nouns, to notions such as purpose, origin, material type, and so forth. Generative devices operate on the meta-entry in order to fill the value of the qualia roles, while a given qualia role need not always be filled in. The advantage of this approach is that it is not static lexical entries that combine in meaning construction, which is the difficulty with a sense-enumerative perspective. Rather, meaning construction occurs, on this account, by virtue of filling in values for and combining qualia roles. This goes some way towards accounting for the protean nature of situated word meaning.

---

[2] See also Pustejovsky 1995.
[3] As we saw in the previous chapter, Sandra has dubbed this tendency the polysemy fallacy.

A significant drawback of Pustejovsky's account, despite its ingenuity, is that it is far from clear that his proposal for lexical meta-entries with qualia structure is psychologically plausible. While psychological validity may not be of paramount concern for cognitive scientists who seek a computationally tractable account of semantic representation, and the way in which words combine—which is one of Pustejovsky's ultimate concerns—the goal of the present work is to develop a psychologically realistic account of semantic representation and meaning construction, one that is consonant with the Generalization and Cognitive Commitments of cognitive linguistics discussed in the previous chapter, and one that is consonant with recent findings from psychology.

The third perspective, the semantics plus pragmatics approach, assumes that while words have the semantic representations that they do, these underspecify for meaning in context due to pragmatic principles which guide the way they are applied in specific utterance contexts. A relatively well-known example of this general perspective includes Herskovits's (1986) account of spatial relations. Herskovits argues that what she terms the **simple-relations model** of spatial prepositions, as presented in formal semantic accounts, fails because it underestimates the role of pragmatic knowledge and the principles of language use which language users deploy when using lexical items such as prepositions. However, Herskovits herself takes a rather narrow view of what the semantic representations associated with prepositions look like. More recent research, for instance by Coventry and Garrod (2004), Deane (2005), Evans and Tyler (2004), Feist (forthcoming), Tyler and Evans (2003) and Vandeloise (e.g., 1994), suggests that in addition to a spatial relation, prepositions also encode functional/qualitative meanings.[4] Adopting this proposal makes redundant many of the pragmatic principles posited by Herskovits.

In general terms, there are two difficulties common to each of these perspectives as they attempt to account for (situated) variation in word meaning. Firstly, each of the accounts assumes that word meanings are stable, circumscribed knowledge structures which can be (relatively) straightforwardly identified—a problem also true of the view of word meaning under literalism. That is, they assume that the semantic values associated with words are relatively rigid, discrete sense units, *qua* mental entities. As we have begun to see in the previous chapter, scholars who take an encyclopaedic perspective on linguistic semantics have suggested that in fact word meaning is less a discrete body of circumscribed knowledge. Rather, words serve as points of access to larger-scale conceptual knowledge structures, cognitive models, which are potentially vast in scope, as I argue in detail in Part II of the book.[5] On this view, words provide access to what I first referred to, in Chapter 1, as a semantic potential, with different sorts of knowledge being potentially **activated**.

---

[4] I develop an LCCM account of spatial particles in Chapter 8.

[5] For related perspectives see, in particular, Allwood 2003; Croft 1993; Cruse 2002; Langacker 1987; Zlatev 2003.

The second difficulty associated with the three perspectives sketched above, notwithstanding their attempt to handle variation in word meaning in language use, is that they do not constitute usage-based accounts of word meaning. That is, they make no serious attempt to relate their theoretical claims to the nature of situated meaning, and thus how words derive from and sanction contextualized usage events. Nor are they concerned with how words are used in context in order to express localized communicative intentions. The semantic contribution of a word, which is to say, which part of its semantic potential is activated, will always be a function of how it is being used in any given context. As we saw in Chapter 1, this includes both the linguistic context—the surrounding words and grammatical constructions—and the extra-linguistic context—including the situated communicative intention of the language user. Thus, we require an account of the nature of the semantic potential that words provide access to, and an account of how this semantic potential is constrained by virtue of the way in which words are combined and their contexts of use (i.e., the cognitive operations that facilitate differential **activation** of a word's semantic potential). Thus, we need a theoretical account of context, and the role of the language user as an intentional agent who employs language, in part, in service of the expression of situated communicative intentions (see Clark 1996; Croft 2000; Sperber and Wilson 1995).[6]

The semantic potential of words

Recent work on knowledge representation in cognitive psychology (e.g., Barsalou 1999, 2003, 2008; Barsalou *et al.* forthcoming)[7] suggests that words provide access to **simulators**: large-scale coherent bodies of body-based (e.g., perceptual, motoric, subjective, etc.) knowledge that can give rise to simulations.[8] From this perspective, one reason for the protean nature of word meaning is due to the large body of non-linguistic knowledge to which words afford access, and the potential for simulations that arise.

In recent work, Rolf Zwaan (2004) has developed a language-processing model which is concerned with modelling how language provides access to simulators, and thus prompts for simulations. This he refers to as the Immersed Experiencer framework. For instance, consider the use of the lexical item *red* in the following examples:

(1) a. The teacher scrawled in red ink all over the pupil's homework exercise
     b. The red squirrel is in danger of becoming extinct in the British Isles

---

6 This is an issue I develop in Chapter 11.

7 For related accounts and discussion of the relationship between aspects of language and simulations see also Bergen and Chang (2005); Glenberg and Kaschak (2002); Kaschak and Glenberg (2000); and Vigliocco *et al.* (2009).

8 Recall that simulations are re-activations of body-based states, as briefly discussed in Chapter 2.

Zwaan makes the point that in linguistic examples such as (1), which are indicative of those he uses in his model, *red* designates two different sorts of sensory experience precisely because the context constrains the sort of simulations derived by language users. That is, while the simulated hue derived from the use of *red* in (1a) is quite a vivid red, the hue of the simulation prompted for by (1b) is likely to be closer to a dun/browny colour. In present terms, *red* has a relatively large semantic potential, which relates to a range of different possible hues (one dimension along which the colour spectrum varies).[9] That aspect of the word's potential which is activated is a consequence, in part, of the way it is constrained by the utterance context, and specifically the scene evoked by the utterance context.[10]

An important lesson from the work of Zwaan, and indeed others who take what I will refer to as a **simulation semantics** approach to language understanding (e.g., Bergen and Chang 2005), is that the semantic potential associated with words is primarily non-linguistic in nature. That is, the semantic potential of *red* is not "there" in the word itself. That is, whatever *red* designates, we are not dealing with purely linguistic knowledge, as the same form prompts for two very different sorts of mental rehearsals of "redness." Rather, the form *red* provides access to perceptual information and knowledge, which can be reconstructed or **simulated**.[11] The general perspective provided by simulation semantics is adopted and integrated with the perspective of cognitive linguistics that is central to LCCM Theory, and developed in more detail in Part II of the book.

Meaning and use

I now turn to a discussion of the relationship between language use and meaning. I do so by adopting a version of the **usage-based thesis** employed in cognitive linguistics (as developed most notably by Langacker e.g., 2000),[12] which I present below.

Language use is integral to our knowledge of language: our language system (or mental grammar). The organization of our language system is intimately related to, and derives directly from, how language is actually used (Croft 2000; Langacker 2000; Tomasello 2003). Through processes of abstraction and schematization (Langacker 2000), based on **pattern recognition** and **intention-reading** abilities (Tomasello 1999, 2003), language users derive symbolic units. These are relatively well-entrenched mental routines consisting of conventional pairings of form and meaning (Langacker 1987).

---

[9] That language serves to prompt for simulations is a point that has been made, albeit in slightly different terms, by a number of other scholars. See in particular Barsalou (1999), and Kaschak and Glenberg (2000).

[10] See Zwaan and Radvansky (1998) for discussion of the importance of constructing and drawing upon **situation models**—knowledge of specific scenes and situations—for language understanding.

[11] For discussion see Barsalou (1999).

[12] See Evans and Green (2006: ch. 4) for a review.

However, the range of symbolic units available to the language user massively underdetermine the range of situations, events, states, relationships, and other interpersonal functions that the language user may potentially seek to use language to express and fulfil. One reason for this is that language users live in a sociophysical matrix that is continually shifting and evolving. No two situations, feelings, or relationships, at any given point in time, are exactly alike. We are continually using language to express unique meanings, about unique states of affairs and relationships, in unique ways. While language has a range of ready-made schemas, or symbolic units which can be combined to express a representative range of the scenarios we may wish to refer to and describe, these necessarily underdetermine the mutability of human experience. Accordingly, the symbolic units employed by language users can only ever partially **sanction** (in Langacker's terms) the situated way in which they are used. As Clark (1996) observes, language use involves solving a **coordination problem**, in which language users must employ non-conventional coordination strategies and devices. That is, language users typically employ the conventional repertoire of linguistic units, including patterns of assembling linguistic units (such as word-order conventions, which are themselves linguistic units), in non-conventional ways.[13] On this view, meaning, which is associated with the utterance (or usage event), is a consequence of combining the symbolic units in novel ways in order to solve the particular coordination problem at hand, thereby facilitating communication.

We saw in the previous section that one reason for the protean nature of word meaning arises from the non-linguistic semantic potential to which lexical concepts afford access, and the range of simulations that can arise. In addition, a second reason arises as lexical concepts—the semantic pole of symbolic units—are only ever realized as part of linguistic utterances. Utterances are necessarily (i.e., by definition) situated, and thus form part of an act of communication. But in being so realized, lexical concepts give rise to context-induced semantic contributions; as we shall see in Part II, the linguistic content encoded by lexical concepts consists of "bundles" of different types of linguistic knowledge. Accordingly, different aspects of this knowledge can become active in different contexts. The consequence of this is that lexical concepts are never actually realized *in toto*. Rather, it is only the contextually relevant aspects which surface in language use.

Borrowing an analogy from phonological theory, we can liken the distinction between lexical concepts on one hand, and their contextualized instantiations on the other as akin to the distinction between phonemes and allophones. Just as with phonemes, lexical concepts *qua* mental representations are never actually perceived. Rather, their existence is inferred based on the variability, and commonalities, in word meaning across (situated) usage events, as judged over many instances of use. In this, then, the job of the

---

[13] This issue is discussed further in Chapter 11.

lexical semanticist is to employ the situated semantic contribution of a given word, by analogy akin to allophones, in order to infer the existence of the underlying lexical concepts—stored mental schemas—akin to phonemes, which partially sanction the semantic contributions which surface. In view of this distinction, in the remainder of the book I will refrain from using the term "word meaning." Rather, I will refer either to the construct of the lexical concept—when I am referring to the underlying semantic structure—or, to the semantic contribution of a given linguistic form—when I am referring to a situated instance of a lexical concept.

In view of the foregoing, we are now in a position to provide some basic distinctions with respect to meaning and use that are central to LCCM Theory. First of all, we need to provide a definition of an utterance. This is less straightforward a task than one might assume. As I will define it, a usage event or utterance has a unit-like status in that it represents the expression of a coherent idea, making (at least partial) use of the **conventions of the language**—informally, the norms of linguistic behaviour in a particular linguistic community, but see Croft (2000). In other words, an utterance is a somewhat discrete entity. However, I use the expressions "unit-like" and "somewhat discrete" because an utterance is not an absolutely discrete, nor a precisely identifiable unit. This follows as utterances involve grammatical forms such as word order and lexical items, lexical concepts, speech sounds, patterns of intonation such as pitch contours, slight pauses, and accelerations and decelerations, and so forth. While these properties converge on discreteness and unity, they do not co-occur in fixed patterns, and therefore do not provide a set of criteria for collectively identifying an utterance. In this respect, utterances differ from the related notion of a **sentence**.

A sentence, as defined in particular by formal linguists, is an abstract entity. In other words, it is an idealization that has determinate properties, often stated in terms of grammatical structure. For example, one definition of (an English) sentence might consist of the formula: $S \Rightarrow NP\ VP$.

The notion of a sentence, while based on prototypical patterns found in utterances, is not the same as an utterance. Utterances typically occur spontaneously, and often do not conform to the grammaticality requirements of a well-formed sentence as understood in formal linguistic theory. For example, in terms of structure, an utterance may consist of a single word (*Hi!*), a phrase (*No way!*), an incomplete sentence (*Did you put the...?*), or a sentence that contains "errors" of pronunciation or grammar because the speaker is tired, distracted, or excited, and so on. While much of formal linguistics has been concerned with modelling the properties of language that enable us to produce grammatically well-formed sentences, utterances often exhibit **graded grammaticality** (see Langacker 1987; see also Evans and Green 2006). In short, while a sentence can be precisely and narrowly defined, an utterance cannot be. While sentences represent the structure associated with a prototypical utterance, utterances represent specific and unique instances of language use. Once a sentence is given meaning, context, and phonetic realization, it becomes a (spoken) utterance. Accordingly, as I am concerned with an account of lexical representation and meaning construction that reflects how language is used, it is ultimately the utterance, rather then the idealized notion of the sentence, with which I am concerned in the present work.

Having provided this (qualified) definition of an utterance, we are now in a position to distinguish meaning from lexical representation. My claim is that the essential distinction between lexical representation and meaning is that while meaning is a property of the utterance, lexical representations consist of the mental abstractions which we infer must be stored as part of the language user's knowledge of language: symbolic units, together with the range of cognitive models, the semantic potential, to which a lexical concept affords access. Hence, lexical representation involves structures of distinct types which inhere in two distinct representational systems: the linguistic system and the conceptual system. The interaction of these distinct types of structures gives rise to meaning associated with an utterance. The meaning associated with an utterance I will refer to as a **conception**.

An architecture for the role of words in meaning construction

The conclusions to emerge from the previous discussion suggest a number of requirements for a theory of lexical and compositional semantics. We require both an account of lexical representation and a theory of semantic composition, which together should contribute to a descriptively adequate and psychologically realistic account of meaning construction. We require a theory of lexical representation which provides a descriptively adequate account of the kind of linguistic knowledge that language users appear to possess. We also require an account which provides a means of understanding how lexical representations interface with conceptual knowledge, which is to say, their semantic potential. That is, we require a theory that shows how the linguistic and conceptual systems interact in order to produce semantic representations. We also require an account of how lexical representations, together with the informational characterizations derived from the semantic potential available, combine in order to provide situated meanings, that is, conceptions. Finally, as the semantic contributions associated with words are a function of specific utterances, and thus a consequence of discrete usage events, the account developed of lexical representation and semantic composition must be thoroughly usage-based in nature. As the two aspects of the theory I present are relatively complex, I present a summary of the architecture below. All of the constructs introduced are argued for in detail in Parts II and III of the book.

LCCM theory

LCCM theory consists of (i) an account of lexical representation (symbolic units and cognitive models) and (ii) an account of semantic composition: integration of lexical concepts in a way which activates, or, in my terms, provides an **access route** through the cognitive models to which a given lexical concept affords access. This can serve to **highlight** particular **attributes**—aspects of a cognitive model, such as properties—and **structural invariants**—relations holding between attributes—of a given cognitive model.

As noted above, the fundamental assumption is that meaning—more technically a conception—is a property of an utterance—a situated instance of language use—which arises, in part, by cognitive operations which apply to the lexical representations—lexical concepts and the cognitive models to which lexical concepts provide access sites—deployed by language users. Thus, meaning arises by virtue of language users forming interpretations based on the lexical concepts employed, the way lexical concepts are combined, and the access routes through the sets of cognitive models—the **cognitive model profile**—accessed by a given lexical concept. Moreover, these interpretations are always guided by linguistic and extra-linguistic context.[14]

Lexical representation

LCCM Theory holds that knowledge of language includes (i) symbolic units, and (ii) cognitive models. Symbolic units consist of bipolar assemblies of form, what, as noted in the previous chapter, I refer to as a phonological vehicle (or vehicle), and a lexical concept. Lexical concepts constitute linguistically encoded concepts—that is, highly schematic knowledge encoded in a form that can be externalized via language. Lexical concepts are conventionally associated with vehicles of all kinds including words—the focus in this book—bound morphemes, idiomatic phrases, and grammatical constructions. Accordingly, lexical concepts, by definition, concern purely linguistic knowledge, as discussed in Chapters 6 and 7. A second important part of the lexical representation is the notion of the cognitive model, which is a large-scale coherent body of non-linguistic knowledge which lexical concepts provide access sites to. The range of cognitive models which are accessed, either directly or indirectly by a lexical concept, as noted above, I refer to as a cognitive model profile. Individual cognitive models consist of attributes and structural invariants.[15] These ideas are developed in more detail in Chapters 9 and 10.

---

[14] The role of context in semantic composition is discussed in more detail at various points in Part III of the book.
[15] See Barsalou (1992a, 1992b); Barsalou et al. (1993).

Lexical concept integration

The linguistically mediated meaning construction process takes place by virtue of **semantic composition**. This process involves two component processes: (i) **lexical concept selection** and (ii) **fusion**. Lexical concept selection involves selecting the most appropriate lexical concepts associated with each vehicle in an utterance, guided by utterance, discourse, and extra-linguistic context. The appropriateness or otherwise of the selected lexical concept is a function of **semanticality**—the semantic acceptability of a conception. This is discussed in Chapter 13. Fusion, the second compositional process, consists of two further constituent processes which are held to occur in tandem: (i) **lexical concept integration** and (ii) **interpretation**. Integration involves the construction of larger lexical entities, driven by linguistic knowledge (lexical concepts). These larger lexical units, which I term **lexical conceptual units**, are then **interpreted**. That is, the larger unit receives what I earlier referred to as an informational characterization. As such, those parts of the cognitive model profiles (semantic potential) associated with each lexical concept in the larger unit are interpreted in a way that is in keeping with the larger unit. Put another way, integration provides (linguistic) instructions which serve to determine how the various lexical concepts are collectively interpreted, and

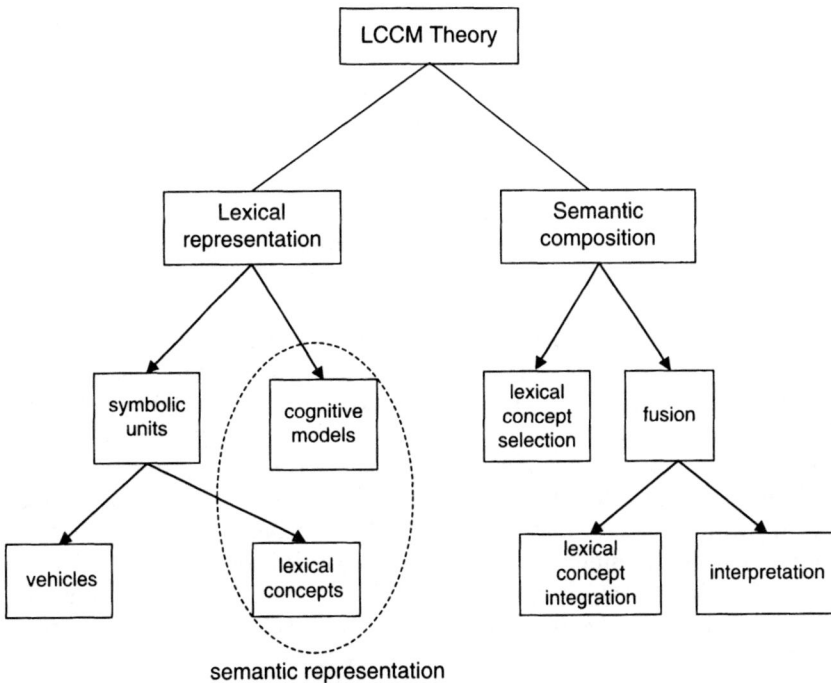

FIGURE 4.1. An overview of the architecture of LCCM Theory

thus, the access route that each individual lexical concept affords through its cognitive model profile. The result is that any given word will provide a unique activation of part of its semantic potential on every occasion of use. This follows as every utterance, and thus the resulting conception, is unique.

Accordingly, this view of compositionality is radically different from the received Fregean view which underpins literalism. While Fregean compositionality assumes that each usage of a word recruits stable, context-independent information, LCCM Theory assumes the semantic contribution associated with a word will vary slightly every time it is used. An overview of the architecture is presented in Figure 4.1.

An illustration

In this section I provide a non-technical illustration of the relationship between a lexical concept and its cognitive model profile, and the way an individual usage sanctioned by a specific lexical concept will give rise to a distinct informational characterization. This follows as each instance of use of a lexical concept contributes to the formation of a distinct conception. Thus, the ensuing is intended to provide an illustration of the way in which lexical concepts activate part of the semantic potential—the cognitive model profile—to which they afford access, which sets the scene for the detailed development of the theoretical constructs of the lexical concept and the cognitive model in the next part of the book.

To begin, consider the following four utterances first discussed in Chapter 1:

(2) a. France is a country of outstanding natural beauty
     b. France is one of the leading nations in the European Union
     c. France beat New Zealand in the 2007 Rugby World Cup
     d. France voted against the EU constitution in the 2005 referendum

In each of these examples the semantic contribution associated with the form *France* is slightly distinct. That is, the semantic contribution provided by *France* varies across these distinct utterances. The key insight of LCCM Theory is that the reason for this variation is due to differential activation of non-linguistic knowledge structures, the cognitive model profile, to which the lexical concept associated with *France* affords access. The linguistic and non-linguistic processes that give rise to this differential activation, which relate, in part, to the differences in the four linguistic contexts in which *France* is embedded are highly complex. LCCM Theory represents a programmatic attempt to identify the sorts of mechanisms involved in this activation process.

In these examples I am concerned with the lexical concept conventionally associated with the vehicle *France*. As noted above, and as we shall see in detail in later chapters, a lexical concept constitutes a relatively complex body of linguistic knowledge which forms a representational unit. I identify these representational units, (the lexical concept), by providing a label in small capitals within square brackets. Thus, the lexical concept associated with the form *France* which appears in the examples in (2) I gloss as [FRANCE]. In addition, a key property is that a lexical concept affords access to a potentially large set of cognitive models: its cognitive model profile. A robust finding from recent work in cognitive psychology on knowledge representation is that the representations which inhere in the conceptual system, while extremely complex, are not an unstructured assemblage.[16] Indeed recent research provides compelling evidence that rather than knowledge being organized in terms of lists of attributes, a key aspect of knowledge representation involves the relations that hold between discrete aspects of knowledge (e.g., Barsalou 1992a). My assumption, therefore, is that a lexical concept provides access to a sophisticated and structured body of non-linguistic knowledge. This body of knowledge I model in terms of a set of cognitive models. LCCM Theory posits that part of the function of a given lexical concept is to provide an access site to a cognitive model profile. In addition, as cognitive models provide coherent and complex bodies of knowledge, and are interlinked, affording access to other cognitive models, and thus, other bodies of complex knowledge, a particular utterance context can serve to activate a subset of knowledge within a single cognitive model, the process which I refer to as **highlighting**.[17]

Returning to the examples in (2), the informational characterization associated with [FRANCE] in each of these examples concerns France as a geographical landmass in (2a), France as a political entity, a nation state, in (2b), the fifteen players who make up the French rugby team in (2c), and in (2d) that proportion of the French electorate who voted "non" when presented, in a recent referendum, with the proposal to endorse a constitution for the European Union. In order to provide these distinct interpretations, this lexical concept must serve as an access site for a cognitive model profile that, at the very least, includes the sort of information indicated in Figure 4.2. This figure represents an attempt to indicate the sort of knowledge that language users must have access to when speaking and thinking about France.

In Figure 4.2, the lexical concept [FRANCE] provides access to a potentially large number of knowledge structures. As each cognitive model consists of a complex and structured body of knowledge which provides access to other sorts of knowledge, we can distinguish between cognitive models which are directly accessed via the lexical concept: **primary cognitive models**, and those cognitive models which form substructures of those which are directly accessed: **secondary cognitive models**. These secondary cognitive models are indirectly accessed via the lexical concept.[18]

---

[16] See Barsalou (1992a) for a review.
[17] Highlighting is discussed in detail in Chapter 13.
[18] I make the case for the distinction between primary and secondary cognitive models in Chapter 10.

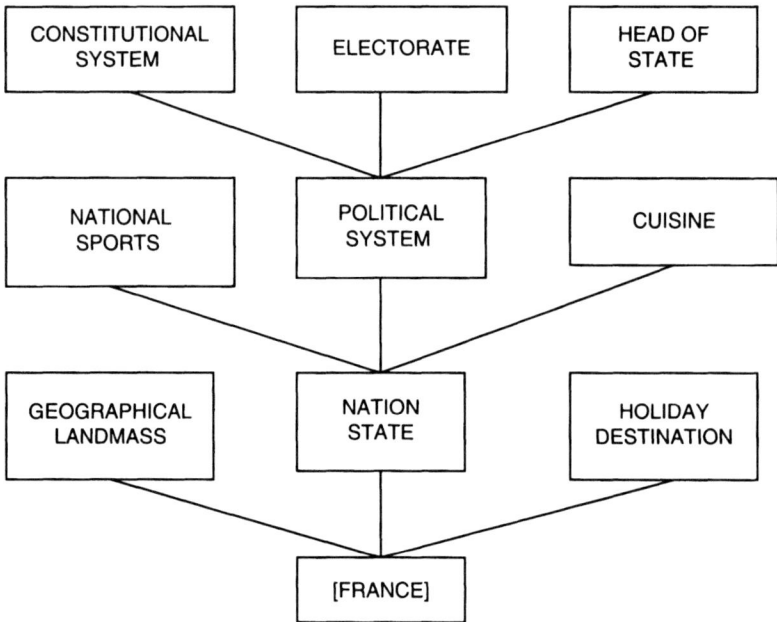

FIGURE 4.2. Partial cognitive model profile for [FRANCE]

The partial cognitive model profile presented in Figure 4.2 constitutes a structured inventory of knowledge—a semantic potential—which the lexical concept [FRANCE] affords access to. Importantly, just as I gloss a lexical concept with a label, so too cognitive models are labelled. An individual cognitive model is labelled using small capitals in a box, as in Figure 4.2. However, it is important to emphasize that these labels are shorthand linguistic glosses which serve to identify large-scale and complex bodies of knowledge, which are non-linguistic in nature.

Figure 4.2 shows that the lexical concept [FRANCE] affords access to a **primary cognitive model profile**. This consists of (at the very least) the following cognitive models: GEOGRAPHICAL LANDMASS, NATION STATE, and HOLIDAY DESTINATION. Each of these cognitive models provides access to further cognitive models. In Figure 4.2 a flavour of this is given by virtue of the various secondary cognitive models which are accessed via the NATION STATE cognitive model. These include NATIONAL SPORTS, POLITICAL SYSTEM, and CUISINE. For instance, we may know that in France, the French engage in national sports of particular types, for instance, football, rugby, athletics, and so on, rather than others. For instance, the French don't typically engage in American football, ice hockey, cricket, and so on. We may also know that as a sporting nation they take part in international sports competitions of various kinds, including the FIFA football World Cup, the Six Nations rugby competition, the Rugby World Cup, the Olympics, and so on. That is, we may have access to a large body of knowledge concerning the sorts of sports French people engage in. We may also have some knowledge of the funding structures and social and economic conditions and constraints that apply to these sports in France, France's international standing with respect to these particular sports, and further knowledge about the sports themselves including the rules that govern their practice, and so on. This knowledge is derived from a large number of sources including direct experience and through cultural transmission.

With respect to the secondary cognitive model of POLITICAL SYSTEM, Figure 4.2 illustrates a sample of further secondary cognitive models which are accessed via this cognitive model. In other words, each secondary cognitive model has further (secondary) cognitive models which it provides access to. For instance, (FRENCH) ELECTORATE is a cognitive model accessed via the cognitive model (FRENCH) POLITICAL SYSTEM. In turn the cognitive model (FRENCH) POLITICAL SYSTEM is accessed via the cognitive model NATION STATE. Accordingly, NATION STATE is a primary cognitive model while ELECTORATE and POLITICAL SYSTEM are secondary cognitive models.

The differential interpretations associated with the examples in (2) arise as follows. In (2a) the interpretation associated with the form *France*, which relates to a particular geographical region, derives from activation of the GEOGRAPHICAL LANDMASS cognitive model. That is, individual language users have knowledge relating to the physical aspects of France, including its terrain, and its geographical location. In this example, the utterance context serves to activate this part of the cognitive model profile accessed by the lexical concept [FRANCE]. In the second example, the utterance context serves to activate a different part of the cognitive model profile to which the lexical concept [FRANCE] affords access. In this example, the informational characterization relates to the cognitive model of France as a political entity. This is due to activation of the NATION STATE cognitive model. In the example in (2c) the use of *France* relates to the group of fifteen French individuals who play as a team and thereby represent the French nation on the rugby field. This involves activation of the NATIONAL SPORTS cognitive model. In the example in (2d) the form *France* relates not to a geographical landmass, nor a political entity, a nation state, nor to a group of fifteen rugby players who happen to be representing the entire population of France. Rather, it relates to that portion of the French electorate that voted against ratification of the EU constitution in a referendum held in 2005. Accordingly, what is activated here is the ELECTORATE cognitive model.

This last example provides an elegant illustration of the way in which activation of a cognitive model serves to provide a situated interpretation of a lexical concept by giving rise to an access route through the semantic potential. In this example, interpretation requires that an access route is established through the cognitive model profile accessed via the lexical concept [FRANCE] in a way that is consistent with the lexical concepts associated with the other linguistic forms and units in the utterance. The interpretation associated with *France* in this example has to do with the French electorate, and specifically that part of the French electorate which voted against ratification of the EU constitution. In other words, [FRANCE] in this example achieves an informational characterization which is facilitated by activating the cognitive models which are shown in bold in Figure 4.3.

Finally, it is important to note, as we shall see in detail in Part IV of the book, that the LCCM approach provides a way of distinguishing between literal versus figurative language understanding. For many linguists, the usage of *France* in (2c) and (2d) would be classed as being instances of figurative language use, and specifically, instances of **metonymy**—one entity, here the landmass known as France, standing for another, in (2d) the portion of the electorate associated with this landmass who voted against the EU constitution. From the LCCM perspective, as a lexical concept provides access to a structured body of knowledge at a particular point in the cognitive model profile, the intuitive distinction between literal versus figurative language understanding that language users make can be related to the sorts of cognitive models that are activated in any given conception. The conceptions associated with the examples in (2a) and (2b) involve activations of cognitive models accessed by [FRANCE] which form part of the primary cognitive model profile. That is, the informational characterizations associated with [FRANCE] in these examples is hypothesized to relate to knowledge structures to which

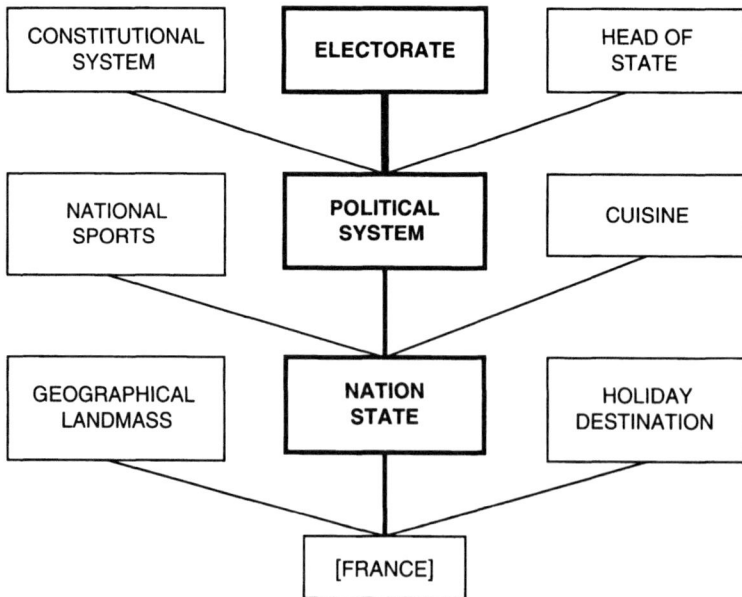

FIGURE 4.3. Access route established by the interpretation of [FRANCE] in the utterance *France voted against the EU constitution*

[FRANCE] affords direct access. In the examples in (2c) and (2d) which intuitively feel more figurative in nature, activation involves cognitive models to which the lexical concept [FRANCE] is hypothesized to provide more indirect access. While the details are complex, especially with respect to the distinction between metaphor and metonymy as we shall see, the LCCM account provides a way not only of accounting for the variability in word meaning evidenced, but as I shall argue later, a means of accounting for the distinction between literal and figurative language use, while showing that both sorts of language use are, in fact, a consequence of a common set of meaning-construction structures and processes.

In essence, this section has not sought to provide technical details. Nor have I addressed the meaning-construction processes that facilitate activation of parts of a cognitive model profile. That is the subject of Part III of the book. Nor have I, at this stage, provided detailed arguments for the distinction between the notion of primary and secondary cognitive models and cognitive model profiles. These issues I address in the rest of the book. However, this section has sought to provide an introduction to some of the key insights of LCCM Theory.

Frequently asked questions

In developing and presenting LCCM Theory, both in lectures and talks at various venues around the world, there are a number of questions that have repeatedly been put to me. At the close of this introductory part of the book it seems fitting that I present a few of the most frequently addressed here and rehearse my responses to them. This is meant to help clarify some of the outstanding issues that I will return to in more detail later in the book.

Q. Are lexical concepts universal?
A. As we will see in detail in the next part of the book, lexical concepts are form-specific. That is, they constitute the semantic pole of a symbolic unit—a conventional pairing of form and meaning. As such, lexical concepts are necessarily language-specific. Central to LCCM Theory is the position that each language, as well as having its own unique repository of vehicles (forms) will, necessarily, have its own language-specific inventory of lexical concepts. Part of the task that awaits a child as it acquires its native language is to acquire the symbolic units, both the vehicles and the lexical concepts associated with each vehicle. While lexical concepts are language-specific, there are, nevertheless, commonalities across the repository of lexical concepts across different languages. This follows as languages serve, broadly, a similar range of communicative functions, and language users, the individuals that make use of language, have, broadly, a common set of coordination problems that they employ language in order, in part, to help resolve. Accordingly, it follows that

a given lexical concept may be broadly similar to (an)other lexical concept(s) across (a) language(s).

Q. All the linguistic examples employed in this and previous chapters relate to modern standard English, rather than other varieties, languages, and time periods. In view of this, is LCCM Theory meant to address how language in general contributes to expressing meaning or is it meant to account just for the situation with respect to English?
A. The theory developed in later chapters in the book presents an account of lexical representation and semantic composition. While the processes involved in semantic composition are held to be universal, the nature of those lexical concepts is specific to each language and indeed each variety of a given language. Thus, the theory does account for the universal nature of meaning construction, while acknowledging that the repository of lexical concepts is language-specific. From this perspective, it is possible to use one variety, namely the language-specific lexical concepts of modern standard English to illustrate the language-general processes of meaning construction.

Q. Is there any inconsistency in the claim at the heart of LCCM Theory that words have semantic units associated with them (lexical concepts) and yet that they do not have meanings associated with them?
A. In fact, this is not quite what I am claiming. I argue that while words are associated with units of semantic structure (lexical concepts), meaning as I define it—and do so using the technical term "conception"—concerns a compositional process. That is, meaning results from integration of semantic representations via processes of meaning construction, guided by context. Thus, words do make a semantic contribution, but this is always associated with a particular utterance. I reserve the term "meaning" for the conception associated with an utterance, to which words contribute. I do so in order to move away from the problematic view apparent in many semantic theories which assumes that meaning construction results from the operations on meanings, *qua* units or atoms of semantic structure associated with words. As I offer a slightly different perspective, viewing meaning not as a thing: a unit of something which is tied to individual word forms, but rather as the result of a compositional process, there is no inconsistency.

Q. LCCM Theory addresses meaning associated with individual utterances. Yet meaning arises from situated exchanges, which is to say extended discourse. Can LCCM Theory be applied to meaning above the level of the utterance?
A. While I am concerned, in this book, with meaning at the level of the utterance (that is, conceptions), it is important to note that a full account of the role of words in meaning construction must also address meaning above the level of the utterance, that is, at the discourse level. Such an account is

beyond the scope of this book, which seeks to present the theoretical architecture of LCCM Theory. Nevertheless, such an endeavour must include, at the very least, an account of the interpersonal and interactional nature of discourse, as studied, for instance, by scholars such as Goffman (e.g., 1981) and Gumperz (e.g., 1982), the structural aspects of discourse, as studied by Sacks, Schegloff, and Jefferson (e.g., 1974), the nature of memory constraints as applied to discourse and topic shifts, as addressed in the work of Chafe (e.g., 1994), the work of Zwaan on the construction of situation models in the comprehension of discourse (e.g., 1999), and the role of backstage cognition as studied by scholars such as Lakoff and Johnson (1980, 1999), Fauconnier (e.g., 1997), Coulson (2000) and Fauconnier and Turner (e.g., 2002). I anticipate that LCCM Theory, by developing a theory of frontstage cognition will serve to contribute to a fuller account of the role of language in discourse-based meaning construction.

Q. Is it necessary to invoke the notion of a simulation, which is somewhat alien to the linguist? After all, you are developing a theory of linguistic semantics, rather than a theory of brain mechanisms involved in knowledge representation or semantic processing.
A. Actually, an account of linguistic semantics will, ultimately, have to be situated in the brain mechanisms and processes that form the basis for meaning construction. The development of LCCM Theory is driven by the premise that we require a psychologically plausible account of meaning construction and the role of language in marshalling linguistic resources to this end. This is in line with the foundational assumptions of cognitive linguistics, reviewed in the previous chapter. Like it or not, there is now an impressive body of work which demonstrates that our conceptual and linguistic systems are grounded in modality-specific areas of the human brain. That is, there is now compelling evidence that perceptual experiences, for instance, are reactivated or simulated when we use language and think (for reviews see Barsalou 2008, Martin 2007, and Pulvermüller 2003). Moreover, recent experimental work has shown that language activates simulations of perceptual experience during language processing (e.g., Glenberg and Kaschak 2002; for reviews see Bergen *et al.* forthcoming, Zwaan and Kaschak 2008, and Taylor and Zwaan 2009). There have as yet been scant attempts to develop a theoretical account of language that takes seriously the recent findings from brain imaging and behavioural studies in the other brain and cognitive sciences. A rare exception is the attempt to develop a version of construction grammar that does exactly this (e.g., Bergen and Chang 2005). LCCM Theory represents a larger-scale attempt to do exactly this. In particular, I argue in detail in the next part of the book that by taking account of the role of simulations in language understanding, we are able to develop an elegant account of the protean nature of word meaning.

Summary

In this chapter I have reviewed a number of perspectives on word meaning which acknowledge the variability in word meaning described in previous chapters. One of the main difficulties with all of the perspectives briefly reviewed is that they fail to explicitly provide a level of conceptual (i.e., non-linguistic) knowledge representation to which the sense units they posit afford access. One of my key points in this chapter has been to suggest that an account which provides a level of non-linguistic knowledge representation to which lexical concepts afford access is crucial in order to account for the observed variability in the semantic contribution of words across utterances. I have introduced an approach, LCCM Theory, which can, in principle, handle the sort of variation observed, together with principles of composition which facilitate differential activation of linguistic and non-linguistic knowledge. LCCM Theory advances the potentially controversial claim that words do not in fact have meaning. Meaning is held to be a function of an utterance, rather than a given mental representation associated with a word, or other linguistic (i.e., symbolic) unit. That is, meaning results from situated acts of communication, in which language plays a part, rather than being a discrete "thing" which can be assembled and manipulated. In this chapter I also made the case for words, and symbolic units in general, being associated with the construct of the lexical concept, a unit of semantic structure. A lexical concept is a representation specialized for being encoded in and externalized by language. Of course, an account of lexical representation would be incomplete without considering the level of conceptual structure to which lexical concepts provide access. This level is populated by what are referred to as cognitive models. Part II of the book addresses lexical representation in detail. In this chapter I also introduced, briefly, the meaning-construction processes which make use of the semantic and conceptual levels of representation in service of situated utterance meaning. These involve an account of how lexical concepts are integrated in specific utterances (i.e., linguistically mediated usage events). Thus, the second key objective of LCCM Theory is to present an account of semantic composition which is compatible with the account of lexical representation developed. This is the subject of Part III of the book.

Part II

Lexical Representation

This part of the book is made up of six chapters and addresses lexical representation. Lexical representation is the substrate deployed in linguistically mediated communication, and is subject to the compositional processes resulting in meaning construction—processes that are addressed in Part III of the book. Lexical representation involves representation types found in two distinct systems: the linguistic system and the conceptual system. The first four chapters in Part II address the representations found in the linguistic system. The final two chapters, Chapters 9 and 10 deal with representations found in the conceptual system. The first chapter, Chapter 5, makes the case for the linguistic system being comprised of symbolic units. This chapter addresses the nature of symbolic units. Chapter 6 focuses on the nature of the semantic structure encoded by symbolic units. In particular, semantic structure is modelled in terms of lexical concepts which are made up of bundles of different types of linguistic content. Chapter 7 provides an overview of many of the key properties and knowledge types associated with lexical concepts. In particular, this chapter also addresses in detail the nature of the lexical profile associated with the lexical concept. In the light of the first three chapters in Part II, Chapter 8 investigates the status and nature of polysemy in LCCM Theory. This is achieved by virtue of a case study of the English prepositions *in*, *on*, and *at*. Chapter 9 provides an overview of conceptual structure, based on a review of recent work on knowledge representation in cognitive psychology. It also re-evaluates the thesis of encyclopaedic semantics in cognitive linguistics. Chapter 10 addresses the construct of the cognitive model, which is held to embody conceptual structure for purposes of access via representations from the linguistic system. It does so in the light of the nature of conceptual structure developed in Chapter 9.

5

Symbolic units

This chapter is concerned with the symbolic unit: the conventional association between a vehicle—a phonological form—and a semantic unit—a lexical concept.[1] In LCCM Theory, the symbolic unit is the type of representation that is hypothesized to populate the linguistic system. LCCM Theory assumes a constructional view of grammar. That is, the view of the linguistic system adopted here assumes the symbolic thesis, as discussed in Chapter 2. In view of this, my presentation of the nature and structure of the symbolic unit in this chapter involves a synthesis of some of the key ideas drawn from Construction Grammar,[2] as well as Cognitive Grammar.[3]

The existence of symbolic units: idioms

Perhaps the most well-known arguments for the symbolic unit constituting the basic form of representation in the linguistic system come from the pioneering work of Charles Fillmore and Paul Kay (e.g., Fillmore *et al.* 1988;

[1] In this chapter, and in the rest of this book, I use the term "symbolic unit" (Langacker 1987) rather than the perhaps more common term "construction"—in cognitive linguistics. I do so as different cognitive-linguistic approaches to grammar have employed the term "construction" in slightly different ways. For instance, Goldberg (1995, 2006), in her theory of Cognitive Construction Grammar, uses the term "construction" to refer to any conventional symbolic assembly including simplex symbolic assemblies, such as *cat*/[CAT], as well as more complex symbolic assemblies such as the so-called ditransitive construction discussed in Chapter 2. In contrast, in his theory of Cognitive Grammar, Langacker (e.g., 1987, 2008) reserves the term "construction" for complex symbolic assemblies. In Cognitive Grammar, the term "symbolic unit" is used to refer to both simplex and complex bipolar assemblies. I follow Langacker in deploying the term symbolic unit to refer to any conventional bipolar assembly involving form and semantic structure.

[2] Construction Grammar is in fact a family of theories—construction grammars—associated with the pioneering work of a number of scholars who have developed a number of distinct theories of construction grammar. These include **Cognitive Construction Grammar** (Goldberg 1995, 2006; Lakoff 1987), **Embodied Construction Grammar** (Bergen and Chang 2005), **Radical Construction Grammar** (Croft 2002), **Sign-based Construction Grammar** (Brenier and Michaelis 2006; Sag 2007), and (**Unification**) **Construction Grammar** (Fillmore *et al.* 1988; Kay and Fillmore 1999; Michaelis 2004; Michaelis and Lambrecht 1996). While there are important points of divergence across these various approaches (see Goldberg 2006: ch. 10), they are broadly similar in key respects. Not least they all assume the symbolic thesis. The theory of Cognitive Construction Grammar, which is centrally placed within and informed by the cognitive linguistics tradition, is the particular version of Construction Grammar which, along with Cognitive Grammar, has been the most influential constructional approach for the development of LCCM Theory.

[3] Cognitive Grammar has been developed by Langacker (1987, 1991*a*, 1991*b*, 1999, 2008).

Kay and Fillmore 1999). While it is uncontroversial in linguistics that the lexical item (i.e., the word) constitutes a symbolic unit, in their now classic 1988 paper, Fillmore, Kay, and O'Connor sought to extend this perspective to complex grammatical constructions (at the level of phrase, e.g., *in the garage*, or the clause, e.g., *the car is in the garage*). They argued that like words, complex grammatical constructions constitute symbolic units: conventional bipolar assemblies of form (or syntax), and semantic structure (semantic and pragmatic information). As such, they argued that the basic unit of grammar, the symbolic unit, is idiomatic, which is to say, idiosyncratic. This serves to blur the more traditional distinction adopted in linguistics between the lexicon—traditionally the repository of the arbitrary and the idiosyn-cratic—and the grammar—traditionally the rule-governed component of linguistic knowledge.[4]

In their 1988 paper Fillmore, Kay, and O'Connor challenge what I will call the **words plus rules model** assumed by the standard Generative model advocated in various versions, in the work of Chomsky (e.g., 1965, 1981, 1995) and others. According to this model, the properties of language can be accounted for by a system of "words and rules," where the words are the individual lexical items in the speaker's lexicon, and these words are subject to rules of different types within the language system. Phonological rules govern the assembly of complex strings of sounds. Syntactic rules govern the assem-bly of words into grammatical structures such as phrases and sentences, while semantic rules assign a semantic interpretation to the sentence, according to the principle of compositionality as advocated by literalism. As we saw in Chapter 1, this gives rise to propositional meaning, a purely semantic meaning that is independent of context. In addition to syntactic and semantic rules, speakers also have knowledge of pragmatic principles that map propositional meaning onto context, and guide the hearer in drawing the relevant infer-ences. Crucially, this approach is modular in that syntax, semantics, and phonology are encapsulated subsystems that only communicate with one another via linking rules. This words plus rules type of model is represented by the diagram in Figure 5.1.

This model of speaker knowledge only accounts for what is regular in language, and leaves aside idiomatic expressions (e.g., *He kicked the bucket*), which, according to Fillmore *et al.* (1988: 504), have the status of an "appendix to the grammar." In other words, in the words plus rule model, the only complex units that are stored whole are those whose properties cannot be predicted on the basis of the regular rules of the grammar. According to Fillmore *et al.*, this appendix is very large, effectively assigning many thou-sands of fixed expressions in any given language the status of "exception."

Fillmore *et al.* reasoned that if such a substantial chunk of the expressions in any given language was being treated as, in some sense, existing "outside"

---

[4] Recall the discussion of the lexicon-grammar continuum in Chapter 2.

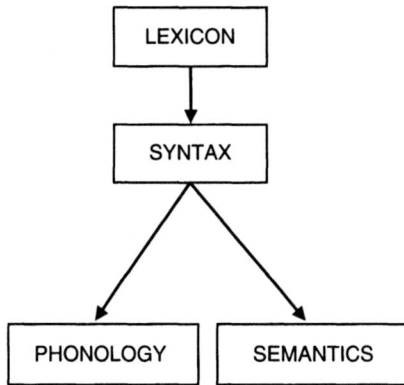

FIGURE 5.1. The words plus rules model of the linguistic system

the rules of the grammar, then perhaps it is the model of grammar, the words plus rules model, rather than the expressions themselves, which is at fault. Given this premise, Fillmore *et al.* decided to focus on the irregular, rather than the regular, in building their model of linguistic representations. In so doing, they began by focusing on idiomatic expressions rather than the apparently rule-governed sentences of language.

The words plus rules model assumes that, what are referred to as **idioms**— expressions that a language user cannot "work out" simply by knowing the grammar and the vocabulary of a language—are simply listed as exceptions. The tack taken by Fillmore *et al.* in developing their constructional account of the linguistic system is to begin with these so-called exceptions. They argued that if it is possible to account, in a principled way, for the "exceptions," then an account of the regular aspects of language should fall out naturally from an account of the irregular.

In their work on idioms, Fillmore *et al.*, reached two important and influential conclusions. Firstly, idioms do display some regular grammatical properties, and can be classified based on how they do and don't conform to regular semantic and grammatical patterns, and hence are not always fully predictable from their subparts. Secondly, idioms can be accommodated within a model of the linguistic system if we jettison the words plus rules model. In its place, they proposed a constructional model, which holds that the linguistic system is made up entirely of symbolic units: bipolar assemblies (or constructions) of form and meaning. This perspective is more parsimonious than the words plus rules model for the following reason. Rather than assuming two types of representations: words plus rules, with the idioms being akin to words, the model of Construction Grammar advocated by Fillmore *et al.* posited just a single kind of representation: symbolic units. In short, they argue that the same theoretical machinery can be held to account for both regular and idiomatic units of the linguistic system.

In developing their account, Fillmore *et al.* developed a typology of idiomatic expressions based on four main parameters, each of which I briefly discuss below:

- decoding and encoding idioms
- grammatical versus extragrammatical idioms
- substantive versus formal idioms
- idioms with and without pragmatic point.

Decoding and encoding idioms

Decoding idioms like *kick the bucket* have to be decoded or "learnt whole" in the sense that the semantic contribution of the expression cannot be worked out on first hearing. In contrast, encoding idioms like *wide awake* may be understood on the first hearing: the adjective *wide* functions as a degree modifier, and it is possible to work out that this expression means "completely awake". However, the speaker would not be able to predict this is the conventional way of encoding a particular idea in the language. In other words, there is nothing in the "rules" of English that enables a speaker to predict the existence of this expression as opposed to, say, *narrow awake, narrow asleep,* or *wide alert.* Encoding idioms also include expressions that are perfectly regular, but just happen to represent the conventional way of saying something. For example, the expression *driving licence* is an encoding idiom in the sense that it represents the conventional way of describing a document that could be (but is not) called a *driving permit* or a *driving document* (Taylor 2002: 547).

Grammatical versus extragrammatical idioms

Grammatical idioms are expressions that obey the usual rules of grammar. For example, in the grammatical idiom *spill the beans*, a verb takes a noun phrase complement. In contrast, extragrammatical idioms such as *all of a sudden* do not obey the usual rules of grammar. In this expression, the quantifier *all* is followed by a preposition phrase, where we would expect to find a noun phrase. Furthermore, an adjective, *sudden*, occurs after a determiner, where we might expect to find a noun.

Substantive versus formal idioms

The third distinction is between substantive and formal idioms. Substantive idioms are **lexically filled**, which means that they have fixed lexical items as part of their composition. For example, *kick the mop* does not have the same communicative function as *kick the bucket*, and *spill the beans* does not have the same communicative function as *spill the champagne*. Both *kick the bucket* and *spill the beans* are substantive idioms because most or all of the substantive or content expressions involved are intrinsic to the idiom. In contrast, formal idioms provide syntactic "frames" into which different lexical items can be "inserted." An example of a formal idiom is the *let alone* construction. As the following examples illustrate, the frame provided by this construction can be filled with all sorts of lexical items. In other words, this type of idiom is productive.

(1) a. Fred doesn't understand women in general, let alone the unique creature that is Holly Golightly
     b. Holly can't wash up, let alone cook
     c. I wouldn't describe Holly's predicament as amusing, let alone hilarious

Idioms with and without pragmatic point

Some idiomatic expressions exhibit a specific **illocutionary force** (Searle 1969), which is to say they have a clear communicative function in a specific extra-linguistic context. This notion Fillmore *et al.* refer to as **pragmatic point**. Examples of idioms which exhibit such a very clear pragmatic function include those which serve as a greeting: *How do you do?* or express a particular (negative) attitude: *What's your car doing in my parking space?* In contrast, other idiomatic expressions appear to be pragmatically neutral, in the sense that they can be used in any pragmatic context. Expressions like *by and large* and *on the whole* fall into this category.

Table 5.1 summarizes these four distinctions. As this table shows, a single idiom can be classified according to each of these four parameters. For example, the expression *by and large* is a decoding idiom that is extragram-

TABLE 5.1. Distinctions in idiom types

Idiom type	Semantic structure	Example
Decoding	Neither semantic contribution nor conventionality can be predicted	*kick the bucket*
Encoding	Semantic contribution may be predicted, but not conventionality	*wide awake*
Grammatical	Obey the rules of grammar	*spill the beans*
Extra-grammatical	Do not obey the rules of grammar	*all of a sudden*
Substantive	Lexically filled	*spill the beans*
Formal	Lexically open	the "let alone" construction
Pragmatic point	Specific pragmatic function	*How do you do?*
No pragmatic point	Pragmatically neutral	*by and large*

matical (a preposition is co-ordinated with an adjective), and is also substantive and pragmatically neutral.

The symbolic unit as the basis of the linguistic system

Having accounted for the exceptions, idiomatic expressions, in terms of the symbolic thesis, we turn to the next stage in developing the symbolic unit as *the* basis for representation in the linguistic system. This involves applying the constructional perspective to all that is regular: the rule-governed component, or the "syntax," of the words plus rules model.

One of the most influential developments in this area has been Adele Goldberg's work, most notably her landmark 1995 book.[5] Influenced both by the work of Fillmore and Kay and by the early work of George Lakoff on the symbolic basis of language,[6] Goldberg developed a theory of Construction Grammar that sought to extend the constructional approach of Fillmore and Kay from "irregular" idiomatic constructions to "regular" constructions. In order to do this, Goldberg focused on **verb argument constructions**. In other words, and as we saw in Chapter 2, she examined ordinary clause-level sentences such as transitives and ditransitives and built a Construction Grammar on the patterns she found there.

The central thesis of Goldberg's theory of Cognitive Construction Grammar is that sentence-level constructions "themselves carry meaning, independently of the words in the sentence" (Goldberg 1995: 1). According to this view, constructions—symbolic units in present terms—are themselves theoretical primitives, rather than "taxonomic epiphenomena" (Chomsky 1991: 417).

As Goldberg observes, the issue of argument structure alternations has received a considerable amount of attention in contemporary work in linguistics. To illustrate, consider the examples in (2) and (3).

(2)   a. Fred brought Holly Golightly some breakfast
      b. Fred brought some breakfast to Holly Golightly

(3)   a. *Fred brought the table some breakfast
      b. Fred brought some breakfast to the table

As these examples illustrate, the ditransitive verb *bring* can occur in two different construction types. Examples like (2a) and (3a) are termed ditransitive or (double object) constructions because the verb is followed by two nominal objects. In examples (2b) and (3b), which is termed the **prepositional construction** (Goldberg 1995: 8), the indirect object (*Holly Golightly* or *the table*) is instead represented by a preposition phrase (PP). The point of

---

[5] See also Goldberg (2006) in which Goldberg revises certain aspects of her earlier theory of Construction Grammar.

[6] Goldberg was influenced in particular by Lakoff's (1987) case study of *there* constructions.

interest here relates to the fact that while the prepositional construction allows the recipient to be either animate (2b) or inanimate (3b), the double object construction requires that it be animate (compare (2a) with (3a)). The issue that arises from this observation is how these differences are best captured in the model of the linguistic system. Goldberg argues that the most explanatory account associates these semantic restrictions directly with the grammatical construction itself, rather than stating the information in the lexical entries of individual verbs. That is, and as we saw in Chapter 2, Goldberg argues that the ditransitive construction, for instance, constitutes a symbolic unit independently of the lexical items which happen to fill it. In so doing she claims that it represents a bipolar unit, which consists of a conventional vehicle, a specifiable syntactic arrangement, with a semantic structure which she glosses as: x CAUSES Y TO RECEIVE Z.

Goldberg argues that the ditransitive symbolic unit is associated with the syntactic frame [SUBJ [V OBJ OBJ$_2$]] (e.g., *Fred gave Holly flowers*), where both objects are noun phrases (NPs). The ditransitive unit is not associated with the syntactic frame [NP [V NP PP]] (e.g., *Fred gave flowers to Holly*), which identifies the distinct prepositional symbolic unit. These two symbolic units are distinct—although related by shared aspects of form and semantic structure—because any difference in either vehicle or semantic structure signifies, in Cognitive Construction Grammar, a distinct symbolic unit.

Goldberg lists a number of properties that are specific to the ditransitive symbolic unit, which cannot be predicted either from the individual words that fill the symbolic unit, or from other symbolic units in the language. The properties of the ditransitive symbolic unit are summarized in Table 5.2.

In more recent work which complements that of Goldberg, William Croft (2002) has developed a constructional account of language informed by research on the grammatical diversity across the world's languages. This approach, which he terms **Radical Construction Grammar**, is noteworthy for completely eliminating syntax (rules relating to word order), and grammatical categories (such as subject and object) from the model of linguistic representation developed. In particular, Croft argues that the symbolic unit

TABLE 5.2. Properties of the English symbolic unit: ditransitive construction (Goldberg 1995)

The English ditransitive: X CAUSES Y TO RECEIVE Z
Contributes TRANSFER semantics that cannot be attributed to the lexical verb
The GOAL argument must be animate (RECIPIENT rather than PATIENT)
Two non-predicative NPs are licensed in post-verbal position
The construction links RECIPIENT role with OBJ function
The SUBJ role must be filled with a volitional AGENT, who intends TRANSFER

(i.e., the "construction") is the only primitive unit in the grammar, and may therefore be either simplex or complex in terms of form, and either specific or schematic in terms of its semantic structure. This means that grammatical categories—for example, word classes such as noun and verb, or grammatical functions such as subject and object—have no independent status, but are defined in relation to the symbolic units within which they occur. This does not mean that word classes, for instance, do not exist, but that word classes cannot be categorized into divisions that have any reality independent of the symbolic units that make up a given language. Hence, what makes Radical Construction Grammar radical is the position that the symbolic unit becomes not only the primary form of linguistic representation but the only constituent of the linguistic system.

From this perspective, it is to be expected that the types of word classes that we observe from one language to another might be significantly different. Moreover, because no universal word classes are posited, this cross-linguistic variation is not only unproblematic but predicted. Croft therefore argues against the traditional distributional approach to word classes, as assumed, for instance, in traditional grammar, structuralism, and the Generative paradigm. Instead, Croft argues in favour of language-specific symbolic units, and in favour of symbolic unit-specific **elements** (grammatical subparts) and **components** (semantic subparts).

Given the fundamental status of the symbolic unit in Radical Construction Grammar, the only syntactic relations admitted are the **part-whole relations** that hold between the symbolic unit as a whole and the syntactic elements that fill it. In other words, the model does not recognize **grammatical relations** (grammatical functions) such as subject and object as having any independent reality outside of individual symbolic units. Instead, to the extent that grammatical functions emerge from symbolic units, these also have the status of construction-specific epiphenomena. In this model, constituency is conceived in terms of **grouping**, where grammatical units are identified in terms of contiguity and prosodic unity, and heads receive a semantic characterization as **primary information-bearing units** or PIBUs (Croft 2002: 258).[7]

In sum, the defining feature of constructional approaches, as adopted by LCCM Theory, is that a symbolic unit as a whole constitutes a conventional assembly of form, a vehicle, and semantic structure, a lexical concept, in the same way as a lexical item is conceived as constituting a symbolic unit in the received view of the lexicon. The types of distinct symbolic units are presented in Figure 5.2. The anatomy of a symbolic unit is presented in Table 5.3.

---

[7] This notion is analogous to Langacker's (e.g., 1987) notion of the head being what he refers to as the **profile determinant**.

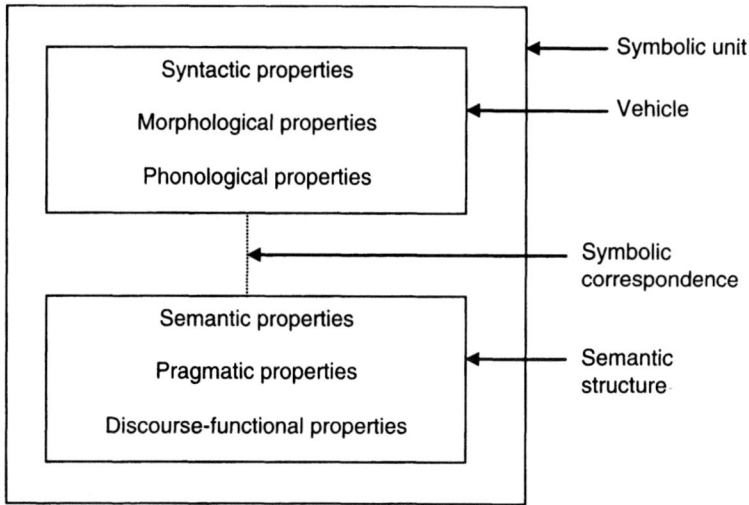

FIGURE 5.2. Anatomy of a symbolic unit (adapted from Croft 2002: 18)

TABLE 5.3. Taxonomy of symbolic units (adapted from Croft 2002: 17)

Type of symbolic unit	Traditional name	Example
Complex and (mostly) schematic	Syntax	NP *be*-TENSE VERB-*en by* NP/[ACTION FROM PERSPECTIVE OF PATIENT]
Complex and (mostly) specific	Idiom	*pull*-TENSE NP's *leg*/[TO TEASE AS A JOKE]
Complex but bound	Morphology	NOUN-*s*/[MORE THAN ONE OF SOMETHING], VERB-TENSE/[TIME REFERENCE WITH RESPECT TO CODING TIME]
Atomic and schematic	Word classes	NOUN/(THING), VERB/[TEMPORALLY GROUNDED RELATION]
Atomic and specific	Lexical items	*the*/[THE], *jumper*/[JUMPER]

The non-reductive nature of symbolic units

An important feature of constructional accounts of the linguistic system—
what is generally referred to, by linguists, as the "grammar"—is their non-
reductive nature. Following Langacker (1987) I assume that one of the factors
involved in the establishment of a symbolic unit is frequency: if a particular

linguistic structure recurs sufficiently frequently, it achieves the status of an entrenched unit.[8] As a result of this process of entrenchment, symbolic units come to have different levels of schematicity. This means that some symbolic units are **instances** (Langacker 1987) of other more abstract units, which Langacker refers to as **schemas.** To illustrate, consider prepositions (P) such as *to, on,* and *in,* which are combined with a complement noun phrase (NP) to form a preposition phrase (PP). In example (4), the NP is bracketed.

(4)   a. to [me]
      b. on [the floor]
      c. in [the garage]

The expressions in (4), *to me, on the floor,* and *in the garage,* are common phrases that probably have unit status for most speakers of English. In other words, they are symbolic units. However, there is another schema related to these symbolic units, which has the highly schematic vehicle "P NP" and the highly schematic semantic structure which I gloss as [DIRECTION OR LOCA-TION WITH RESPECT TO SOME PHYSICAL ENTITY]. The symbolic units in (4) are thus specific instances of this more abstract symbolic unit. This is illustrated in Figure 5.3 which identifies the symbolic units based on their vehicles.

   This view of the linguistic system is non-reductive in the following way. The symbolic units in (4) can be predicted by the more general schema of which they are instances. However, the fact that they can be predicted does not mean that they can be eliminated from the linguistic system—the mental repository of symbolic units. On the contrary, the fact that expressions of this kind are frequently occurring ensures that they retain unit status as distinct symbolic units. Moreover, that fact that they share a similar structure and a common abstract semantic structure ensures that the more abstract schema also co-exists with them in the linguistic system.

   This non-reductive model stands in direct opposition to the words plus rules model. This is because the words plus rules model assumes that the rapid

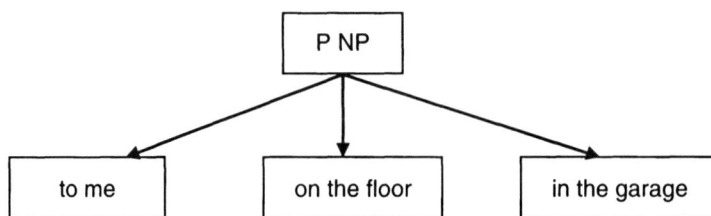

FIGURE 5.3. Schema-instance relations holding between symbolic units

[8] For a review of the role of frequency in the storage of symbolic units see Croft and Cruse (2004).

acquisition of an infinitely creative system of language can only be plausibly accounted for by a small and efficient set of principles. In particular, the words plus rules model seeks to eliminate redundancy: the same information does not need to be stated in more than one place, as this makes the system non-parsimonious. According to this view, the fact that the expressions in (4) are predictable from the more abstract symbolic unit means that these instances can be eliminated from the linguistic system, and "built from scratch" each time they are used. In the words plus rules model, the only construction that would be stored in the linguistic system is the abstract schema. However, this schema would lack schematic meaning, and would instead have the status of an "instruction" about what kinds of vehicles can be combined to make grammatical units. In the words plus rule model, then, what I am here calling a schema is actually a rule. While schemas are derived from language use and thus incorporate semantic structure—a lexical concept—rules are minimally specified structural representations that predict the greatest amount of information possible in the most economical way possible.

The structure of symbolic units

Lexical concepts are associated with vehicles, a consequence of their status as the semantic pole of bipolar symbolic units. As the vehicles can be complex, made up of simpler vehicles, lexical concepts can be simpler or more complex. Moreover, just as a vehicle can be construed as having part-whole organization, so too lexical concepts have part-whole organization. In other words, there are relations that hold between distinct symbolic units.[9] To illustrate, consider the following examples:

(5) a. Vehicle: "*France*"
        Lexical concept: [FRANCE]
     b. Vehicle: "NP *kick*FINITE *the bucket*"
        Lexical concept: [AN ANIMATE ENTITY DIES]
     c. Vehicle: "NP FINITE VERB NP NP"
        Lexical concept: [THING X CAUSES THING Y TO RECEIVE THING Z]

It is necessary to make mention of the formatting conventions I will be deploying in the rest of the chapter, and the book. I use italics to represent a **phonetically overt vehicle**, such as *France, the bucket*, or *kick*—this is akin to the notion of the substantive idiom discussed above. I use capitals to represent **phonetically implicit vehicles**—akin to the notion of a formal idiom—such as FINITE to indicate a finite construction, e.g., the nature of the tense

---

[9] This corresponds to Langacker's (1987) **content requirement**. This holds that the only entities permissible within the grammar are: (1) phonological, semantic, and symbolic units; (2) the relations that hold between them; and (3) the schemas that represent those units.

involved, or NP, which stands for "noun phrase." Vehicles which are phonetically implicit are those that have a highly schematic phonetic representation relating to a **phonetic potential**, rather than being lexically filled.

In the example in (5a), the vehicle relates to the lexical item *France*, while the lexical concept I gloss as [FRANCE]. This symbolic unit, by virtue of consisting of a phonetically overt vehicle, is lexically filled. Lexical concepts conventionally paired with phonetically overt vehicles I refer to as being **internally closed**.

The example in (5b) involves the vehicle "NP *kick*FINITE *the bucket*", which relates to the lexical concept which I gloss as [AN ANIMATE ENTITY DIES]. This lexical concept is **internally open**: as it is conventionally paired with a vehicle that is not fully lexically specified. That is, other lexical concepts can be integrated with it.[10]

A further distinction relates to those lexical concepts which can be described as **internally simple** versus those that are **internally complex**. An internally simple lexical concept is one that has no part-whole structure and hence cannot be analysed in terms of more than one lexical concept. An example of such a lexical concept is [FRANCE] associated with the vehicle *France*. At this point it is worth emphasizing that being internally simple is not the same as being internally closed (or open). For instance, the lexical concept [THING] is internally open being an abstract lexical concept and hence one that is associated with a vehicle which is phonetically implicit, namely the vehicle NOUN. Yet this lexical concept is internally simple.

An example of an internally complex lexical concept is [THING X CAUSES THING Y TO RECEIVE THING Z], associated with the vehicle: "NP FINITE VERB NP NP" as in (5c). As the vehicle which corresponds to the lexical concept is itself complex, associated with simpler lexical concepts, the overall lexical concept is itself complex. This, of course, relates to what Goldberg refers to as the ditransitive construction, as discussed in Chapter 2.[11]

Integration of symbolic units

One of my central concerns in this book is semantic compositionality. A constructional perspective to grammar offers a promising point of departure for such an account as symbolic units are integrated in nested fashion[12] via an operation known as **unification** in unification-based Construction Grammar (e.g., Kay and Fillmore 1999), **fusion** in Cognitive Construction Grammar (e.g., Goldberg 2006), and **elaboration** in Cognitive Grammar

---

[10] This is an issue that I will address in more detail in Part III, in particular Chapter 12.

[11] The distinction between internally open versus closed, and simple versus complex lexical concepts will be discussed in more detail in Chapter 12.

[12] Recall the discussion of nested integration in Chapter 2.

(e.g., Langacker 1987).[13] For instance, Goldberg (2006: 21) observes that the utterance given in (6) is made up of all the symbolic units in (7):

(6)   A dozen roses, Nina sent her mother!

(7)   a. Ditransitive symbolic unit
      b. Topicalization symbolic unit
      c. VP symbolic unit
      d. NP symbolic unit
      e. Indefinite determiner symbolic unit
      f. Plural symbolic unit
      g. *dozen, rose, Nina, send, mother* symbolic units

Of course, my concern in this book is with the way in which units of semantic structure—lexical concepts—are combined in order to prompt for the construction of simulations. Nevertheless, LCCM Theory takes from constructional approaches the perspective that symbolic units provide slots that facilitate the composition of lexical concepts. This is an issue that I return to in Part III of the book.

Summary

In this chapter I have provided a brief overview of the nature and structure of the symbolic unit, as developed in constructional accounts of the linguistic system in cognitive linguistics. In LCCM Theory the symbolic unit is the representation type that is held to populate the linguistic system. A symbolic unit is comprised of a bipolar assembly of phonological content, what I refer to as a vehicle, and semantic structure, which I term a lexical concept. Hence, it is a bipolar symbolic assembly. In internal structure, the vehicles and lexical concepts that make up a symbolic unit have distinct, albeit related, characteristics. A vehicle can be phonetically overt: lexically filled; or phonetically implicit: possessing schematic phonetic content, which is to say phonetic potential. A lexical concept can be internally open, such that it can be integrated with other lexical concepts or internally closed, when it cannot. Both vehicles and lexical concepts can also be simplex or complex, reflecting the view that symbolic units exhibit part-whole relations.

[13] See Kay and Michaelis (forthcoming) for discussion of constructional perspectives on semantic compositionality.

6

Semantic structure

This chapter is concerned with developing an account of the nature of semantic structure. In particular, I examine the distinctive character of semantic structure, contrasting it with conceptual structure. In LCCM Theory semantic structure is modelled in terms of the theoretical construct of the lexical concept. Hence, this chapter also lays the foundation for the lexical concept, focusing in particular on the kind of content that it encodes.

The main claim that I make in this chapter is that lexical concepts have **bipartite structure**. Firstly, lexical concepts encode information that can be directly encoded in, and externalized via, language. Hence, information of this sort is unique to language. This relatively stable information I refer to as **linguistic content**. In addition, a subset of lexical concepts (as discussed below) serves as access sites to a representational type which is non-linguistic in nature: conceptual structure—modelled in terms of the construct of the cognitive model.[1] The non-linguistic information encoded by cognitive models I refer to as **conceptual content**. Content of this type is not directly encoded by lexical concepts, which is to say it is not encoded *in* language. Rather it can be accessed by lexical concepts, and hence *via* language. Thus, the bipartite structure of lexical concepts means that they *encode* linguistic content and *facilitate access to* a potentially unlimited array of conceptual content—the semantic potential discussed in Chapter 4. This situation is summarized in Figure 6.1.

In the next section, which synthesizes and builds on work by Leonard Talmy (e.g., 2000), I lay the foundation for an account of semantic structure. In his approach to semantic representation, Talmy argues for two levels of representation facilitated by language: a schematic level and a rich level. After presenting Talmy's account, I then argue, in the following section, that Talmy's separation of two levels of representation in fact relates to the distinction between linguistic content on the one hand and conceptual content on the other. In subsequent sections I examine the distinction between linguistic and conceptual content in detail, as well as the basis for the distinction. Finally, I present a fairly detailed examination of the distinct types of linguistic content encoded by the lexical concept. I argue that the

---

[1] Conceptual structure is the subject of Chapter 9.

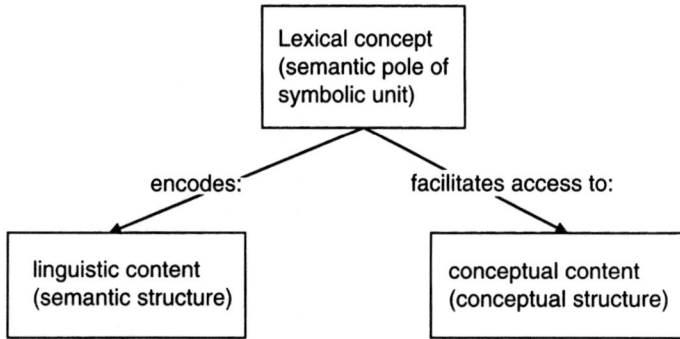

FIGURE 6.1. The bipartite structure of a lexical concept

lexical concept can be best thought of as a **bundle** of different types of linguistic content.

Rich versus schematic content

According to Talmy (2000) a central design feature of language is that the concepts expressed are divided into two subsystems. As we first saw in Chapter 2, Talmy characterizes this in terms of what he refers to as the grammatical subsystem and lexical subsystem. These two subsystems serve to express the experiential complex—what Talmy refers to as the **cognitive representation**—that a speaker attempts to evoke in the listener by virtue of deploying language. The range of concepts expressed by the grammatical subsystem is highly restricted cross-linguistically, providing a basic framework for the structuring of the experiential complex that language users seek to evoke in their interlocutors. Put another way, the lexical concepts associated with the grammatical subsystem have **schematic content**, providing a structuring function. Thus, the lexical concepts with schematic content provide a "scaffolding" so to speak, across which the rich content associated with the lexical concepts of the lexical subsystem can be draped. In contradistinction to this, the lexical concepts associated with the so-called lexical subsystem provide **rich content**, giving rise to the details (rather than structural aspects) of the cognitive representation. Talmy expresses this idea in the following way:

Together, the grammatical elements of a sentence determine the majority of the *structure* of the CR [cognitive representation], while the lexical elements together contribute the majority of its *content*... The grammatical specifications in a sentence, thus, provide a conceptual framework or, imagistically, a skeletal structure or scaffolding, for the conceptual material that is lexically specified.

(Talmy 2000: 21).

An important aspect of Talmy's work is the claim that the distinction between rich versus schematic content corresponds to a bifurcation between vehicle types: open-class versus closed-class vehicles. Closed-class vehicles are so-called because it is considered more difficult to add members to this set. This set of lexical items includes the so-called "grammatical" or "functional" words such as conjunctions, determiners, pronouns, prepositions, and so on. In contrast open-class vehicles include words belonging to the lexical classes: noun, verb, adjective, and adverb.

While the concepts expressed by closed-class vehicles encode schematic content, they are nevertheless essential for the expression of the cognitive representation. To make this point clear, consider the following semantic analysis of the range of open- and closed-class elements which comprise the utterance in (1):

(1)   A *rockstar smash*ed the *guitar*s

The forms in bold: **a**, **-ed**, **the**, and **-s** are associated with the grammatical subsystem. Their semantic contribution relates to whether the participants (rockstar/guitars) in the experiential complex evoked by (1) can be easily identified by the hearer (the use of the indefinite article **a** versus the definite article **the**), that the event took place before now (the use of the past-tense marker **-ed**), and how many participants were involved (the absence or presence of the plural marker **-s**).

In contrast, the forms in italics: *rockstar*, *smash*, and *guitar* are associated with the lexical subsystem. That is, their semantic contribution relates to the nature of participants involved in the experiential complex, and the relationship holding between them, namely one involving smashing. In other words, while the closed-class vehicles encode content relating to structural aspects of the experiential complex evoked, the open-class vehicles are associated with detailed information concerning the nature of the participants, scenes involving the participants, and the states and relationships that hold.

To make this point even clearer, consider the example in (2):

(2)   A *waiter serv*ed the *customer*s

While the utterance in (2) involves exactly the same closed-class elements, and hence schematic content as (1), the cognitive representation evoked by (2) is radically different. According to Talmy, this is because the content evoked by the lexical subsystem—the example in (2) involves different open-class vehicles from the example in (1)—involves very different content than that associated with schematic content encoded by the closed-class vehicles. The lexical subsystem relates to things, people, places, events, properties of things, and so on. The grammatical subsystem on the other hand relates to content having to do with topological aspects of space, time, and number (discussed in further detail below), whether a piece of information is old or

TABLE 6.1. Schematic content associated with closed-class vehicles

Closed-class vehicles	Schematic semantic content
a	Introduces a referent which the hearer is held to be unable to readily identify (from context or preceding discourse)
a	Designates a unitary instantiation of the referent
the	Introduces a referent which the hearer is held to be able to readily identify (from context or preceding discourse)
-s	Designates multiple instantiations of a referent
-er	Designates performer of a particular action or activity
lexical class: verb (for *serve*)	Designates entity as an event (as one possibility)
lexical class: noun (for *waiter/customer*)	Designates entity as an object (as one possibility)
grammatical relation: subject (for *waiter*)	Designates entity as being the primary or focal entity in a designated relationship
grammatical relation: object (for *customers*)	Designates entity as less important or secondary entity in a designated relationship
active voice (through verb form)	Designates point of view being situated at the agent
declarative word order	Speaker knows the situation to be true and asserts it to the hearer

TABLE 6.2. Rich content associated with open-class vehicles

Open-class vehicles	Rich semantic content
waiter	Person with a particular function, and sometimes appearance, who works in a particular setting
serve	Particular mode of activity involving two or more people and, typically, an entity with which one of the participants is provided by the other
customer	Person who is provided with a particular object or service (of various sorts) in exchange for, typically, money

new, and whether the speaker is providing information or requesting information and so on, as illustrated by (3) in which information is being requested:

(3)   Which *waiter* served the *customers*?

The closed-class vehicles I have discussed thus far have an overt phonetic realization. However, each of the examples discussed also includes closed-class vehicles that are phonetically implicit. Examples include lexical classes: e.g., noun, verb; lexical subclasses: e.g., count noun, mass noun; grammatical relations: e.g., subject, object; declarative versus interrogative forms, active voice versus passive voice, and clause-level symbolic units such as the ditransitive construction, and so forth.

In order to capture the range of concepts associated with both overt and implicit closed-class vehicles, as well as those encoded by open-class vehicles, Tables 6.1 and 6.2 present a Talmy-style analysis in order to illustrate the distinction in schematic versus rich content. The tables are based on the example in (2).

As is evident from a comparison of Tables 6.1 and 6.2, there is a clear distinction between the nature of the content associated with closed- versus open-class vehicles. While the number of closed-class vehicles required to evoke the experiential complex designated by (2) are more numerous, they relate to structural aspects of the scene, and serve to relate different aspects of the

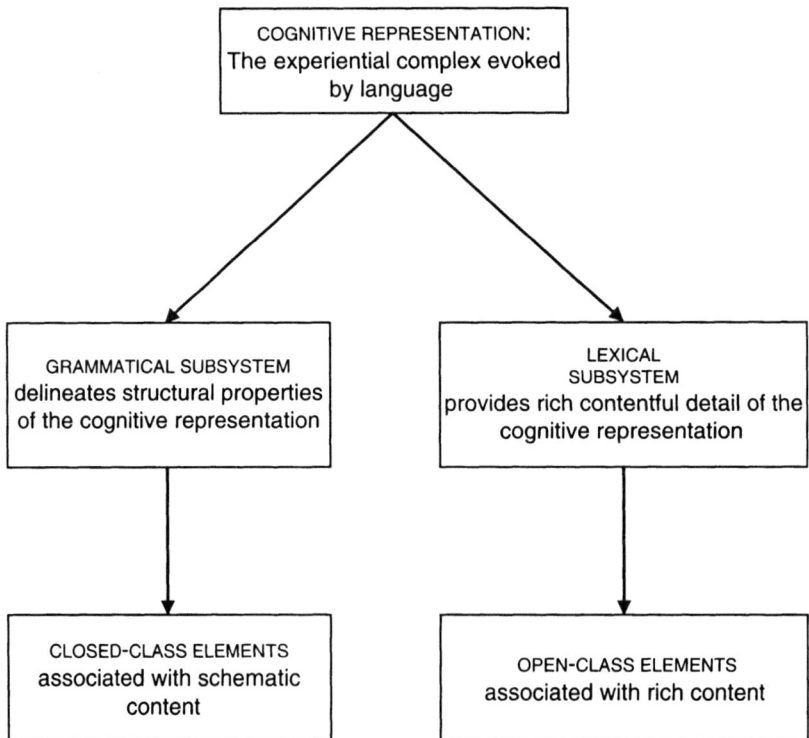

FIGURE 6.2. The bifurcation in the expression of the cognitive representation in language

cognitive representation. In contrast, there are fewer open-class vehicles, but the level of detail associated with these is much greater, involving social, physical and interpersonal function, details of the nature of the relationship holding between participants, as well as rich perceptual details concerning substance, shape, size, and so forth. This distinction is summarized in Figure 6.2.

Recasting the distinction between rich versus schematic content in LCCM terms

Having considered Talmy's distinction between schematic versus rich content, I now address the way in which this insight is recast by LCCM Theory. As we saw in Chapter 2, LCCM Theory makes a principled distinction between semantic structure on one hand, and conceptual structure on the other. This distinction in the kind of knowledge—in present terms, **content**—evoked, is of two quite different kinds. While conceptual structure has to do with conceptual (i.e., non-linguistic) content, to which language, and specifically lexical concepts, afford access, semantic structure has to do with linguistic content.

I argue that the distinction in content evoked by language, pointed to by Talmy, relates to the distinction between linguistic and conceptual content. The rich content evoked by open-class vehicles relates to conceptual content—a level of knowledge representation "above" language. Information of this kind is multimodal in nature. As such, it derives from sensory-motor systems—those sensory systems that recruit information relating to the external environment and the human individuals' interaction with the environment—as well as proprioception—the systems that recruit information relating to the motor aspects of the body's own functioning—and subjective experience—which includes experiences ranging from emotions, temporal and other cognitive states, to the visceral sense (see Barsalou 1999). Conceptual content provides records of perceptual states, in the sense just given. Accordingly, it is **analogue** in character. That is, conceptual content encodes information that parallels the multimodal body-based (perceptual, motoric, subjective, etc.) experience that it constitutes a representation of.[2] As such, conceptual structure is not suitable for being encoded in language. After all, language as a representational system consisting of symbolic units is simply not equipped to directly encode the rich, multimodal character of sense-perceptory and subjective experience. While lexical concepts do not encode multimodal information of this sort, as suggested in Part I of the book they do provide access to content of this sort.

In contrast, the schematic content discussed by Talmy is not an analogue representation of multimodal experience. Rather, it represents an abstraction

---

[2] Conceptual content is not an exact record of the multimodal states that are captured. Rather, it is somewhat attenuated. See Barsalou (1999) for discussion.

over multimodal content of various sorts, provided in a form that can be directly encoded in language, i.e., by lexical concepts. Content of this kind constitutes what I refer to as linguistic content, and forms part of the information encoded by a lexical concept.

While the distinction between rich and schematic aspects of the cognitive representation provides evidence for the distinction in linguistic and conceptual content just outlined, the distinction in open-class and closed-class vehicles provides evidence for a closely related distinction in the nature of the associated lexical concepts.[3] The distinction in vehicle types provides evidence that lexical concepts fall into two distinct categories. Closed-class vehicles are associated with lexical concepts which are specialized for encoding linguistic content. Lexical concepts of this sort I refer to as **closed-class lexical concepts**. Open-class vehicles, while also encoding linguistic content, are, in addition, specialized for serving as access sites to conceptual content. Lexical concepts of this sort I refer to as **open-class lexical concepts**.

In sum, the distinction between open-class lexical concepts versus closed-class lexical concepts embodies the bipartite organization of lexical concepts introduced at the outset of the chapter, as captured in Figure 6.3. To reiterate, while both types of lexical concepts *encode* linguistic content, I hypothesize that only open-class lexical concepts *afford access* to conceptual content. The distinction between "encode" and "afford access" is critical here. Linguistic content is encoded by lexical concepts precisely because this is the content which makes up lexical concepts. However, conceptual content, as we have begun to see above, and as we will see in more detail in the next section, is associated with a different representational type, the cognitive model, which is non-linguistic in nature. Thus, conceptual content is not directly encoded in language, although the linguistic system has developed the means to access

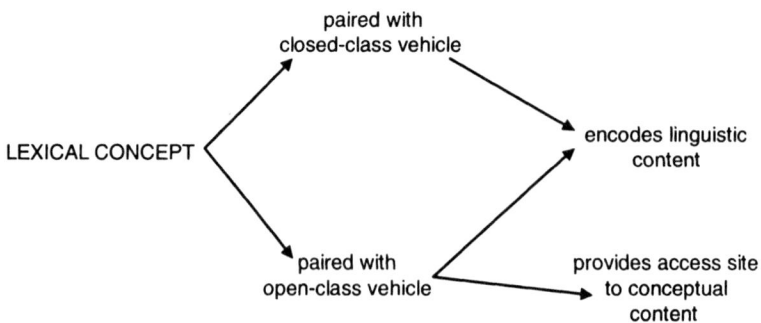

FIGURE 6.3. The distinction in content associated with lexical concepts

[3] Recall that symbolic units are made up of forms which serve as vehicles for the associated lexical concepts.

TABLE 6.3. A summary of key terms in LCCM Theory

Term	Description
Linguistic system	The collection of symbolic units comprising a language, and the various relationships holding between them.
Symbolic unit	A conventional pairing of a phonological form or vehicle and a semantic element.
Lexical concept	The semantic element that is paired with a phonological vehicle in a symbolic unit.
Linguistic content	The type of content encoded by a lexical concept. This content is of a highly schematic type that can be directly encoded *in* language.
Conceptual system	The body of non-linguistic knowledge captured from multimodal experience. This knowledge derives from sensory-motor experience, proprioception, and subjective experience.
Cognitive model	The representational form that knowledge in the conceptual system takes, as modelled in LCCM Theory. Consists of frames which give rise to a potentially unlimited set of simulations.
Conceptual content	The nature of the knowledge encoded by a cognitive model.
Lexical representation	The primary substrate deployed in linguistically mediated meaning construction, and modelled in terms of symbolic units and cognitive models.
Semantic representation	The semantic dimension of lexical representations, consisting of semantic structure and conceptual structure.
Semantic structure	That part of semantic representation encoded by the linguistic system. Semantic structure is modelled, in LCCM Theory, by lexical concepts.
Conceptual structure	That part of the semantic representation encoded by the conceptual system. Conceptual structure is modelled, in LCCM Theory, by cognitive models.

conceptual content via **association areas**, discussed in more detail in Chapter 10. Table 6.3 provides a summary of the way some of the key terms introduced so far are used in LCCM Theory.

Before concluding this section, it is important to spell out one of the consequences of the distinction between lexical concepts types identified. As pointed out by Croft (2007), the bifurcation between open- and closed-class vehicles and hence the content versus structuring distinction, as presented by Talmy, is problematic if we assume that there is a sharp distinction between open- and closed-class vehicles. Rather, the distinction between the lexical and grammatical subsystems should be thought of more as a continuum.[4] Hence, while I make a sharp distinction between closed- and open-class lexical concepts, it is less clear that it is possible to equate, in a straightforward way, the ability to facilitate access to conceptual content solely to open-class vehicles. For this reason, I express this ability as a tendency: identifying a vehicle as being open-class will signal a likelihood, rather than an assurance, that the lexical concept associated with the form in question will facilitate access to conceptual structure. Nevertheless, the notional distinction between open- and closed-class vehicles is useful for analytic purposes.[5]

The distinction between linguistic and conceptual content

In order to obtain a more detailed sense of the distinction between the nature of linguistic and conceptual content, consider the expression given in (4):

(4)   a red ball in the box

This expression features three open-class vehicles: *red, ball,* and *box.* These vehicles are paired with lexical concepts which I will gloss as [RED], [BALL], and [BOX] respectively. Each of these lexical concepts (i) encodes linguistic content, and (ii) provides access to conceptual content. To illustrate, let's briefly examine the lexical concept [RED]. Dealing with the linguistic content first, [RED] encodes schematic information: namely that we are dealing with a property of an object-like entity.

Now turning to the issue of conceptual content, the lexical concept [RED] provides access to rich perceptual information: in other words, information which is non-linguistic in nature. In order to illustrate, reconsider the following utterances, first discussed, briefly, in Chapter 4:

(5)   a. The teacher scrawled in red ink all over the pupil's homework exercises
       b. The red squirrel is in danger of becoming extinct in the British Isles

As we have already seen, in each of these utterances the use of *red* gives rise to a distinct simulation. A simulation is an analogue mental rehearsal of a multimodal experience that is recorded and represented in the conceptual

---

[4] Recall the discussion of the lexicon-grammar continuum in Chapter 2. For discussion of the nature of the continuum holding between open- and closed-class vehicles and some reasons for it see Gentner and Boroditsky (2001).

[5] The foregoing discussion has implications for the process of **grammaticalization**: the evolution of closed-class vehicles and lexical concepts from open-class vehicles and lexical concepts. It has been well documented that grammaticalization involves what has been termed **semantic bleaching**: the loss of access to the rich or contentful aspects of semantic representation, as vehicles evolve from being open-class to being closed-class. From the perspective of LCCM Theory, grammaticalization results both from a change in form, as well as the loss of a lexical concept's ability to afford access to conceptual structure.

system. As such, a simulation is a type of experience that can be prompted for by virtue of linguistically mediated communication, which is to say, in the absence of an external stimulus. As such, simulations are types of experience which are **imageable**. In terms of a given simulation of "redness", the form that the imageable experience takes relates to visual experience. For instance, if I close my eyes I can mentally rehearse or "picture" the kind of red evoked by each utterance in (5). As we have already seen, the simulation derived for the use of *red* in (5a) involves a bright, vivid red, while the simulation derived in response to the use of *red* in (5b) is more of a dun/browny red. The point, of course, is that the perceptual experience of redness derived in response to each utterance is not a matter of language. By this I mean that the perceptual experience is not somehow encoded by the semantic structure associated with the word *red*. Rather, [RED] provides access to a (multiplicity of) cognitive model(s), as we shall see in Chapter 10, which encode(s) conceptual content: perceptual experience relating to that part of the colour spectrum which is categorized as being "red".

Now let's consider the nature of the content encoded by open-class lexical concepts. To illustrate, consider the distinction between the open-class lexical concepts [SLIPPER] and [CHAMPAGNE] associated with the vehicles *slipper* and *champagne* respectively. Both these lexical concepts, designating physical entities, relate to the domain of space. In so doing, they facilitate access to complex conceptual content. [SLIPPER] for instance, relates to knowledge having to do with a type of footwear, worn in a restricted context and typically, at particular times of the day. Such knowledge is based on abstracting across episodic experiences—that is, experience which is personal and situated, including personal observation—as well as cultural experience—knowledge gleaned through narrative, story, and so on. As such, knowledge of this sort is extremely rich in nature, and hence is conceptual—that is, non-linguistic—in nature. Similarly, the lexical concept [CHAMPAGNE], relates to knowledge concerning an alcoholic beverage, of a particular type, served and drunk in a particular way, for particular reasons, and in particular venues. Similarly, this sort of knowledge constitutes conceptual content.

In addition, both lexical concepts also encode linguistic content. For instance, and as we shall see below, they are both **nominal lexical concepts**, which means they refer to a **thing** (cf. Langacker 1987)—an entity which is held to relate to a region in some conceptual domain (in Langacker's terms)—rather than encoding a relation, and hence constituting a **relational lexical concept**. This distinction is discussed later.

Moreover, both [SLIPPER] and [CHAMPAGNE] encode different aspects of the category **plexity** (Talmy 2000). Plexity is a category that relates to the domains of both TIME and SPACE, although as it concerns [SLIPPER] and [CHAMPAGNE] it relates to SPACE. Plexity encodes whether a quantity of SPACE consists of one (uniplex) or more than one (multiplex) equivalent elements. The lexical concept [SLIPPER] encodes **uniplex structure**. Evidence for this comes from the fact that [SLIPPER] can undergo integration with the plural lexical concept as encoded by the vehicle *-s*, as in *slippers*. In contrast, [CHAMPAGNE] encodes **multiplex structure**, evidenced by the fact that it cannot be integrated with the plural lexical concept. In other words, the nature of the plexity encoded by each of these lexical concepts determines, in part, the range of other lexical concepts with which they can undergo integration.

Now let's turn to a brief consideration of the lexical concepts associated with closed-class vehicles. Returning to our example in (4), above, this includes the vehicles: *a*, *in*, and *the*, which are associated with the lexical concepts [A], [ENCLOSURE], and [THE] respectively. I focus here, briefly, on one of these, the lexical concept [ENCLOSURE] associated with *in*. In fact, we need, at this point, to anticipate a discussion which follows in a later chapter.[6]

Firstly, it is important to note that the lexical concept [ENCLOSURE] encodes linguistic content. That is, it provides highly schematic spatial information: it fails to provide precise geometric details relating to size or distance, shape or substance. This I refer to as being **magnitude-**, **shape-**, and **substance-neutral**—to be discussed in detail in the next section, below. This lexical concept specifies a relationship holding between one entity, the Figure (F), and a second entity which I refer to, following Tyler and Evans (2003) as a **bounded landmark**.[7] The lexical concept [ENCLOSURE] specifies that a bounded landmark must have the structural properties interior, boundary, and exterior, and that the F must be smaller than the landmark (LM), such that the LM encloses the F. However, beyond this schematic topological information it specifies no perceptual information relating to the precise nature of the F or LM, nor to the precise spatial relationship, for example, in terms of where, in the bounded LM, the F must be located, whether there must be contact between the F and LM, and so on.

Empirical evidence for the dissociation between linguistic and conceptual content comes from psycholinguistic and neuropsychological work relating to representations for space. For instance, Munnich *et al.* (2001) suggest that there are divergences between the linguistic and perceptual encoding of spatial location, and that the language-specific semantic structures captured by, for instance, prepositions—and other closed-class spatial markers—are employed primarily when a language user has to package a spatial representation in a form that can be easily expressed in words. A similar idea is advocated by Landau *et al.* (forthcoming) who argue that spatial language is of a different format from conceptual representation of space, and serves to

---

[6] A given linguistic form can be associated with more than one lexical concept, the phenomenon of polysemy, introduced in Chapter 2. As we will see in Chapter 8, the English vehicle *in* is associated with a range of lexical concepts. The lexical concept that is selected—see Chapter 11 for a discussion of selection—in (4) I refer to as [ENCLOSURE].

[7] The notion of a (bounded) landmark, as I use it with respect to spatial semantics, is akin to the notion of reference object (RO) introduced in Chapter 2.

enhance our representational power of space. Further evidence for the distinction comes from a neuropsychological study by Kemmerer and Tranel (2000) which shows that the meanings of locative prepositions can be selectively impaired depending upon the nature of the non-linguistic spatial task being engaged in. In a more recent study, Tranel and Kemmerer (2004) additionally found that subjects with lesions in the left interior prefrontal brain region and the left inferior parietal region while severely defective on tests involving the use of locative prepositions were robustly intact on non-linguistic tests involving visuo-spatial and visuo-constructional skills. This is suggestive that different brain processes and/or regions are responsible for semantic and conceptual representations of space.

The nature of linguistic content

As the property common to all lexical concepts is that they encode linguistic content, in this section I outline the nature of linguistic content in more detail. Linguistic content concerns the information available to a language user, encoded by language. Put another way, it represents the informational form that conceptual structure takes for *direct* representation *in* language. That is, linguistic content takes a form that can be encoded in a format that is externalized in an auditory stream (or a manual gestural stream in the case of signed language), which is severely time-pressured—which is the case with language. Such a format presumably requires filtering out the complexity associated with the range of multimodal experiences—in the sense defined above. There are a number of distinct features associated with linguistic content. These include the following, all of which, except the lexical profile, are examined in detail below:

- parameterization
- non-analogue nature
- topological reference
- restricted set of domains and categories
- a distinction between nominal and relational lexical concepts
- referentiality
- pragmatic point
- lexical profile[8]

A lexical concept—a unit of semantic structure—can be thought of as a bundle of different types of highly schematic content which is thereby specialized for being encoded in language. As such, semantic structure provides a distinct representational format which is, as I have argued, highly schematic vis-à-vis the rich perceptual basis of conceptual structure. One consequence

---

[8] I address this aspect of linguistic content in the next chapter.

of the highly schematic nature of the content directly encoded in language is that language exhibits representational limitations. However, this is to be expected, given the inherent limitations of language as a representational format, which must encode content in a time-pressured auditory-physical stream—in Chapter 9 I make the argument that the linguistic system evolved by taking advantage of an extant representational format, the conceptual system, which is much richer in nature. It is by virtue of facilitating access to the conceptual system that language can prompt for simulations, taking advantage of rich representations which are non-linguistic in nature, in service of linguistically mediated communication.

Parameterization

The first key feature of linguistic content I address is that of **parameterization**. One way in which knowledge, in general terms, can be represented is in terms of richly inflected nuances that serve to reflect the complexity of experience. An alternative way is to "compress" such fine distinctions into two, three, or more, much broader, and hence, far more general distinctions. These I refer to as **parameters**. Linguistic content serves to encode content by adopting the latter strategy, which is to say, to employ parameterization. Parameters are hence part of the bundle of information that a lexical concept serves to encode.

To illustrate this notion, consider the complex range of expressions that a language user might employ, in English, in order to "locate" themselves with respect to time, thereby facilitating time reference. Any one of the following could conceivably be employed depending upon context: *today, January, 2008, the day after yesterday, the day before tomorrow, this moment, now, this second, this minute, this hour, today, this week, this month, this quarter, this year, this half century, this century, this period, the 8th day of the month, this era, this millennium*, and so on. A potentially unlimited set of finer and finer distinctions can additionally be made (e.g., *1 second ago, 2 seconds ago, 1 hour 4 minutes and 3 seconds ago, 2 days ago*, etc.), reflecting any manner of temporal distinctions we might care to make.

In contrast, parameterization functions by dividing all the possible permutations relating to a given category, such as time reference, into a small set of divisions: parameters. Such parameters might distinguish between the Past, for instance, and the Non-past. Indeed, this is the basis for the tense system in English, as illustrated by the following:

(6)   a. He kicked the ball   Past
      b. He kicks the ball   Non-past

English encodes just two parameters that relate to time reference: Past versus Non-past, as exhibited by the examples in (6), and thus manifests a binary distinction. Some languages, such as French, have three parameters: Past,

Present, and Future. Some languages have more than three parameters, distinguishing additionally Remote Past from Recent Past, for instance. The language with the most parameters thus far reported is an African language: Bamileke-Dschang with eleven. Crucially, parameters are encoded by specific lexical concepts, and thus form part of the knowledge bundle that constitutes a lexical concept. For instance, the parameter Past is encoded by the lexical concept associated with the -ed form in (6a). However, other lexical concepts also include the parameter Past such as the lexical concepts associated with the following forms: *sang, lost, went,* etc.

I argue, then, that a key feature of linguistic (as opposed) to conceptual content is that it encodes knowledge in parametric fashion. Parameterization is a highly reductive form of abstraction: it serves to abstract across the complexity exhibited by a particular category. In consequence the parameters encoded by linguistic content serve to "strip away" most of the differences apparent in the original experience, thereby reducing it to a highly limited number of parameters.

Non-analogue

As conceptual content relates to records of multimodal states captured directly from a variety of experience types including sense perception, proprioception, and subjective experience, it therefore consists of perceptual states recorded in analogue fashion: in a format that is similar to the perceptual experiences that gave rise to them. Indeed, there is a good deal of evidence, in the neuroscience literature, that sensory-motor representations, for example, are stored in the same areas of sensory-motor cortex that process sensory-motor experience (Pulvermüller 1999, 2003).

In contrast, I argue that linguistic content is so highly schematic in nature that it is **non-analogue:** it takes a format that is not analogous to the multimodal experiences that it is a schematization of. Hence, due to the reduction of rich perceptual information to highly impoverished parameters, this gives rise to a qualitatively very different type of information from the kind captured by conceptual structure. To illustrate, take the parameters Past and Non-past discussed with respect to example (6) above. These parameters are highly schematic abstractions drawn from the complex range of temporal relationships that hold between our experience of past, and our experience of now: our temporal location as experiencing centres of consciousness. Temporal experience, a form of subjective experience, is extremely rich in perceptual terms (Evans 2004a). Yet the parameters Past and Non-past are not rich at all.

An important consequence of the observation that linguistic content is non-analogue in nature is the following. I claim that linguistic content does not give rise, directly, to simulations. By this I do not mean that linguistic content cannot contribute to simulations, for instance, as part of an utterance. The meanings—conceptions—which arise from utterances are specialized for facilitating simulations. As linguistic content provides the structural or schematic dimension of semantic representation, facilitating the way in which conceptual structure is interpreted (see Chapter 13), the content represented by parameters can be said to play a role in giving rise to simulations.

Nevertheless, in the absence of an appropriate utterance context[9] my claim is that a closed-class lexical concept fails to even give rise to a **diffusely activated simulation**. This situation contrasts with open-class lexical concepts. For instance, the lexical concept [RED] does give rise to a diffusely activated simulation, even without a rich utterance context. That is, upon hearing the vehicle *red*, a language user activates a generic experience of redness. As Zwaan (2004) observes, diffuse activation involves activating a complex functional web of conceptual knowledge—the word's semantic potential in present terms—which "comprises the totality of our experiences with a certain entity or event" (*ibid.* 39). The degree of diffuseness will depend upon a range of issues including the frequency of the representations of the entity, in this case redness, across relevant cognitive models in the language user's conceptual system, recency of our interaction with the given referent, and so on. As we have seen, in the examples in (5) a specific utterance context serves to constrain the diffuse activation of the referent giving rise to a discrete simulation. This narrowing process involves different processes of semantic composition, discussed in Part III of the book.[10] In essence, the inability of linguistic content—and hence closed-class lexical concepts—to directly evoke simulations is another way of saying that closed-class lexical concepts do not facilitate access to the conceptual system.

In sum, parameters (i) encode highly schematic linguistic content abstracted from far richer multimodal experience, as recorded in the conceptual system, and (ii) provide a means for encoding recurrent "digitized" dimensions of humanly relevant experience in an efficient way, and as such (iii) may not, of themselves, directly give rise to simulations. In contrast, conceptual content which is accessed via open-class lexical concepts, gives rise to (i) perceptually rich aspects of experience, and, as such (ii) is likely to give rise to simulations directly.

Topological reference

A further consequence of the highly reductive nature of the parameters encoded as linguistic content, first pointed to by Talmy (e.g., 2000), is that they provide **topological reference** rather than **Euclidean reference**. That is, linguistic content encodes schematic aspects of sensory-motor, proprioceptive, and subjective

---

[9] As Zwaan (2004) notes, experiencing a word without a semantic context is not normally the case, outside the cognition lab or the game of Scrabble.

[10] Cf. Zwaan (2004) who provides an account of how this narrowing process works in terms of three stages termed: activation, construal, and integration.

experience, while conceptual content, to which open-class lexical concepts facilitate access, relates to precise, metric distinctions.

To illustrate consider the closed-class lexical concepts associated with the demonstrative vehicles *this* and *that*. These lexical concepts encode a distinction between an entity construed as proximal to the speaker, glossed as [THIS], versus an entity construed as distal, glossed as [THAT]. Consider (7):

(7)   "Sit on this chair not that one!"

In this utterance, the chair that the addressee is being asked to sit on is the one closer to the speaker: "this chair" as opposed to "that one". Nevertheless, the distinction between [THIS] versus [THAT] does not rely upon precise metric details such as the exact distance from the speaker, in terms of metres, centimetres, and millimetres. After all, it is immaterial how far the chairs are from the speaker (within reason), as long as one is closer to the speaker than the other. In other words, linguistic content and hence closed-class lexical concepts are **magnitude-neutral**, where magnitude has to do with metric properties relating to distance. This is what it means to say that linguistic content and thus closed-class lexical concepts provide topological reference. In contrast, the open-class lexical concepts facilitate access to conceptual content, and hence can be employed to express metric details of distance giving rise to Euclidean reference, as illustrated by (8):

(8)   "Sit on the chair 2.54 metres away from me!"

The expression "254 metres" involves open-class lexical concepts rather than closed-class lexical concepts, and serves to evoke the chair precisely.

The parameters encoded as linguistic content exhibit a range of other **Euclidean neutralities**: notably with respect to the domains of SPACE and TIME. In terms of SPACE, in addition to being magnitude-neutral, closed-class lexical concepts are also **shape-neutral** and **substance-neutral**. To illustrate consider the examples below, adapted from those used by Talmy:

Shape-neutrality
(9)   a. I zigzagged through the forest
      b. The road circled through the forest

The lexical concept glossed as [TRANSECTION] associated with *through* in these examples is shape-neutral. That is, the shape of the motion trajectory derives not from [TRANSECTION] but from conceptual content accessed via the open-class lexical concept associated with the verb *zigzagged* or *circled*. These, of course, are open-class lexical concepts.

Substance-neutrality
(10)   The laser beam passed through the window/steel sheet/planet's crust

The example in (10) again deploys the lexical concept associated with *through* that I gloss as [TRANSECTION]. In this case, [TRANSECTION] is substance-neutral: it can be applied to landmarks involving substances of any kind. Hence, the application of this closed-class lexical concept does not require or specify a particular substance. Rather, the permissible set of substances is a function of the range of substances that a laser beam can penetrate, based on conceptual structure associated with laser beams, as accessed via the open-class lexical concept [LASER BEAM].

In terms of the domain of TIME, linguistic content also serves to encode topological reference. As we saw above, in LCCM Theory tense systems are conceived in terms of parameterization. In English there are two such parameters: Past versus Non-past. These parameters are time-neutral with respect to Euclidean reference, and hence provide topological reference. Indeed, precise metric details, as we saw earlier, can only be expressed by virtue of open-class lexical concepts which facilitate access to conceptual structure, as illustrated by the following examples:

(11)   a. Two days ago
        b. The day before yesterday
        c. Forty-eight hours ago

A restricted set of domains and categories

A consequence of parameterization is that the range of **domains**, and the member **categories** that populate them, are highly restricted in terms of their encoding as parameters in linguistic content (cf. Talmy 2000). In using the term domain I have in mind large-scale and coherent bodies of knowledge such as the following: TIME, SPACE, COLOUR, MOTION, FORCE, TEMPERATURE, MENTAL STATES, and so on. By category I have in mind the member notions that populate a particular domain. For instance, in terms of the domain of TIME, categories consist of notions such as Punctuality, Durativity, Sequentiality, Simultaneity, Synchronicity, Boundedness, Time reference (e.g., Past versus Non-past etc.), Time-reckoning (e.g., 10.05 pm, etc.), and so forth. While *all* the domains of the sort just mentioned, and the categories which populate them, are evident at the conceptual level, only a restricted subset are encoded at the linguistic level, in terms of linguistic content.

For instance, some domains to which open-class lexical concepts facilitate access, such as COLOUR, do not appear at all in terms of linguistic content in English or any other language. That is, there are no parameters, in the sense defined above, that relate to this domain. This follows as many (perhaps most) domains do not relate to experience that can be straightforwardly parameterized in a humanly relevant way. There are at least two likely explanations for this. Firstly, the nature of the domain in question may not lend itself to being "reduced" to highly schematized digitized parameters.

After all, the reduction to content that does not directly give rise to simulations results in a reduction that, for some domains such as COLOUR, may eliminate the essential character of the information thereby making it uninterpretable. A second reason is that some domains do not relate in a ubiquitous way to the humanly relevant scenes that language serves to encode. For instance, categories that relate to the domain of MEDIAEVAL MUSICOLOGY, or even parameters that relate to less esoteric domains such as LOVE or JOURNEYS are not as ubiquitous in human experience as parameters relating to domains such as SPACE, TIME, MOTION, and MENTAL STATES.

The range of domains encoded by linguistic content appears to be highly restricted. As already intimated, domains encoded in linguistic content include TIME, SPACE, MOTION, and MENTAL STATES. In addition to the restricted set of domains encoded, linguistic content also features only a small number of categories within each domain. To illustrate, consider a few of the categories associated with the domain TIME:

> Domain: TIME
> Category: Time reference   Parameter:
(12) a. He kicked the ball   Past
>   b. He kicks the ball   Non-past
>
> Category: Boundedness
(13) a. Holly has left the party   Bounded
>   b. Holly is leaving the party   Unbounded
>
> Category: Plexity
(14) a. Fred coughed   Uniplex
>   b. Fred coughed for 10 minutes Multiplex

The category that I refer to as time reference is more traditionally referred to as tense. Each category exhibits a small number of parameters. As already noted, English encodes just two parameters: Past versus Non-past, as exhibited by the examples in (12), and thus manifests a binary distinction. As noted earlier, other languages have more than two parameters such as French with three, and Bamileke-Dschang with eleven.

Of the other two categories illustrated, these are normally treated as relating to what is commonly referred to as aspect. The more usual terms for uniplex and multiplex, as they relate to TIME are "semelfactive" and "iterative" respectively. The examples in (13) are usually referred to as perfective and imperfective aspect. Some examples of categories and parameters associated with other domains encoded in linguistic content are provided below:

DOMAIN: SPACE
Category: Number   Parameter:
(15) a. Holly lost a slipper   Singular
      b. Holly lost both her slippers   Plural

(16) Category: Unitizability (or countability)   Parameter:
      a. She gave him slippers for his birthday   Unit
      b. She gave him champagne for his birthday   Mass

Domain: MOTION
(17) Category: Windowing of motion path (cf. Talmy's 2000 notion of
      the "windowing" of attention)   Parameter:
      a. The crate fell out of the plane   Initial windowing
      b. The crate fell through the air   Medial windowing
      c. The crate fell into the ocean   Final windowing

With respect to a path of motion of the sort diagrammed in Figure 6.4,
linguistic content serves to encode different portions of the path, as evidenced
by lexical concepts associated with the prepositional phrases headed, respectively, by *out of, through,* and *into.*

Domain: MENTAL STATE
(18) Category: Mood   Parameter:
      a. She bought him slippers   Indicative
      b. Buy him slippers!   Imperative

The category Mood relates to the speaker's intention or mental state. English
exhibits only three parameters in linguistic content: including Indicative,
Imperative, and Subjunctive. However, cross-linguistically a variety of parameters belong to this category, ranging from the Admirative in languages such
as Bulgarian and Ukrainian, which encodes surprise, to the Hypothetical,

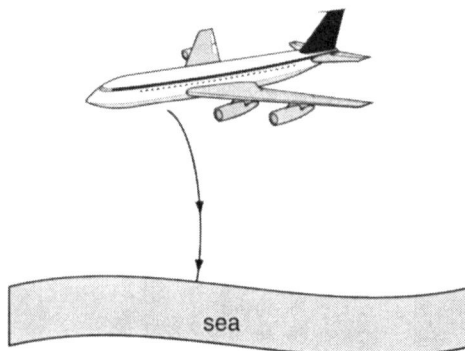

FIGURE 6.4. The path associated with an object falling out of a plane

which encodes the speaker's belief that a situation is counterfactual yet possible, as in a language such as Russian.

Nominal versus relational

Another aspect of linguistic content is that it encodes a bifurcation between **nominals** and **relations** (Langacker 1987). The distinction in type of lexical concepts is as follows. Nominal lexical concepts are **conceptually autonomous**: they relate to entities which are independently identifiable, such as "chair", or "shoe". In contrast, relations are **conceptually dependent**: they constitute a relation holding between other entities, and are thus "dependent" on those other entities in order to fully determine the nature of the relationship. For instance, in an utterance such as the following:

(19)   Max hid the mobile telephone under the bed

The lexical concept associated with the vehicle *hid*, which I shall gloss as [HID], relates the conceptually autonomous lexical concepts associated with the vehicles *Max, mobile telephone*, and *bed*, establishing a relationship involving "hiding" between the conceptually autonomous participants in the conception: namely [MAX] and [BED]. Analogously, the lexical concept associated with the vehicle *under* establishes a spatial relation between lexical concepts associated with *mobile telephone* and *bed*.

The conceptually dependent structure of relational lexical concepts is modelled, in LCCM Theory, in terms of a schematic participant role (Goldberg 1995). The lexical concept [HID] as exemplified in (19) encodes three schematic participant roles.[11] The rich content relating to the participant roles is not specified in linguistic content. This arises from access to conceptual structure. That is, conceptual structure encodes rich content relating to hiding: that it involves someone who does the hiding for particular reasons, and that an entity of a particular sort, often an object, is hidden. Non-linguistic knowledge also includes what facilitates something being hidden, such as perceptual inaccessibility of the object being hidden and/or its being placed in a novel location. Conceptual structure also encodes information relating to the motor processes involved in hiding, which involves moving the object from one location to another. The participant roles encoded as part of the linguistic content for [HID] do not encode such details. Rather, what is encoded is a highly abstract representation, derived from the rich perceptual details of a hiding scenario.[12] As such we have three roles that serve to

---

[11] Notice that the vehicle *hid* is polysemous. For instance, *hid* is also associated with the "reflexive" lexical concept in which an entity hides oneself, as in: *John hid in the wardrobe*. This lexical concept, which I gloss as [REFLEXIVE HID] encodes two schematic participant roles.

[12] The schematic participant roles are integrated with the rich content derived from conceptual structure in a process referred to as **interpretation**, discussed in Chapter 11.

distinguish between the three entities involved at the most general level of detail. These participant roles are: Hider, Object, and Location.[13]

Just as the bifurcation in lexical concepts discussed above—that holding between lexical concepts which solely encode linguistic content and those which additionally facilitate access to conceptual content—corresponds to a distinction in the formal encoding of lexical concepts—the distinction between open- and closed-class vehicles—so too the distinction between nominal and relational lexical concepts has a formal reflex in terms of linguistic vehicles. In a language such as English, for instance, this distinction relates to lexical concepts associated with what are commonly referred to as nouns and noun phrases (nominals) on the one hand, and lexical concepts associated with other lexical forms, including verbs, prepositions, adjectives, adverbs, and non-finite verb forms such as infinitives and participles (relations) on the other (see Langacker 1987 for details).

In view of the foregoing, LCCM Theory assumes that every **externally open lexical concept**, i.e., a lexical concept which, informally, holds at the level of the phrase or below[14] encodes either **nominal structure** or **relational structure**. I suggest that this bifurcation in linguistic content emerges from perceptual experience, and hence relates to a highly salient, humanly relevant, dimension of **embodied experience**.

The idea is as follows. In seminal work, Rosch (1978) argued that aspects of perceptual experience give rise to inevitable conflations due to correlations or clumping of the perceptual array. Building on this insight, Gentner (1982; see also Gentner and Boroditsky 2001) posits that objects and animate beings are thus perceived as being individuated on the basis of perceptual experience. That is, entities such as these are non-relational, in that they emerge as coherent and discrete conceptual entities from the perceptual-cognitive sphere.

Gentner refers to the claim that embodied experience gives rise to the distinction between nominal versus relational notions as the **Natural Partitions Hypothesis**. This states that "there are in the experiential flow certain highly cohesive collections of percepts that are universally conceptualized as objects, and . . . these tend to be lexicalized as nouns across languages" (Gentner 1982: 324).

Given the Natural Partitions Hypothesis, it follows that certain notions encoded by language in the form of lexical concepts will arise from distinctions apparent in the stream of physical experience. Those notions which are likely to emerge most easily in the perceptual stream are those which are **individuable**. Hence, apparent **ease of individuation** is a function of perceptual coherence. According to Gentner and Boroditsky (2001) there are two factors which contribute to ease of individuation. The first factor relates to

---

[13] The way in which the participant roles encoded by [HID] are integrated with other lexical concepts in the utterance in (19) results from the compositional mechanisms discussed in Part III of the book.

[14] See Chapter 12 for further details.

continued "objecthood." This relates to the maintenance of a stable perceptual structure moving against a background. Hence, entities which can undergo motion are likely to be highly individuable. Accordingly, animate entities are likely to be more easily individuated based on this criterion.

The second factor relates to what Gentner and Boroditsky refer to as **perceptual coherence**. That is, "[h]ighly coherent objects have densely interconnected representations" (*ibid.* 222). This means that the range and number of internal links between component parts of a given object is, in relative terms, greater than the number of components that make up the object. For instance, a stool with a seat and four legs has multiple connections between each component, and these are greater than the total number of component parts. A second contributing issue to perceptual coherence concerns the well-formedness of the overall structure. For instance, a symmetrical structure is more likely to be perceived as perceptually coherent than one which is asymmetric.

While many entities are pre-individuated based on perceptual experience, individuation itself constitutes a continuum. For instance, animate entities, like inanimate entities, exhibit strong perceptual coherence. However, by virtue of remaining perceptually stable during motion, animate entities are more easily individuated. Conversely, amorphous objects such as substances are likely to be less easily individuated than discrete objects because they are less perceptually coherent. Figure 6.5 presents these conclusions in the form of an Individuability Continuum as applied to physical entities.

By encoding a given entity as a nominal lexical concept, linguistic content serves to provide a particular construal, one which relates to individuability. Langacker (1987), in his Cognitive Grammar framework, argues for a similar perspective. He claims that what he refers to as **nominal predications** (nominal lexical concepts in present terms) serve to designate a region: a delimited portion, in some domain: a coherent body of conceptual knowledge. This very general definition serves to distinguish the construal provided by nominals from those of relations, which are concerned with the relationships between regions of domains, rather than the regions themselves.

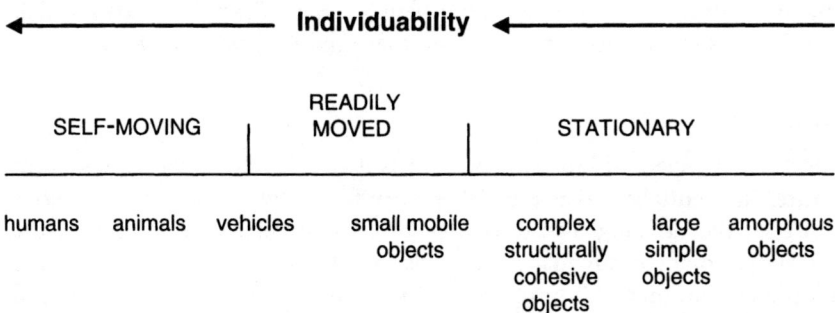

←───────────── **Individuability** ←─────────────

	SELF-MOVING		READILY MOVED		STATIONARY		
humans	animals	vehicles	small mobile objects	complex structurally cohesive objects	large simple objects	amorphous objects

FIGURE 6.5. The Individuability Continuum as applied to physical entities (Adapted from Gentner and Boroditsky 2001: 230)

For instance, while [CAR] and [EXPLOSION] represent very different sorts of lexical concepts, the lexical concept conventionally associated with the lexical vehicle *explosion* is distinct from the lexical concept associated with *to explode*. That is, [EXPLOSION] is concerned with an event *qua* discrete occurrence in SPACE and TIME. The relational lexical concept [EXPLODE], by contrast, is concerned with a particular process as it relates to a specific entity such as a dam, as in the event evoked by the following utterance:

(20)   The dam exploded

Thus, the essence of a nominal lexical concept is that the linguistic content encoded concerns the schematic property of individuability. In contrast, the conceptual content to which nominals provide access may be diverse, as is evident by the examples, below (the nouns are underlined):

(21)   a. His car was making a funny noise
       b. The galaxy is made up on more than one solar system
       c. She sent a letter to her lover
       d. His uncle was a kind man
       e. Fred tried to teach Holly the Arabic alphabet
       f. The explosion in her engine made her late for work
       g. Holly's love for Fred began on a Tuesday
       h. The team played appallingly

Nevertheless, there is commonality in terms of the linguistic content that each nominal lexical concept encodes. Each nominal is construed as encoding content that has to do with individuability. In contrast, lexical concepts which are conceptually dependent, such as those associated with verbal vehicles, for instance, encode linguistic content which constitutes a relation of some kind. The range of relations encoded by relational lexical concepts is likewise diverse, as evidenced, for example, by the range of lexical classes which encode relational lexical concepts. Nevertheless, there is a clear basis, based on linguistic content, for distinguishing between those lexical concepts which exhibit conceptual autonomy and those that exhibit conceptual dependency.

Referentiality

Another key aspect of linguistic content is that it is inherently referential in nature. Referentiality takes a number of different forms, as detailed below. However, the defining feature is that lexical concepts serve to encode the following: an intention that a particular entity is being indexed or, more informally, "pointed to." In using the term "entity" I have in mind physical entities that inhabit the world such as people, as well as physical artefacts, such as "Sam" and "ball" in (22a), abstract notions such as ideas, for example "peace" in (22b), as well as relations that hold between physical entities and abstract ideas, such as "kicked" in (22a) and "thought about" in (22b), as well as highly schematic relations, as encoded by "to" in (22c).

(22)   a. Sam kicked the ball
       b. Sam thought about peace
       c. Sam walked to the park

I identify at least three distinct types of **reference** encoded by lexical concepts.

The first type relates to what I will refer to as **denotational reference**. Many lexical concepts serve to index a physical entity of some sort, whether real or imagined. In this sense, part of what the lexical concepts associated with the vehicles *John* and *unicorn* serve to do is to signal an intention, on the part of the speaker, to refer to a given entity, whether real or imagined.

The second type I refer to as **cognitive reference**. This relates to relatively abstract notions or ideas that have no physical substance, whether real or imagined, and relate to lexical concepts associated with forms such as *love*, *war*, *phonology*, and so forth. Hence, lexical concepts that serve to encode cognitive reference signal an intention, on the part of the speaker, to refer to a non-physical idea.

The third type I refer to as **contextual reference**. This involves reference to an entity that is present in the linguistic or extra-linguistic discourse context. Hence, reference of this sort involves the encoding, by a lexical concept, of an intention to refer to an entity that the addressee can recover from context.

One type of contextual reference is **textual reference**. One form of textual reference involves reference to an entity already mentioned. This is traditionally termed **anaphora**. Textual reference that relates to an entity yet to be mentioned is termed **cataphora**. Examples of textual reference are provided in the examples below.

(23)   a. John is smart. **He** had a reading age of 14 by the time **he** was just 8.
       b. I want to say just **this**: I love you.
       c. The new target to reduce carbon emissions by 20% by 2020 will be
          a tough **thing** to achieve.

In the examples in (23), the lexical concepts associated with the forms *he*, *this*, and *thing* are specialized for referring to other entities (underlined) in the text.

There are many kinds of lexical concepts which encode an intention to signal contextual reference as it relates to extra-linguistic context. Many of these are often treated under the heading of **deixis**. Previous research has identified a range of diverse sorts of deictic lexical concepts including phenomena referred to as **spatial deixis**, **temporal deixis**, and **social deixis** (for details see Fillmore 1997; Levinson 1983).

Pragmatic point

While the taxonomy of dimensions presented in this chapter most likely does not exhaust the properties of linguistic content, the final dimension of linguistic content that I address relates to what I refer to as pragmatic point. This is a term I borrow from Fillmore *et al.* (1988). I use this term to refer to schematic aspects of extra-linguistic context encoded in linguistic content by a given lexical concept. As I use it, this term relates, broadly, to two aspects: (i) the contexts of use in which a given lexical concept is conventionally employed, including settings and participants, and (ii) some aspects of what has traditionally been referred to as the **illocutionary point** (Searle 1969) of a given lexical concept: which is to say the communicative purpose for which a lexical concept is employed.[15]

To illustrate the notion of pragmatic point consider the form *declared* in the examples below. This is associated with at least three lexical concepts, each of which exhibits a different pragmatic point.

(24)   a. She declared her love for him
       b. Neville Chamberlain declared war on Germany on September 3rd 1939
       c. Despite being over the limit on the amount of dollars in cash eligible to be taken into the country, she declared nothing as she crossed the US border

The use of *declared* in (24a) serves to encode an intention to provide information of a particular sort, with an above-average level of assertiveness. Hence, the lexical concept which sanctions this use of *declared* can be glossed as [FORTH-RIGHT INFORMATIONAL ASSERTION]. In contrast, the lexical concept associated with the use of *declared* in (24b) relates to an assertion which either changes, or otherwise revises, an institutional state. Crucially, not only is the illocutionary point distinct from the lexical concept responsible for the use of *declared* in (24a), but the context of use is distinct too. This follows as the context of use for the [ANNOUNCEMENT OF NEW LEGAL STATUS] in (24b) can only be successfully deployed by suitably qualified participants. For instance, Neville Chamberlain was able to successfully deploy this lexical concept because on September 3rd 1939 when he declared war, he was the legally appointed Prime Minister of the United Kingdom, and under the terms of the Royal Prerogative—powers invested in the monarch and deployed by the Prime Minister on behalf of the monarch—he was legally entitled to take the country to war.

---

[15] It is worth re-emphasizing here that linguistic content is schematic in nature. Hence, while making a speech act (Searle 1969), such as declaring a state of war, for example, involves being able to call upon highly detailed bodies of conceptual knowledge relating to the sorts of scenarios and participants involved, linguistic content involves only the most generic aspects, including schematic information concerning the types of context in which a particular lexical concept can be deployed, the nature of the participants involved and the conditions which must hold.

Finally, the lexical concept which sanctions the use of *declared* in (24c) relates to the [ANNOUNCEMENT OF DUTIABLE GOODS AT CUSTOMS] lexical concept. This is distinct both in terms of illocutionary point and context(s) of use from the previously mentioned lexical concepts. This lexical concept is specialized for use in contexts involving customs provision at international border crossings. Its communicative function has to do with signalling as to goods being transported, or caused to be transported by the person issuing the "declaration" in this specific context, with respect to restrictions on the nature and/or amount of goods that may be transported into the country which establishes the customs provision, and/or tax payable on particular goods.

Based on the foregoing discussion, I present in Table 6.4 a summary of the key components of pragmatic point that are encoded as part of the linguistic content of each of the three lexical concepts. Much of the content associated with the three lexical concepts for *declared* comes from the conceptual content to which they afford access. That is, as lexical concepts have bipartite structure, they are each associated with a rich semantic potential. However, pragmatic point, which concerns linguistic content, is highly schematic in nature. In these terms then, the distinction between the three lexical concepts relates to whether they stipulate that the setting is restricted or not, whether the participants are restricted or not, and the nature of the communicative function: the illocutionary point. Hence, by way of illustration, the lexical concept [ANNOUNCEMENT OF NEW LEGAL STATUS] encodes the following: there is no restriction on where the utterance can take place for it to realize its illocutionary point; the participants involved are, however, restricted, and the communicative purpose is to change some institutional state. This information is clearly highly schematic. However, it adequately captures, I argue, the highly stable aspects of the content encoded by this lexical concept, which is to say, its linguistic content. The details regarding the precise nature of the participants involved in making the declaration, the setting, and the precise communicative function, including the wider consequences and implications of the declaration, are a function of conceptual content. That is, the utterance context in (24b) facilitates narrowing the range of semantic potential—the non-linguistic content—so that the conceptual content activated for *declared*

TABLE 6.4. Pragmatic point for three lexical concepts of *declared*

Lexical concept	Setting	Participant(s)	Illocutionary point
[FORTHRIGHT INFORMATIONAL ASSERTION]	Unrestricted	Unrestricted	Make statement
[ANNOUNCEMENT OF NEW LEGAL STATUS]	Unrestricted	Restricted	Change official state
[ANNOUNCEMENT OF DUTIABLE GOODS AT CUSTOMS]	Restricted	Restricted	Make official statement

in (24b) gives rise to a rich informational characterization, much in the same way as the examples relating to France discussed in Chapter 4.

Summary

This chapter has been concerned with developing an account of the nature of semantic structure, relating to the linguistic system, and contrasting it with conceptual structure, the representational format of the conceptual system. I model semantic structure in terms of the lexical concept. The main claim that I made was that lexical concepts have bipartite structure: lexical concepts encode information that can be directly encoded in and externalized via language. This information, which is unique to language, and which is relatively stable, I refer to as linguistic content. In addition, a subset of lexical concepts—open-class lexical concepts—serve as access sites to conceptual structure. I model conceptual structure in terms of the theoretical construct of the cognitive model, addressed in detail in a later chapter. The non-linguistic information encoded by cognitive models I refer to as conceptual content. This is not directly encoded by lexical concepts, which is to say it is not encoded *in* language. Rather it can be accessed by lexical concepts, and hence *via* language. Thus, the bipartite structure of lexical concepts means that they *encode* linguistic content and *facilitate access to* a potentially unlim-ited array of conceptual content—the semantic potential discussed in Chapter 4. The linguistic content encoded by any given lexical concept constitutes a bundle of distinct types of knowledge, which is characterized as being highly schematic in nature. The final part of the chapter addressed content of this sort. The aspects of linguistic content considered included: parameterization, the non-analogue nature of linguistic content, the position that it affords topological rather than Euclidean reference, that the parameters involved relate to a restricted set of domains and categories, the view that there is a distinction between nominal and relational lexical concepts, that lexical concepts facilitate reference of various sorts, and finally, that lexical concepts encode pragmatic point.

7

Lexical concepts

This chapter is concerned with providing an overview of the main properties and characteristics of lexical concepts. As such, it serves to complement the study of the linguistic content encoded by lexical concepts in the previous chapter. This chapter is comprised of two main sections. The first provides an overview of the main properties of lexical concepts. The purpose of this section is to pull together the key attributes of the lexical concept presented in earlier chapters. The second section is concerned with providing a methodology for identifying lexical concepts based on usage data. Lexical concepts are units of semantic structure. Hence, they inhere in the mental grammar and so, strictly, do not arise in language use. Rather they sanction specific instances of use. Nevertheless, they leave a "footprint" in usage data: their lexical profile, the selectional tendencies which form part of the linguistic content encoded by a lexical concept. As a lexical concept's lexical profile is held to be unique, this provides a principled basis for employing actual instances of use, utterances, in order to identify the lexical concept involved in sanctioning a given instance of use. As such, this chapter is also concerned with harnessing the construct of the lexical profile as a methodological tool for identifying lexical concepts.

The nature of lexical concepts

My starting point in this chapter is to briefly survey a number of the most notable properties of lexical concepts. These are as follows and are addressed in more detail below:

- lexical concepts are elements of mental grammar
- lexical concepts sanction instances of language use
- lexical concepts are vehicle-specific
- lexical concepts are language-specific
- vehicles are not lexical concept-specific
- lexical concepts are associated with different vehicle types
- lexical concepts have bipartite structure
- lexical concepts have an encapsulation function
- lexical concepts have a lexical profile

- lexical concepts can be combined
- lexical concepts have relativistic consequences for non-linguistic representation

Lexical concepts are elements of mental grammar

Lexical concepts are units of semantic structure. That is, they provide the semantic pole of a bipolar symbolic assembly. As LCCM Theory adheres to the symbolic thesis, symbolic units of the sort discussed in Chapter 5 are held to be the fundamental units of grammar. As such, lexical concepts are themselves units of mental grammar.

However, being units of mental grammar lexical concepts do not arise in language use. Rather, they are units of linguistic knowledge abstracted from across usage events (i.e., utterances) that encode linguistic content and facilitate access to conceptual (i.e., non-linguistic) knowledge. Thus, a lexical concept is a unit of linguistic knowledge that populates the "mental grammar," deriving from commonalities in patterns of language use. In Chapter 4 I likened lexical concepts to phonemes in phonological theory. Like phonemes, lexical concepts are abstractions over multiple instances of language use.

Lexical concepts sanction instances of language use

Lexical concepts sanction—which is to say license—instances of language use (Langacker 1987). While the semantic contribution of any given vehicle—word or linguistic expression—in a particular utterance is licensed by a given lexical concept, the nature of the semantic contribution associated with that expression will always be a function of the unique context in which it is embedded. In other words, any usage of a given vehicle constitutes a unique instantiation of a lexical concept, and is thus subject to processes of semantic composition—discussed in Part III of the book—due to the specific context, which, in part, determines the semantic contribution of the lexical concept in question.

Given that lexical concepts do not occur in language use, but rather sanction instances of use, it is often the case that more than one lexical concept may be sanctioning a particular use of a vehicle. This state of affairs I refer to as **multiple sanction**. To illustrate, take the vehicle *fast* which I first discussed in Chapter 1. The way in which this vehicle is used by language users often appears to assume a number of distinct lexical concepts, including those that can be glossed as [PERFORM SOME ACT(ION) QUICKLY], as evidenced by (1a), and [REQUIRE LITTLE TIME FOR COMPLETION], as evidenced by (1b):

(1)   a. She's a fast typist
      b. Which courier company would you recommend to get a package from Brighton to London fast?

Now consider the following example:

(2)   We need a fast garage for our car, as we leave the day after tomorrow

The example in (2) appears to be a "blend" of both the lexical concepts which sanction the examples in (1). In other words, the semantic contribution of *fast* in (2) involves nuances relating to both these lexical concepts. A garage is required in which the mechanics can perform the relevant repairs quickly, and which takes little time for completion of repairs, given that the car will be required the day after tomorrow.

Lexical concepts are vehicle-specific

Lexical concepts are **vehicle-specific**. That is, they are conventionally associated with specific linguistic vehicles. While it is, perhaps, obvious that the vehicles *cat* and *car* would be associated with distinct lexical concepts, it is perhaps less obvious that the vehicles *sing* and *sang* would also be associated with distinct lexical concepts. Nevertheless, this is indeed the claim made by LCCM Theory, in keeping with constructional approaches to grammar. A distinction in form spells a distinct lexical concept.

Notwithstanding this claim, some approaches to lexical representation make the assumption that vehicles such as *run* and *ran*, and so forth, relate to essentially the same semantic representational unit, what is traditionally referred to as a lexeme. On this account, vehicles such as *run* and *ran* essentially provide equivalent semantic content—the lexeme RUN—and only differ in terms of the grammatical information they encode, which is held to be non-semantic in nature. In other words, the traditional view attempts to account for the intuition that the semantic units associated with vehicles such as these are closely related.

LCCM Theory accounts for the intuition that *run* and *ran* are associated with closely related semantic units in the following way. As we saw in the previous chapter, lexical concepts have bipartite organization, encoding linguistic content and facilitating access to conceptual content. Hence, lexical concepts as units of semantic structure can differ in at least one of two ways. Firstly, lexical concepts may provide differential access to the cognitive model profile to which they facilitate access. That is, they may provide access at different points in conceptual structure. The second way in which lexical concepts may differ relates to the nature of the linguistic content they encode. The difference between the lexical concepts associated with *run* and *ran* has less to do with a difference in terms of access to cognitive model profiles. Rather, the difference relates to linguistic encoding, in particular, the nature of the parameters relating to time reference encoded by the respective lexical concepts. Hence, in LCCM Theory, *run* and *ran* are associated with distinct lexical concepts, which facilitate access to similar cognitive model profiles but encode a different bundle of linguistic content. As such their linguistic content is similar but not identical.

Lexical concepts are language-specific

An important corollary of the position that lexical concepts are vehicle-specific is that lexical concepts are necessarily language-specific. Thus, each language, by virtue of comprising language-specific vehicles which populate the language, necessarily provides an inventory of language-specific lexical concepts. A difference in form results in a difference in the lexical concept associated with the vehicle. In short, what might be dubbed the naïve view, which holds that a language represents an inventory of language-specific vehicles for encoding cross-linguistically identical semantic units is rejected by LCCM Theory.

To illustrate this point, consider the way in which two unrelated languages, English and Korean, encode ostensibly the same spatial relationship. This discussion is based on the work of Choi and Bowerman (1991; Bowerman and Choi 2003). In order to prompt for the spatial scenes evoked by the utterances in (3), the English lexical concept that I gloss as [PLACEMENT OF ONE ENTITY ONTO ANOTHER] associated with the English vehicle *put on* can be deployed.

(3) a. She put the cup on the table
     b. She put the magnet on the refrigerator
     c. She put the hat on
     d. She put the ring on her finger
     e. She put the top on the pen
     f. She put the Lego block on the Lego stack

The lexical concept [PLACEMENT OF ONE ENTITY ONTO ANOTHER] encodes placement of the figure in contact with a surface of some kind. The reader familiar only with English might be forgiven for thinking that this is the only way these spatial scenes can be encoded by a linguistic system. However, the situation in Korean is very different. The English examples in (3) are categorized into lexical concepts of four different kinds in Korean. This is achieved using the four distinct symbolic units, as in (4):

(4) a. vehicle: *nohta*
        lexical concept: [PLACEMENT ON HORIZONTAL SURFACE]
     b. vehicle: *pwuchita*
        lexical concept: [JUXTAPOSITION OF SURFACES]
     c. vehicle: *ssuta*
        lexical concept   [PLACEMENT OF APPAREL ON HEAD]
     d. vehicle: *kkita*
        lexical concept: [FIT TWO ENTITIES TIGHTLY TOGETHER]

TABLE 7.1. Korean lexical concepts and their correspondence to English spatial relations

nohta [PLACEMENT ON HORIZONTAL SURFACE]	Corresponds to...	[PLACEMENT OF ONE ENTITY ONTO ANOTHER] e.g., *put cup on table*
pwuchita [JUXTAPOSITION OF SURFACES]	Corresponds to...	[PLACEMENT OF ONE ENTITY ONTO ANOTHER] e.g., *put magnet on refrigerator*
ssuta [PLACEMENT OF APPAREL ON HEAD]	Corresponds to...	[PLACEMENT OF ONE ENTITY ONTO ANOTHER] e.g., *put hat on*
kkita [FIT TWO ENTITIES TIGHTLY TOGETHER]	Corresponds to...	[PLACEMENT OF ONE ENTITY ONTO ANOTHER] e.g., *put ring on finger/put top on pen/put Lego block on Lego stack*

While the situation just described makes the point clearly that lexical concepts, as well as vehicles, are language-specific (see Table 7.1), my claim is that more mundane examples, for instance, the lexical concept associated with the vehicle *cat* in English and *chat* in French are also distinct. This follows as lexical concepts have bipartite organization, as discussed in the previous chapter and as summarized below. Hence, even in cases where lexical concepts share similar linguistic content cross-linguistically, the nature of the conceptual structure to which lexical concepts afford access will always be distinct. This follows as the individuals that make up distinct linguistic communities have divergent bodies of knowledge based on experiences that are divergent due to linguistic, cultural, and areal divergences.[1]

Vehicles are not lexical concept-specific

Although lexical concepts are vehicle-specific, a single vehicle can be conventionally associated with a potentially large number of distinct lexical concepts, which may or may not be semantically related. Hence, vehicles are not lexical concept-specific. Lexical concepts that are related, either in terms of similar linguistic content, or in terms of facilitating access to related cognitive model profiles—by virtue of providing proximal access sites to conceptual content—or both, are held to exhibit a **polysemy relationship**. For example, in the utterances below in (5), the form *flying* is associated with four distinct lexical concepts, each of which facilitates access to distinct, but closely related, cognitive model profiles:

---

[1] The nature of conceptual structure and some of the factors involved in providing it with its distinctiveness, at the individual level, will be explored in Chapter 10.

(5) a. The plane/bird is flying (in the   [SELF-PROPELLED   AERODYNAMIC
        sky)   MOTION]
     b. The pilot is flying the plane (in   [OPERATION OF ENTITY CAPABLE
        the sky)   OF AERODYNAMIC MOTION]
     c. The child is flying the kite (in   [CONTROL OF LIGHTWEIGHT EN-
        the breeze)   TITY]
     d. The flag is flying (in the breeze)   [SUSPENSION OF LIGHTWEIGHT
                                              OBJECT]

Lexical concepts are associated with different vehicle types

As lexical concepts are conventionally associated with a given linguistic vehicle, it follows that lexical concepts are conventionally associated with a wide
range of vehicle types. As we saw in Chapter 5, the range of vehicles with which
lexical concepts are conventionally associated include phonetically overt vehicles, such as *cat*, and phonetically implicit vehicles, such as the ditransitive
vehicle: (SUBJECT VERB OBJ1 OBJ2), e.g., *John baked Mary a cake*; *John gave
Mary the cake*; *John refused Mary the cake*. Moreover, explicit vehicles that have
distinct lexical concepts conventionally associated with them include bound
morphemes, "simplex" words, "complex" or polymorphemic words, and
idiomatic expressions and phrases.

Lexical concepts have bipartite structure

Lexical concepts are units of semantic structure with bipartite organization.
They encode linguistic content and facilitate access to conceptual structure.
Linguistic content represents the form that conceptual structure takes for
direct encoding in language. There are a large number of different properties
encoded by linguistic content which serve to provide a schematic or skeletal
representation that can be encoded in language. The various characteristics
involved, the majority of which were discussed in detail in the previous
chapter, include the following:

- parameterization
- non-analogue in nature
- topological reference
- restricted set of domains and categories
- a distinction between nominal and relational lexical concepts
- referentiality
- pragmatic point
- lexical profile

In addition, a subset of lexical concepts serve as access sites to conceptual
structure. Conceptual structure relates to non-linguistic information to which

lexical concepts potentially afford access. The potential body of non-linguistic knowledge: a lexical concept's semantic potential, is modelled in terms of a set of cognitive models. Recall that I refer to the body of cognitive models and their relationships, as accessed by a given lexical concept, as the cognitive model profile.

A design feature of language is that it involves a bifurcation of lexical concepts into two types: open-class lexical concepts and closed-class lexical concepts. While both encode linguistic content it is only open-class lexical concepts which facilitate access to conceptual structure.

Lexical concepts have an encapsulation function

Lexical concepts provide what I refer to as an **encapsulation function**. This is achieved by virtue of open-class lexical concepts providing an access site to conceptual knowledge which is often complex and informationally diffuse. This provides the illusion that words have semantic unity, and that it is language which is directly encoding the complex body of knowledge which I refer to as a cognitive model profile. Indeed, what I refer to as an access site is, in fact, made up, typically, of a large number of association areas which hold between a single open-class lexical concept and the conceptual system. Thus, the encapsulation function is a function of two distinct systems being related such that the linguistic system provides a means of interfacing at specific points with the knowledge "matrix" that is conceptual structure.[2]

An example of the encapsulation function of lexical concepts comes from the following culture-specific example from Korean which cannot be easily and/or simply expressed in another language. This is the lexical concept encoded by the vehicle *nunchi*, which might be translated into English as "eye-measure." This lexical concept relates to the idea that one should be able to judge how others are feeling, such as whether a guest in one's home is hungry or not, and thus be in a position to offer food so that the guest is not embarrassed by having to request it. Hence, the lexical concept facilitates access to complex ideas which are typically diffusely grounded in an intricate cultural web of ideas and information. But by virtue of providing a unique access site to this complex body of conceptual content the lexical concept provides an encapsulation function.

Lexical concepts have a lexical profile

Many, perhaps most, lexical concepts have a lexical profile. A lexical profile constitutes knowledge relating to the range of other lexical concepts and vehicles with which a particular lexical concept regularly co-occurs. This constitutes what we might refer to, informally, as its **use potential**.[3] As such,

---

[2] These are ideas that I explore in more detail in Chapter 10.

[3] See Zlatev (1997, 2003) for a related, albeit distinct, notion of the use potential of words. See also Allwood (2003).

as each lexical concept is unique, so too its lexical profile is unique. Moreover, the lexical profile relates to knowledge, stored as part of the linguistic content encoded by a lexical concept.

The sorts of other lexical concepts and vehicles with which a lexical concept can co-occur, and which thereby make up its lexical profile, I term selectional tendencies, first introduced in Chapter 1. A lexical profile's selectional tendencies can be **restricted** or **non-restricted**. For instance, the lexical profile of the lexical concept [KITH] is "X *and kin*" where "X" is the position occupied by the vehicle *kith* which is paired with [KITH]. This is the only occurrence of [KITH] in the language. As such this restricted lexical profile I refer to as an instance of **extreme restriction**. In this case, the lexical concept is indissociable from the larger lexical concept, and hence vehicle with which it is associated.

Extreme restrictions of this kind in a lexical concept's selectional tendencies are in fact rare, as are selectional tendencies which are wholly non-restricted. The kind of restricted selectional tendencies which are somewhat less rare relate to what are otherwise known as **collocations**. For instance, the lexical concepts associated with the following vehicles: *stale, rotten, sour,* and *rancid,* as applied to particular foodstuffs, exhibit the following restrictions in terms of their selectional tendencies:

(6) a. stale bread/cake/cheese, etc.
     b. rotten fruit/eggs/vegetables, etc.
     c. sour milk/yoghurt, etc.
     d. rancid butter/oil, etc.

In terms of the examples in (6) we see that the lexical concepts associated with the vehicles *stale, rotten, sour,* and *rancid* exhibit quite distinct selectional tendencies. The pattern associated with each can thus be said to be restricted.

A selectional tendency for any given lexical concept, for convenience, can be divided into **semantic selectional tendencies** and **formal selectional tendencies**. Semantic selectional tendencies have to do with the (range of) lexical concepts with which a lexical concept co-occurs and in which it can be embedded. Formal selectional tendencies have to do with the (range of) vehicles with which a given lexical concept co-occurs, or in which it can be embedded. I illustrate each kind with an example adapted from Goldberg (2006: 56). Consider, first of all, the semantic selectional tendencies associated with the [PLACEMENT] lexical concept encoded by *put on*:

(7) a. Jane put the butter on the table
     b. <actor> *put* <thing> <location>

The [PLACEMENT] lexical concept selects for semantic arguments that can be construed as, respectively, an actor, a thing, and a location. In other words, part of our knowledge concerning this lexical concept involves knowing what kinds of lexical concepts it can co-occur with. In terms of formal selectional tendencies, part of our knowledge of the same lexical concept is knowing the order in which the vehicles associated with the actor, thing, and location lexical concepts occur, with respect to the vehicle *put on*. That is, part of knowledge involves knowing where the actor, thing, and location slots are located relative to the vehicle. Together these two types of knowledge form the lexical profile for the [PLACEMENT] lexical concept.[4]

In addition, formal selection tendencies needn't be restricted to knowledge of word order. It can also include knowledge concerning the nature of the permissible vehicles that can co-occur with a given lexical concept. For instance, and again adapting an example from Goldberg (2006: 57), the [LOCATED] lexical concept associated with the vehicle *found* exhibits a distinct formal selectional tendency from the [REALIZED] lexical concept exhibited by the same vehicle:

(8)   a. Jane found the cat   [LOCATED]
      b. Jane found that the cat was missing   [REALIZED]

The [LOCATED] lexical concept selects for a direct object, whilst the [REALIZED] lexical concept selects for a sentential complement.

Thus far I have primarily addressed the selectional tendencies associated with lexical concepts associated with vehicles that have overt phonetic content. I now briefly consider the lexical profile associated with lexical concepts that are internally open. Recall that internally open lexical concepts are paired with vehicles which have implicit phonetic content, such as the lexical concept [THING X CAUSES THING Y TO RECEIVE THING Z] conventionally paired with the ditransitive vehicle. The lexical profile of such lexical concepts relates to what I refer to as **internal selectional tendencies**. That is, as the lexical concept is internally open, it can be integrated with other less abstract lexical concepts paired with vehicles that do have phonetically explicit phonetic content. Yet, such lexical concepts are constrained in certain ways, as specified by the lexical profile that forms part of the linguistic content encoded by the [THING X CAUSES THING Y TO RECEIVE THING Z] lexical concept. In particular, part of the knowledge captured by lexical profiles for internally open lexical concepts involves which kind of lexically closed lexical concepts can align with particular slots in the internally complex vehicle. For instance, in terms of the [THING X CAUSES THING Y TO RECEIVE THING Z] lexical concept, its lexical profile specifies that only animate entities capable of causing transfer can be integrated with the NP1 slot. Some of the internal selectional tendencies associated with this lexical concept are summarized in Table 5.2 in Chapter 5.

There is now well-established empirical evidence for the notion of a lexical profile associated with lexical concepts. Compelling evidence comes from

---

[4] See Goldberg (2006) for discussion of how the item-based knowledge which comprises the lexical profiles of lexical concepts are acquired.

work in corpus linguistics which reveals that part of the knowledge language users have of words, for instance, includes what I am referring to as a lexical profile. In particular, this notion has been empirically explored in the work of Atkins (1987) who uses the term "ID Tag." Developing ideas from Hanks (1996), Gries and Divjak (2009) employ the term "behavioural profile." Other empirical work that is consonant with the theoretical construct of the lexical profile is represented in the work of Dąbrowska (2009): her notion of "words as constructions." Still other work that supports this perspective is discussed in Goldberg (2006).

Finally, some lexical concepts do not have a lexical profile associated with them. This is a feature of lexical concepts which constitute semantically well-formed utterances in their own right. Such lexical concepts I refer to as being **externally closed**. Lexical concepts of this kind include greetings such as *Hello!*, *How do you do?*, *Hi!*, and exclamatives such as *Shit!*.

However, being externally closed does not inevitably mean that a lexical concept must lack a lexical profile. For instance, many lexical concepts, which I refer to, informally, as "clause-level" lexical concepts—traditionally referred to as "independent clauses," or alternatively "simple sentences"—such as the [THING X CAUSES THING Y TO RECEIVE THING Z] lexical concept, as observed above, do indeed have a lexical profile. If they didn't, we wouldn't know how such lexical concepts could be combined with other, more specific, symbolic units, in order to produce a well-formed utterance.

Finally, it is also important to observe that being externally closed does not imply, however, that a given lexical concept cannot be combined with other lexical concepts above the level of the utterance. After all, the ditransitive symbolic unit can be combined with other lexical concepts to make more complex utterances:

(9)   Fred gave Holly flowers, and she smelled them.

Traditionally an utterance of the sort provided in (9) is referred to as a "compound sentence," involving two independent clauses related by a coord-inator, which, in this case, is *and*.

In sum, a lexical profile constitutes a body of more or less restricted linguistic knowledge relating to its use potential that is specific to a given lexical concept. It expresses sets of tendencies: patterns of co-occurrence abstracted from usage events. Moreover, as the lexical profile is apparent in language use, it provides a "footprint" that can serve in identifying the specific lexical concept that sanctions a given instance of use. As such, we might think of the lexical profile as providing a distinct "biometric" identifier for each lexical concept. This is particularly useful in cases of polysemy, where a single vehicle is associated with a number of semantically related lexical concepts. Polysemy provides an analytical challenge for the linguist, as it is not always clear where sense boundaries begin (and end). Later in the chapter

I will illustrate how the lexical profile can be applied in adducing distinct polysemous lexical concepts. In the next chapter I will, among other things, apply this methodology to a case study of polysemy.

Lexical concepts can be combined

One consequence of lexical concepts encoding a lexical profile as part of their linguistic knowledge bundle is that lexical concepts can be combined. While the lexical profile expresses schematic tendencies, lexical concept combination involves the integration of actual instances of specific lexical concepts in a way that serves to combine both the linguistic content encoded by lexical concepts and a subset of the cognitive model profiles that each open-class lexical concept facilitates access to. The general process of combination of both linguistic and conceptual content is referred to, in LCCM Theory, as fusion.

There are two mechanisms which relate to the different sorts of content associated with a lexical concept: linguistic content versus conceptual content. The mechanism which governs the combination of the various types of linguistic content encoded by lexical concepts is termed lexical concept integration. This involves a process termed **unpacking**, and results in a word (or other linguistic expression) receiving a **semantic value**. The mechanism which relates to the way in which conceptual content is then accessed via open-class lexical concepts, following lexical concept integration, is termed interpretation. This is guided by lexical concept integration, and results in the formation of an informational characterization. The combination of lexical concepts resulting in the formation of a semantically well-formed utterance gives rise to a conception. The two types of mechanism that give rise to fusion are, in LCCM Theory, constraint-based, expressed in terms of a set of principles that facilitate and govern the combination of lexical concepts in the construction of meaning.[5]

Of course, lexical concepts are components of symbolic units. They can be combined precisely because symbolic units can be combined. One of the main claims of LCCM Theory, in keeping with the constructional approach to grammar presented in Chapter 5, is that symbolic units, and hence lexical concepts, are combined in nested fashion. In Part I of the book I referred to this as nested integration. By way of illustration, consider the following utterance, based on one similar discussed in the previous chapter:

(10)   Max hid the mobile telephone

The basic insight is that there are (at least) three distinct levels of lexical concept apparent in this particular utterance. Proceeding from the most abstract level, there is a lexical concept that specifies an asymmetric

---

[5] This is the subject of Part III of the book.

relationship holding between two related entities. This corresponds to the intuition that many utterances in English (and indeed many other languages) assign focal prominence to one entity, rather than another in a **profiled relationship** (Langacker 1987). A profiled relationship involves a linguistically encoded relationship holding between two entities, the trajector (TR) and the landmark (LM). This corresponds to the intuition that there is a subject/ object asymmetry encoded by sentence-level symbolic units (in English). The symbolic unit in question is provided in (11):

(11) a. vehicle   "NP1 VERB PHRASE NP2"
      b. lexical concept [A PROFILED RELATIONSHIP HOLDS BETWEEN A TR AND AN LM]

At the next level, there is a lexical concept which establishes that the perspective from which the profiled relationship is viewed is that of the agent. Hence, this lexical concept encodes an asymmetric relationship between an agent and a patient, and in so doing serves to align the agent role with that of TR and the patient role with that of the LM in the lexical concept provided in (11b). That is, the lexical profile encoded by the lexical concept in (11b) stipulates that the internally closed lexical concept that is construed as agentive in a profiled relationship is integrated with the TR role. Hence, the lexical concept provided in (11b) relates to what is more commonly referred to as active voice:

(12) a. vehicle   "NP1 VERB+TNS NP2"
      b. lexical concept [PROFILED RELATIONSHIP INVOLVING AGENT AND PATIENT VIEWED FROM PERSPECTIVE OF AGENT]

The lexical profile for the lexical concept in (12b) stipulates that the agent role aligns with NP1 while the patient role aligns with NP2.

Finally, the third level of lexical concepts involves those which are internally closed, and are hence conventionally paired with vehicles that have overt phonetic content. For the utterance in (10) these relate to lexical concepts associated with the vehicles: *Max, hid, the,* and *mobile telephone.*

While asymmetric focal prominence, as captured by the lexical concept in (12b) is a feature of all linguistically overt (i.e., profiled) relationships, the "active" lexical concept in (12b) need not be. That is, there are situations in which the agent is not associated with the TR. This happens in utterances involving what is commonly referred to as passive voice. Consider the utterance in (13):

(13) The mobile phone was hidden by Max

In this utterance, the internally closed lexical concept: [MOBILE PHONE] is aligned with NP1 This is a consequence of the lexical profile of the "passive" lexical concept which determines that the lexical concept which is construed as being the patient receives focal prominence. Hence, the patient aligns with the NP1 slot associated with the symbolic unit provided in (14). I formalize the "passive" symbolic unit as follows:

(14) a. vehicle   "NP1 BE VERB+PPT *by* NP2"
      b. lexical concept [PROFILED RELATIONSHIP INVOLVING AGENT AND
                           PATIENT VIEWED FROM PERSPECTIVE OF PATIENT]

Full details of how lexical concepts are integrated, and the constraints that apply, are provided in Chapter 12.

Lexical concepts have relativistic consequences for non-linguistic

representation

The integration and interpretation of lexical concepts serves, in part, to contribute to simulations. This follows as semantic representation involves representations from both the linguistic and conceptual systems. The simulations which arise can, in turn, serve to dynamically update conceptual structure. That is, language can contribute to the modification of conceptual structure. As lexical concepts are language-specific, as discussed earlier, each language is likely to affect the modification of conceptual structure in language-specific ways. That is, one of the consequences of the disjunction between the linguistic and conceptual systems posited in LCCM Theory is the prediction that languages will differentially affect non-linguistic representation, i.e., conceptual structure. Hence, we should expect to see relativistic effects of language on non-linguistic cognition.[6]

A summary of the various characteristics associated with lexical concepts is provided in Table 7.2.

TABLE 7.2. Summary of the characteristics of lexical concepts

Property	Details
Lexical concepts are units of mental grammar	Lexical concepts are units of linguistic knowledge: the semantic pole of a symbolic unit, abstracted from across usage events (i.e., utterances). They comprise a bundle of different knowledge types, collectively referred to as linguistic content

(*Continued*)

---

[6] For influential collections which address the notion of linguistic relativity see Gumperz and Levinson (1996) and Gentner and Goldin-Meadow (2003).

TABLE 7.2. (Continued)

Property	Details
Lexical concepts sanction instances of language use	Lexical concepts, *qua* mental knowledge structures, don't appear in utterances, but rather are realized as contextualized semantic contributions. As such, they license instances of language use
Lexical concepts are vehicle-specific	Lexical concepts are conventionally associated with a specific vehicle
Lexical concepts are language-specific	Each language, by virtue of comprising language-specific vehicles which populate the language, necessarily provides an inventory of language-specific lexical concepts
Lexical concepts are associated with different vehicle types	Lexical concepts are associated with vehicles of various kinds, including forms with overt phonetic content as well as those with implicit phonetic content
Vehicles are not lexical concept-specific	Lexical concepts are associated with a "semantic network" of related lexical concepts, and thus exhibit polysemy
Lexical concepts have bipartite structure	Lexical concepts encode linguistic content and facilitate access to conceptual structure. Linguistic content represents the form that conceptual structure takes for direct encoding in language. Conceptual structure relates to non-linguistic information to which lexical concepts potentially afford access
Lexical concepts have an encapsulation function	By virtue of lexical concepts facilitating access to conceptual structure they serve to encapsulate often complex and informationally diffuse ideas
Lexical concepts have a lexical profile	A lexical profile constitutes a body of more or less restricted linguistic knowledge relating to its use potential that is specific to a given lexical. It 'expresses' sets of tendencies: patterns of co-occurrence abstracted from usage events. Moreover, as the lexical profile is apparent in language use, it provides a "footprint" that can serve in identifying the specific lexical concept that sanctions a given instance of use. As such, we might think of the lexical profile as providing a distinct 'biometric' identifier for each lexical concept
Lexical concepts can be combined	Lexical concepts can be combined in various predictable ways in service of activating semantic potential and thus facilitating meaning construction. Combination of lexical concepts involves the integration of linguistic content—a process termed

| | lexical concept integration—and the activation of a subset of the semantic potential accessed via the open-class lexical concepts in the utterance—a process termed interpretation. Lexical concept integration and interpretation—collectively termed fusion—are governed by various constraints modelled in terms of a set of principles |
| Lexical concepts have relativistic consequences for non-linguistic representation | As lexical concepts are language-specific, and contribute to simulations which can serve to modify conceptual structure, each language has relativistic effects on non-linguistic representation |

A methodology for identifying lexical concepts

We now return to one of the key characteristics of the linguistic content encoded by a lexical concept: its lexical profile. There are three reasons for providing such a relatively detailed treatment of this issue here. Firstly, I illustrate the procedure by which distinct selectional tendencies can be employed to identify distinct lexical concepts associated with particular lexical forms. Secondly, as word forms typically have multiple lexical concepts conventionally associated with them, identifying the lexical profiles associated with instances of a given vehicle across discrete utterances serves to disambiguate the range of lexical concepts associated with any given vehicle. And thirdly, as the lexical profile is an important part of the linguistic content encoded by all those lexical concepts (that have one), there is intrinsic merit in providing a more detailed treatment here.

As we saw above, the lexical profile is made up of selectional tendencies of two kinds: semantic selectional tendencies and formal selectional tendencies. I develop two criteria below, relating to the distinct types of knowledge that make up these two sorts of selectional tendencies.[7] I then apply these criteria in order to identify a number of distinct lexical concepts associated with the open-class vehicles: *time*, and *flying*.[8] I do so based on usage data. The two criteria are as follows:

- The Semantic Selectional Criterion:
  A distinct lexical profile—by definition encoded by a distinct lexical concept—provides unique or highly distinct patterns in terms of the

---

[7] In previous work (Evans 2004a, 2005), I formalized criteria for distinguishing between polysemous sense units in somewhat different terms. These were the Meaning Criterion and the Formal Criterion developed as part of the refinement of the Principled Polysemy model presented in that work. The present criteria build on the insights developed in (Evans 2004a), but operate within the new context of LCCM Theory.

[8] Note that I use the same examples of *flying* first introduced in Chapter 2.

nature and range of the lexical concepts with which a lexical concept can co-occur or in which it can be embedded, or in the case of an internally open lexical concept, which occur within it.

- The Formal Selectional Criterion:
  A distinct lexical profile—by definition encoded by a distinct lexical concept—provides unique or highly distinct patterns in terms of the vehicles with which a lexical concept can co-occur or within which it can be embedded, or in the case of an internally open lexical concept, the nature of the alignment between vehicles and the internally closed lexical concepts that lexically fill the internally open lexical concept.

While successful application of only one of the two criteria will normally be sufficient to point to the likelihood of a distinct lexical concept, in the final analysis, identifying the existence of a given lexical concept requires converging evidence employing a number of lines of support and deploying a complementary set of methodologies. Recent work in this regard, which can be used to support the evidence from linguistic analysis presented below, include techniques from psycholinguistic testing (see e.g., Cuyckens *et al.* 1997) as well as corpus-based tools and methodologies (Gries 2006).

Lexical concepts for time

Before being able to apply the two selectional criteria just introduced, it is first necessary to develop a hypothesis as to the nature of the distinct lexical concepts involved in particular utterances. That is, how many lexical concepts are involved across the utterances to be examined? To this end, consider the following examples which involve the form *time*:

(15)   Time flies when you're having fun

(16)   The time for a decision is getting closer

(17)   The old man's time [= death] is fast approaching

(18)   Time flows on (forever)

These instances of the lexical form *time* all appear in the "subject" phrase. Moreover, the verb phrase which complements the subject phrase relates to a motion event. Thus, motion is being ascribed to the entities that *time* contributes in prompting for, in each example. In addition, the semantic contribution associated with *time* appears to be distinct in each example. In the first example in (15), *time* appears to relate to an assessment of temporal magnitude. Thus, we might provisionally gloss the lexical concept which sanctions this instance of *time* as [DURATION]. In (16) the lexical concept sanctioning *time* might be glossed as [MOMENT]. This follows as the conception associated with the utterance as a whole relates to a specific temporal moment when a particular decision is to be taken. Thus, the contribution of *time* in this example appears not to relate to a durational elapse, but rather a discrete instant. In (17) the lexical concept which sanctions this use of *time* appears to relate to an event, which extra-linguistic context informs us is death. Thus, the lexical concept involved here might be glossed as [EVENT]. Finally, in (18), the lexical concept which sanctions this use of *time* appears to relate to an unending temporal elapse. In earlier work (Evans 2004a, 2004b) I described this as the "matrix" lexical concept associated with *time*, in which we understand time to be *the* event within which all other events occur. Thus, the gloss we might apply to describe the lexical concept involved here is [MATRIX].

Indeed, this preliminary analysis suggests that distinct lexical concepts underpin the usages of *time* in each of these examples (see Evans 2004a). In order to test this hypothesis, I apply the selectional criteria. For a distinct lexical profile (and hence a distinct lexical concept) to be confirmed, at least one of these two criteria must apply. In order to confirm whether the instances of *time* in (15) to (18) inclusive are sanctioned by distinct lexical concepts, I begin by applying the Formal Selectional Criterion. To do this, let's consider the kind of noun phrase in which each use of *time* appears. I start by noting that the examples in (15) and (18) appear, on the face of it, to be similar. Neither is pre-modified by a determiner. However, further examples reveal that what I have hypothesized to be a distinct [DURATION] lexical concept of *time* as in (15) can be determined by the definite article when the assessment of temporal magnitude is specific rather than generic, while the use that I hypothesize to be sanctioned by the [MATRIX] lexical concept cannot be. To see that this is the case, consider the following instances of *time*, which are similar to those in (15) and (18):

(19)   During the dinner date, the time seemed to fly   [DURATION]

(20)   *The time flows on (forever)   [MATRIX]

The asterisk in (20) here indicates that a usage that I hypothesize to be sanctioned by the [MATRIX] lexical concept cannot co-occur with the definite article. In contrast, an instance of *time* I hypothesize to be sanctioned by the [DURATION] lexical concept can be. Indeed, this formal patterning appears consistent with the linguistic content encoded by the [MATRIX] lexical concept. The [MATRIX] lexical concept is hypothesized to relate to a unique referent: the event which subsumes all others, and thus further specification which the lexical concept associated with the definite article would provide is superfluous.

The examples in (16) and (17) also exhibit unique patterns in terms of formal selectional tendencies: both from each other and from the examples in (15) and (18). The use of *time* hypothesized to be sanctioned by the [MOMENT] lexical concept appears to pattern straightforwardly as a count noun, allowing determination by the definite article, as in (16), or by the indefinite article, as in (21) below:

(21)   A time will come when we'll be forced to make a decision   [MOMENT]

In this, its behaviour is distinct from the use of *time* in (15), hypothesized to be sanctioned by the [DURATION] lexical concept, which cannot be pre-modified by the indefinite article:

(22)   *During the dinner date a time seemed to fly   [DURATION]

The [EVENT] lexical concept, which I suggest sanctions the use of *time* in (17) appears to require a pre-modifying genitive noun phrase followed by the enclitic possessive "-s", or else an attributive pronoun, serving a similar function:

(23)   His time [=death] is fast approaching.

Thus, in subject position, these uses of *time* all appear to have quite distinct formal selectional tendencies.

Let's now turn to the semantic selectional tendencies associated with these uses *time*. I do so by applying the Semantic Selectional Criterion. The point here is that the nature of the motion event encoded by the lexical concept associated with the verb-phrase vehicle is distinct for each of the uses in a significant way. Moreover, the choice of motion-event type is compatible with the nature of the various lexical concepts hypothesized to sanction the distinct uses of *time*.

For instance, the [DURATION] lexical concept which I suggest underpins the use of *time* in (15), and the particular variant—which in previous work I refer to as the [TEMPORAL COMPRESSION] lexical concept, as it relates to an assessment of temporal magnitude which proceeds more "quickly" than usual (Evans 2004a)—co-occurs with lexical concepts that encode motion events which are rapid in nature, as evidenced by the example in (15).[9] In contrast, what I hypothesize to be the [MOMENT] lexical concept appears to possess a lexical profile which allows a wider range of motion events to co-occur with it, including imperceptible motion as in (24), rapid motion, as in (25), and terminal motion, as in (26):

---

[9] The temporal compression variant of duration associated with *time* can also co-occur with lexical concepts that encode motion events which imply a lack of perceptual awareness, such as the following: *Where has the time gone? The time seemed to have vanished*, etc.

(24) The time for a decision has gone/vanished/disappeared

(25) The time for decision is racing towards us/fast approaching

(26) The time for a decision is approaching/getting closer/has arrived

The [EVENT] lexical concept appears to possess a lexical profile which restricts the range of motion lexical concepts which can co-occur with it to terminal motion events, i.e., motion events which terminate "at" the experiential locus, typically a human experiencer. Finally, the [MATRIX] lexical concept appears to possess a lexical profile which requires lexical concepts encoding motion events which are non-terminal in nature. That is, it requires motion events which are ongoing, a paradigm example being the lexical concept associated with the vehicle *flow*.

Thus, each of the examples of *time* in (15) to (18) inclusive, based on the Semantic Selectional Criterion and the Formal Selectional Criterion, behaves as if sanctioned by distinct lexical concepts with distinct lexical profiles. Table 7.3 summarizes the semantic and formal selectional tendencies which comprise the lexical profiles for the lexical concepts considered.

Lexical concepts for flying

While the lexical concepts associated with the vehicle *time* are nominal in nature, I now provide a further illustration, this time involving relational lexical concepts. Hence, I now consider the lexical profile relating to distinct lexical concepts associated with the verbal vehicle: *flying*. To do so, consider the examples in (5) presented earlier in the chapter and reproduced below:

(5) a. The plane/bird is flying (in   [SELF-PROPELLED AERODYNAMIC MO-
        the sky)   TION]
     b. The pilot is flying the plane   [OPERATION OF ENTITY CAPABLE OF
        (in the sky)   AERODYNAMIC MOTION]
     c. The child is flying the kite   [CONTROL OF LIGHTWEIGHT ENTITY]
        (in the breeze)
     d. The flag is flying (in the   [SUSPENSION OF LIGHTWEIGHT OB-
        breeze)   JECT]

For convenience I have provided the lexical concepts which I hypothesize to sanction each of the uses of *flying* alongside the examples. These data, and the glosses, suggest that each instance is sanctioned by a distinct lexical concept associated with the vehicle *flying*. If so, we should expect to be able to adduce a distinct lexical profile associated with each use. Unlike many (English) nominal lexical concepts, for which a salient grammatical feature is how they are determined, a salient grammatical feature for relational lexical concepts, associated with verb forms, is transitivity.

TABLE 7.3. Lexical profiles associated with lexical concepts which sanction the uses of *time* considered

Gloss	Brief description of conceptual content	Nature of semantic selectional tendencies	Nature of formal selectional tendencies
[DURATION] two variants:	Assessment of magnitude of duration		Mass noun; can appear with definite article
[PROTRACTED DURATION]	Duration "slower" than usual	Slow motion, e.g., *time drags*	and some quantifiers
[TEMPORAL COMPRESSION]	Duration "faster" than usual	Fast motion, e.g., *time flies*	
[MOMENT]	A discrete temporal "point"	Ego-centred motion, e.g., *the time is approaching...*	Count noun; can appear with definite and indefinite articles
[EVENT]	A boundary-event of some kind	Ego-centred motion, e.g., *Her time is approaching...*	Count noun; cannot take articles, but can be preceded by pronouns and possessive noun phrases
[MATRIX]	An unbounded elapse conceived as the event subsuming all others	Non-terminal motion, e.g., *Time flows on forever*	Mass noun; cannot be preceded by definite or indefinite articles

Hence, in terms of formal selectional tendencies, and hence the Formal Selectional Criterion, the hallmark of the lexical concepts which license the uses of *flying* in (5a) and (5d) is the lack of a direct object—what is traditionally referred to as an intransitive verb. This contrasts with the lexical concepts which sanction the examples in (5b) and (5c) which both require a direct object—making them transitive verbs. This distinction in transitivity fails to distinguish (5a) from (5d) and (5b) from (5c). For this we must rely on semantic selectional tendencies, and the Semantic Selectional Criterion.

The hallmark of each of these lexical concepts is that they stipulate distinct types of lexical concepts. For instance, the [SELF-PROPELLED AERODYNAMIC MOTION] lexical concept, which, I suggest, sanctions the use of *flying* in (5a), only applies to entities that are capable of self-propelled aerodynamic motion.

Entities that are not self-propelled, such as tennis balls, cannot be used in this sense (*the tennis ball is flying in the sky).

The lexical concept which underlies the use of *flying* in (5b): [OPERATION OF ENTITY CAPABLE OF AERODYNAMIC MOTION] is restricted to operation by an entity which can be construed as an agent, and moreover, to entities that can undergo self-propelled aerodynamic motion. Further, the entity must be able to accommodate the agent and thereby serve as a means of transport. This explains why aeroplanes and hot air balloons are compatible with uses sanctioned by this lexical concept, but entities unable to accommodate an agent are not. This is illustrated by example (27).

(27)   ??He flew the sparrow across the English Channel

Nevertheless, entities which can be construed as being guided, or at least susceptible to being trained, by a volitional agent, yet which cannot accommodate an agent, are partially sanctioned by this lexical concept, as the following example illustrates:

(28)   He flew the homing pigeon across the English Channel

In the case of the use sanctioned by the [CONTROL OF LIGHTWEIGHT ENTITY] lexical concept, as evidenced by the use of *flying* in (5c), this lexical concept appears to be restricted to entities that are capable of becoming airborne by turbulence, and can be controlled by an agent on the ground. This lexical concept appears to be specialized for objects like kites and model/remote-controlled aeroplanes.

Interestingly, as we saw in our discussion of the lexical concepts associated with the vehicle *fast* in examples (1) to (3) earlier, particular instances of *flying* appear to rely on multiple sanction. In the following example:

(29)   The kite is flying (in the sky)

this use appears to be partly sanctioned by both the [SELF-PROPELLED AERODYNAMIC MOTION] and the [CONTROL OF LIGHTWEIGHT ENTITY] lexical concepts. It exhibits the formal selectional tendencies of the former lexical concept, but we understand that it must be controlled by an agent, rather than being self-propelled.

The final use of *flying*, sanctioned by the lexical concept which I gloss as [SUSPENSION OF LIGHTWEIGHT OBJECT], selects for entities that can be supported by virtue of air turbulence, but remain "connected to" the ground. This lexical concept applies to flags as well as hair and scarves, which can "fly" in the wind.

In sum, this discussion of lexical concepts which sanction distinct uses of *flying* can be identified by virtue of examining formal and semantic selectional tendencies, which relate to the Formal and Semantic Selectional Criteria. As each use of the vehicle patterns in a markedly different way across the utterances in (5), based on application of these criteria, we can conclude that a distinct lexical profile underpins each use and hence, each use is indeed sanctioned by a distinct lexical concept.

Summary

This chapter has provided an overview of the main properties of lexical concepts. I argued that lexical concepts, by virtue of constituting units of semantic structure—the semantic pole of a symbolic unit—are thereby central elements of a language user's mental grammar. As such, lexical concepts sanction instances of language and are conventionally associated with a lexical form. Accordingly, they are vehicle-specific. A corollary of this is that lexical concepts are necessarily language-specific. While lexical concepts may encode related and hence similar linguistic content across languages, they will always facilitate access to a distinct body of conceptual structure: their semantic potential. This is a consequence of lexical concepts having bipartite structure: encoding linguistic content while facilitating access to the contents of the human conceptual system. One consequence of lexical concepts facilitating access to conceptual structure is that they provide an access site—consisting of multiple association areas, to be discussed in Chapter 10—for a diffuse body of non-linguistic knowledge. As such, they provide an encapsulation function. As we shall see later, it is by virtue of lexical concepts providing a unique access site on the conceptual system that words give rise to the illusion of semantic unity. Another important aspect of the linguistic content encoded by a lexical concept is its lexical profile. This constitutes knowledge relating to the semantic and formal tendencies: the (types of) lexical concepts and vehicles with which a given lexical concept co-occurs. Moreover, as the lexical profile is abstracted from across usage events, it can be applied to usage data in order to provide evidence as to whether a given lexical concept is sanctioning a particular usage of a vehicle. The procedure for employing the lexical profile in this way was formalized in terms of the Semantic and Formal Selectional Criteria. The application of these was illustrated by virtue of an analysis of nominal lexical concepts associated with the vehicle *time*, and relational lexical concepts associated with the verbal vehicle *flying*. The chapter also briefly addressed the compositional processes that give rise to the combination of lexical concepts in service of meaning construction. This particular issue is addressed in detail later, in Part III of the book. Finally, it was suggested that as lexical concepts contribute, in part, to simulations which can come to be stored as part of conceptual structure, they thus have relativistic consequences for non-linguistic knowledge representation.

8

Polysemy

In this chapter I address the issue of polysemy: the phenomenon whereby a single vehicle has multiple related sense-units associated with it. Polysemy constitutes an important topic in language science. Traditionally, lexical semanticists have taken the view that polysemy is a "surface" phenomenon: a consequence of a relatively abstract underlying mental representation giving rise to a plethora of manifestations in specific contexts of use. The emergence of cognitive lexical semantics, a branch of cognitive linguistics, with work by Brugman and Lakoff (1988) and Lakoff (1987), reconceptualized polysemy as being an "underlying" phenomenon. That is, words exhibit polysemy as a consequence not of a single abstract mental representation, but because polysemy is inherently conceptual in nature: distinct sense-units inhere in semantic memory independently of contexts of language use. More recent work in cognitive lexical semantics has sought to nuance and modify this position to take account of the role of the interactive nature of language use in mediating the construction of meaning (e.g., Allwood 2003; Croft and Cruse 2004; Zlatev 2003). One of the functions then, of this chapter, is to present a perspective on the semantic relatedness holding between the semantic units associated with a single word, i.e. polysemy, in the light of LCCM Theory. Accordingly, this chapter can be viewed as an application of some of the theoretical machinery relating to semantic structure developed in the last two chapters.

Polysemy, in LCCM Theory, relates not to the variation evident in the situated semantic contribution of a word—which arises due to the compositional principles considered later in the book. Rather, polysemy in LCCM Theory is a consequence of a single vehicle being associated with distinct lexical concepts which are semantically related. Semantic relatedness is a matter of degree and is determined by the bipartite structure of lexical concepts. The way in which open-class as well as closed-class polysemous lexical concepts can be related is by virtue of shared or overlapping linguistic content, for instance in terms of shared parameters. The second way concerns the nature of the conceptual structure that open-class lexical concepts afford potential access to. That is, there may be significant overlap between parts of the cognitive model profile[1] accessed via open-class lexical concepts associated with the same vehicle.

---

[1] The notion of a cognitive model profile is discussed in detail in Chapter 10.

The main way in which I examine polysemy in this chapter is by way of a detailed case study of the "state" lexical concepts associated with the English prepositions *in*, *on*, and *at*. Hence, I will be concerned with the semantic relatedness in the linguistic content encoded by lexical concepts associated with the same vehicle. There is a significant tradition of employing prepositional analyses in cognitive linguistics, and in other areas of cognitive science—see many of the papers in Evans and Chilton (forthcoming). One of the main reasons for employing prepositions is because they are presumably grounded in spatial interactions, and yet are highly polysemous in all languages that feature them. They also give rise to a wide range of non-spatial sense units from the temporal, to the aspectual, to the abstract. To illustrate, consider the divergence of the conventional semantic contributions associated with the English preposition *on*:

(1) a. The book is on the table   "spatial"
     b. I heard it on the radio   "abstract"
     c. The house is on fire   "state"
     d. She arrived on time   "temporal"

One of the main points of interest for cognitive linguists in studying the polysemy of prepositions, and the trajectory of the emergence of non-spatial semantic representations derived from historically earlier spatial ones, relates to the thesis of embodied cognition briefly discussed in Chapter 3.[2] In particular, evidence that spatial representations give rise to related but more abstract representations, as is evidenced by studying the polysemy of prepositions, provides compelling support for the foundational basis of embodiment in terms of representations that populate the conceptual system as well as those that populate the linguistic system. In this spirit, this chapter builds towards and concludes with a detailed case study of the "state" lexical concepts of several English prepositions: lexical concepts which are non-spatial in nature.

Polysemy in cognitive linguistics

While both polysemy and homonymy give rise to **lexical ambiguity**—two or more lexical concepts associated with a lexical item—the nature of the ambiguity is different in each case. Polysemy is the phenomenon whereby a vehicle is associated with two or more lexical concepts that appear to be semantically related. Consider the following examples containing the English preposition *over*.

---

[2] See Evans and Green (2006) for an overview; see also Johnson (1987, 2007); Lakoff (1987); Tyler and Evans (2003). For other views on embodiment see Gibbs (2006); Varela *et al.* (1991); Clark (1998). For useful reviews see Ziemke (2003); Wilson (2002).

(2) a. The picture is over the sofa   [ABOVE]
     b. The ball landed over the wall   [ON THE OTHER SIDE]
     c. The arrow flew over the target   [ABOVE AND BEYOND]
         and landed in the woods

According to Tyler and Evans (2001, 2003), each of these instances of *over* is associated with a slightly different lexical concept (listed on the right), but these are nevertheless relatively closely related. This illustrates that *over* exhibits polysemy.

Polysemy contrasts with **homonymy**, which relates to two distinct lexical concepts that happen to share the same vehicle. For example, the vehicle *bank* relates to two different lexical concepts that are otherwise semantically unrelated: [FINANCIAL INSTITUTION] and [SIDE OF A RIVER]. These two lexical concepts are not only synchronically unrelated: unrelated in current usage, but also historically unrelated. The lexical concept [SIDE OF RIVER] has been in the English language for much longer, and is related to the Old Icelandic word for "hill", while the lexical concept [FINANCIAL INSTITUTION] was borrowed from Italian *banca* (via French) originally with the sense: "money changer's table".

While formal linguists have long recognized the existence of polysemy, it has generally been viewed as a "surface" phenomenon, in the sense that lexical entries are underspecified—abstract and lacking in detail—and are "filled in" either by context (Ruhl 1989), or by the application of certain kinds of lexical generative devices (Pustejovsky 1995). According to this view, polysemy is epiphenomenal, emerging from **monosemy**: a single relatively abstract semantic representation from which other senses—such as the range of semantic contributions associated with *over*—are derived on the basis of context, speaker intention, recognition of that intention by the hearer, and so on. A monosemy account is plausible in principle when accounting for semantic contributions such as those in the utterances in (2), which are all spatial in nature and could therefore be accounted for in terms of a single abstract spatial semantic representation. However, *over* is also associated with a range of non-spatial lexical concepts. Consider example (3).

(3) Jane has a strange power over him

While the semantic contribution associated with the use of *over* in (3) might be glossed as "control", it is difficult to see how a single abstract semantic unit could derive the three spatial lexical concepts in (2) as well as this non-spatial [CONTROL] lexical concept. After all, the utterance in (3) does not describe a spatial scene—*Jane* is not located above *him* in space—but has an abstract sense relating to a power relationship between two people.

One way of analysing the semantic contribution of *over* in (3) would be to treat it as a distinct and unrelated semantic unit associated with the form *over*. This would amount to the claim that *over* in (3) is a homonym: a symbolic unit which is distinct and hence unrelated to the symbolic unit which is associated with the uses evident in (2). A second possible analysis, which preserves the monosemy position, might claim that a single abstract under-lying semantic unit sanctions both the spatial and non-spatial senses, but that while the spatial senses are literal, the non-spatial sense is metaphorical, and is interpreted by applying pragmatic principles to retrieve the speaker's in-tended meaning.

In their work on cognitive lexical semantics Claudia Brugman (1988; Brug-man and Lakoff 1988) and George Lakoff (1987) claimed that *over* is stored as a category of distinct polysemous sense units, rather than a single abstract monosemous sense. It follows from this position that polysemy reflects underlying distinctions stored in long-term semantic memory rather than being a purely surface effect. In this respect, this earliest work in cognitive lexical semantics diverged both from traditional and from more recent formal approaches to word meaning, in particular in developing the position that polysemy is a fundamentally conceptual phenomenon, and that lexical or-ganization at the mental level determines polysemy as it is manifested in language use.

While the work of Brugman and Lakoff has been highly influential, it led to a perspective on lexical representation which, in Chapter 2, I referred to as the Sense Enumerative Lexicon perspective. That is, Lakoff and Brugman mod-elled word senses (i.e., lexical concepts) in terms of what are often referred to as **semantic networks**, making the assumption that such lexical concepts are relatively stable knowledge structures deployed by language users in utter-ances. The difficulty with this perspective lies in the observable fact that, as we saw in Part I of the book, word meaning is protean: it shifts in context. The consequence of treating situated word meaning as being a function of stored word senses is that a huge number, perhaps an infinite range of distinct word senses are required, even for a single vehicle.

Some recent cognitive linguistic accounts of lexical representation have reacted against some of the clear difficulties with the tack taken by Brugman and Lakoff. Such approaches (e.g., Allwood 2003; Croft and Cruse 2004; Zlatev 2003) argue that the semantic contribution associated with words is construed in context. That is, rather than words having pre-specified senses, *qua* Lakoff, they have what has been variously termed a "meaning potential" (Allwood 2003), a "purport" (Croft and Cruse 2004), or a "use potential" (Zlatev 2003). While it is not entirely clear what semantic structures of this sort look like, the idea appears to be that semantic structures relate to the range of potential knowledge to which words relate, based in part, on the history of a word's use, as well as encompassing conceptual structure.

Two important issues arise from this. Firstly, and in contrast to the Lakoff/ Brugman account of lexical representation, semantic structures are not stable and pre-defined in the way envisaged by Lakoff. Secondly, such approaches are thoroughgoingly usage-based in character. The semantic contribution of a given word is always a function of a situated interpretation in a unique context of use. Hence, a word's semantic contribution, what Croft and Cruse refer to as its "sense-boundary," is construed in context. A further consequence of such approaches is that the theoretical dichotomy between polysemy versus monosemy disappears. As Zlatev (2003) points out, from this perspective, wondering whether lexical representations should be modelled in terms of one or other of these two extremes is no longer a question worth asking. After all, semantic structures are not in and of themselves discrete entities, but come to have a particular semantic contribution as a function of their precise context of use.

The difficulty with this more recent perspective, as pointed out by Harder (2009), is that it places all the responsibility for meaning construction on language output (comprehension), but ignores (or underplays) the role of the input (production). Hence, it runs the risk of what Harder refers to as usage fundamentalism: the risk of eliminating the role of words as instructions or prompts for meaning construction.[3] That is, language users must have pre-existing mental representations of some sort in order to deploy words in the way they do.

In essence, claiming that language provides "instructions," in Harder's (2009) terms does not logically exclude the position that linguistically mediated meaning construction involves the construal of sense boundaries in context. The two are not mutually exclusive. Indeed, LCCM Theory requires both stable units of semantic structure—lexical concepts—which encode stable bundles of linguistic content, and a meaning potential, which consists of dynamically evolving non-linguistic knowledge—a cognitive model profile—and posits integrative and interpretative processes which ensure that word "meanings" are always construed in context—the subject of the next part of the book.

The "state" lexical concepts of English prepositions

The analytical focus in the remainder of the chapter is what we might loosely refer to as "state" lexical concepts. In particular, I examine the "state" lexical concepts associated with the prepositional vehicles *in*, *at*, and *on*. My overarching purpose is to provide a sense of the nature and status of polysemy, as a phenomenon, from the perspective of LCCM Theory. I do this by way of a detailed illustration employing the "state" lexical concepts. Representative examples are provided below:

(4) We are in love/shock/pain   "state" sense
     cf. We are in a room   "spatial" sense

---

[3] Recall the discussion in Chapter 1.

(5)   We are at war/variance/one/daggers drawn/loggerheads   "state" sense
      cf. We are at the bus stop   "spatial" sense

(6)   We are on alert/best behaviour/look-out/the run   "state" sense
      cf. We are on the bus   "spatial" sense

In these examples, *in*, *at*, and *on* mediate a relation between human experien-
cer(s) and a particular state. While some of these expressions, for instance, to be
"at daggers drawn" are clearly idiomatic, the contention of cognitive lexical
semantics is that while such expressions may be highly conventionalized, and
the source of the idiom may not be accessible to contemporary language users, the
fact that *at* is employed, is, diachronically at least, motivated.

If the perspective offered by cognitive linguistics is correct, namely that the
use of *in*, *at*, and *on* is sanctioned by a "state" lexical concept, then there is one
important issue that awaits explanation: each of the "state" lexical concepts
associated with the prepositional vehicles in (4)–(6) exhibit distinct patterns in
terms of their semantic selectional tendencies. For instance, the "state" lexical
concept associated with *in* selects for co-occurring open-class lexical concepts
which access conceptual structure concerning emotional or psychological
"force" such as being "in love", "in pain", and so on. In contrast, the open-
class lexical concepts which co-occur with *at* have to do, not with emotional
force but, rather, with mutual (or interpersonal) relations, such as being "at
war". Meanwhile, *on* selects for lexical concepts that relate to content that has
to do with time-restricted activities, as well as actions which involve being
currently active. These include being "on alert", "on duty", and so forth. That
is, the types of co-occurring lexical concepts selected by each of the "state"
senses for these prepositions is of a quite different kind. This suggests, as
predicted by LCCM Theory, that each of the prepositional vehicles is associated with a distinct lexical concept, which accordingly exhibits a distinct lexical
profile, as manifested in usage patterns. Hence, although I have hitherto
applied the label "state" to refer to the lexical concepts which underpin the
specific instance of the distinct prepositional vehicles, *in*, *at*, and *on*, it is
important to recognize that the so-called "state" lexical concepts are distinct,
as evidenced by their distinct selectional tendencies.

In view of this, in what follows I employ linguistic data in order to provide a
reasonably detailed illustration of how LCCM theory accounts for the complexity of the closed-class "state" lexical concepts for *in*, *at*, and *on*. I suggest
that LCCM theory facilitates the following:

- a revealing descriptive analysis of the "state" lexical concepts of these
  three prepositional vehicles, including the way in which the "state" lexical
  concept(s) associated with one prepositional vehicle are distinct from
  the state lexical concept(s) associated with other prepositional vehicles;
- a revealing account of the range of "state" lexical concepts within a given
  preposition showing how they are distinct; that is, some vehicles, notably
  in and *on* exhibit more than one distinct "state" lexical concept;

- an account of the spatio-geometric and functional knowledge encoded by the core "spatial" lexical concepts associated with *in*, *at*, and *on*;
- and in view of this, a revealing account of how each of the "state" lexical concepts involved is motivated by, and related to, the core "spatial" lexical concepts associated with each prepositional vehicle.

There are a number of claims that I make, and which the findings presented serve to substantiate:

- Polysemy is a phenomenon that holds at the level of semantic structure: at the level of lexical concepts. As such it is not a "surface" phenomenon: a matter of contextual variation in the semantic contribution of words. We shall see that the "state" lexical concepts described, both within and between prepositional vehicles, vary in terms of their linguistic content: the nature of their parameters and their lexical profiles. Hence, polysemy relates to the stable linguistic knowledge encoded by lexical concepts prior to language use.
- The derivation of new lexical concepts arises from extant lexical concepts by virtue of inferential processes, relating to situated instances of language use. Hopper and Traugott (2003) refer to such a mechanism as **pragmatic strengthening**: an inferential process whereby a new semantic unit is abstracted from an extant semantic unit, arising in a **bridging context** (Evans and Wilkins 2000): a context of use in which the new lexical concept emerges as a situated inference (or an "invited inference," Traugott and Dasher 2004). A polysemous relationship thereby holds between the extant and the derived lexical concept. From the perspective of LCCM Theory, a new lexical concept arises for one of two reasons: (i) due to a reanalysis of linguistic content and/or (ii) a shift in the access site to a cognitive model profile that the derived open-class lexical concept provides.
- In the case of the closed-class lexical concepts associated with the prepositional vehicles addressed in this chapter, the derived lexical concepts arise from a change in the nature of the linguistic content being encoded, rather than a shift in access site. Specifically, I argue that the polysemous lexical concepts arise due to new parameters being encoded, giving rise to distinct lexical concepts. These parameters arise due to the functional consequences of spatio-typological properties in situated language use. That is, and as we shall see, functional parameters arise inferentially, a consequence of antecedent spatial lexical concepts. Hence, the derivation of new lexical concepts is motivated rather than arbitrary.

The functional nature of spatial semantics

My purpose in this section is to briefly make the case for a functional characterization of the spatial lexical concept associated with a given preposition.[4] By "spatial" I mean lexical concepts that encode a spatio-topological relation of some sort, as illustrated for *over* in the examples in (2), above. By "functional" I mean the following. To understand how language users employ the spatial lexical concept of a prepositional vehicle we must also allow for non-spatial parameters which form part of the linguistic content encoded by the lexical concept. The use of the term "functional" is motivated by the observation that such non-spatial parameters are a functional consequence of humanly relevant interactions with the spatio-topological properties in question. Moreover, the way spatial lexical concepts are ordinarily employed by language users would appear to require such a functional understanding if spatial lexical concepts are to be correctly interpreted in context.

Providing a functional account is of further importance as the derived lexical concepts—such as the "state" lexical concepts—which result from extant spatial lexical concepts, arise from humanly relevant **spatial scenes** (Tyler and Evans 2003), in which the functional consequences—what I refer to as **functional categories**—are more salient than the spatio-topological relation encoded by the linguistic content of the spatial lexical concept. Through the process of pragmatic strengthening, derived (i.e., functionally motivated) lexical concepts arise. This involves new functional parameters becoming added to the linguistic content of the derived lexical concept(s).

In her work, Annette Herskovits (e.g., 1996, 1988) observes that, traditionally, work on spatial representation in language assumed that the "basic" function of the spatial lexical concepts associated with prepositional vehicles is to encode purely spatial relations.[5] The traditional view, which she terms the **simple relations model**, assumes that the semantic contribution of any given spatial use of a prepositional vehicle relates to spatio-geometric properties, typically designating a relation involving notions such as dimensions, axes, or proximity (e.g., Bennett 1975; Miller and Johnson-Laird 1976 for representative examples). However, the simple relations model is descriptively inadequate. That is, the "simple" spatial relations posited are unable to account for the range of spatial representations that prepositions ordinarily designate.[6]

A related, and influential, perspective has been presented by Vandeloise in his work. Vandeloise (1991, 1994) argues compellingly that any account of spatial semantics that leaves out the functional nature of prepositional lexical concepts fails to properly account for how they are actually employed. That is, spatio-topological relations have functional consequences, consequences which arise from how we interact with objects and entities in our physical environment, and in our daily lives. To illustrate, take the mundane example of a cup of coffee. Imagine holding it in your hand. If you move the cup slowly

---

[4] For more detailed arguments see Evans (forthcoming *a*).

[5] See also Coventry and Garrod (2004), Deane (2005), Feist (forthcoming), and Tyler and Evans (2003) for a related perspective.

[6] See Herskovits (1988) for a survey of some of the descriptive inadequacies of the simple relations model.

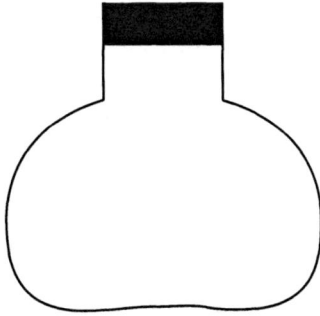

FIGURE 8.1. A bottle or a light bulb? (adapted from Vandeloise 1994)

up and down, or from side to side, the coffee moves along with the cup. This follows as the cup is a container with a bottom and sides and thus constrains the location of any entity within these boundaries. Tyler and I (2003) referred to this property of bounded landmarks as "location with surety."

The force-dynamic properties associated with a cup as a container also show up in linguistic content, as illustrated by the semantic contribution of the preposition *in*. Consider the diagram in Figure 8.1, drawn from the work of Vandeloise (1994).

Vandeloise observes that the image depicted in Figure 8.1 could either represent a bottle or a light bulb. As example (7) shows, we can use the preposition *in* to describe the relation between *the light bulb* (Figure) and *the socket* (Reference Object).

(7)   The bulb is in the socket

In contrast however, we cannot use *in* to describe the relation between a bottle and its cap, as illustrated by (8). The hash sign indicates that the utterance is semantically odd.

(8)   #The bottle is in the cap

Vandeloise points out that the spatial relation holding between the figure (F) and reference object (RO) in each of these utterances is identical, and yet while (7) is a perfectly acceptable sentence (8) is semantically odd. Vandeloise suggests that it is not the spatial relation holding between the F and RO that accounts for the acceptability or otherwise of *in*. He argues that the relevant factor is one of force-dynamics: "[W]hile the socket exerts a force on the bulb and determines its position, the opposite occurs with the cap and the bottle" (Vandeloise 1994: 173). In other words, not only is the position and the successful function of the bulb contingent on being *in* (contained by) the socket, but the socket also prevents the bulb from succumbing to the force of gravity and falling to the ground. In contrast, the position and successful functioning of the bottle is not contingent on being *in* the cap. This suggests that our knowledge of the functional consequences associated with what it means to be enclosed affects the contextual acceptability of a preposition such as *in.*

Lexical concepts associated with *in*

In this section I present an LCCM analysis of the "state" lexical concepts associated with *in.* That is, I argue that there is more than one distinct "state" lexical concept conventionally associated with the prepositional vehicle *in.* I also show how these "state" lexical concepts relate to, and are motivated by, the functional consequences attendant upon the range of spatial scenes which involve usages of *in* sanctioned by the core spatial lexical concept which I gloss as [ENCLOSURE].

The two aspects of linguistic content, in particular, that I will be focusing on below, in adducing distinctions between lexical concepts, are the lexical profile and the parameters encoded by a given lexical concept. In terms of parameters, the prototypical spatial lexical concept associated with *in,* namely [ENCLOSURE], encodes the parameter Enclosure, as evidenced by the example in (9), for instance. In contrast, the [PSCYHOSOMATIC STATE] lexical concept—one of the "state" lexical concepts associated with *in*—encodes the parameter Psycho-somatic State, as evidenced in (10), but not the Enclosure parameter.

(9)   The kitten is in the box   Parameter: Enclosure

(10)   John is in love   Parameter: Psychosomatic state

That is, the [ENCLOSURE] lexical concept which sanctions the use of *in* in (9) encodes a schematic dimension abstracted from sensory-motor experience in which the F is contained by the RO. Notice that the relation encoded is highly schematic in nature; it says nothing about whether there is contact or not between the F and RO as in (11), nor whether the F represents part of the RO or not as in (12):

(11)   a. The fly is in the jar (i.e., flying around)
       b. The fly is in the jar (i.e., stationary on one interior surface)

(12)   There's a crack in the vase

Indeed, the precise spatio-topological nature of the F, RO, and their relation-ship is a function of the F and RO and their possible forms of interaction, rather than the abstract parameter encoded by the [ENCLOSURE] lexical concept. This information derives from the semantic potential accessed via the open-class lexical concepts, and as mediated by the compositional processes discussed later in the book.

In contrast, the [PSYCHOSOMATIC STATE] lexical concept encodes the parameter Psychosomatic state. This information is highly schematic in nature. That is, the parameter encoded does not determine which sorts of psychosomatic states can collocate with this lexical concept. This is a function of the lexical profile: for instance, knowledge relating to the semantic selectional tendencies associated with this lexical concept, and hence the range of psychosomatic states which can co-occur with the [PSYCHOSOMATIC STATE] lexical concept. Hence, while the parameters encoded by a lexical concept determine the possible range of lexical concepts (and hence semantic arguments) that can co-occur, the lexical profile provides information relating to the range of permissible states which can co-occur with this lexical concept.

[ENCLOSURE] *and its parameters*

As noted above, the [ENCLOSURE] lexical concept encodes a spatio-topological relation holding between a schematic F, the entity enclosed, and a bounded landmark, the RO. Bounded landmarks themselves consist of many types even in everyday experience. A bounded landmark includes an interior, which further subsumes an interior surface, and the volumetric interior bounded by the interior surface. It also subsumes a boundary, which can be rigid, as in a metal safe, or non-rigid, as in a plastic carrier bag. The boundary also has other physical characteristics such as permeability and degrees of opacity. Finally, the bounded landmark has, by definition, an exterior: that region which constitutes the inverse of the volumetric interior. Accordingly, part of the exterior includes the exterior surface. The spatio-topological attributes just described relate to enclosure. They are encoded in linguistic content in terms of what I refer to as the Enclosure parameter.

As observed earlier, due to human interaction involving enclosures, the [ENCLOSURE] lexical concept, as manifested in usage events, is associated with a number of functional consequences. That is, there are a number of identifiably distinct sorts of functional categories associated with spatial scenes involving enclosure in addition to the spatio-topological relation of Enclosure just described. These include Location with Surety, Occlusion, and Affecting Conditions, summarized in Figure 8.2.

Bounded landmarks that are specialized for providing a Location with Surety function are known as "containers." This functional category is encoded in linguistic content in terms of what I refer to as the Location with Surety parameter. Containers can provide a support function by virtue of locating by fixing (i.e., holding and restricting) the location of the F. This was illustrated with the discussion of the light bulb in the socket example earlier. Alternatively, containers can restrict access (and escape), as in the case of prisons and safes.

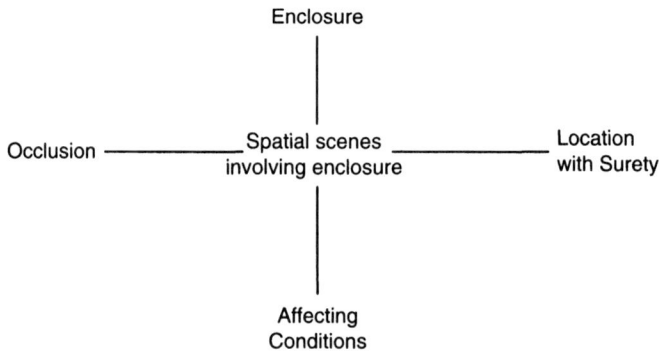

FIGURE 8.2. Parameters deriving from spatial scenes involving the spatio-topological relation: Enclosure

The second functional category mentioned relates to Occlusion. A consequence of certain bounded landmarks, due to the opacity of the material which forms the boundary, is that the figure located on the volumetric interior is occluded, and hence hidden from view. This functional category gives rise to the Occlusion parameter.

The third functional category, that of Affecting Conditions, relates to the fact that an enclosure provides a delimited environment which thereby affects the F located on the volumetric interior. For instance, a prisoner held in solitary confinement in a windowless sound-proofed room is thereby subjected to a particular sensory environment that is a direct consequence of the nature of the bounded landmark in which s/he is located.

In other words, by virtue of interacting in humanly relevant ways with the spatio-topological relation Enclosure, a number of distinct functional consequences arise, which I formalize as distinct and identifiable categories. These functional categories give rise to schematic parameters which come to be encoded as part of the bundle of linguistic content encoded by the [ENCLOSURE] lexical concept. In essence, the lexical concept [ENCLOSURE] encodes the spatio-topological relation Enclosure, a schematic unit of knowledge akin to a parameter, and the parameters—arising from the encoding of distinct functional categories—Containment, Occlusion, and Affecting Conditions. This is summarized in Table 8.1.

Polysemy emerges in the following way. Due to the multiplicity of parameters encoded by a single lexical concept, under certain conditions, a parameter (or parameters) that is particularly salient in a given context of use can become reanalysed as a distinct sense-unit, giving rise to a new lexical concept in its own right. This does not mean, for instance, that the [ENCLOSURE] lexical concept loses the Affecting Conditions parameter from its linguistic content. Rather, the Affecting Conditions parameter can become established as the core parameter of a new lexical concept.

TABLE 8.1. Linguistic content encoded by [ENCLOSURE] deriving from spatial scenes and functional categories

Consequences of spatial scene and humanly relevant interaction with aspects of scene:		Linguistic content of [ENCLOSURE]:
Spatio-topological relation:		*Parameter:*
Enclosure	encoded as:	Enclosure
Functional categories:		*Parameter:*
Location with Surety	encoded as:	Location with Surety
Occlusion	encoded as:	Occlusion
Affecting Conditions	encoded as:	Affecting Conditions

Evidence for the disjunction in parameters for [ENCLOSURE]

In this section I present linguistic evidence in support of the position that [ENCLOSURE] encodes a number of distinct parameters. That is, I provide evidence for a disjunction in the nature of this aspect of the linguistic content encoded by [ENCLOSURE]. As my claim relating to the emergence of new lexical concepts, and hence polysemy, rests on such a disjunction, it is important to briefly provide the evidence before proceeding further. I illustrate this with the examples below which reveal the disjunction between the Enclosure and Location with Surety parameters encoded by [ENCLOSURE].

Accordingly, consider the following examples:

(13)   The toy is in the box

(14)   a. The bulb is in the socket
       b. The flower is in the vase
       c. The umbrella is in his hand

The example in (13) is, I suggest, a consequence of the two parameters: Enclosure and Location with Surety. That is, by virtue of being located in the interior portion of the bounded landmark, the F is thereby enclosed. Moreover, by virtue of being enclosed, the F is located with surety: if the box is moved, so also is the F—the toy—as a direct consequence. That is, Location with Surety is entailed by Enclosure.

Evidence for thinking that the Location with Surety and Enclosure parameters are, nevertheless, distinct units of knowledge encoded as part of [ENCLOSURE]'s linguistic content comes from spatial scenes involving partial enclosure. In the examples in (14), the F is only partially enclosed by the bounded landmark: only the base of the bulb is enclosed by the socket as illustrated in Figure 8.1 above; only the stem, and not the whole flower, is enclosed by the vase (see Figure 8.3); and only the umbrella handle is enclosed by the hand (see Figure 8.4). Indeed,

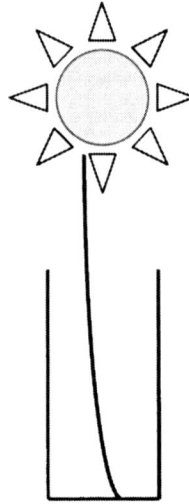

FIGURE 8.3. *The flower is in the vase*

FIGURE 8.4. *The umbrella is in his hand*

the reason that the vehicle *in* can relate to spatial scenes involving partial, as well as full, enclosure is due to the parameter of Location with Surety. It is precisely because the bounded LM that partially encloses the TR serves to provide location with surety that the vehicle *in* is sanctioned in these instances.

On the basis of the examples in (13) and (14), there is no reason, however, to be convinced that Enclosure and Location with Surety constitute distinct parameters, and hence distinct units of knowledge encoded as part of the linguistic content associated with the [ENCLOSURE] lexical concept.

However, the example in (8) above illustrates a crucial disjunction between the two. While the F, the bottle, is partially enclosed by the bounded LM, the cap, in exactly the same way as the relationship between the bulb and the socket in (7), the use of *in* in (8) is semantically anomalous. In the spatial scene designated by (8) the bottle is not located with surety by virtue of being partially enclosed by the cap. That is, the bottle's location is not determined by being partially enclosed by the cap—although access to its contents are. Hence, in a situation where partial enclosure applies, but location with surety does not, the [ENCLOSURE] lexical concept associated with *in* cannot be applied. This reveals that in the absence of the Location with Surety parameter, *in* cannot be applied to spatial scenes involving only partial enclosure.

So far we have discovered that the Enclosure parameter entails Location with Surety. Moreover, we have seen that in spatial scenes in which there is no location with surety, yet there is (partial) enclosure, as in the spatial scene to which (8) refers, the use of the [ENCLOSURE] lexical concept cannot apply.

We must next examine whether the Location with Surety parameter can be employed independently of the Enclosure parameter. If so, we can posit that there is a distinct lexical concept, which we can gloss as [LOCATION WITH SURETY], a lexical concept which encodes the Location with Surety parameter as part of its linguistic content but does not also feature the Enclosure parameter. Evidence for such a state of affairs is provided by the following example, which relates to the spatial scene depicted in Figure 8.5.

(15)   The pear is in the basket

In this example, the pear—in the centre of the image—is not enclosed by the basket, as it is supported by other fruit; although the supporting fruit are enclosed by the basket. Yet, the form *in* can be applied to this spatial scene, as is evident in (15). I argue that this is due to a [LOCATION WITH SURETY] lexical concept which sanctions this particular usage. While the [ENCLOSURE] lexical concept apparent in (13) and (14) encodes the Enclosure and Location with Surety parameters, the [LOCATION WITH SURETY] lexical concept encodes the Location with Surety parameter but not the Enclosure parameter as part of its linguistic content. This difference in linguistic content between the two lexical concepts explains the difference in linguistic behaviour in the

FIGURE 8.5. *The pear is in the basket*

examples just considered. The [ENCLOSURE] lexical concept requires full enclosure, or partial enclosure *plus* location with surety. However, in (15) neither full nor partial enclosure is apparent, yet *in* is sanctioned. This follows as the independent, but semantically related (and hence polysemous), [LO-CATION WITH SURETY] lexical concept sanctions this use. Thus, we see that there are, plausibly, at least two spatial lexical concepts associated with *in*: [ENCLOSURE] and [LOCATION WITH SURETY], which encode different con-figurations of parameters, and hence, subtly distinct linguistic content.[7]

"State" lexical concepts for in

I now turn to the "state" lexical concepts, in order to see how these arise from the spatial lexical concepts. Consider the following examples involving *in*.

(16)   a. He is in good health
        b. The girl is in love
        c. John is in trouble/debt
        d. He's in banking [i.e., works in the banking industry]

While each relates to a "state" of some kind, these examples in fact relate to slightly different "states": those that have a physical cause, as in (16a)—the state of being "in good health", which is a consequence of the physical condition of an organism's body—those that have a psychological or emo-tional cause, as in (16b)—the state is a consequence of a subjective state, which may (or may not) have physical, i.e., observable, manifestations—those that have a social/interpersonal cause, as in (16c)—resulting from social/interpersonal interactions which result in an externally maintained state—and those that are a result of a habitual professional activity, as in (16d). Put another way, each of these "states" co-occurs with distinct lexical concepts—they take distinct semantic arguments—which relate a particular entity to quite different sorts of states. Hence, there are four distinct sorts of semantic selectional tendencies in evidence, supporting the view that we are dealing with four distinct lexical profiles. In essence, I argue that these examples are sanctioned by four distinct "state" lexical concepts associated with the prep-ositional vehicle *in*. This is illustrated more clearly in the examples below:

          [PHYSIOLOGICAL STATE] (i.e., bodily state)
(17)   a. He's in poor/good health
        b. The woman is in labour

---

[7] The [LOCATION WITH SURETY] lexical concept appears to be restricted to use in contexts in which the location with surety is an indirect result of enclosure, as depicted in Figure 8.5 for instance. In view of this, the parameter encoded by this lexical concept might be better stated as Location with Surety due to Enclosure. It remains an empirical question as to whether this lexical concept will evolve such that it can be employed in a wider range of contexts.

[PSYCHOSOMATIC STATE] (i.e., subjective/internal state)
(18)   a. John is in shock/pain (over the break-up of the relationship)
       b. John is in love (with himself/the girl)

[SOCIO-INTERPERSONAL STATE] (i.e., externally maintained state)
(19)   a. The girl is in trouble (with the authorities)
       b. John is in debt (to the tune of £1000)

[PROFESSIONAL STATE] (i.e., professional activity habitually engaged in)
(20)   a. He is in banking
       b. She is in insurance

In addition to evidence based on semantic selectional tendencies, the position that there must be a number of distinct "state" lexical concepts associated with *in*, along the lines captured by the examples in (17) to (20) inclusive, can also be demonstrated by virtue of ambiguities associated with an utterance of the following kind:

(21)   She's in milk

The utterance in (21) could potentially be interpreted as relating to a woman who is nursing a baby, and thus lactating, or as relating to a woman who works in the dairy industry. That is, given an appropriate extra-linguistic context, an example such as this can be interpreted in at least two ways. The potential for divergent interpretations is a consequence, in part, of our knowledge that *in* has a number of distinct lexical concepts associated with it: what is relevant for this example is the distinction between a [PHYSIOLOGICAL STATE] lexical concept and a [PROFESSIONAL STATE] lexical concept. Moreover, ambiguities can be generated even when a relatively well-entrenched example is employed. For instance, even examples of the following kind:

(22)   She is in labour

(23)   He is in love

can be interpreted in alternate ways. For instance, (22) could be interpreted as relating to childbirth or to a professional activity, e.g., the trade union movement. Similarly, (23) could be interpreted as relating to an emotional state or a professional activity, e.g., marriage-guidance counselling. The former reading is only possible by virtue of assuming something akin to a [PSYCHOSOMATIC STATE] lexical concept which is distinct from a [PROFESSIONAL STATE] lexical concept. That is, both lexical concepts must exist if "love" can be interpreted in these ways in this example.

Derivation of the "state" lexical concepts

In this section I consider how the "state" lexical concepts for *in* exemplified in (17) to (20) inclusive may have been extended from the prototypical [ENCLOSURE] lexical concept.

I observed above that in previous work, Tyler and I (2003) argued that polysemy derives from regular processes of semantic change, in which situated implicatures associated with a particular context can become reanalysed as distinct sense-units—lexical concepts in present terms. That is, Tyler and I argued for a usage-based approach to language change, a position adopted by LCCM Theory.

In terms of an LCCM account of the emergence of the "state" lexical concepts for *in*, the trajectory is as follows. Situated implicatures arise in bridging contexts, as briefly discussed earlier. These are contexts in which a usage sanctioned by the relevant "spatial" lexical concept, such as the [EN-CLOSURE] lexical concept also gives rise to a situated implicature, such as an affecting condition. If the prepositional vehicle is repeatedly used in such bridging contexts, the situated implicature may give rise to the formation of a new parameter, or the detachment of an existing parameter as the core parameter of a new lexical concept. I argue below that bridging contexts involving the functional category of Affecting Conditions may have given rise to the formation of a number of related but distinct "state" parameters, and hence lexical concepts.

In order to trace the development of the functional category Affecting Conditions, we need to consider spatial scenes that might provide appropriate bridging contexts. To illustrate, consider the following expressions:

(24)   a. in the dust
       b. in the sand
       c. in the snow

While dust, sand, and snow are physical entities which can "enclose," they cannot normally fulfil the functions provided by, for instance, containers. That is, they do not typically serve to locate with surety, exceptional circumstances such as quicksand and avalanches excepted. For instance, dust, sand, and snow, by virtue of enclosing, do not normally have the structural attributes that allow an entity to be supported and thus transported (cf. a bucket), nor do they normally restrict access in the way a prison cell does, for instance.

Nevertheless, these examples exhibit some of the spatio-topological properties associated with the [ENCLOSURE] lexical concept. This is a consequence of the properties associated with these "bounded" landmarks: they provide an affecting condition, an environmental influence which affects our behaviour. For instance, they determine the kinds of apparel we wear, and how we behave when we are exposed to the dust/sand/snow, and so on. As such, these contexts of use provide bridging contexts: both enclosure and affecting conditions are implicated, and either (or both) may be understood. While examples such as sand, snow, and dust can be construed as enclosures with boundaries, there are other related examples of what we might refer to as Prevailing Conditions which are much less clear-cut in terms of the nature of the boundaries involved:

(25)   a. the flag in the storm
       b. the flag in the wind

   I suggest that these instances of *in* are sanctioned by virtue of there existing a distinct parameter Affecting Conditions, which forms part of the linguistic content encoded by a distinct [PREVAILING CONDITIONS] lexical concept. That is, the next stage in the development of a new lexical concept is for the parameter Affecting Conditions to be re-analysed as a core component of an independent lexical concept. Clearly a storm and wind are much less prototypically enclosures, and more saliently provide prevailing conditions which thereby constitute an environment which affects us. As such, spatial scenes involving more prototypical enclosures have given rise to the functional category Affecting Conditions, which has led to the formation of a distinct Affecting Conditions parameter in semantic memory. The existence of a distinct [PREVAILING CONDITIONS] lexical concept, as evidenced by examples in (25), provides suggestive evidence that such a distinct Affecting Conditions parameter exists.

   I argue that the distinct "state" lexical concepts associated with *in* evidenced in (17) to (20) encode the parameter Affecting Conditions, rather than Enclosure. Indeed, these lexical concepts are what I have referred to as "state" lexical concepts, as the states invoked all provide, in some sense, affecting conditions. Moreover, all these "state" lexical concepts are relatively, and to degrees, far removed from the physical notion of enclosure from which they most likely originally evolved. In essence, once an Affecting Conditions parameter becomes conventionalized, it can be applied to distinct kinds of affecting conditions, even those that are non-spatial in nature, such as states. This leads to the development of new lexical concepts.

   The first such "state" lexical concept relates to the physical condition of an organism which thus provides an affecting condition. Such physical conditions include good/ill health, pregnancy, and any salient physical aspect of the organism's condition which affects and thus impacts on the organism's functioning. This lexical concept I gloss as [PHYSIOLOGICAL STATE]. In addition to environmental and physical conditions, affecting conditions can be caused by psychosomatic states, such as grief, happiness, and sadness which are internal in nature. This "state" gives rise to a [PSYCHOSOMATIC STATE] lexical concept associated with *in*. In addition, social interactions which give rise to social or

Enclosure

|

Occlusion ——————— Spatial scenes ——————— Location with
Surety
involving enclosure

|

Affecting
Conditions

[PREVAILING   [PHYSIOLOGICAL   [PSYCHOSOMATIC   [SOCIO-INTERPERSONAL   [PROFESSIONAL
CONDITIONS]   STATE]   STATE]   STATE]   STATE]

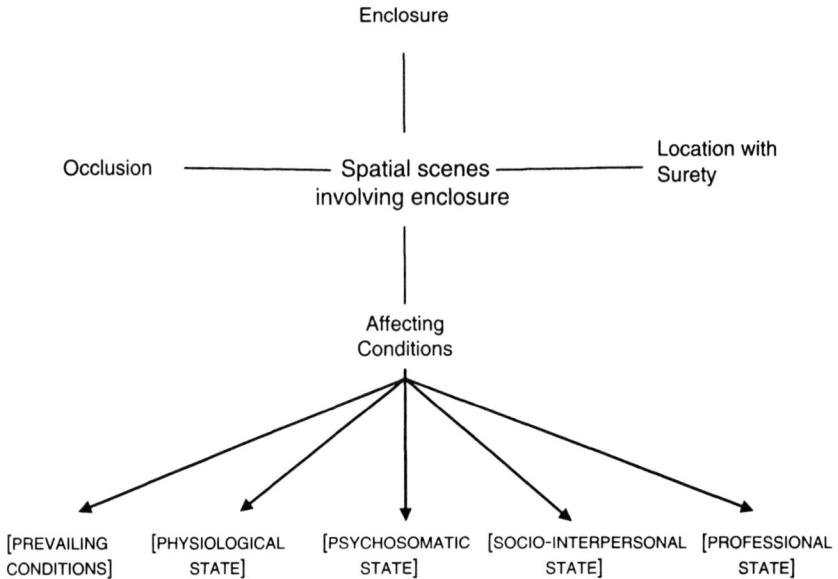

FIGURE 8.6. Parameters and their relationship with the "state" lexical concepts for *in*

interpersonal relationships lead to conditions which may affect the individual.
Such extrinsic or socially induced affecting conditions might include debts, or
other sorts of difficult situations which impose conditions on the behaviour
of an individual. This set of affecting conditions gives rise, I suggest, to what
I gloss as the [socio-interpersonal state] lexical concept associated with *in*.
Finally, one's habitual professional activity provides an affecting condition by
virtue of the physical and social interactions that are attendant upon such
activities. This provides an affecting condition giving rise to a lexical concept
glossed as [professional state] associated with *in*. The relationship between
the Affecting Conditions functional category and the range of non-spatial lexical
concepts for *in* discussed is summarized in Figure 8.6.

Lexical concepts for *on*

In this section I deal, somewhat more briefly, with lexical concepts associated
with the prepositional vehicle *on*.

[contact] *and its parameters*

The spatial relation designated by *on* involves the relation of contact or
proximity to the surface of a RO, and so the functional consequence of

being supported or upheld by it. I gloss the prototypical spatial lexical concept conventionally associated with *on* as [CONTACT]. This serves to encode the spatio-topological relation Contact and the parameter Support, derived from the corresponding functional category. The [CONTACT] lexical concept sanctions an example of the following sort:

(26)   the apple on the table

Note that evidence that the parameters Contact and Support are both encoded by the lexical concept [CONTACT] comes from the fact that *on* can only felicitously be employed to describe spatial scenes in which both parameters are apparent. For instance, if an apple is held against a wall by someone, the utterance in (27) is semantically anomalous. However, if the apple is affixed to the wall, for instance by glue, then (27) is entirely appropriate.

(27)   the apple on the wall

That is, while the apple is in contact with the wall in both scenarios, in the first scenario it is the person, rather than the wall, that affords support, while it is the wall, and the glue, which employs the wall as a means of affixing the apple, in the second. Hence, the example in (27) applies when there is both physical contact between the F and the RO, and when the latter has a role in supporting the former.

Indeed, there are a number of distinct "support" lexical concepts associated with *on* which privilege the Support parameter at the expense of the Contact parameter, as illustrated by the following examples:

[SUPPORTING BODY PART]
(28)   a. on one's feet/knees/legs/back
        b. on tiptoe
        c. on all fours

In the examples in (28), the use of *on* relates to that part of the body which provides support, rather than being concerned with contact. That is, *on all fours*, for instance, does not mean that something is in contact with all fours. Rather, the conventional interpretation is that "all fours" provides the means of support.

[MEANS OF CONVEYANCE]
(29)   a. on foot/horseback
        b. on the bus

With respect to the example in (29b), it is worth pointing out, as Herskovits (1988) does, that if children were playing on a stationary bus, for instance, that had been abandoned, then it would not be appropriate to say *on the bus*, but rather *in* would be more natural. This supports the view that the [MEANS OF

CONVEYANCE] lexical concept is a distinct "support" lexical concept encoded by *on*.

[SUPPORTING PIVOT]
(30)   The Earth turns on its axis

Again, in this example, being 'on' an axis has to do with being supported and thus, in this case, being able to turn. Other examples of more abstract support, ranging for chemical reliance, to rational support are illustrated below:

[CHEMICAL RELIANCE]
(31)   a. Are you on heroin?
        b. She's on the pill

[PSYCHOLOGICAL SUPPORT]
(32)   You can count/rely on my vote

[RATIONAL SUPPORT]
(33)   on account of/on purpose

The [ACTIVE STATE] *lexical concept*

There is just one "state" lexical concept for *on*, which I gloss as [ACTIVE STATE]. This lexical concept derives not from the functional category of Support. Rather, it pertains to a functional category concerning "functionality" or "activity." That is, in many spatial scenes, a consequence of contact is that the F, as it comes into contact with a particular surface, becomes functional. This category I refer to as Functional Actioning. Removing contact precludes functional actioning. Such forms of contact, for instance, invoke scenarios involving physical transmission, such as the very salient one of electricity. Many times a day we plug-in or switch "on" electrical appliances. It is by facilitating contact between the appliance and the electrical circuit that an appliance is rendered functional. A "switch" provides a means of facilitating this contact, which is why we employ the term "switch on" in English. In other words, I suggest that the [ACTIVE STATE] lexical concept associated with *on* encodes a Functional Actioning parameter as part of its linguistic content. It is this which makes it distinctive from the spatial lexical concepts of *on* discussed in the previous examples.

The [ACTIVE STATE] lexical concept associated with *on* relates to lexical concepts which concern a particular state that can be construed as "active" or "functional," as contrasted with a perhaps normative scenario in which the state does not hold. In other words, states described by instances of *on* sanctioned by this lexical concept are often temporally circumscribed and thus endure for a prescribed or limited period of time. In this, the states referred to are quite distinct from those that the "state" lexical concepts

Contact ——————— Spatial scenes ——————— Support
                 involving contact

                        |
                        |
                        |

            Functional Actioning

                        |
                        |
                        |

                [ACTIVE STATE]

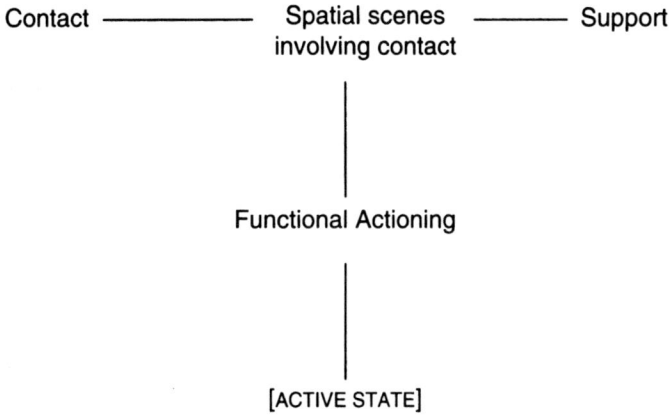

FIGURE 8.7. Parameters and their relationship with "state" lexical concepts associated with *on*

associated with *in* relate to. Here, the notion of being 'affected', apparent with *in*, is almost entirely absent. Consider some examples:

(34) a. on fire
      b. on live (i.e., a sports game)
      c. on tap (i.e., beer is available)
      d. on sleep (as in an alarm clock on a particular mode)
      e. on pause (as in a DVD player)
      f. on sale
      g. on loan
      h. on alert
      i. on best behaviour
      j. on look-out
      k. on the move
      l. on the wane
      m. on the run

Figure 8.7 depicts the parameter associated with this lexical concept.

The "state" senses for *at*

This section briefly examines the "state" lexical concepts associated with *at*.

[CO-LOCATION]: *the prototypical lexical concept for at*

The lexical concept which licenses spatial uses of *at* affords the most general expression of localization in space in English, expressing the relation between a F and a point of space that it is contiguous or proximal with. This lexical concept I gloss as [CO-LOCATION]. Consequently, it is one of the most polysemous of all English prepositions. Indeed, this lexical concept for *at* forms a **contrast set** (Tyler and Evans 2003) with the 'place' identifying lexical concepts associated with other prepositions. The [CO-LOCATION] lexical concept encodes the Co-location parameter, designating a highly abstract spatial relation between the F and a place, when the relation is not more precisely expressed by spatial lexical concepts associated with the following prepositional vehicles: *near, by, on, in, over, under,* all of which, at times, can be paraphrased by the situated use of the [CO-LOCATION] lexical concept.

Perhaps the most salient functional category associated with *at* constitutes what I will refer to as that of Practical Association. That is, a functional consequence of being co-located with a particular RO is that the F has some practical association with the reference object. This is evidenced in the following examples:

(35)   a. the man at the desk
       b. the schoolboy at the bus stop

In these examples, the relation that holds between the F and the RO is more specific than a spatio-topological relation. That is, the example in (34a) implies, and is understood to mean, that not only is the F in question, *the man*, in close proximity to his desk, but he is also working at his desk (or at least in a position to do so). Similarly, in (34b), in addition to the co-location relation, this expression implies that the schoolboy is "waiting" at the bus stop, presumably for a bus. In other words, part of the linguistic content associated with the [CO-LOCATION] lexical concept appears to be derived from functional consequences of spatial scenes.

The "state" lexical concepts for *at*

There are three distinct lexical concepts associated with the prepositional vehicle *at* that might be described as relating to "states." These are illustrated below:

       [STATE OF EXISTENCE]
(36)   at rest/peace/ease/liberty
       (e.g., *He stood at ease,* or *He is at peace* [=dead])

       [STATE OF MUTUAL RELATIONS]
(37)   at war/variance/strife/one/daggers drawn/loggerheads
       (e.g., *The EU is at war with the US over the imposition of steel tariffs*)

       [AFFECTING EXTERNAL STATE]
(38)   at peril/risk/hazard/expense/an advantage/a disadvantage
       (e.g., *The company is at risk of going under*)

The "state" lexical concepts associated with *at* appear to be motivated by the functional consequence of close proximity between two point-like entities giving rise to the formation of a parameter: Practical Association. The "state" lexical concepts appear to have arisen from specific contexts in which a practical association holds.

In the case of the [STATE OF EXISTENCE] lexical concept, the practical association resulting from the co-location is the state of existence which holds. That is, there is a practical association which holds between a given entity and its state of existence.

The second lexical concept I gloss as [STATE OF MUTUAL RELATIONS], as evidenced by (37). This lexical concept arises due to a salient practical association resulting from co-location of two entities involving mutual relations. For instance, while warfare often involves combatants who must be proximal to one another, the state of being "at war" need not, as evidenced by the so-called "phoney war" which held during 1939 when the United Kingdom, France, and Germany were officially "at war", and yet no troops engaged. Thus, the use of *at* to designate a state of mutual relations, independent of spatio-topological co-location, is due to the parameter of Practical Association being invoked as part of the linguistic content encoded by this lexical concept. Put another way, this lexical concept encodes a state of a particular kind, rather than the spatial notion of proximity.

Finally, states pertaining to external circumstances may relate to evaluations concerning circumstances associated with mutual relations. This is instantiated by the lexical concept which I gloss as [AFFECTING EXTERNAL STATE], as evidenced by the examples in (38). The relationship between the

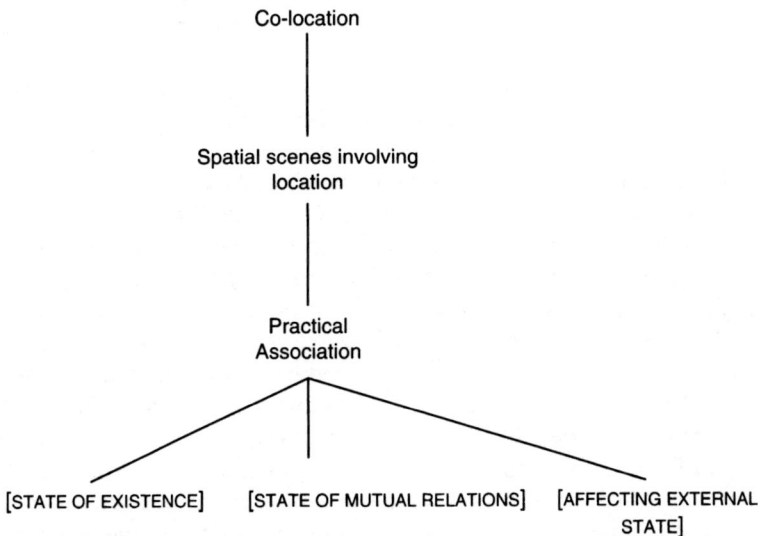

FIGURE 8.8. Parameters and their relationship with "state" lexical concepts for *at*

parameter of Practical Association and the "state" lexical concepts is dia-grammed in Figure 8.8.

Summary

In this chapter I have addressed the phenomenon of polysemy in the light of LCCM Theory. In LCCM Theory, polysemy relates not to the variation evident in the situated semantic contribution of a word. Rather, it is a consequence of a single vehicle being associated with distinct lexical concepts which are semantically related. Semantic relatedness is a matter of degree and is determined by the bipartite structure of lexical concepts. The way in which open-class as well as closed-class polysemous lexical concepts can be related is by virtue of shared or overlapping linguistic content, for instance in terms of shared parameters. The second way concerns the nature of the conceptual structure that open-class lexical concepts afford potential access to. I exam-ined polysemy by way of a detailed case study of the spatial and "state" lexical concepts associated with the English prepositional vehicles *in*, *on*, and *at*. The main conclusions arising from this case study are as follows.

Firstly, the perspective offered here, particularly with respect to the con-struct of the lexical concept, allows us to establish in a reasonably precise way the nature of the distinction between the "state" lexical concepts associated with the vehicles *in*, *on*, and *at*. That is, given that lexical concepts are vehicle-specific and moreover have distinct lexical profiles—for instance they have distinct semantic selectional tendencies—we are able to quite clearly see that the "state" lexical concepts (within and between) prepositions are distinct.

Secondly, by taking seriously the functional nature of spatial relations, and the formation of parameters: highly abstract knowledge structures specialized for being directly encoded *in* language, this allows us to understand the sorts of functional motivations, and thus distinctions, between the "state" lexical concepts across different prepositional vehicles.

Thirdly, prepositional vehicles, particularly *in* and *at* have more than one "state" lexical concept associated with them. We have seen that the prototyp-ical spatial lexical concept associated with a given vehicle is associated, typically, with a number of parameters, derived from what I referred to as functional categories. Providing an LCCM analysis gives us a way of estab-lishing the sorts of distinctions that exist between the "state" lexical concepts associated with the same vehicle. That is, we have a means of understanding how these lexical concepts are distinct—based on a distinction in parameters encoded. We also have a means of empirically verifying hypotheses as to distinctions in the underlying lexical concepts which are assumed to sanction instances of use. This is due to the construct of the lexical profile. In this chapter I employed the notion of semantic selectional tendencies, one of the two types of linguistic content which make up the lexical profile, in order to distinguish between putatively distinct lexical concepts.

9

Conceptual structure

A defining assumption of LCCM Theory is that knowledge representation in humans makes use of multiple forms of representation. In particular, I assume that there are (at least) two distinct core systems which are necessary both for knowledge representation and for linguistically mediated communication: a linguistic system and a conceptual system. Previous chapters in this part of the book have addressed the first of these systems, and have been concerned with linguistic knowledge, which takes the form of symbolic units, encompassing phonological vehicles and lexical concepts. In this chapter, and the next, I turn to the second core system: the conceptual system, the repository of human concepts.

In this chapter I am concerned, in broad terms, with conceptual structure: the nature and organization of concepts. I am also concerned with the way in which language interfaces with the conceptual system in service of situated meaning construction. A key feature of knowledge representation in humans is that the linguistic system interacts with the conceptual system in order to facilitate access to conceptual knowledge. Indeed, as the philosopher of cognitive science Jesse Prinz (2002: 14) has observed:

Concepts must be capable of being shared by different individuals and by one individual at different times. This requirement...must be satisfied if concepts are to play some of their most important explanatory roles...it is almost universally assumed that concepts play a pivotal role in linguistic communication.

Indeed, a fundamental design feature of human cognition is that linguistic representations provide an indexing and control function, greatly increasing the range of uses and flexibility of the human conceptual system. However, this does not mean that linguistic representations are equivalent to the concepts which populate the conceptual system.

I assume that the human conceptual system is, *en grandes lignes*, continuous with the primate conceptual system. Recent findings suggest that such an assumption is not unreasonable (e.g., Barsalou 2005; Hurford 2007). Given the relatively recent emergence of language, and the far greater antiquity of the conceptual system[1] I assume that linguistic representations evolved to

---

[1] For discussion, a sample of relevant book-length treatments from various perspectives include Corballis (2003), Deacon (1997), Donald (1991), Dunbar (1996), Mithen (1996), Hurford (2007), and Renfrew (2007). See also the excellent collection of papers in Christiansen and Kirby (2003).

complement and enhance the existing form of representations that inhere in the conceptual system, rather than duplicating them. The approach to encyclopaedic semantics widely assumed in cognitive linguistics, discussed in Chapter 2 and addressed in further detail below, has tended to assume that the semantic structures encoded by language are equivalent to conceptual representations, i.e., concepts. That is, it has often been assumed that semantic structure is equivalent to, or at least, not significantly distinct from conceptual structure.[2] Indeed, this is a perspective that is shared by a wide range of scholars in other traditions too.[3] Hence, part of my task in this chapter is to suggest a revised perspective on encyclopaedic semantics. I do so by providing an overview of the distinctive nature of conceptual structure. Accordingly, I draw on recent work in cognitive psychology, in particular, the Theory of **Perceptual Symbol Systems** (PSS Theory) developed by Lawrence Barsalou (1999, 2003).

The overarching purpose of this chapter is to present an overview of what I mean by conceptual structure. It is, in large part, for this reason that I introduce Barsalou's PSS Theory, which is the best-developed, and most complete, theory of simulation semantics currently available. PSS Theory is not without its drawbacks, however. For instance, the use by Barsalou (1999) of the term "perceptual" to cover a wide range of body-based states, including experiences which are patently not perceptual, such as affective, cognitive, and emotional states, is potentially confusing. Moreover, the use of the term "perceptual symbol" is suggestive that percepts can serve to re-present perceptual (in Barsalou's sense) knowledge. This begs the question as to what perceptual symbols re-present to, throwing up the spectre of approaches to knowledge representation which assume (or imply) an internal homunculus. Notwithstanding the potentially problematic nature of some aspects of Barsalou (1999), I present below a version of PSS Theory in order to illustrate the sort of substrate that inheres in the conceptual system, as envisioned by LCCM Theory.

Future work in simulation semantics may reveal that some (or even all) aspects of Barsalou's theory require revision. And, in important respects, it is not a requirement of LCCM Theory that Barsalou's account stands the test of time. What is important for LCCM Theory, however, is the perspective that a simulation account plays at least some role in our model of how knowledge is represented in the mind. This commitment to a simulation-type account follows for two reasons. Firstly, findings from cognitive linguistics provide compelling evidence that language and mind are embodied. This being so, an account of conceptual structure that is grounded in the specific modalities of

---

[2] In fairness, cognitive linguists have primarily been concerned with developing cognitively realistic accounts of linguistic representation. Hence, they have not always been unduly concerned with the architecture of the conceptual system. However, such accounts cannot achieve psychological plausibility unless they mesh with recent findings on the nature of conceptual structure from cognitive psychology and the other relevant cognitive sciences.

[3] See Barsalou *et al.* (1993) for discussion.

the brain is more plausible than an amodal account. Secondly, simulation accounts, such as Barsalou's, explicitly assume, and posit, that representations are componential. This is also a finding of LCCM Theory based on linguistic evidence. For instance, I argued in earlier chapters that lexical concepts comprise, in part, distinct and often (typically) multiple parameters. Hence, a simulation-style account of conceptual structure is compatible with findings from LCCM Theory. Accordingly, with the provisos given above, I illustrate what conceptual structure might look like by presenting Barsalou's PSS theory. In so doing, this chapter thus sets the scene for the detailed development of the cognitive model—the unit of conceptual structure relevant for language—in the next chapter.

Embodied cognition

Theories of knowledge representation, dominant for much of the twentieth century, possess what Barsalou (e.g., 1999) refers to as an **amodal character**. Such theories assume that knowledge representation involves the manipulation of abstract symbols which are purely propositional in nature, and hence are not grounded in bodily states.[4] Recent accounts of knowledge representation are **modal** or embodied, because they treat knowledge as being grounded in the perceptual experiences and mechanisms that result from having the kinds of bodies we, as humans, have. Hence, conceptual knowledge arises from the modal systems that give rise to specific sorts of information. Barsalou (2008), in a recent review, refers to this perspective on knowledge representation as grounded cognition (as I noted in Chapter 2). Work on the embodied (or grounded) basis of cognition in cognitive linguistics, especially as associated with the work of George Lakoff and Mark Johnson (Lakoff and Johnson 1980, 1999; Lakoff 1987; Johnson 1987, 2007) has emphasized the role of sensory-motor experience, and hence perception—the processing of external stimuli via sensory (or modal) systems (vision, audition, olfaction, haptics, and gustation)—action—which provides motor information relating to bodily states via proprioception—information about movements involving joints and muscles—as well as the vestibular system—which provides information as to position in space and motion trajectories.[5]

However, other cognitive scientists have argued that, in addition, subjective (or introspective) experiences are just as important for grounding cognition. For instance, Damasio (1994) in his review of some of his groundbreaking work on emotion has emphasized a number of categories of feelings that arise from internal body states. For instance, body states (emotions) that we label as Happiness, Sadness, Anger, Fear, and Disgust, give rise to phenomenologically

---

[4] See Lakoff (1987) for a detailed critique of such disembodied accounts.
[5] See Evans (forthcoming *b*) for a review of the operation of the sensory mechanisms responsible for sense perception.

real, in the sense of directly experienced **feelings**. Damasio identifies a further category of feeling, what he terms **background feelings,** which derive from internal body states. Background feelings arise from, among other things, interoceptive experience, which is to say the visceral sense—our felt sense of the internal organs and other internal bodily states. Other subjective experiences, which are directly felt, include various aspects of temporal experience which arise from bodily states (circadian rhythms such as the wake–sleep cycle), as well as perceptual processing, which is subserved by a wide range of neurologically instantiated temporal mechanisms (see Evans 2004a, 2004b and references therein), and consciousness (Chafe 1994; Grady 1997). Hence, and as we shall see later when I discuss abstract concepts, cognition is grounded in both sensory-motor experience and subjective experience: experience of internal bodily and cognitive states, including emotion, mood, and affect.

In sum, contemporary accounts of embodied (or grounded) cognition assume that recordings of perceptual states form the basis of the representations that populate the conceptual system. Further, as the conceptual system has, on this view, evolved in order to facilitate perception, as well as situated action (including social interaction), and provides the necessary platform for higher-order cognitive operations such as categorization, inferencing, and conceptualization (Barsalou *et al.* forthcoming), perceptual states must be recoverable. Many recent accounts of embodied cognition postulate that recorded perceptual states are activated in service of the various functions the conceptual system supports. As already noted earlier in the book, these activations are referred to as simulations (e.g., Barsalou 1999, 2003; Gallese and Lakoff 2005; Kaschak and Glenberg 2000; Prinz 2002; Glenberg and Kaschak 2002; Zwaan 1999, 2004). Simulation represents, on this view, a general-purpose computation performed by the brain in order to recover bodily states and to perform operations deploying such multimodal states. As we shall see below, multimodal states can be manipulated in simulations in order to provide conceptualizations that are not present in the recorded perceptual states themselves. For instance, phenomena such as analogical counterfactuals are a case in point, as when we say: "In France, Bill Clinton would never have been harmed by his affair with Monica Lewinsky."[6] The account of Conceptual Blending Theory (Fauconnier 1997; Fauconnier and Turner 2002) represents one attempt to show how simulations deploy a range of existing knowledge representations in order to produce novel scenarios, categories, and inferences.

Perceptual Symbol Systems

The theory of Perceptual Symbol Systems (PSS Theory), as presented in Barsalou (1999), is a theory of grounded cognition which aims to account for how

---

[6] See Evans and Green (2006: ch. 12) for a discussion of this analogical counterfactual from the perspective of Conceptual Blending Theory.

perceptual and other body-based states come to be captured in memory, and to be available for (re)activation as simulations. It is well known from research on attention that during perceptual experience, the cognitive system can focus attention on individual components of the stimulus array. For instance, attention can selectively focus on the colour of an object, filtering out, for instance, its shape, or texture, and even the surrounding objects (Garner 1974, 1978).

The essential insight of PSS Theory is that, through selective attention, individual perceptual components derived from modality-specific experience are recorded, in bottom-up fashion, in sensory-motor areas of the brain.[7] The components are stored in schematic fashion. This means that it is not individual perceptual states that are stored, but rather commonalities are abstracted across specific instances of perceptual states providing individual memories (e.g., individual memories for *red, hot,* and *purr*). In addition, knowledge is captured from other types of perceptual state, including proprioception (e.g., *lift, run*) and subjective experience (e.g., *compare, similar, hungry*). Accordingly, Barsalou uses the term "perceptual" more widely than has traditionally been the case.[8] These schematic memories Barsalou refers to as **perceptual symbols**. They are symbols in the sense that, later, in top-down fashion, they can be reactivated, or simulated, and can be used to support the range of symbolic behaviours that subserve a fully functional conceptual system.

Perceptual symbols implement a conceptual system as follows. Barsalou argues that memories of similar and related components become organized into a system of perceptual symbols which exhibit coherence. This perceptual symbol system he refers to as a frame. A frame is an information structure consisting of large collections of perceptual symbols, encoding information which is stable over time as well as incorporating variability. Hence, a frame provides a unified, and hence coherent, representation of a particular entity. For instance, a frame involves numerous components that have a perceptual basis, that are related in various ways. In addition, the perceptual symbols that collectively comprise the frame can be combined in a range of ways, giving rise to an infinite variety of simulations. Hence, a system of perceptual symbols gives rise to both a frame: a relatively stable knowledge matrix and dynamic simulations.[9] Together, the frame and simulations are referred to as a simulator (a term I first introduced in Chapter 4).

---

[7] There is compelling neuropsychological and neuroimaging evidence which supports the view that human conceptual representations are grounded in the modalities, and hence are perceptual in nature. For instance, categorical knowledge is grounded in sensory-motor regions of the brain (for reviews see Damasio 1989; Gainotti *et al.* 1995; Pulvermüller 1999, 2003). Damage to a particular sensory-motor region serves to impair the processing of categories that use the region in question to perceive physical exemplars.

[8] I will henceforth use "perceptual" in Barsalou's more inclusive sense, while pointing the reader to the provisos outlined at the outset of the chapter.

[9] Detailed examples of frames are provided in the next chapter.

Properties of perceptual symbols

Perceptual symbols are characterized by six key properties:

- perceptual symbols are neural representations in the brain's sensory-motor areas
- perceptual symbols are schematic
- perceptual symbols are dynamic, not rigid
- perceptual symbols are componential, not holistic
- perceptual symbols need not represent specific entities
- perceptual symbols can be indeterminate and generic

I briefly discuss each of these properties below.

Perceptual symbols are neural representations in the brain's sensory-motor areas

In PSS Theory, perceptual symbols constitute the records of the neural states that underlie perceptual experience (i.e., perception, proprioception, and subjective experience). Following Damasio (1989), Barsalou argues that **convergence zones** serve to integrate information from outside sense perception—for example, perceptual states relating to subjective experience—in sensory-motor maps. Hence, subjective experience also gives rise to perceptual symbols represented in the brain's sensory-motor systems.

Perceptual symbols are schematic

Perceptual symbols arise from abstracting across instances of particular perceptual states to provide memories of points of similarity. Hence, perceptual symbols are not exactly the same as perceptual states, but are rather somewhat schematic memories of them.

Perceptual symbols are dynamic, not rigid

Perceptual symbols constitute associative patterns of neurons. The subsequent amendment of a perceptual symbol, by virtue of updating, means that connections between neurons may not be reinstated in the same way prior to updating. Hence, perceptual symbols constitute dynamic, rather than rigid representations, whose character changes as ongoing perceptual states are incorporated into the perceptual symbol.

Perceptual symbols are componential, not holistic

Perceptual symbols represent components of a given modal stream, rather than a holistic representation. This position is supported by findings relating to the neuro-anatomy of the visual system, for instance. As is well established the visual system separates different kinds of visual information into distinct types of representations (e.g., Livingstone and Hubel 1988; Zeki 1992; Zeki and Shipp 1988). For instance, according to Zeki (1992) there are multiple representations for shape, including distinct representations for static form and dynamic form, and so on. There are also distinct channels for processing other dimensions of visual information including colour, movement, and location.

Perceptual symbols need not represent specific entities

As perceptual symbols are schematic representations, the same perceptual symbol can represent a variety of referents, for instance, multiple instances of *purr* or *red*.

Perceptual symbols can be indeterminate and generic

Perceptual symbols encode qualitative as well as quantitative information. This follows as some neurons are specialized for encoding qualitative information. For example, a qualitative neuron can encode the presence of an entity without encoding its shape, position, or orientation. In this way, perceptual symbols can be indeterminate with respect to metric details and hence also generic.

Properties of simulators

Simulators are characterized by five key properties:

- simulators consist of frames
- frames are multimodal, analogue representations
- frames are structured
- simulators facilitate simulations
- simulators implement fully functional conceptual processes

I briefly address each of these properties below:

Simulators consist of frames

Simulators are comprised of coherent constellations of perceptual symbols, in the sense described above, which are organized into frames. Frames are large-scale coherent knowledge structures of different types, as described in more detail in the next chapter.

Frames are multimodal, analogue representations

Frames incorporate perceptual symbols captured from across the sensory modalities, as well as introspection and subjective experience. Hence, they are multimodal in nature. In addition, as the perceptual symbols are recordings of perceptual experience, they constitute analogue representations: they are directly grounded in embodied experience (both sensory and subjective experience), and hence have the same form as the experiences they are records of.

Frames are structured

Frames are not unstructured bodies of perceptual knowledge. On the contrary, they are highly structured and exhibit diverse types, as discussed in the next chapter.

Simulators facilitate simulations

A simulator provides a means of reactivating the recorded perceptual states. These reactivations are known as simulations. Simulations serve to implement conceptual processes, as discussed next.

Simulators implement fully functional conceptual processes

A simulator is not just a record of various perceptual states. A simulator implements fully functional conceptual abilities. This is achieved via simulations, which serve to combine perceptual symbols in order to produce novel activations which subserve a complex range of conceptual processes. These include the following:

- Categorization: individual entities (tokens) can be matched with frames (types).
- Productivity: complex concepts can be constructed from simpler ones via simulations which combine sets of perceptual symbols in novel ways. That is, perceptual symbols are compositional in that they can combine to produce larger wholes. To illustrate this, imagine a circle. Now imagine a red circle. Now imagine a dotted red circle. PSS Theory posits that to form a red circle you combined perceptual symbols for circle and red. To form a dotted red circle, you added, in addition, a perceptual symbol for dots. That is, these "additions" are transformations on the perceptual symbol for circle, akin to the kind of transformations observed in the literature on imagery (e.g., Finke 1989; Shepard and Cooper 1982).
- Inferencing: simulations can be deployed in order to draw inferences regarding associations of various sorts.
- Reason: simulations can be employed in order to reason about various states of affairs on the basis of a particular premise.
- Choice: simulations can be deployed in order to create imagined or counterfactual scenarios in order to facilitate choice.

Encyclopaedic semantics revisited

The previous sections in this chapter have been concerned with providing a brief overview of the nature and organization of conceptual structure in the light of recent work in cognitive linguistics and, in particular, cognitive psychology. In this section, I briefly review the key aspects associated with the thesis of encyclopaedic semantics first presented in Chapter 2. I do so in order to prepare the ground for a revision of this approach later in the chapter, in the light of what we now know about the nature of conceptual structure.

The thesis of encyclopaedic semantics

The thesis of encyclopaedic semantics is one of the central assumptions of cognitive linguistics, and is fundamental for much research that is conducted within the two sub-branches of cognitive linguistics: cognitive semantics and cognitive approaches to grammar (see Evans and Green 2006 for a review).

More than any other researcher in cognitive linguistics, Langacker (1987, 1991a, 2008) has been responsible for developing the thesis of encyclopaedic semantics. He does this in adducing a "conceptual" semantics that underpins his theory of Cognitive Grammar. Langacker's view of encyclopaedic semantics is based on two assumptions: (i) that the semantic structure associated with words directly accesses conceptual structure, and (ii) words and other symbolic units cannot be understood independently of the larger knowledge structures, the encyclopaedic domains of conceptual knowledge, to which words serve as "points of access." In essence, Langacker's claim is that semantic structure is equivalent to conceptual structure; that is, the semantic structure associated with a lexical form *is* conceptual structure. In the next section, I explore the details of this claim.

Profile/base organization in cognitive grammar

As we briefly saw in Chapter 2, in Cognitive Grammar the semantic structure conventionally associated with a symbolic unit, such as a word, is equated with a subset of conceptual structure. For Langacker, conceptual knowledge is organized into domains: conceptual entities of varying levels of complexity and organization, which are organized in terms of a hierarchical network of knowledge. The set of domains to which a word provides access is referred to as a domain matrix.[10]

For example, consider the concept with which the word form *knuckle* is equated. This concept is understood with respect to the domain HAND, which is to say all the knowledge we have concerning what a hand is: for instance, its shape, its component parts, how it functions, and so on. In turn, the domain

---

[10] Recall the discussion in Chapter 3.

HAND is understood with respect to the domain ARM, which, in turn is understood with the respect to the domain BODY. This domain is understood, ultimately, with respect to the domain of SPACE. In this way, the relationship between domains reflects meronymic (part-whole) relations, with one domain being part of a larger more inclusive domain. The most inclusive domains are what Langacker refers to as **basic domains**. Basic domains are directly grounded in embodied experience, and thus have a pre-conceptual basis, as illustrated in Table 9.1.

As we saw in Chapter 2, Langacker argues that the semantic structure conventionally associated with a given vehicle, such as *knuckle*, consists of profile/base organization. The profile for knuckle, for instance, what is designated, consists of the various joints in one's fingers, thumb, or hand. A human hand contains fourteen knuckles. The base constitutes a larger structure, within the domain matrix, which is essential for understanding what the knuckle designates. Put another way, the conventional semantic representation associated with the form *knuckle* consists of a substructure (the profile) of a larger conceptual structure (the base), within a domain matrix (a series of hierarchically linked domains of knowledge). Langacker suggests that evidence that the base relates to the hand, rather than some other structure, e.g., the arm, comes from examples such as the following:

(1)   a. My hand has 14 knuckles
       b. #My arm has 14 knuckles

While it is semantically acceptable to provide the utterance in (1a), the utterance in (1b) is decidedly odd, as represented by the hash sign. In sum, the position adopted by Langacker is that semantic structure directly relates to conceptual knowledge.

TABLE 9.1. Partial inventory of basic domains (after Langacker 1987)

Basic Domain	Pre-conceptual Basis
SPACE	Visual system; motion and position (proprioceptive) sensors in skin, muscles, and joints; vestibular system (located in the auditory canal; detects motion and balance)
COLOUR	Visual system
PITCH	Auditory system
TEMPERATURE	Tactile (touch) system
PRESSURE	Pressure sensors in the skin, muscles and joints
PAIN	Detection of tissue damage by nerves under the skin
ODOUR	Olfactory (smell) system
TIME	Temporal awareness
EMOTION	Affective (emotion) system

A more complex example of profile/base organization is illustrated by the relational lexical concept associated with the form *uncle*. In Cognitive Grammar, the semantic structure associated with *uncle* profiles an entity with a complex domain matrix. This includes at least the following abstract domains: GENEALOGY, PERSON, GENDER, SEXUAL INTERCOURSE, BIRTH, LIFE CYCLE, PARENT/CHILD RELATIONSHIP, SIBLING RELATIONSHIP, EGO. The base for the semantic representation for *uncle* is drawn from across a number of these domains to provide the conceived network of FAMILIAL RELATIONS represented in Figure 9.1. Against this base, *uncle* profiles an entity related to the EGO by virtue of being a MALE SIBLING of EGO's mother or father.

FIGURE 9.1. The familial network which forms the base against which the entity designated by *uncle* is profiled (Adapted from Evans and Green 2006: 239)

The distinctiveness of the linguistic and conceptual systems

In certain respects, the thesis of encyclopaedic semantics developed by Langacker and others in cognitive linguistics provides an extremely useful way of thinking about linguistic semantics and its relationship with conceptual structure. The claim that words directly encode conceptual structure serves to distinguish Cognitive Grammar and other cognitive linguistic accounts of linguistic semantics and grammar from formal approaches which assume, like literalism,[11] that words pattern after reference to an objective reality "out there." In this then, Cognitive Grammar, and cognitive linguistic theories more generally take a **representational** rather than a **denotational** perspective on semantic representation. Moreover, by virtue of assuming that semantic structure encoded by language directly activates conceptual knowledge, cognitive linguistic theories can get on with the business of conducting linguistic semantic analyses that are claimed to be cognitively realistic, without being unduly concerned about possible distinctions between the representational format of language and other representational systems.[12]

Yet while such an approach is reasonable, there exists evidence that the representational formats in the linguistic and conceptual systems significantly diverge. In Chapter 6, for instance, I reviewed linguistic evidence which points to a bifurcation in the nature of the content associated with linguistic expressions: the distinction between schematic and rich content. This distinction, and moreover, the existence of lexical patterns that are variously termed "grammatical," "functional," or "closed-class," points to the view that there is something distinct about the representational format that language affords, vis-à-vis the way in which concepts are represented.[13]

The thrust of my argument is that it is now apposite to confront the possibility—I would argue, the reality—that linguistic and conceptual representations diverge, precisely in order to achieve a (genuinely) cognitively realistic account of language. Moreover, such an account provides the means for investigating the way in which semantic structure and conceptual structure interface, in order to provide a joined-up theory of semantic representation: an account of the interface between the linguistic and conceptual systems. Such an account will, I suggest, additionally facilitate the development of theories of backstage cognition—for example Conceptual Blending Theory—which can thus be stated with greater precision than is possible presently.

---

[11] Recall the discussion in Chapter 1.

[12] There are exceptions to this of course. Recent work under the rubric of the Neural Theory of Language (NTL) has begun attempting to model language in a framework that takes seriously the various representational systems that the brain appears to make use of. For a general statement on the NTL project see Feldman and Narayanan (2004). For one attempt to sketch the formalism necessary to model linguistic representations in the light of how they interface with non-linguistic representations see Bergen and Chang (2005).

[13] This is an issue we shall revisit below.

Accordingly, in this section I deploy a recent theory relating to the inter-action between the linguistic and conceptual systems—the **Theory of Language and Situated Simulation** (Barsalou *et al.* forthcoming). This theory is, in fact, a reformulation of, and based upon, PSS Theory presented above. Its distinctiveness lies in the way it seeks to account for the interaction between the conceptual and linguistic systems. I introduce this account here in order to provide a basis for developing in detail the LCCM perspective on the nature and distinctiveness of the conceptual system, vis-à-vis the linguistic system. As such, I seek to evaluate and revise the thesis of encyclopaedic semantics presented in the previous section.

Language and Situated Simulation Theory

Language and Situated Simulation Theory (**LASS Theory** for short), as developed in Barsalou *et al.* forthcoming) is based on, and in certain respects revises, Barsalou's theory of Perceptual Symbol Systems (PSS Theory), dis-cussed above. LASS Theory holds that knowledge is made up of distinct types, notably representations which inhere in a **simulation system**—that is a conceptual system[14]—and representations which inhere in a linguistic system. Crucially, the representations which make up each of these two systems are of a wholly different format, and hence the systems constitute distinct forms of knowledge available to the human organism.

As with PSS Theory, LASS Theory assumes that the conceptual system is made up of representations which are grounded in the modal systems of the brain. These representations are derived from perceiving, from action and from subjective experience. To illustrate, take the example of perceiving a cat. The brain records perceptual information derived from modalities relating to vision, audition, and the somatosensory system. This provides information relating to how cats look, sound, and feel. In addition, as the human experi-encer interacts with cats, for example, stroking or feeding, information relating to appropriate and relevant actions is captured from motor actions and proprioception. The brain additionally records information relating to subjective states such as the experiencer's affective response to the interaction with the cat. On later occasions, the experience, or experiences, which gave rise to one (or more) of the perceptual states, can be simulated in the sense described earlier. Hence, the conceptual system is analogue in nature, as the representations that populate it are captured directly from perceptual experi-ence and therefore have a perceptual character.[15]

One reason for thinking that the conceptual and linguistic systems are distinct derives from the fact that while other organisms must have conceptual

[14] I shall continue to use the term "conceptual system" rather than "simulation system," and treat the two as synonymous.

[15] It is precisely because the conceptual system gives rise to reactivations of perceptual states, namely simulations, that it is referred to, in LASS Theory, as a simulation system.

representations, only humans possess language. Recent research in primatology reveals continuity across species, both human and other primates in terms of the conceptual system. Hurford (2007), for instance, reviews a welter of evidence which suggests that other species, and particularly primates, construct rich representations of the world around them, including the ability to refer to objects, to represent entities in their absence, to remember past events, and also appear to have elements of propositional thought. Barsalou (2005) also reports on recent findings in which evidence has emerged that Macaque monkeys have a modality-specific circuit in their brains for representing conceptual knowledge associated with social knowledge. Barsalou argues that this finding shows striking parallels with human conceptual representations: macaques appear to represent conceptual knowledge in modality-specific ways, as appears to be the case for humans. In other words, there is good evidence supporting the view that there is continuity between the conceptual systems exhibited by humans and other primates.

Barsalou *et al.* (forthcoming) argue that the conceptual system that evolved in humans and other primates did so in order to process non-linguistic stimuli, notably perceptual, motor, and introspective dimensions of experience. This being the case, it makes sense that the relatively recent emergence of language in modern humans—full-blown language is likely to only have emerged in the last 200,000 years[16]—relates to a system which is distinct from that of the evolutionarily more ancient conceptual system.

According to LASS Theory, the linguistic system evolved in order to provide an executive control function with respect to the conceptual system. That is, the representations which populate the linguistic system involve linguistic vehicles—which might be auditory, orthographic, or signed—and encode selectional tendencies, in the sense of the theoretical construct of the lexical profile developed in Chapter 6.[17] In addition, linguistic representations serve to index representations in the conceptual system with which they are associated.

LASS Theory makes two specific proposals with respect to lexical processing and knowledge representation which are noteworthy. Firstly, LASS Theory claims that the time course in terms of activation of the linguistic versus conceptual representations exhibit distinct and non-simultaneous patterns. This follows, as argued by Barsalou *et al.*, precisely because there are two distinct systems: while they interface, the two systems involve distinct trajectories of activation. In particular, LASS Theory assumes that when a word is perceived, the linguistic system (LS) becomes engaged immediately in order to categorize the linguistic representation. An associated simulation in the conceptual system (CS) becomes engaged slightly later, with the activation of the linguistic system

---

[16] See the following for discussion: Burling (2007), Johansson (2005), Mithen (1996), Renfrew (2007).

[17] On this account, semantic structure is somewhat more impoverished than is claimed by LCCM Theory—about which I will have more to say later in the chapter.

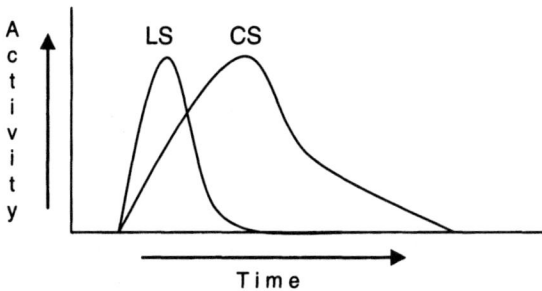

FIGURE 9.2. The respective activation of linguistic and conceptual knowledge associated with the linguistic and conceptual systems in the processing of a word (adapted from Barsalou *et al.* forthcoming)

peaking before the associated simulation. This is illustrated in Figure 9.2, where the respective peaks, labelled LS (= Linguistic System) and CS (= Conceptual System) are depicted as being non-simultaneous.

Secondly, Barsalou *et al.* argue that lexical processing involves a shallow, or superficial, level of processing. That is, for many lexical processing tasks, such as lexical association tasks, processing takes place solely in the linguistic system. For instance, the prime *cat* will generate the vehicles *fur*, *purr*, and *pet*. LASS Theory predicts that such lexical associations are due to statistical relations which are encoded as part of linguistic representations.[18] That is, part of the knowledge we have regarding words has to do with the other words with which a vehicle commonly co-occurs—the lexical profile. Put another way, the claim made by LASS Theory is that lexical associations of this kind are not due to "deep" conceptual processing, which retrieves conceptual information.[19]

In sum, LASS Theory claims that there are two basic representational systems (among others), the linguistic system, and the conceptual system, the latter grounded in the modalities. These systems underpin knowledge processing in service of linguistically facilitated meaning construction.

The relationship between semantic structure and conceptual structure in LCCM theory

The proposals developed by Barsalou *et al.*, described above, diverge from the thesis of encyclopaedic semantics assumed in cognitive linguistics. After all, LASS Theory argues that the linguistic and conceptual systems, while they interact, involve different types of representation and different types (and levels) of processing.

[18] See also Boroditsky and Prinz (forthcoming) for discussion of related issues.

[19] The position that situated communication relies on distinct types of knowledge inhering in distinct representational systems: the linguistic and conceptual system, is consistent with other approaches in the cognitive psychology literature, for which there is empirical support. For instance, LASS Theory is consistent with some of the key claims of Paivio's Dual Coding Theory (1971, 1986).

However, one of the consequences of LASS Theory is that much of what linguists normally think of as semantic structure is removed from the linguistic system. In the linguistic system we are left with vehicles stripped of semantic content, save for the statistically established associations between vehicles—the lexical profile in present terms. On this account, the linguistic system has impoverished representations, which are pale reflections of the bipolar assemblies involving a phonological vehicle and semantic structure developed in previous chapters. Barsalou *et al.* argue, correctly, I submit, that simulations—the bread and butter, so to speak, of meaning construction—constitute a computation which arises from a different representational type than that found in language. Language, they suggest, serves to index and prompt for simulations, but does not directly encode the perceptual records, the perceptual symbols, upon which simulations are based. In so doing, they place what I referred to, in earlier chapters, as the "rich content" associated with language in the conceptual system. So far so good. However, semantic representation also involves "schematic content." As I have argued, one of the important findings to emerge from empirical work on linguistic semantics by scholars such as Talmy and Langacker is that grammar is meaningful in its own right.[20] That is, in addition to the "rich content" that language prompts for, language encodes a level of schematic content—recall the discussion of Talmy's notion of the bifurcation in the way the Cognitive Representation is represented via language, in Chapter 6. Hence, my claim is that while LASS Theory is correct to place the "rich content" in the conceptual system, and identify it in terms of records of perceptual states—for example, the situated perceptual experience associated with the vehicle *red* arises not from linguistic representation, but rather is based on conceptual representation—this is not the whole story.

As discussed in previous chapters, there is an additional level of relatively rich, in the sense of multifaceted, knowledge directly encoded by language. The lexical concept *qua* theoretical construct represents an attempt to characterize this level of knowledge. The linguistic content that makes up the lexical concept is highly schematic, and hence is non-analogue, in the sense that it is hypothesized not to directly prompt for simulations. Another way of

[20] Indeed, the perspective that language directly encodes schematic meaning of the kind I have been describing, in the context of much of twentieth-century linguistics, has been a relatively minor perspective, until recently. Since Chomsky (1957), with his influential arguments for the dissociation between grammar and semantics, it has been common to assume that grammatical structure, knowledge of linguistic forms, is distinct—in the sense of being separable from—semantic knowledge. One of the outstanding contributions of Langacker's work, for instance, has been to show that such a view is erroneous. Consider the vehicles *explode* and *explosion*. While the former is a verb the latter is a noun. The traditional view has been to assume that both forms encode the same semantic structure and differ only in the syntactic information encoded by the two forms. Langacker, in contrast, argues that these vehicles do contrast in terms of their semantics. This follows as he assumes grammatical categories such as lexical class have a semantic basis. For Langacker, verbal vehicles, such as *explode*, encode a relation and hence a schematic trajector and landmark (in his terms). As such they are conceptually dependent. In contrast, nominal vehicles (i.e., noun forms) encode things—prototypically physical entities—and hence are non-relational. The discussion of nominal and relational lexical concepts in Chapter 6 is based on Langacker's pioneering work on lexical classes.

saying this is that the level of knowledge I have been referring to as linguistic content assumes a format that can be encoded directly by language, and hence, inheres not in the conceptual system, but rather the linguistic system.

On my account then, the thesis of encyclopaedic semantics, discussed above, oversimplifies matters. It blurs the boundaries between linguistic and conceptual knowledge. While marking such boundaries may not be necessary in Cognitive Grammar, for instance, which is ultimately concerned with accounting for formal properties of linguistic organization, such a situation is unsatisfactory when attempting to account for the role of language in meaning construction, and specifically, the apparent variation in word "meanings" across contexts of use.

The claim at the heart of LCCM Theory, and one enshrined in the distinction between its two foundational theoretical constructs—the lexical concept and cognitive model—is that what has, in cognitive linguistics, been treated as two qualitatively distinct, albeit related, aspects of semantic structure—schematic versus rich aspects of semantic content—in fact relate to very different types of representation that constitute different kinds of knowledge. While these two knowledge types interact in order to produce simulations, as we shall see in detail in the next chapter, they nevertheless constitute different knowledge formats. LCCM Theory takes from Langacker, and other researchers in cognitive linguistics, the view that linguistic representations constitute bipolar assemblies of form and semantic structure. Moreover, based in large measure on the work of Langacker and Talmy, I have sketched the nature of the linguistic content that makes up the semantic pole of the bipolar symbolic unit: the lexical concept. The knowledge that makes up an individual lexical concept is highly schematic in nature, and highly impoverished, in terms of perceptual information, vis-à-vis the rich information associated with conceptual representations.

In addition, lexical concepts facilitate access to conceptual content, perceptual information in the sense of Barsalou's (1999) PSS Theory. Information of this type I model in terms of the construct of the cognitive model, elaborated in the next chapter. However, unlike Langacker's assumption in Cognitive Grammar, lexical concepts are not equated with cognitive models. That is, lexical concepts encode linguistic content—a direct relationship—while a subset of lexical concepts facilitate access to cognitive models—an indirect association. This insight is drawn from LASS Theory. In the next chapter I turn to a consideration of the cognitive model—based on proposals by Barsalou (e.g., 1999)—which is the theoretical construct that is held to populate the conceptual system, and to which open-class lexical concepts are hypothesized to facilitate access.[21]

---

[21] That said, a caveat is in order. To claim that there are two distinct forms of representation that give rise to linguistically mediated conceptions is not to claim that we have modular systems which fail to interact. That is, I am not claiming that the output of one system serves as input to another, and the internal operations of each system are not visible to that of the other. Rather, and as we shall see in Part III when I address semantic composition, the two systems interact in continuous and dynamic fashion in service of producing simulations and hence situated meaning construction.

Summary

In this chapter I have been concerned with outlining, in general terms, the nature of conceptual structure as assumed by LCCM Theory. I have also been concerned with the way in which language interfaces with the conceptual system in service of situated meaning construction. I argued that a fundamental design feature of human cognition is that linguistic representations provide an indexing and control function with respect to the conceptual system, greatly increasing the range of uses and flexibility of the human conceptual system. However, this does mean that linguistic representations are equivalent to the concepts which populate the conceptual system. In particular, I have suggested that linguistic representations, namely symbolic units, evolved to complement and enhance the existing form of representations that inhere in the conceptual system, rather than duplicating them. One of the consequences of assuming two distinct systems: a linguistic and a conceptual system, has been the need to revise the thesis of encyclopaedic semantics widely assumed in cognitive linguistics. In doing so, I built on the Theory of Perceptual Symbol Systems (PSS Theory), developed by Barsalou (e.g., 1999, 2003), and its application with respect to language in the Theory of Language and Situated Simulation (LASS Theory), developed by Barsalou *et al.* (forthcoming).

10

Cognitive models

This chapter is concerned with outlining the construct of the cognitive model. I do this in light of the perspective on conceptual structure developed in the previous chapter. In LCCM Theory a cognitive model is, in broad terms, similar to Barsalou's (1999) notion of a simulator, which encompasses a frame and simulations, discussed in more detail below. The use of a novel term, "cognitive model," is done for three reasons.

Firstly, at this stage in our understanding, it is not clear to what extent units of semantic structure—lexical concepts—facilitate access to the conceptual system. For instance, the common experience of "not being able to put thoughts into words," particularly as applied to subjective experiences, suggests that the linguistic system may be less well connected to certain types of conceptual representations than others. Indeed, this is a point made by Jackendoff (e.g., 1992). It is conceivable that some aspects of conceptual structure may only be partially accessible or even inaccessible to the linguistic system. I introduce the theoretical construct of the cognitive model, then, to distinguish between those simulators which are accessible via linguistic representations, and those which are not. Simply put, while the conceptual system is populated by simulators (Barsalou 1999), cognitive models are simulators which are specialized for being accessed by lexical concepts. Hence, the rationale for introducing the term "cognitive model" is to identify those simulators with which the linguistic system interacts.

The second reason is as follows. In his Theory of Perceptual Symbol Systems, Barsalou is primarily focused on the perceptual basis—in the wider sense as described in the previous chapter—of conceptual structure. While he acknowledges that other forms of information are likely to feed into conceptual representations, he is primarily exercised by accounting for the perceptual grounding of cognition. In my account, I explicitly acknowledge that propositional (i.e., non-perceptual) information may also become incorporated in cognitive models, which supplements the perceptual information already present. Such propositional information is likely to accrue via linguistically mediated routes, including narrative, exchange of news, and gossip. For these reasons, it is useful to distinguish the theoretical construct under development here, by applying the novel term cognitive model.

Finally, while I employed PSS Theory in the previous chapter to illustrate what a simulation-style account of conceptual structure could look like, much work remains to be done. PSS Theory arose in the context of behavioural work on how people represent concrete objects and actions – things that are perceptible. Other sorts of subjective and cognitive states are still not well understood—a point acknowledged by Barsalou (1999) in referring to what he terms "introspective experience." As work proceeds, the state of our knowledge, particularly relating to non-perceptual knowledge, is likely to require significant revisions of our account(s) of how simulation takes place, and the nature of other cognitive states. Accordingly, an additional reason for using the novel term cognitive model is to dissociate LCCM Theory from PSS Theory. While I have employed PSS Theory for purposes of illustration, LCCM Theory is not contingent upon it.

Knowledge representation in the conceptual system

In this section, I consider in more detail the way in which perceptual symbols are organized within the conceptual system to provide larger-scale knowledge structures. In short, I argue that there are a number of distinct kinds of cognitive models—frames and the possible set of simulations associated with the frame—that populate the conceptual system. Distinctions in types of cognitive models arise due to distinctions in the frames that provide the cognitive model with its organizational structure. Hence, in this section I identify a number of frame types. I do so based on Barsalou's work on frames (e.g., Barsalou 1991, 1992a; Barsalou et al. 1993).[1] In general terms, frames can be identified which relate to things and to situations. Further, within each of these broad divisions there are frames which are episodic, relating to specific types of experience and/or knowledge, and frames which are generic, relating to schematizations over broadly similar aspects of experience and/or knowledge. The distinct frames (and hence cognitive models) identified below are **individuals** (episodic) and **types** (generic), which relate to things, and **episodic situations** and **generic situations**, which relate, self-evidently, to situations. I begin by focusing on the frames for things: individuals and types, before proceeding with a discussion of the frames for situations.

The world model

Barsalou (1991) provides an ontology for a theory of knowledge representation based on what he refers to as the **world model**. This comprises a person's beliefs about the current state of the world. These beliefs relate to individuals, their current states and where they are located. Barsalou suggests that people employ a hierarchically arranged core of spatial frames. That is, people represent the world and its contents in a spatial fashion, corresponding to

---

[1] Barsalou's work on frames was developed prior to the development of PSS Theory, but is compatible with it.

continents, countries, cities, neighbourhoods, individual buildings, rooms, and locations within rooms. They further locate entities within these locations, and integrate the spatial frames with temporal knowledge, for instance, relating to cycles and time frames of various sorts including the seasons, the calendar, and temporal intervals such as years, months, weeks, and days, as well as content-based temporal structures such as knowledge relating to one's own and family members' daily routine, development over the life span, stages in career progression, and so on. Temporal information serves to organize past, present, and future information in the world model and, Barsalou argues, does so orthogonally to the spatial core. Moreover, in this world model, people represent other people's interactions and movements, updating the model continuously. For instance, while at work, a person might represent their partner's movements: going to the shops, returning home, or their children's activities while at school, and so on. People also represent other ongoing activities taking place in the various regions represented in their world model. For instance, one might know about a meeting of a University Exam Board taking place in a committee room near one's office, it being Tuesday afternoon, Prime Minister's Question Time taking place at the House of Commons, knowing—based on having read today's newspaper—that the Queen is currently staying at Windsor Castle rather than Buckingham Palace, that Big Ben in London is currently undergoing repairs and hence not presently chiming, and so on.

In the world model two distinct kinds of frames can be distinguished which relate to things: individuals and types (Barsalou et al. 1993).[2] Individuals are frames that relate to animate and inanimate entities that are held to persist continuously in the environment. As such, individuals are central to the ontology of the world model. Individuals provide relatively stable information about a given entity: information that is both stable over time, as well as incorporating episodic information. Hence, the new information for a given individual is added to the frame thereby updating it on an ongoing basis. An individual is updated based on encounters with the entity it represents. For instance, the frame for "my car" might include the petrol gauge reading the last time I interacted with it, and the fact that I have noticed there is an oil leak, and that the car needs cleaning. This information is merged into the frame to provide an updated representation.

Crucially, although the same individual may be encountered in the world on many occasions, often in the same day, in terms of the world model all the episodic information extracted during these encounters is integrated into the individual frame. This follows from the **one-entity one-frame principle** (Barsalou et al. 1993). This principle holds that only one frame can relate to any given entity. Hence, all the information extracted from experience that

---

[2] Barsalou et al. (1993) use the term "model" to refer to what I am here calling "type." I prefer the more intuitively accessible term "type" and also seek to avoid any confusion with the construct of the cognitive model. Hence, I do not use the term "model."

relates to a particular individual is merged into the frame for that entity. As such, the frame for a particular colleague at work may include information relating to his or her location the last time I interacted with them, and so on.

In addition to individuals, Barsalou *et al.* (1993) argue that there is another frame type which inheres in the world model. This type of frame, which I refer to as type, is an abstraction across frames for individuals, providing a frame for a type of individual. As such, types are not conceptualized as having corresponding entities in the world. For example, while the individual for "my car" in the world model corresponds to my car in the world, the frame for "car" is a type, and relates to a type of individual, abstracted from across a range of individuals. Hence, people understand their frames for types to inhere only in the world model, but not, crucially, in the world itself.

One of the features of individuals in the world is that they change location. In the world model, this feature is captured in terms of the phenomenon referred to as **transcendence** (Barsalou *et al.* 1993). Transcendence has to do with the number and range of locations at which individuals and types are represented. For instance, a colleague from work will be represented at work. However, a chance meeting at the local supermarket will ensure that the individual frame for the colleague becomes additionally stored at the supermarket location in the world model. When the colleague goes on vacation to Paris, and sends a postcard in to the office to report on the vacation, the individual is additionally stored as part of the Paris location in the world model.

Barsalou *et al.* (1993) argue that transcendent frames for individuals and types, while being located at multiple sites in the world model, become **functionally detached** from the world model. That is, they give rise to a level of information about the nature of individuals and types, and the interactions they can engage in which become abstracted from the spatial frames that form the core of the world model. In other words, transcendence gives rise to de-contextualized representations which form **transcendent taxonomies**. For example, the type for "heart" is a feature of all mammals. Hence, its presence as part of the frame for numerous individuals and types gives rise to transcendence.

This property serves two important functions. Firstly, transcendence provides an important means of organizing beliefs about the nature of entities in the world. It does so as it serves to capture similarities between individuals and models. As such, it facilitates inferences. For instance, we can infer that lions have hearts on the basis of knowing that all mammals possess hearts. Secondly, transcendent taxonomies may constitute important building blocks in the construction of the world model. This follows as transcendent information can be inserted into frames for new individuals upon first encounter. For instance, on encountering an unfamiliar cat, information from the model for cats is retrieved and copied, in order to form the basis for the new individual in the world model. This process serves to minimize the amount of learning about new entities before they can be adequately represented.

Situations

Having briefly described the ontology for individuals and types, I now consider how situations are modelled from the perspective of Barsalou's work on frames. The basic insight is that in addition to individuals and types, humans additionally represent situations, there being two kinds of situation: episodic situations and generic situations. The distinction between episodic and generic situations is orthogonal to the distinction between individuals and types.

According to this approach, situations are part of larger **events**—events are composed of situations—while being made up of discrete **images**. As with situations, events and images—as I deploy these terms—are mental representations. The notions of event, situation, and image are somewhat akin to the notions of scripts, scenes, and states developed in Schank (1975, 1982) and Schank and Abelson (1977), with the difference being that events, situations, and images are made up of perceptual symbols, and hence are perceptual and thus embodied in nature.

One of the key insights of this approach is that it takes a **situated cognition** perspective. That is, people's frames for individuals and types are **situated** and **local** rather than being de-contextualized and universal. An individual or type is situated in the sense that it is represented in the situations in which it occurs. For instance, the individual frame for "my sofa" is represented as being located in my living room. Hence, the frame for my sofa is related to the situation frame for "my living room". Similarly, individuals and types are local in the sense that they relate only to exemplars actually encountered, rather than being generalized to entities universally. For instance, the type for "sofa" incorporates information relating only to sofas that have been encountered. In this way, this approach to knowledge representation assumes that the conceptual system is directly grounded in situated action and interaction.

Barsalou *et al.* (1993) propose that the mental representations they refer to as images are static spatial scenes (cf. Tyler and Evans 2003). These may consist of frames for individuals and/or types, viewed from a particular viewpoint, with a particular geometric, topological, and functional relationship holding between them. Crucially, an image is composed of numerous perceptual symbols. For instance, a person may represent a picture hanging on the wall above the sofa in their living room.

A situation is comprised of a series of images. Hence, and as with an image, a situation may consist of a relatively stable set of individuals and types. The difference is that a situation, while occupying a relatively constant region of space, is dynamic, in the sense that entities may interact and move around, and there is change over time. For instance, a situation might involve a person approaching the sofa, sitting down, turning their head to look at the picture on the wall, turning their head away again, sitting for a while before getting up and moving away from the sofa.

An event comprises a series of two or more situations which are related in coherent fashion. The key difference between an event and a situation is that an event involves a significant outcome, often involving a change in regions of space and/or the individuals and/or types involved in the event. For instance, an event might involve a person going to a department store and purchasing a picture, bringing it home in their car, fetching a hammer and nail from the garage, selecting a spot on the wall above the sofa to hang the picture, knocking a nail in the wall at the desired location, and hanging the picture above the sofa. A table summarizing the differences between image, situation, and event *qua* mental representations is provided in Table 10.1.

As observed above, there are distinct sorts of frames relating to both episodic and generic situations, which parallels the distinction between individuals and types. An episodic situation arises from perceiving a situation in the world, the situation *qua* frame constituting a mental representation of the perceived situation. Moreover, humans represent situations at the locations in their world model where the situation occurs. For instance, in the example of the situation involving the hanging of a picture above the sofa, the frame for the episodic situation is linked to the frame for the conceptualizer's living room. On this account, and just as we saw with frames for individuals above, episodic situations are not wholly episodic. They also include a potentially large amount of generic information. This is due to the phenomenon of transcendence, which facilitates cognitive economy: generic knowledge can be shared between related frames. As with frames for things—individuals and types, discussed above—frames for situations are associated with temporal knowledge structures such as those relating to daily routines, life periods, hours of the day, and so on.

There are two special cases of episodic situations. The first example relates to **counterfactual situations**. A counterfactual situation is a situation that hasn't and/or won't occur. These are often alternatives to episodic situations that have occurred or are likely to occur. The difference is that in the counterfactual

TABLE 10.1. Features of images, situations, and events

Features of Images	Features of situations	Features of events
(i) a set of perceptual symbols	(i) a series of images	(i) a series of two or more situations
(ii) represents individuals and/or types	(ii) depicts a relatively constant set of individuals and/or types	(ii) the situations are related in a coherent manner
(iii) a static spatial configuration	(iii) depicts some significant change over time	(iii) the situations lead to a significant outcome
(iv) viewed from a particular perspective	(iv) occurs in a relatively constant region of space	

TABLE 10.2. Identification of commonalities in the formation of an abstract situation (after Barsalou *et al.* 1993)

Two situations are related when the following occur:

(i)   They share a common number of images.
(ii) They share common individuals and/or types.
(iii) The configuration of individuals/types in each similar image across situations is qualitatively the same.
(iv) The transformations of individuals/types between similar images across situations is qualitatively the same.
(v)   The two situations culminate in a common end state.

situation, the individuals and/types, their states, and the actions they perform vary with respect to the **realis situation**, which is to say, the mental representation of the situation which did occur or is likely to occur.[3] As with other frames, these are linked to a particular location in the world model, typically that associated with the location associated with the realis situation. The second special case is that of **prospective situations**. Like counterfactual situations these are situations that haven't occurred, however, they are future-oriented, and hence are predicted to occur.

In contrast, frames for generic situations do not include episodic information. Rather they develop by virtue of abstracting away points of difference, in order to distill the commonalities that persist in different frames for episodic situations. Like frames for types, discussed above, generic situations do not have direct counterparts in the world. Barsalou *et al.* (1993) propose that frames for a generic situation are formed when two or more episodic situations share a number of commonalities. These are presented in Table 10.2. These commonalties serve to indicate that two episodic situations are related. The episodic situations in question are then abstracted in order to form a generic situation for this type of situation.

Cognitive models

As noted above, I use the term cognitive model to refer to a coherent body of knowledge—consisting of a frame or related frames—and the potential for simulations arising from this body of knowledge. A number of distinct kinds of frames can be identified, as discussed above. There are two types of frames that I have distinguished, those that represent things and those for events. I have identified two kinds of frames for things: individuals and types. The

---

[3] In his work on mental spaces, Fauconnier (e.g., 1997) makes the point that mental representations of counterfactual scenarios always emerge by virtue of constructing representations for a realis scenario. That is, counterfactual scenarios are always relativized to representations of what is taken as reality.

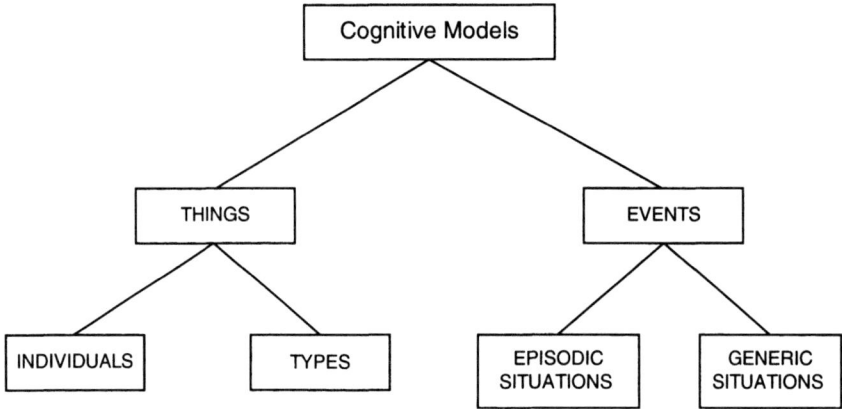

FIGURE 10.1. Types of cognitive model

relationship between individuals and types is captured in terms of representations of events. Events are comprised of situations, there being two types of
frame: episodic situations and generic situations. Figure 10.1 summarizes
these proposals.

The structure of frames

Before moving on to a discussion of the way in which lexical concepts interact
with cognitive models, we first need to establish the nature and structure of
frames: the collections of perceptual symbols and images which comprise the
frame types identified above: individuals and types versus episodic and
generic situations. Frames have three basic constituents: **attribute-value
sets**, **structural invariants**, and **constraints**. In this section, which draws on
Barsalou (1992a) I examine each of these in turn.

Attribute-value sets

Frames consist of sets of attributes and values. An attribute concerns some
aspect of a given frame, while a value is the specification of that aspect. For
example, in terms of the vastly simplified frame for CAR depicted in Figure
10.2, ENGINE represents one aspect of the CAR, as do DRIVER, FUEL, TRANS-
MISSION, and WHEELS. An attribute is therefore a concept that represents one
aspect of a larger whole. Attributes are represented in Figure 10.2 as ovals.
Values are subordinate concepts which represent subtypes of an attribute. For
instance, SUE and MIKE are types of DRIVER, PETROL and DIESEL are types of
FUEL, MANUAL and AUTOMATIC are types of TRANSMISSION, and so on. Values
are represented as dotted rectangles in Figure 10.2. Crucially, while values are
more specific than attributes, a value can also be an attribute, because it can

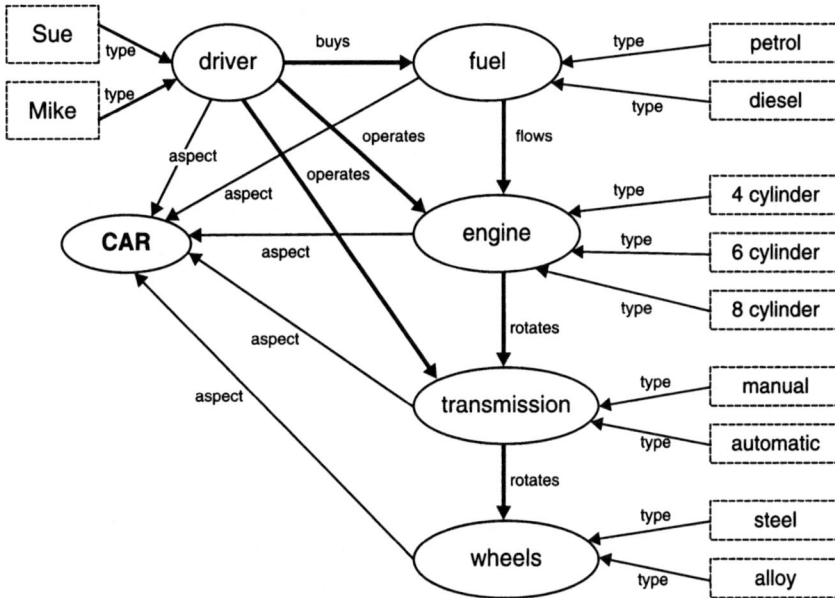

FIGURE 10.2. Frame for CAR (adapted from Barsalou 1992a: 30).

also have subtypes. For instance, PETROL is an attribute to the more specific concepts UNLEADED PETROL and LEADED PETROL, which are values of PETROL. Attributes and values are therefore superordinate and subordinate concepts within an **attribute taxonomy**: subordinate concepts, or values, which are more specific, inherit properties from the superordinate concepts, or attributes, which are more general.

In addition, attributes within a frame can be associated with their own **attribute frame**, providing an embedded form of framing. For instance, the attribute DRIVER in the CAR frame may have a number of attributes associated with it, including AGE, SEX, STATUS OF DRIVING LICENCE (i.e., whether it is "clean" or not), NUMBER OF YEARS' EXPERIENCE, and so on. As frames are dynamic entities, undergoing continuous updating, attributes can be added to frames based on new encounters, or in order to achieve a particular goal. For instance, in the light of the recent introduction of a new banding scheme for road tax—an annual tax paid on all vehicles in the UK to use the public highway which is based on petrol consumption and emissions ratings—UK car owners are likely to have added a new attribute to their frame type for CAR relating to CAR-TAX LEVEL. It is also worth emphasizing that attribute-value sets, as with other aspects of knowledge representation, are likely to be idiosyncratic, and hence to vary from person to person.

A final property of attribute-value sets that I mention relates to what Barsalou and Billman (1989) have referred to as **attribute systematicity**. This concerns the idea that certain attributes are core, in the sense that they frequently recur across contexts.[4] This can facilitate frame formation. For instance, if a particular value for an attribute is not known when setting up a new frame of the type individual, a value for a core attribute can be ascribed based on the core attribute set retrieved from memory. For instance, imagine your friend is proudly showing off his new bright red sports car to you. A core attribute of the type frame SPORTS CAR is FUEL with the value PETROL. Hence, even though there may be no direct evidence that the car takes fuel, for instance, because you haven't noticed a petrol cap, or seen evidence of a fuel tank, this is something that will be added to the frame for this individual, and the value PETROL will be added as a consequence.

Structural invariants

According to Barsalou, "[A]ttributes in a frame are not independent slots but are often related correlationally and conceptually" (Barsalou 1992a: 35). In other words, attributes within a frame are related to one another in consistent ways across **exemplars**: instances of a given frame in the world. For example, in most exemplars of the frame CAR it is the driver who controls the speed of the ENGINE. This relation holds across most instances of cars, irrespective of the values involved, and is therefore represented in the frame as a structural invariant: a more or less invariant relation between attributes DRIVER and ENGINE. In Figure 10.2 structural invariants are indicated by bold arrows. Hence, a structural invariant constitutes what Barsalou (1992a) terms "a normative truth" holding between attributes within a frame.

Constraints and factors

Like structural invariants, constraints and factors are relations that hold between attributes, or more specifically, between attribute values. However, rather than capturing normative relations, constraints and factors give rise to variability in the values associated with attributes. This follows as values in a given frame are interdependent on the values associated with other attributes. There are two kinds of constraints, which I briefly review below, and two factors. The constraints are **global constraints** and **local constraints**. The two factors are **contextual factors** and **goal factors**. I deal with each of these below.

Global constraints

Global constraints serve to constrain attribute values globally. This means that a modification in one value entails a proportional modification in a related

---

[4] As is well known, correlations in experience give rise to associative strength in memory: co-occurrence gives rise to a core set of attributes, which thus exhibit systematicity. See references in Barsalou *et al.* (1993) for instance.

value. For instance, consider the example of a TRANSPORTATION frame involving a journey involving a passenger in a taxi, for instance, being transported from one location to another. In this frame there is a negative attribute constraint which holds between the attributes SPEED and DURATION. That is, as the value for the attribute SPEED increases (and transportation becomes faster), so the value for the attribute DURATION decreases.

Local constraints

These constrain sets of values locally, rather than globally. That is, the presence of a given value entails the presence of a related value, while the absence of one entails the absence of another. For instance, consider a frame for VACATION. If the attribute ACTIVITY has the value SKIING, then this requires that the attribute HOLIDAY DESTINATION has the value SKI RESORT. Similarly, if the attribute ACTIVITY has the value SURFING, then the destination attribute must have the value OCEAN BEACH.

Contextual factors

Contextual factors relate to aspects of context which serve to influence attribute values. For instance, the activity of SKIING requires a SKI RESORT, while increasing SPEED of travel reduces the DURATION of the journey. As aspects of situations are related rather than being independent, context constitutes a factor which can influence both global and local constraints.

Goal factors

In addition to context, an agent's goal(s) also provides a factor that influences the interaction between values associated with related attributes. For instance, in a PHYSICAL WORKOUT frame, the agent's goal, to get fit, serves to ensure that the attribute EXERTION forms part of the frame.

Chaining within the conceptual system

In this section I briefly consider the phenomenon of **chaining** (Barsalou *et al.* 1993; see also Lakoff 1987). The conceptual system is not a haphazard collection of cognitive models. Rather, cognitive models exhibit a range of often complex interconnections. As such, cognitive models are linked in a web of interconnections, of diverse sorts: hence, chaining. The consequence of this, in terms of linguistic interaction, is that access sites established by lexical concepts provide a deep semantic potential for purposes of linguistically mediated communication.

Chaining is a consequence of a number of different types of interconnections and relationships holding between frames. One such interconnection arises due to the phenomenon of attribute frames, discussed above. That is, frames are embedded within larger frames. Take the frame CAR, discussed above. A salient attribute associated with this type is ENGINE. The knowledge of engines possessed by one group of conceptualizers, namely car mechanics, is highly complex, and this attribute includes many subordinate attributes each with corresponding values, which are themselves subordinate attributes with further values, and so on. In this way, a frame subsumes multiple frames which are embedded, capturing aspects of the larger units of which they are subparts.

Another way in which chaining occurs arises from the phenomenon of transcendence. This relates to the situated nature of cognitive models for things: individuals and types. Recall that cognitive models of this kind are "located" in situations. In other words, cognitive models for things are located in the world model at the points at which they are encountered. Hence, cognitive models for episodic and generic situations include representations for individuals and types. The greater the number of situations to which individuals and types are linked, the greater their transcendence is held to be. Hence, transcendence is a function of how interconnected cognitive models for things are with those for situations, and hence the events with which they are connected.

Another motivation for chaining arises due to the componential nature of the conceptual system itself. Recall that cognitive models are comprised of sets of perceptual symbols. As perceptual symbols are records of discrete perceptual states (e.g., *purr*, *red*, *hot*, etc.), similar perceptual symbols (e.g., *red*) form part of many different cognitive models within the conceptual system. As such, unique records of similar perceptual states persist throughout the conceptual system. The consequence of this is that the conceptual system is thoroughgoingly redundant in terms of the nature of the representations which make up the range of cognitive models which populate it. This provides, naturally, commonalities across cognitive models, and is a consequence of a fundamental design feature of the conceptual system.

Another way in which chaining arises is due to the relationships that exist between cognitive models, due to, broadly, the distinction between episodic versus generic cognitive models. For instance, in terms of cognitive models for things, we have the distinction individuals and types. While individuals may be related to each other based on the dimensions of chaining mentioned in the preceding paragraphs, a type is related to all the individuals from which it is formed. Similarly, a generic situation is related to all the episodic situations that it resembles, and from which it has abstracted across to provide a generic situation.

Interaction between the linguistic and conceptual systems

I now turn to a consideration of the way in which the linguistic and conceptual systems interact. From the perspective of LCCM Theory, this concerns the interaction between a subset of lexical concepts, the open-class lexical concepts, and the range of cognitive models that have been identified in this chapter. I discuss the nature of the interaction by examining some of the relevant issues below.

Access sites

The primary way in which the linguistic and conceptual systems interact is by virtue of access sites—introduced informally earlier in the book. An access site, as I use the term, is a theoretical construct which represents a composite of the range of association areas that hold between an open-class lexical concept and the conceptual system. An association area is a location in the conceptual system with which a specific lexical concept is associated. In other words, an association area provides a point of convergence between the two systems facilitating interaction between content from both. As a given lexical concept has typically many association areas, an access site constitutes the set of association areas for a given lexical concept. For example, and as we shall see below, the lexical concept [RED] is associated with many representations for individuals and types, each with its own distinctive hue throughout the conceptual system. All the association areas collectively form the access site for this lexical concept. Yet this gives rise to considerable complexity, providing access, as we shall see, to a large semantic potential.

The purpose of an access site is to facilitate integration of linguistic and conceptual content in order to provide an **integrated simulation**. An integrated simulation is what I have referred to earlier in the book as a conception. Hence, the evolutionary motivation, on this account, for the linguistic and conceptual systems to interact is in order to make use of conceptual structure inhering in the conceptual system in service of linguistically mediated communication. The mechanism whereby composite semantic structures from the linguistic system interact with conceptual structure I refer to as interpretation: the subject of Chapter 13.

The association areas that comprise an access site arise by virtue of usage patterns: vehicles sanctioned by specific lexical concepts being used in the context of perceived things and situations. Based on such patterns of use, statistical frequencies are extracted which serve to associate lexical concepts with the regions of the conceptual system where the relevant things and situations are represented, giving rise to association areas. Access sites are thus probabilistic, in the sense that the greater the frequency with which a language user experiences a sanctioning lexical concept and a thing/situation as co-occurring, the greater the strength of the association area.[5]

---

[5] See Barsalou *et al.* (forthcoming) for discussion of a related proposal. See also Boroditsky and Prinz (forthcoming).

Semantic potential

One consequence of the chaining exhibited by the conceptual system is that lexical concepts, by being associated with access sites, facilitate access to a large semantic potential. Indeed, one of the main reasons for the protean nature of word meanings, the starting point for the present enquiry (in Chapter 1), is due to the large body of conceptual knowledge, the "potential" which they facilitate access to.

To illustrate, let's briefly consider an example from an earlier chapter, the lexical concept [RED] associated with the vehicle *red*. To do so, reconsider the following utterances:

(1)   a. The teacher scrawled in red ink all over the pupil's homework exercise
      b. The red squirrel is in danger of becoming extinct in the British Isles

The lexical concept [RED] facilitates access to a bewildering number of distinct perceptual symbols which contribute to a vast number of cognitive models in the conceptual system of any language user of English. To get a sense of the semantic potential involved, consider all the individuals and types that a single person will represent in their world model that feature the perceptual state I gloss as *red*.

Limiting ourselves to types we might list Royal Mail post boxes, red squirrels, foxes, roses, blood, lipstick, Santa Claus's clothes, a robin's throat, strawberries, the red stop sign, tomatoes, red traffic lights, the Red Cross, red ink, the flag of St George, celebrity carpets, Babybel cheese wax, chilli peppers, fire engines, the Chinese flag, red wine, fire, henna, and so on. Notice that the represented hue associated with these types may vary from person to person, based on cultural experience, and so on. Nevertheless, we can imagine contexts in which we would apply the vehicle *red* in order to evoke the colour associated with these types.

In addition, we have further situations, both episodic and generic, that involve the individuals and types which include a perceptual symbol that I gloss as *red*. However, each of these perceptual symbols is unique to the individual and/or type and hence the situation of which it forms part. After all, it is the generic situation in which a teacher scrawls red ink on a pupil's exercise book, evoking a different perceptual symbol than the one evoked when we simulate a red squirrel scurrying up a tree. Nevertheless, the lexical concept [RED] is associated with, and hence facilitates access to, both. Put another way, the semantic potential for the lexical concept [RED] comes from the diverse range of perceptual symbols that are encoded by these cognitive models, and many others. Moreover, it is precisely because [RED] facilitates access to such a diverse potential that the vehicle *red* exhibits such variation in the way it can be used, as exhibited by the very different simulations we achieve for "red" in the examples in (1).

The illusion of semantic unity

In Chapter 7 I discussed the notion of encapsulation: a property of lexical concepts. From the perspective of the body of cognitive models—the semantic potential—to which a lexical concept potentially affords access, the encapsulation function of a lexical concept provides the illusion of semantic unity.[6]

For instance, the lexical concept [CAR] associated with the vehicle *car* provides access to a wide array of different types, including cognitive models for makes (e.g., Land Rover), models (e.g., Land Rover Defender), and model types (e.g., standard versus deluxe versions, and so on), as well as individuals (e.g., "my car", "my neighbour's car", "the DB5 Aston Martin" used by James Bond in the film *Goldfinger*), and the range of situations relevant to the types and individuals represented. That is, the lexical concept [CAR] serves as an access site to all the specialized cognitive models associated with cars.

I refer to this phenomenon as encapsulation, as a lexical concept serves to relate a diverse range of cognitive models, establishing a degree of unity across the cognitive models in question. It is by virtue of linguistically mediated encapsulation that cognitive models *appear* to exhibit greater similarity than they would otherwise. This is what I refer to as the *illusion* of semantic unity.

Primary versus secondary cognitive models

The range of cognitive models—the semantic potential—to which a lexical concept facilitates access I refer to as its cognitive model profile—a term I first introduced in Chapter 4. As we saw earlier in this chapter, in discussing the nature of chaining within the conceptual system, the cognitive model profile is not an unstructured inventory of knowledge: conceptual structure is highly structured. I distinguish between two aspects of a lexical concept's cognitive model profile: the primary cognitive model profile, and the secondary cognitive model profile—terms also introduced in Chapter 4.

The primary cognitive model profile consists of all those cognitive models with which a lexical concept is directly associated: the association areas which make up its access site. Hence, the primary cognitive model profile may constitute many discrete cognitive models—as an access site may be made up of many distinct association areas—dispersed across various regions within the conceptual system.[7] The cognitive models which make up the primary cognitive model profile I refer to as primary cognitive models, as we also saw in Chapter 4.

In contrast, the **secondary cognitive model profile** consists of all those cognitive models—what I refer to as secondary cognitive models—with which a lexical concept is not associated. Hence, secondary cognitive models do not comprise part of the access site of a cognitive model. Put another way,

---

[6] See also Barsalou *et al.* (forthcoming) for discussion.

[7] As we saw earlier in the discussion of the notion of an access site, the cognitive models with which a lexical concept is associated are established probabilistically.

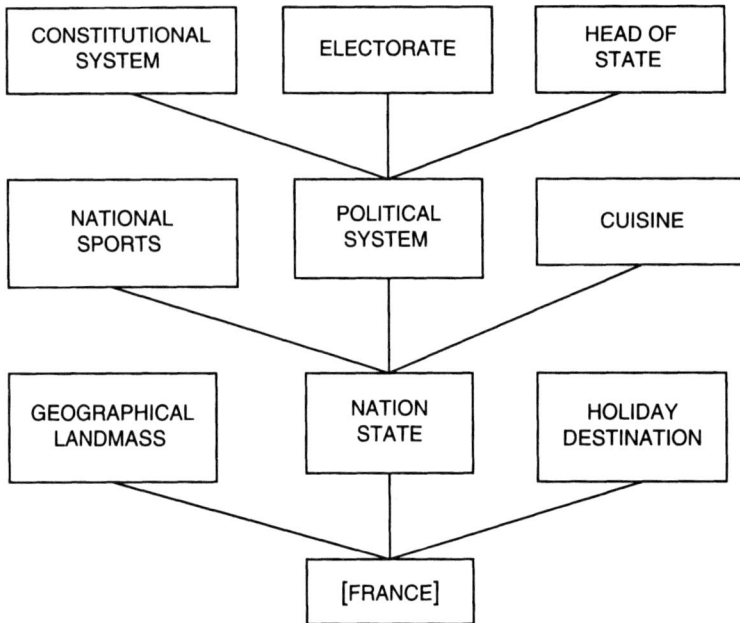

FIGURE 10.3. Partial cognitive model profile for [FRANCE]

secondary cognitive models are those that are chained, with respect to the primary cognitive models. Hence, they form part of the semantic potential to which a given lexical concept potentially affords access, although there is not an established association between the lexical concept and secondary cognitive models.

By way of illustration, let's reconsider the cognitive model profile for [FRANCE] first presented in Chapter 4. The diagram for the very partial cognitive model is provided in Figure 10.3.

The access site for the lexical concept [FRANCE] consists of (at the very least) the following cognitive models: GEOGRAPHICAL LANDMASS, NATION STATE, and HOLIDAY DESTINATION. That is, the linguistic system is associated with each of these sites in the conceptual system: the lexical concept [FRANCE] facilitating access to conceptual structure via these cognitive models.[8] Moreover, each of the three primary cognitive models to which [FRANCE] facilitates direct access is an individual. That is, the cognitive model GEOGRAPHICAL LANDMASS relates to knowledge about the specific geographic region coincident with the borders of the political entity France. Similarly, NATION STATE relates to knowledge of the nation state France, while HOLIDAY DESTINATION relates to knowledge about what it means to holiday in France.

[8] As noted in Chapter 4, a cognitive model is represented in LCCM Theory in highly abbreviated fashion: a rectangular box with a gloss in small capitals. However, this gloss, e.g., GEOGRAPHICAL LANDMASS relates to a simulator: a frame which gives rise to limitless simulations.

Each of these cognitive models provides access to further cognitive models as a result of chaining within the conceptual system. The chained cognitive models arise for the reasons described above, and constitute the secondary cognitive models. While the primary cognitive models are represented diagrammatically as adjacent to one another in Figure 10.3, this in no way constitutes a commitment to their actual location in the conceptual system; after all, the location of primary cognitive models may be distributed throughout the conceptual system, as in the case of [RED], for example. Equally, while secondary cognitive models are diagrammed as being organized hierarchically, with respect to the primary cognitive models in a given cognitive model profile, this mode of representation serves to distinguish secondary from primary cognitive models, rather than constituting a commitment to how primary and secondary cognitive models are actually represented within the conceptual system.[9]

In Figure 10.3, a flavour of some of the secondary cognitive models in the cognitive model profile for [FRANCE] is given by virtue of the various secondary cognitive models which are accessed via the NATION STATE cognitive model. These include NATIONAL SPORTS, POLITICAL SYSTEM, and CUISINE. For instance, we may know that in France, the French engage in national sports of particular types, for instance, football, rugby, athletics, and so on, rather than others. As I observed in Chapter 4, we may also know that as a sporting nation the French take part in international sports competitions of various kinds. That is, we may have access to a large body of knowledge concerning the sorts of sports French people engage in. We may also have some knowledge of the funding structures and social and economic conditions and constraints that apply to these sports in France, France's international standing with respect to these particular sports, and further knowledge about the sports themselves including the rules that govern their practice, and so on.[10]

The uniqueness of the access site

While lexical concepts are typically associated with a number of primary cognitive models—often many—which thereby make up the access site, the exact nature of the access site with which a lexical concept is associated is unique. Put another way, no two lexical concepts share the same access site. While the range of primary cognitive models to which lexical concepts facilitate access may be similar, they will never be exactly the same. The consequence of this is that

[9] Cognitive models are interconnected in a range of ways, and hence, it is not always clear where a cognitive model begins and ends. For instance, knowledge representations are typically embedded structures, with an attribute serving as a value for another attribute, and giving rise to its own attribute frame, with connections to other cognitive models. Matters are further complicated by conceptual metaphors, which serve to establish long-term stable connections between cognitive models, as discussed in Chapter 15.

[10] While the basis for much of this knowledge is perceptual in nature, in the sense assumed by the Theory of Perceptual Symbol Systems, much of this information additionally has a propositional basis, in the sense that it derives from linguistically mediated communication.

each lexical concept has a unique cognitive model profile, as the exact make-up of primary cognitive models determines which chained cognitive models make up the secondary cognitive model profile of a given lexical concept. From the perspective of the linguistic system, this means that there can be no true synonymy between lexical concepts. To illustrate, consider the lexical concepts which I gloss as [SHORE] and [COAST] associated with the vehicles *shore* and *coast*, respectively. As observed by Fillmore (1982), while the semantic representation for these two words is very similar, it is not the same. This follows, in present terms, as while each of these lexical concepts exhibits partial overlap in the primary cognitive models, there are also distinctions. For instance, both lexical concepts facilitate access to a cognitive model profile relating to the strip of land that borders land and sea. However, each lexical concept accesses a cognitive model relating to a generic situation from which this land region is viewed. In the case of [SHORE] this concerns a sea-based perspective, which is to say, on board a ship. In contrast, [COAST] does so from the perspective of a land-based location. For this reason, a shore-to-shore trip is across water while a coast-to-coast trip is over land.

The development of cognitive models

Cognitive models, as we have seen, are simulators in the sense of Barsalou (e.g., 1999). That is, they are located in the sensory-motor regions of the brain, and they consist of perceptual symbols: records of perceptual states. However, cognitive models also involve information from other sources (Barsalou 1999), which is incorporated into sensory-motor representations by virtue of convergence zones (Damasio 1989). In LCCM Theory I assume that the output of the interaction between the linguistic and conceptual systems, namely conceptions—linguistically mediated simulations—can be integrated with existing cognitive models in order to provide an additional source of information which serves to update relevant cognitive models. That is, simulations are perceptual in nature, albeit internally generated perceptual states. In essence, linguistic interactions with the conceptual system can modify the representations held in the conceptual system, by virtue of the products, simulations, serving to modify the representational states which generated them in the first place. Simply put, linguistically mediated simulations can serve to modify the conceptual system, by updating existing cognitive models. I refer to non-modal modification of this sort as **propositional modification.**[11]

Relativistic effects of language on the conceptual system

One of the consequences of linguistic indexing of the conceptual system, and the modification of the conceptual system as a consequence, is the prediction that we should expect relativistic effects. That is, linguistic relativity is

---

[11] See Boroditsky and Prinz (forthcoming) for a related proposal.

predicted by LCCM Theory. Recall that lexical concepts are language-specific. Hence, each language consists of a unique set of linguistically encoded concepts. As lexical concepts have unique access sites, this means that each language interacts with the conceptual system in a language-specific way. As the conceptual system can be modified as a result of the simulations arising from the interaction between language and conceptual structure, LCCM Theory predicts that speakers of different languages should have distinct conceptual representations.

The thesis that language can influence non-linguistic aspects of cognitive function and representation, the **linguistic relativity principle**, is also commonly referred to as the **Sapir–Whorf hypothesis** after the two twentieth-century linguists, Edward Sapir and Benjamin Lee Whorf, who advanced versions of this principle. Classic work which has sought to empirically test a version of the Sapir-Whorf hypothesis has been conducted by Lucy (1992). More recent empirical work has been conducted in the domains of Space (e.g., Levinson 2003) and Time (e.g., Boroditsky 2001). Their findings are suggestive that language does indeed influence aspects of non-linguistic cognition.[12] LCCM Theory makes a proposal which might form part of an account as to why this is so.

The emergence of non-interacting lexical concepts

In this section, I briefly consider why there is a bifurcation in lexical concept types, i.e., between open-class versus closed-class lexical concepts. Language as a system comprising symbolic units, with lexical concepts as the **interacting elements** with the conceptual system, evolved in order to facilitate access to the conceptual system. Two questions emerge from this:

- Why is it that non-interacting lexical concepts emerged?
- How did non-interacting lexical concepts emerge? That is, what is the trajectory of the emergence of closed-class lexical concepts?[13]

Recent work on grammaticalization—the study of the evolution of closed-class symbolic units—suggests that in their initial form linguistic representations did indeed take the form of open-class lexical concepts (Heine and Kuteva 2007). Heine and Kuteva argue that evidence from grammaticalization points to a number of stages in the emergence of closed-class symbolic units, and hence grammar, which suggest that such units developed out of open-class elements. Indeed, given the contention provided here, that the linguistic

---

[12] Recent work by January and Kako (2007) has called into question the findings reported on by Boroditsky (2001). Needless to say, further work is required to empirically investigate the principle of linguistic relativity.

[13] In slightly different terms, these are also the central questions asked by Leonard Talmy (2000) in his work.

system emerged in order to provide access to the conceptual system, it is to be expected that open-class lexical concepts should have emerged first. But what then motivates the development of closed-class lexical concepts? In other words, what drives the process of grammaticalization?

A plausible solution seems to be that as language developed into a fully fledged system, independent of the conceptual system, its specialization—lexical concepts, which encode schematic linguistic content and are borne by physical vehicles, whether signed or oral—allowed it to fulfil a function that better facilitated the linguistic system's primary function: to interact with the conceptual system. In other words, some lexical concepts specialized for encoding solely linguistic content, and hence lost the ability to serve as access sites and hence interact with the conceptual system. Yet, by developing in this way, the linguistic system was able to develop greater precision in the way it interacted with the conceptual system and thereby develop greater control over the integrated simulations, the conceptions, it was able to give rise to. This came about, as I shall argue in Chapter 12, by providing a skeletal framework, through the process of lexical concept integration, thereby providing more precise guidance and hence more finely nuanced simulations. That is, the development of grammar—closed-class symbolic units—facilitated the exercise of greater control over the conceptual system. This is achieved by providing integrated lexical concepts, with unit-like status,[14] which form the input for the process of interpretation: the development of linguistically mediated simulations, as described in Chapter 13.

Abstract concepts

Before concluding this chapter, it is important to very briefly address the issue of abstract concepts. Abstract concepts relate to cognitive models for notions such as JUSTICE, TRUTH, LOVE, and, of course, TIME. Notions such as these have been labelled abstract by scholars such as Lakoff and Johnson (1980, 1999) and by other scholars in other traditions (e.g., Barsalou 1999), as they are held not to be directly grounded in sensory motor experience. In Conceptual Metaphor Theory, for instance, such concepts are often assumed to be structured largely in terms of content derived from sensory-motor experience, rather than in their own terms.

However, a number of scholars have emphasized that part of the content of so-called abstract concepts is likely to include what we might refer to, informally, as **inherent content**, arising from what Barsalou refers to as introspective experience, and I have referred to as subjective experience. After all, while temporal concepts such as DURATION, SIMULTANEITY, and so on are structured in terms of perceptual information derived from sensory-motor experience, their essence derives from our direct experience of what

---

[14] As discussed in Chapter 12.

duration and simultaneity feel like (Evans 2004a; see also Moore 2006). Indeed, as Barsalou (1999) has argued,[15] abstract concepts are likely to be constituted, in part, in terms of inherent content. I will provide an LCCM account of lexical concepts for time in Chapter 15.

Summary

This chapter has developed, in some detail, the theoretical construct of the cognitive model. The cognitive model is a unit of conceptual structure which consists of a frame—or related and/or embedded frames—and gives rise to a potentially limitless set of simulations. Frames have complex structure. This chapter has examined in detail the nature of two types of frames: frames for things and situations. A subset of lexical concepts—open-class lexical concepts—facilitate access to cognitive models, what is referred to as a cognitive model profile. A cognitive model profile consists of primary cognitive models: the cognitive models with which a lexical concept is associated, established through usage. Cognitive models of this sort constitute what is referred to, in LCCM Theory, as the access site of a lexical concept. In addition, the cognitive model profile consists of secondary cognitive models. These are all those cognitive models which are related to the primary cognitive models by virtue of chaining. Cognitive models constitute units of conceptual structure which are accessible to the linguistic system. Hence, lexical concepts, and as a consequence the linguistic system, provide an indirect means of giving rise to simulations.

---

[15] See also Barsalou and Wiemar-Hastings (2005).

Part III

Semantic Compositionality

This part of the book, which consists of three chapters, is concerned with exploring in more detail the role of language in facilitating simulations. This involves purely linguistic processes as well as interaction between linguistic structures and conceptual structures. The processes involved are lexical concept selection and fusion. Lexical concept selection is the process, in language understanding, of identifying the most appropriate lexical concepts associated with the phonological vehicles which populate a given utterance. This is the subject of Chapter 11. Once selection has occurred, the lexical concepts must be integrated: the process of fusion. Fusion manifests itself in two distinct forms. The first, lexical concept integration, involves the integration of linguistic content associated with the selected lexical concepts. This is the subject of Chapter 12. Once this has occurred, the open-class lexical concepts serve to activate a subset of their semantic potential, guided by the output of lexical concept integration. This process, referred to as interpretation, is the subject of Chapter 13.

11

Lexical concept selection

As we saw in the previous part of the book, the linguistic system consists of symbolic units: conventional pairings between phonological vehicles and lexical concepts. As a vehicle may potentially be associated with a large number of distinct lexical concepts, for instance, as seen with the prepositional vehicles *in*, *on*, and *at* in Chapter 8, language understanding involves a process whereby an appropriate lexical concept is identified. This process of lexical concept identification I refer to as lexical concept selection, or selection for short.[1] Of all the lexical concepts associated with a given vehicle, what makes one appropriate, rather than another, can be attributed loosely to the notion of context, although this subsumes a number of more specific factors that influence lexical concept selection, as we shall see in later sections.

Selection proceeds by identifying the lexical concepts associated with each vehicle in a given utterance. Once this has taken place, the output of selection, which is to say the range of lexical concepts identified, are subject to fusion, a compositional process of semantic integration. Fusion involves a further two processes: a compositional process that applies to semantic structure, which is to say linguistic content. This I refer to as lexical concept integration (Chapter 12), and results in each lexical concept receiving a semantic value. The next step is for the semantic values of all open-class lexical concepts to undergo a further process of semantic composition which I refer to as interpretation. This results in interaction between these lexical concepts and conceptual structure via access sites, in order to derive an informational characterization of each relevant lexical concept. Crucially, the nature of the interpretations achieved, and hence which aspects of an open-class lexical concept's cognitive model profile becomes activated, is a consequence of the output of lexical concept integration. The end result is a conception: a simulation achieved by virtue of selection and the subsequent compositional processes.[2]

---

[1] The notion of selection discussed in the present chapter is orthogonal to the notion of sanction discussed in Chapter 2. Selection relates to identification of an appropriate lexical concept from the perspective of language understanding, i.e., comprehension. Sanction relates to the way in which a particular instance of use is motivated by the existence of a lexical concept. Hence the use of the term sanction situates things from the perspective of the producer. For the most part, I am concerned with language understanding.

[2] Although the compositional processes described in this and subsequent chapters are informed by findings from psycholinguistics, LCCM Theory is not a psycholinguistic theory. That is, it does not make specific claims about the details of language processing issues. Rather, it is an attempt to develop a

Selection in meaning construction

Recall that the motivation for the development of LCCM Theory is to account for the inherent semantic variation exhibited by words in contexts of use. The specific problem that I seek to account for is how words take on a specific reading in any given context of use. That is, in this book we are ultimately concerned with how words obtain their specific context-bound interpretation. Selection is the first step in serving to narrow down, so to speak, the reading associated with a context-bound word.

One way of thinking about the process involved in arriving at the specific reading a word achieves in any given utterance, and about the perspective adopted here, is as follows. A word form has a range of distinct lexical concepts associated with it. For instance, *in* exhibits extensive polysemy, as described in Chapter 8.[3] This **lexical concept potential** must be narrowed to (typically) a single lexical concept. This process of narrowing is a consequence of lexical concept selection.

To illustrate, consider the following examples involving the prepositional vehicle *in*:

(1)   a. The kitten is in the box
      b. The flag is flapping in the wind
      c. John is in love

In each of these examples, a distinct lexical concept is selected for. The lexical concepts for *in* selected are [ENCLOSURE] for (1a), [PREVAILING CONDITIONS] for (1b), and [PSYCHOSOMATIC STATE] for (1c).

Selection relies on a number of **constraining** factors to determine the **appropriate** lexical concept: the lexical concept which best fits the conception under construction, discussed later in the chapter. Once a lexical concept has been selected, it must be integrated with other selected lexical concepts of the utterance, and, if it is an open-class lexical concept, interpreted in the light of conceptual structure to which it affords access, and the other open-class lexical concept(s) with which it has been integrated. That is, the selected lexical concept undergoes the second compositional process: namely fusion. Once this has occurred, the word achieves what we might informally refer to as a reading: a situated interpretation, specific to the context in which it is embedded. We might think of the stages involved as involving passage through an ever narrowing cone, as illustrated in Figure 11.1, in which compositional processes serve to restrict the potential of the word in order to specify the semantic contribution it makes to the utterance.

psychologically plausible account of lexical representation and meaning construction that, in principle, is compatible with what is known about the processes involved in semantic composition. For excellent reviews that deal with psycholinguistic processing see Harley (2008) and Whitney (1998). One of the goals of LCCM Theory is to develop a significantly robust theoretical architecture which will give rise to testable predictions that can be subject to empirical investigation by psycholinguists.

    [3] See also Tyler and Evans (2003: ch. 7).

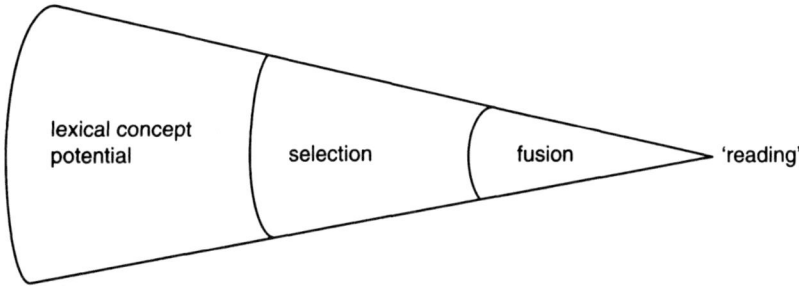

FIGURE 11.1. Narrowing in the situated interpretation of words

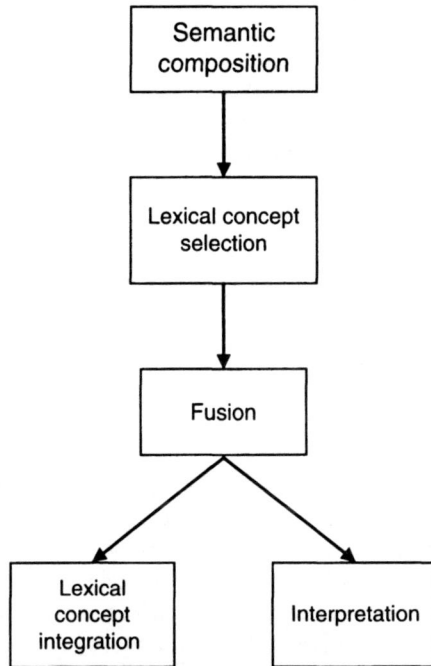

FIGURE 11.2. Processes of semantic composition in LCCM Theory

The relationship between selection and the other processes of meaning construction in LCCM Theory are diagrammed in Figure 11.2.

Having provided a preliminary notion of what is involved in selection, it is important to briefly say what selection is not. Selection applies in order to distinguish between lexical concepts. However, once a lexical concept has been identified, the processes which apply in order to further narrow the reading are lexical concept integration and interpretation. Hence, while selection serves to identify distinct lexical concepts associated with *in*, in the examples in (1), selection does not apply to *France* in the examples in (2), which we first met in Chapter 1:

(2) a. France is a country of outstanding natural beauty
     b. France is one of the leading nations in the European Union
     c. France beat New Zealand in the 2007 Rugby World Cup
     d. France voted against the EU constitution in the 2005 referendum

This follows as the vehicle *France* is sanctioned by the same lexical concept in each of these examples. Hence, while *France* provides a different semantic contribution in each of the utterances in (2), this is not a consequence of selection, but the two constituent compositional processes associated with fusion, discussed in the next two chapters. Accordingly, my claim is that *France*, in these examples, is associated with a single lexical concept, with a single access site and a single coherent cognitive model profile. In contrast, the instances of *in*, in the examples in (1), are associated with distinct lexical profiles, and hence count as instances of distinct lexical concepts.[4]

Types of selection

Selection can be divided into two distinct types: **broad selection** and **narrow selection**. Broad selection involves the identification of a lexical concept. For instance, in an utterance such as (1a) above, reproduced below:

(1a) The kitten is in the box

the hearer has to select the appropriate lexical concept for *in* from amongst the range of available lexical concepts—as we have seen, *in* is highly polysemous with a large number of distinct lexical concepts stored in semantic memory. Typically, the language user will select a single lexical concept in order to build a conception. This is the canonical situation, which I refer to as **single selection**. In the example in (1a) the hearer selects the [ENCLOSURE] lexical concept from the lexical concept potential associated with the vehicle *in*. However, in certain contexts more than one lexical concept can be selected. This I refer to as **multiple selection**: the selection of more than one lexical concept for a single vehicle.

There are at least two distinct types of multiple selection. This we first met in an earlier chapter. Reconsider the following examples involving the vehicle *fast*:

(3) a fast car   [RAPID LOCOMOTION]

(4) a fast typist   [RAPID PERFORMANCE OF ACTIVITY]

(5) a fast decision [REQUIRES LITTLE TIME FOR COMPLETION]

---

[4] Recall that as lexical concepts associated with *in* are closed-class lexical concepts they do not have an access site to the conceptual system.

In each of these examples, a distinct lexical concept for *fast* is selected, as indicated by the lexical concept glosses next to each utterance. However, as indicated by Pustejovsky (1995) in his discussion of *fast*, the following example appears to be a blend of the [RAPID PERFORMANCE OF ACTIVITY] and [REQUIRE LITTLE TIME FOR COMPLETION] lexical concepts:

(6)   We need a fast garage for our car, as we leave the day after tomorrow

That is, to construct the conception that most native speakers will ordinarily derive, based on this utterance, this use of *fast* seems to involve two lexical concepts. That is, the reading derived relates to a garage whose mechanics are able to carry out the repairs rapidly, and that takes little time to do so. After all, a garage whose mechanics worked fast would be to no purpose if the garage also had a backlog of work so that the mechanics in question couldn't get to the repairs without delay. Multiple selection of this kind I refer to as **single instance multiple selection.** That is, there is a single instance of a vehicle, i.e., *fast*, in (6) which requires selection of multiple lexical concepts.

The second type of multiple selection I refer to as **multiple instance multiple selection.** This occurs when a single vehicle occurs or is implicated multiple times in a single utterance giving rise to distinct lexical concepts on each instance of use. An example of this arises in elliptical utterances as exemplified by the following:

(7)   On the day my old dad expired, so did my driving licence

In this utterance, there are two distinct instances of *expired*: an actual occurrence of the vehicle in the first clause, and an implied instance in the second or elliptical clause: the clause with the omitted, but understood, instance of *expired*. Moreover, each instance is associated with a distinct reading, giving rise to a humorous effect. Indeed, the example in (7) where the two clauses are related by virtue of employing (or implying) the same verb in each is an instance of the figure of speech known as **zeugma**—I shall have more to say about zeugma later in the chapter by way of a detailed case study illustrating the mechanics of selection. In the first clause *expired* relates to an event involving death, while in the second, *expired* relates to expiry of the term for which an individual's right to drive on the public highway was sanctioned or "licensed." That is, there are multiple instances of *expired*, each instance selecting distinct lexical concepts.

Having addressed broad selection I now consider narrow selection. While broad selection concerns selection of a distinct lexical concept from among a number of possible lexical concepts conventionally associated with a particular vehicle, narrow selection involves selection *within* a single lexical concept.

As we saw in the previous part of the book, while it is convenient to speak of lexical concepts as if they were discrete entities, and to gloss them with a label, it is crucial to remember that they constitute a complex array of different sorts of linguistic content. That is, a lexical concept comprises a bundle of different types of knowledge. For instance, lexical concepts often encode multiple parameters. We saw an instance of this in Chapter 8 when discussing the [ENCLOSURE] lexical concept associated with the prepositional vehicle *in*. This lexical concept, I argued, encodes (at least) two distinct parameters: Enclosure and Location with Surety. Which parameter is selected is a function of context. For instance, contexts involving full enclosure, such as that in (8) select the Enclosure parameter, while contexts involving only partial enclosure, as exhibited by the examples in (9), select the Location with Surety parameter.

(8)   The toy is in the box

(9)   a. The bulb is in the socket
      b. The flower is in the vase
      c. The umbrella is in his hand

In fact, it is likely that narrow selection relates to a **gradient of activation**; for example, instances of full enclosure may in fact activate both parameters, with the Enclosure parameter achieving greater (or primary) activation. This serves to **foreground** the Enclosure parameter. Analogously, contexts involving partial enclosure result, I suggest, in the foregrounding of the Location with Surety parameter.[5]

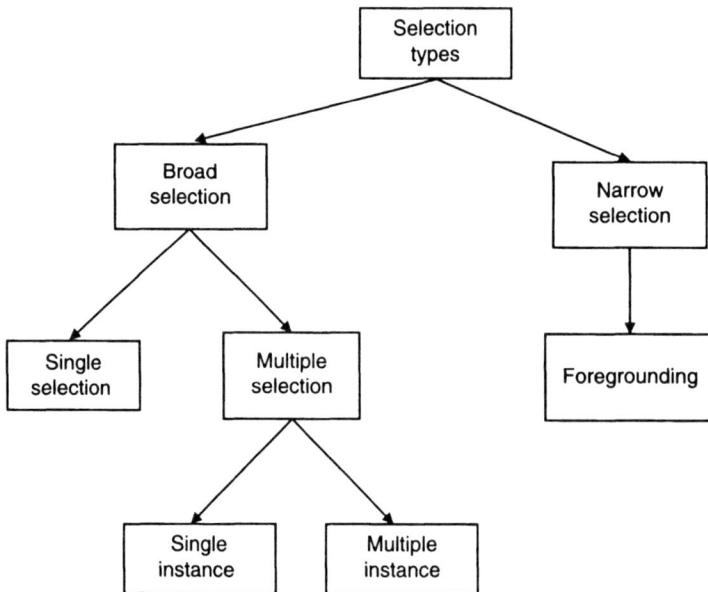

FIGURE 11.3. Selection types

---

[5] Ultimately, this remains an empirical question, of course.

The distinction in selection types discussed in this section is represented diagrammatically in Figure 11. 3.

Before concluding this section I briefly discuss a further phenomenon: **selection revision**. A key claim made by LCCM Theory is that meaning construction—which is to say, the formation of utterance-level meaning: a conception—involves the recruitment and integration of a range of distinct types of information drawn from different sources. These include linguistic content encoded by the various lexical concepts selected for in an utterance, conceptual content associated with the cognitive model profiles to which the selected open-class lexical concepts potentially afford access, as well as various aspects of context including the discourse context, extra-linguistic context, and what we might refer to as background knowledge—discussed in greater detail below.[6] Indeed, and as we shall see in later chapters, LCCM Theory claims that the various processes of semantic composition occur in tandem, and recursively, in building the conception. Hence, it is to be expected that a conception is revised, as further information is incorporated.

One way in which a conception can be revised is due to revising which lexical concept is selected: selection revision. To illustrate this process consider the following attested exchange:

(10) 1. A. Let's make a MARGARITA.
      2. B. What?
      3. A. For lunch . . . for Isabella.
      4. B. Oh, pizza!

In this attested exchange, two speakers were discussing lunch arrangements and specifically what each person should have: two adults and two children aged 6 and 2. The previous day speaker A had been talking about making margaritas: the alcoholic cocktail drink. In the exchange in (10), upon hearing the vehicle transcribed as "MARGARITA" person B took this to relate to the drink: *margarita*. However, person A in fact intended *margherita*, a type of pizza. While "margherita" and "margarita" have distinct orthographic representations, they share the same phonological vehicle. Hence, lexical concept selection is required.

Upon hearing the utterance in (10.1) person B selected the lexical concept [TYPE OF ALCOHOLIC DRINK]. The utterance in line 2 seeks clarification, given the unusual nature of making cocktails for lunch. In line 3 person A clarifies that the "margherita" is intended for Isabella, a 2-year-old child, whose favourite food is margherita pizzas, a fact known by both A and B. Person B then revises the lexical concept that the vehicle selects for, and instead selects the lexical concept [TYPE OF PIZZA]. This is confirmed in line 4.[7]

---

[6] See the discussion of joint activities and the accumulation of common ground.

[7] It is worth observing that this example illustrates that lexical concept selection applies to cases of homonymy, as evidenced by *margherita* and *margarita*, as well as to instances involving polysemy, as in the case of the distinct lexical concepts associated with the prepositional vehicle *in*.

The nature of linguistically mediated communication

LCCM Theory constitutes an attempt to account for meaning construction at the level of the utterance. That is, it is concerned with the formation of conceptions. Following previous research in cognitive linguistics, notably Croft (2000), Langacker (1987, 1991a, 2008), and Tomasello (2003), I refer to an utterance as a usage event (recall the discussion in Chapter 3). Yet usage events occur within larger chunks of discourse. Moreover, discourse involves language users, who have particular communicative intentions. In the words of Herbert Clark: "Language is used by individuals at particular times and places for particular purposes" (*ibid.* 1996: xi). In short, usage events, and the words which populate them, are not plucked out of thin air. The conception associated with a particular usage event is a function of the communicative intention expressed by a speaker and understood by a hearer. Put another way, a conception is always situated and hence unique, arising in service of the expression of a communicative intention, mediated, in part, by the resources made available by language. But we cannot hope to fully get to grips with the nature of the linguistic resources available, and how they contribute to meaning-construction processes without, if only briefly, considering usage events as an outcome of situated linguistically mediated communication, namely, communicative events. The compositional processes at the heart of LCCM Theory, including lexical concept selection, assume a particular view of the nature of language and its role in communication. In this section, which represents an excursis of sorts, I spell out this perspective. In so doing, I draw in particular on the seminal work of Herbert Clark (e.g., 1996).

Joint activities

Clark argues that language users deploy language in order to do things. That is, language is primarily used for social purposes. For instance, we use language to engage in gossip, to get to know someone, to conduct business, to make a purchase in a shop, to declare love, to propose marriage, to get married, to quarrel, to make up afterwards, to get divorced, and so on and so forth. Clark argues that the way we deploy language, in order to facilitate these social functions, takes place by engaging in what he terms **joint activities**. A joint activity involves two or more participants, who engage in some culturally recognized activity in order to achieve some, typically, mutually understood goal. Moreover, for Clark, language use arises *in* joint activities, which are *impossible without* language.

Clark suggests that joint activities vary on a number of dimensions, thus exhibiting **dimensions of variation**. The dimensions of variation include the following:

- *Scriptedness*: while some activity types are highly scripted, such as a marriage ceremony, others, such as a chance meeting in a supermarket are unscripted. There are other activities which lie between these two poles of scriptedness, which is what it means to say that scriptedness is a dimension of variation.

- *Formality*: activities also vary in terms of formality between two extremes; while activities can be highly formal, such as a court hearing, the other extreme is that of complete informality, such as a gossip session.
- *Verbalness*: this dimension relates to the degree to which language is integral to a given activity. Again, there are extremes and event types in-between. For instance, a telephone call is constituted solely by language, while a football match is primarily not linguistic in nature. The degree to which a joint activity relies on language is referred to as a **discourse continuum**. This continuum is illustrated in Table 11.1.
- *Cooperativeness*: activities range from those that are wholly cooperative, to those that are adversarial in nature. For instance, making a purchase in a shop is cooperative as it relies on both the customer and the shop assistant working cooperatively in order to effect the purchase. In contrast, a tennis match, at least in one sense, is adversarial, rather than cooperative, as the players seek to cause their opponent(s) to lose.
- *Governance*: the final dimension of variation relates to the respective roles of the participants involved in the joint activity, in particular whether their roles are equally balanced or not in terms of significance and contribution towards realizing the goal of the activity. For instance, making a purchase in a shop involves **egalitarian governance**: both participants, the customer and the shopkeeper, must work equally in order to effect the sale. In contrast, some activities involve **autocratic governance**, whereby one participant is especially dominant, such as in a university lecture.

In addition, joint activities also exhibit **constituent elements** which serve to provide them with structure. These include the following:

- *Participants*: A joint activity involves two or more participants who carry out the activity. For instance, in a shop purchase, the participants consist of the customer and the sales assistant.

TABLE 11.1. The discourse continuum (After Clark 1996: 50).

Mostly linguistic	Telephone conversations, newspaper articles, radio reports, and so on.
	Face-to-face conversations, television reports, tabloid news items
	Business transactions, plays, films, coaching demonstrations
	Football matches, tennis matches, two people moving furniture, making love
Mostly non-linguistic	Playing a violin in a duet, waltzing, playing catch

- *Activity roles*: In a joint activity, each participant takes on particular public roles. These determine how each participant proceeds in service of facilitating the joint activity. For instance, in a commercial event transaction such as a purchase in a shop, one participant assumes the role of seller, the other of customer.
- *Public goals*: These are the mutually known goals which result from the joint activity, such as effecting a purchase.
- *Private goals*: In addition, participants in a joint activity may harbour private goals, which are unknown to the other participants(s).
- *Joint actions*: Joint activities are comprised of, and advance through, joint actions. These are the discrete action components that make up a joint activity. For instance, in making a purchase in a shop, the sales assistant or customer may initiate the activity by enquiring as to whether assistance is required, or can be provided, deciding on the items wanted, confirming the price, exchanging payment in return for goods, producing and receiving a receipt and finally closing the transaction. Each of these discrete components constitutes a joint action.
- *Hierarchies*: A joint activity involves a hierarchy of joint actions (and indeed other joint activities). That is, as we have seen in the example of a shop purchase, joint actions naturally lead to others, in a hierarchical sequence: one cannot proceed to the next activity until another is first completed. Equally, extended event sequences involve hierarchies of joint activities.
- *Procedures*: Participants in a joint activity achieve their public and private goals by deploying procedures of various sorts. These include using language as well as other non-linguistic procedures specialized for, or adapted to, the joint activity in question. For instance, in football non-linguistic procedures may include those which are recognized by the laws of the game, such as kicking the ball in various ways, passing the ball to team-mates, dribbling past opposing players, and those which are not, such as attempting to win free kicks in goal-scoring position by virtue of simulation, which is to say, pretending to have been fouled.
- *Phases*: A joint activity involves a number of distinct phases. Clark identifies three:

i. an *entry*: the participants go from not being in the joint activity to being in it, as when a customer approaches a shopkeeper to ask for help in selecting an item for purchase;
ii. the *body*: the participants are engaged in the joint activity;
iii. an *exit*: the participants go from being in the joint activity to not being in it.

- *Dynamics*: joint activities are dynamic in the sense that they may occur simultaneously with, or overlap, other joint activities. In addition they may also feature a varying number of participants at different points in the achievement of the activity's goal(s).

Common ground

Joint activities proceed in incremental steps which are cumulative in nature. These incremental steps serve to accumulate what Clark refers to as **common ground**, borrowing a term from Richard Stalnaker (1978). For Clark, common ground constitutes the shared knowledge between participants that is built up incrementally during the course of a joint activity. Clark argues that joint activities are driven by the accumulation of common ground.

Three stages can be adduced in the accumulation of common ground:

- Initial common ground: This involves the knowledge that participants bring with them before engaging in a joint activity, and hold at the point of entry to the activity. This knowledge includes the set of background assumptions and presumed facts that participants have about each other, and their presumptions about their respective goals, how these will be achieved including knowledge and assumptions about their joint activity roles.
- Current state of the joint activity: At any given point in a joint activity, participants represent the current state of the activity. This relates to knowledge concerning how the activity is progressing and what stage it is at.
- Public events so far: Participants also represent the various events that have thus far taken place in realizing the joint activity.

By way of illustration, let's reconsider the shop purchase event, and imagine that the customer enters a shoe shop in order to buy a pair of boots. At the moment the shop assistant approaches the customer, in order to enquire whether she requires assistance in effecting her purchase, both the customer and sales assistant hold a large body of knowledge. This involves knowledge about the procedures involved in making a purchase of footwear, and about each other, including assumptions. For instance, the sales assistant assumes that the customer wishes to purchase an item or items of footwear, and the customer assumes that the sales assistant is available for, and offers, assistance in effecting the selection and purchase of footwear. These assumptions made by the participants represent the initial state of the common ground. The joint activity progresses by virtue of the participants jointly and collaboratively navigating their way through a series of joint actions which collectively make up the joint activity. These include the sales assistant offering assistance, the customer indicating the kind of item required, the sales assistant perhaps measuring the customer's feet, fetching boots and the customer trying them on, making a decision on the boots required, confirming on price, payment for the boots, wrapping the purchase, and closing the transaction. Each of these joint actions can proceed in a range of ways, and constitutes a hierarchical sequence, as described above. The current state of the common ground includes knowledge as to which stage has been reached, while participants

Common Ground

Discourse Representation	
Textual Representation	Situational Representation

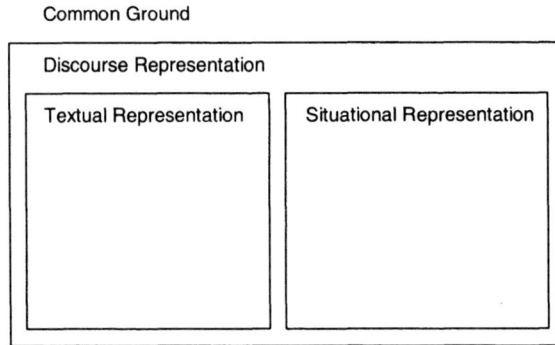

FIGURE 11.4. Common ground and the discourse representation

also represent knowledge relating to all the joint actions that have thus far occurred.

According to Clark, common ground accumulates by virtue of participants maintaining a **discourse representation**. This consists of two other sorts of representation. The first is a **textual representation**. During the joint activity, participants keep track of all the utterances issued and other signals, such as accompanying gestures, prosody, and so on, during the various joint actions. The record of all the utterances made constitutes the textual representation. In addition, participants maintain a **situational representation**.[8] This comprises the participants, the time, venue, and physical environment, the referents of the linguistic expressions deployed, the social commitments implied by the participants' utterances—for example, the offer to help made by the sales assistant—and the relationship between the various joint actions in accomplishing the joint activity. The relationship between the components of the discourse representation are captured in Figure 11.4.

Joint actions

Joint activities proceed by virtue of the joint actions which make them up, as we have seen. The hallmark of joint actions is that they require coordination between the two (or more) participants. In this they are **participatory**: they involve two or more participants who each perform a part in order to achieve the joint action. Joint actions can be contrasted with **autonomous actions** which are non-participatory, such as playing a flute solo. Joint actions progress by virtue of the **coordination** of actions between participants in order to overcome a coordination problem. A coordination problem arises when two or more people have common interests and/or goals which can only be achieved by virtue of

[8] See the related notions of the situation model (van Dijk and Kintsch 1983) and mental model (Johnson-Laird 1983) developed in the psycholinguistic literature, and addressed in slightly more detail in Chapter 13.

coordinating their actions. In joint actions the coordination problem is resolved by virtue of employing **coordination devices**. One kind of coordination device, and the one employed by language, is convention.

A linguistic system (e.g., English) represents a conventional signalling system that facilitates coordination in joint actions. This system is comprised of symbolic units—bipolar assemblies comprising vehicles and lexical concepts—which are established by convention in a given linguistic community. However, and as observed in Chapter 4, the range of symbolic units available to the participants in joint actions underdetermine the range of situations, events, states, relationships, and other interpersonal functions that participants may potentially seek to use language to express and fulfil. Language users are continually using language to express unique meanings, about unique states of affairs and relationships, in unique ways. While each language has a range of "ready-made" schemas—symbolic units which can be combined to facilitate coordination in joint actions—these necessarily underdetermine the mutability of human experience. As Langacker puts it, "Linguistic convention cannot provide a fixed, unitary expression for every conceivable situation that a speaker might wish to describe" (*ibid.* 1987: 278). As Clark argues, in order to overcome this, language use involves employing the conventional repertoire of symbolic units in non-conventional ways in order to overcome coordination problems (see also Croft 2000). That is, words do not have stable and fixed semantic representations which surface each time they are used. Rather, words exhibit semantic variation, a function of situated language use in service of joint actions.

From the perspective of LCCM Theory, the protean nature of semantic representation is, in part, a function of (i) selecting the appropriate lexical concept, and (ii) deriving a context-specific reading due to the processes of lexical concept integration and interpretation; as lexical concepts facilitate access to the conceptual system, and hence possess a vast semantic potential, this potential must be narrowed in service of the formation of a conception.

Factors in selection

In this section I provide a brief overview of some of the main factors in selection. Selection, like the other compositional processes in LCCM Theory, is guided by context. In order to identify some of the main contextual factors involved, I divide the discussion as follows:

- factors associated with linguistic context, and
- factors associated with extra-linguistic context.

Selection is influenced by both these distinct types of context.

Linguistic context

We can think of linguistic context as involving three levels. The first level is that of the utterance, the primary concern of LCCM Theory. Above this is the discourse level, which involves an arrangement of more than one, typically many, utterances. Above the discourse level is the speech event. A speech event can be thought of as the highest level of linguistic context, in which more than one, sometimes many distinct episodes of discourse are embedded. While speech events might be co-extensive with events of other sorts, such as a dinner party, sometimes an event is entirely constituted by the speech event, as in a lecture.[9] In terms of the example of a dinner party, which might last for several hours, this may consist of a large number of separate discourses, involving different configurations of participants as they range over different topics, in different locations in the house or other venue of the dinner party. Similarly, a lecture is not simply a monologue involving a single unbroken discursive unit. Lectures often involve questions, and interactions between members of the audience and the lecturer, the lecturer may indulge in asides, anecdotes, and a lecture is typically organized into separate parts with distinct themes and organizational structures. Hence, even a lecture, *qua* speech event, can be thought of as involving distinct discourse episodes. Each level, the utterance level, the discourse level, and the level of the speech event, provides a context which facilitates, in slightly different ways, lexical concept selection.

i. Utterance context: The utterance itself provides a linguistic context which guides selection. This linguistic context includes all aspects of linguistic information that appear in a given utterance. These include all the lexical concepts implicated in the utterance, as well as features of prosody—rhythm, stress, and intonation. To illustrate the way in which utterance context serves to guide selection, consider the following attested example:

(11) Send your girlfriend somewhere really cool, the fridge for a pork pie.

The utterance in (11) derives from a billboard advertisement for the alcopop WKD Original Vodka. The point of interest in this example relates to the lexical concept selected for the vehicle *cool*. The first part of the utterance leads the language user to select the [POSITIVE EVALUATION] lexical concept. One reason for this follows from the lexical profile for this lexical concept. That is, part of the knowledge we have of the [POSITIVE EVALUATION] lexical concept is that there is a formal selectional tendency for *cool* to be pre-modified by *really*, as in the expression *really cool*. This leads to selection of the [POSITIVE EVALUATION] lexical concept. Hence, the first part of the utterance gives rise to a reading in which the advert is interpreted as suggesting sending the addressee's girlfriend to an exciting location, perhaps on vacation.

---

[9] Indeed, the degree to which a speech event is integral to the event with which it is co-extensive corresponds to the discourse continuum (Clark 1996); see Table 11.1.

However, the second part of the utterance relates to a fridge, a specific location which is designed for refrigerating foodstuffs. Hence, by definition a fridge is cold. This prompts for selection revision, in which the [LOW TEMPERATURE] lexical concept is selected. This then gives rise to a reading in which it is not an exciting location to which the addressee's girlfriend should be sent, but rather a cold location, namely the fridge, in order to fetch a pork pie. The advertising campaign for WKD Vodka typically concludes with the slogan: "Have you got a WKD (pronounced 'wicked') side?" In the UK where WKD Original Vodka has been heavily promoted, this particular alcoholic drink is aimed at the under 25 age group. The humour of the advert plays, in part, on the distinct lexical concepts associated with *cool*, and the fact that for a certain audience it is amusing to seemingly hold out the prospect, to one's girlfriend, of an exotic location, only to reveal that an errand is required; presumably a pork pie goes nicely with a bottle of WKD Original Vodka. The humour also plays, in part, on the selection for the [LOW TEMPERATURE] lexical concept, while **evoking** the [POSITIVE EVALUATION] lexical concept. That is, in so far as the utterance is amusing, this is so because it evokes one lexical concept—advantageous to the addressee's girlfriend—only to revise it with another—which is not advantageous—thereby revealing a "wicked side".

ii. Discourse context (aka common ground): The discourse context can be equated with the construct of common ground, developed by Stalnaker (1978) and especially Clark (1996), as summarized above. This includes knowledge "above" the level of the utterance, and relates to the accumulated knowledge, both textual and situational, that is shared by interlocutors due to the ongoing discourse. The discourse context serves to guide the process of lexical concept selection.

To illustrate, reconsider the exchange in (10) reproduced below:

(10) 1. A. Let's make a MARGARITA.
      2. B. What?
      3. A. For lunch ... for Isabella.
      4. B. Oh, pizza!

As is evident in this exchange, as the common ground accumulates, it becomes clear to speaker B that person A is referring to [TYPE OF PIZZA] in line 1 rather than [CITRUS-FLAVOURED TEQUILA COCKTAIL]. Crucially, the discourse itself provides the context which facilitates the selection of the lexical concept intended by speaker A.

iii. Speech event: Moving "above" the discourse level we have the speech event. The speech event can provide a context which facilitates lexical concept selection. For instance, a student who attends a linguistics lecture on "word-formation processes" will select the lexical concept [THE STUDY OF WORD PARTS] upon hearing the phonological vehicle *morphology*. However, a student attending a lecture on human anatomy will select the lexical concept [THE STUDY OF BODY PARTS] when exposed to the same vehicle. In other words, the nature of the speech event can provide a context which facilitates lexical concept selection regardless of the utterance or discourse contexts.

Extralinguistic context

Extra-linguistic context is a complex construct which plays a significant role in the compositional process of interpretation. However, for our purposes here two examples will suffice to illustrate its more limited function in lexical concept selection. Firstly, consider the following example:

(12)   "The woman approached the bar."

The phonological vehicle of interest in this utterance is *bar*. Crucially, this vehicle has a number of distinct lexical concepts associated with it, including [VENUE OF PURCHASE IN PUBLIC HOUSE] and [DEMARCATION OF AREA RE-SERVED FOR JUDGE IN COURT OF LAW]. Hence, this utterance could relate to a woman approaching a "bar" in a public house, presumably in order to purchase alcohol, or to a woman approaching the area where the judge is seated in a court of law. In an utterance such as this, the venue in which the utterance is made, which is to say the setting, provides the extra-linguistic context which facilitates lexical concept selection. If uttered in a pub, the lexical concept selected will be that of [VENUE OF PURCHASE IN PUBLIC HOUSE]. If uttered in or near a court of law, the lexical concept selected will be [DEMARCATION OF AREA RESERVED FOR JUDGE IN COURT OF LAW].

Now consider this second example:

(13)   Satisfaction with every erection!

The lexical vehicle *erection* has a number of lexical concepts associated with it. However, this attested phrase represents the slogan of a scaffolding contractor, and was seen on a company vehicle belonging to the contractor. Here, then, the setting provides the extra-linguistic context which is sufficient to identify the lexical concept in question: [ACT OF ASSEMBLING A MAN-MADE VERTICAL STRUCTURE].

An illustration: *declare*

In this section I illustrate some of the issues relating to selection by examining an example of single-instance multiple selection involving the vehicle *declare*.[10]

---

[10] Note that as lexical concepts are vehicle-specific, in this section I will only be addressing the form *declare*, rather than other related forms, such as *declared*. Lexical concepts associated with *declare* as opposed to *declared* differ in terms of (at least) their linguistic content, as they encode different parameters for the category Time reference.

Consider the following example, attributed to Oscar Wilde, the Irish playwright, novelist, and poet, when questioned at US customs in 1882:

(14)   "I have nothing to declare but my genius."[11]

The vehicle *declare* has a number of distinct lexical concepts associated with it. To illustrate consider just a few of these:

[FORTHRIGHT INFORMATIONAL ASSERTION]
(15)   a. He wanted to declare his undying love for her
       b. The convict wishes to declare his innocence

[ANNOUNCEMENT OF NEW LEGAL STATUS]
(16)   a. Neville Chamberlain was forced to declare war on Germany on
           September 3rd 1939
       b. The Junta is set to declare martial law

[PROVISION OF AN OFFICIAL RULING]
(17)   a. The referee will declare him the winner
       b. The judge decided to declare the inmate legally insane
       c. The building inspector won't declare the building fit for habitation

[ANNOUNCEMENT OF DUTIABLE GOODS AT CUSTOMS]
(18)   a. 'I have nothing to declare'
       b. The traveller was forced to declare having more than his allocated
           cigarette allowance

Each of the examples above are licensed by distinct lexical concepts associated with the vehicle *declare*. That is, as a lexical concept has bipartite organization, encoding linguistic content and facilitating access to conceptual content—collectively its semantic representation—each lexical concept associated with *declare*—being an open-class lexical concept—involves distinct linguistic content and a unique access site to conceptual content, as described in Part II of the book. In terms of linguistic content, one obvious difference between the lexical concepts for *declare* relates to their pragmatic point (recall the discussion in Chapter 6), in particular the social consequences associated with each lexical concept, the settings in which they can occur and the participants involved. In terms of conceptual content, each of these lexical concepts has a unique access site. That is, each lexical concept has a unique semantic potential, facilitating access, potentially, to a large body of non-linguistic knowledge. For instance, part of the knowledge of the [ANNOUNCEMENT OF

[11] The discussion in this section is based on suggestions for analysing the Oscar Wilde quotation, involving *declare*, by my graduate student Kyle Jasmin. These were presented in an unpublished term paper which I refer to as Jasmin (2008). I am grateful to Kyle for bringing this quotation to my attention.

NEW LEGAL STATUS] lexical concept involves the cognitive models, which I refer to as individuals and types, with which this lexical concept is associated. For instance, many people, particularly in the United Kingdom, will know that the Prime Minister is able to bring about a state of war between the UK and another country without consulting parliament. This is a function of the Royal Pre-rogative whereby the British Prime Minister is endowed by the monarch with the monarch's rights, for example to wage war. Hence, the lexical concept [ANNOUNCEMENT OF NEW LEGAL STATUS] facilitates access to both individuals and types that have the institutional power to effect a new legal state. For many people the type of cognitive model for British Prime Minister will include knowledge relating to the Prime Minister's ability to take the country to war. Others will have an individual cognitive model for the Prime Minister Neville Chamberlain, who failed in his bid to appease Hitler, leading to the invasion by Nazi Germany of Poland in 1939. Neville Chamberlain subsequently declared war on Germany before standing aside for an all-party "National" government and the premiership of Winston Churchill.

Now returning to the example in (14), the humour apparent in this example turns on the fact that a single instance of the vehicle *declare* facilitates the selection of two distinct lexical concepts: [FORTHRIGHT INFORMATIONAL ASSERTION] and [ANNOUNCEMENT OF DUTIABLE GOODS AT CUSTOMS]. These two lexical concepts are selected for in slightly different ways. The selection of the [FORTHRIGHT INFORMATIONAL ASSERTION] lexical concept is facilitated by linguistic context. This follows as "my genius" is a property being ascribed to an individual, namely Oscar Wilde, by Oscar Wilde. Accordingly, this counts as an informational assertion, and therefore guides the selection of the [FORTHRIGHT INFORMATIONAL ASSERTION] lexical concept associated with *declare*. However, both linguistic and extra-linguistic context serve to select for the lexical concept: [ANNOUNCEMENT OF DUTIABLE GOODS AT CUSTOMS]. In terms of linguistic context, the [ANNOUNCEMENT OF DUTIABLE GOODS AT CUSTOMS] lexical concept collocates with the expression *I have nothing to*, which forms part of the lexical profile associated with this lexical concept. In addition, the extra-linguistic context, a US customs post, serves to facilitate selection of this lexical concept. The humour that derives from this expression relies, in part, on the dual selection of two distinct lexical concepts from a single instance. Moreover, this usage provides evidence for Wilde's assertion regarding his genius. Oscar Wilde was well known for his wit and clever wordplay. In asserting his genius he also provides evidence of it.

Summary

This chapter has been concerned with lexical concept selection, or selection for short. Selection involves the identification of the lexical concepts associ-ated with each vehicle in a given utterance. Selection is thus one of the compositional processes central to meaning construction in LCCM Theory.

Indeed, the output of selection, which is to say the range of lexical concepts identified, are subject to fusion, a compositional process of semantic integration. Selection can be divided into two distinct types: broad selection and narrow selection. Broad selection involves the identification of one specific lexical concept, rather than the range of others conventionally associated with the same phonological vehicle. Narrow selection involves selection "within" a single lexical concept, for example, the selection of distinct parameters from amongst the range of parameters encoded by a given lexical concept. In addition, there are two types of broad selection. Typically, the language user will select a single lexical concept in order to build a conception. This is the canonical situation, and is referred to as single selection. However, in certain contexts more than one lexical concept can be selected. This is referred to as multiple selection: the selection of more than one lexical concept for a single vehicle. Finally, selection is influenced and guided by context. In particular, factors associated with both linguistic and extra-linguistic context were described which serve to constrain the application of selection.

12

Lexical concept integration

This chapter is concerned with the first of the two constituent processes associated with fusion, namely lexical concept integration. Lexical concept integration, or integration for short, involves the integration of the linguistic content encoded by the full range of lexical concepts in a particular utterance. Hence, integration is concerned solely with the integration of linguistic content, and as such is guided by the linguistic context of the utterance rather than any other sort of context, for instance extra-linguistic context.

Integration applies once the lexical concepts in a given utterance have been selected, based on the mechanism described in the previous chapter. Integration involves what I refer to as the unpacking[1] of the linguistic content associated with the lexical concepts being integrated in order for integration to take place. Integration gives rise to the formation of **lexical conceptual units**: integrated units of linguistic content. Once lexical concepts have been integrated, those lexical concepts which afford access to cognitive model profiles, open-class lexical concepts, are then subject to the process of interpretation. However, and as we shall see in greater detail in the next chapter, the relationship between the mechanisms of lexical concept integration and interpretation is best characterized as constituting a dynamic interplay, rather than two discrete processes that are "blind" to the workings of each other. In part, this is a consequence of the way fusion proceeds: lexical conceptual units in different parts of the utterance may undergo interpretation prior to undergoing lexical concept integration with other lexical conceptual units that make up the utterance.

As we saw in Chapters 6 and 7, the linguistic content encoded by a lexical concept constitutes a bundle of distinct types of knowledge which is highly schematic in nature. The unpacking and integration of this schematic knowledge serves to provide scaffolding, so to speak, for structuring the rich conceptual content to which the open-class lexical concepts afford access. In short, the linguistic content ("grammatical" knowledge) which arises from lexical concept integration is essential for providing conceptual content with structure, thereby informing the nature of the informational characterizations which arise during interpretation, as we shall see in the next chapter.

---

[1] I first introduced the term "unpacking" in Chapter 7.

Previous approaches to compositionality in cognitive linguistics

In cognitive linguistics, semantic compositionality has been addressed head on by approaches which model grammar.[2] This follows as cognitive approaches to grammar assume the symbolic thesis.[3] Consequently, as units of grammar consist of pairings of a phonological vehicle (or form) with units of semantic structure then an account of grammar which is concerned with addressing the combinatorial potential of language, by necessity, also addresses the issue of semantic compositionality.

The accounts of compositionality that have been most influential in the development of LCCM Theory are those associated with the theory of Cognitive Grammar (Langacker 1987, 1991*a*, 1991*b*, 1999, 2008) and Cognitive Construction Grammar (Goldberg 1995, 2006). Both theories include accounts of constituency structure—the combinatorial property of grammar which facilitates the building of grammatical constituents, such as noun phrases from nouns and determiners, and clauses and sentences from noun, preposition, and verb phrases, and so on. Crucially, as both these theories of grammar assume the symbolic thesis, by virtue of dealing with constituency and combinatorality, these theories also directly address compositionality.

In Cognitive Grammar semantic compositionality arises due to a distinction between conceptually independent and conceptually dependent lexical structures. Conceptually dependent lexical structures are relational in the sense that they have schematic trajectors (TRs) and landmarks (LMs) which form part of their semantic representation. The distinction between a TR and an LM relates to a distinction in focal prominence in what Langacker refers to as a profiled relationship—as discussed earlier in the book. Profiling concerns the attribution of attention to a particular entity or relationship by virtue of encoding in language. To illustrate, consider the utterance in (1):

(1)   The boy smashed the vase

The TR relates to the participant in the relationship being profiled which receives focal prominence. That is, in (1) the TR is the participant designated by *the boy*. In contrast, the LM is the participant in the profiled relationship which receives secondary prominence. In (1) the LM corresponds to the entity designated by *the vase*. One consequence of this is that what counts as a TR or an LM is encoded as part of linguistic content by the relational or conceptually dependent lexical concept (e.g., *smashed*), rather than the

[2] This situation stands in stark contrast to the position in formal approaches to linguistics. For a review see Evans and Green (2006). See Kay and Michaelis (forthcoming) for a review of compositionality in constructional approaches to grammar.

[3] Recall the discussion in Chapters 3 and 5.

conceptually independent or nominal lexical concepts (e.g., *boy, vase*).[4] To illustrate consider (2).

(2)   The vase fell

In this example *the vase* corresponds to the TR. This follows as it occupies the schematic TR slot encoded by the relational lexical concept associated with the vehicle *fell*. Langacker refers to the schematic TRs and LMs encoded by conceptually dependent lexical concepts as **elaboration sites** (or **e-sites** for short), and the filling of these e-sites as **elaboration**. From the perspective of Cognitive Grammar, then, compositionality is a consequence of conceptually dependent lexical concepts becoming elaborated by nominal lexical concepts which are conceptually autonomous.

This is not the whole story, of course. Any cognitively realistic account of compositionality must provide an account of how the level of semantic structure that is encoded by language, or that results from the integration of grammatical structures, as in the case of elaboration in the sense of Langacker, interfaces with what I am referring to as conceptual content. In Cognitive Grammar, this latter level of semantic representation is broadly referred to as encyclopaedic knowledge. Langacker argues that words directly encode what I operationalize in terms of conceptual content. As we have seen,[5] conceptual content is modelled in Cognitive Grammar in terms of domains, with a word encoding a profile against some base, which relates to a subset of some domain or domains. Yet, not only is the notion of a domain not worked out in any great detail, it is not clear how the result of integration at the linguistic (or grammatical) level then interfaces with this encyclopaedic knowledge at the level of an utterance in order to produce an utterance-level meaning: a conception.

With respect to Cognitive Construction Grammar, as exemplified in Goldberg (1995) for instance, compositionality is modelled in terms of correspondence between word-level constructions, for example verbs, and sentence-level constructions: verb-argument constructions. Goldberg distinguishes between what she refers to as argument roles—the schematic slots encoded by the phonetically implicit verb-argument constructions[6]—and participant roles—the schematic slots encoded by the schematic verb-argument constructions. Compositionality arises from the integration—Goldberg uses the term "fusion"—of the argument-level and participant-level roles. While this level of integration accounts for linguistic or grammatical information, this doesn't account for the rich level of multimodal information which I refer to as conceptual content.

---

[4] Recall the discussion of the distinction between nominal and relational lexical concepts in Chapter 6.

[5] Langacker's notion of domains was discussed in Chapters 3 and 10. See also Evans and Green (2006: ch. 7) for an introductory overview.

[6] Recall the discussion of the ditransitive construction in Chapter 3.

As with Langacker, Goldberg has an encyclopaedic account for this, appealing to Fillmore's (1982, 1985) notion of frame semantics. According to Goldberg, each verb that fuses with a verb-argument construction is relativized with respect to a rich semantic frame—a body of conceptual knowledge relating to the perceptual details associated with the various verbs in question. However, as with Langacker's account, it is not clear how this level of knowledge representation interfaces with the linguistic or grammatical level, and what the mechanisms are whereby structure from the perceptually rich semantic frames becomes incorporated with fused grammatical structures.

To be fair to the accounts developed by Langacker and Goldberg, the models they each developed were not primarily concerned with the details of semantic composition. Rather, they were primarily exercised by attempting to develop a semantically based account of linguistic organization and structure (a "grammar"), which could account for issues such as constituency, and the combinatorial properties of the formal aspects of language. LCCM Theory can then be viewed, in certain respects, as complementing the research perspectives provided by such constructional accounts of grammatical organization. LCCM Theory differs from Cognitive Grammar and Cognitive Construction Grammar in that it *is* concerned precisely with the nature of semantic representation and the mechanics of semantic composition. Moreover, given its foundational assumption that semantic structure and conceptual structure constitute distinct kinds of representation, it follows that I posit two distinct processes of composition: lexical concept integration, which relates to fusion of linguistic content, and interpretation, which concerns fusion of conceptual content.

Fusion

My purpose in this section is to provide an overview of fusion, and the respective roles of lexical concept integration and interpretation as specific mechanisms of fusion, before proceeding, in the remainder of the chapter, with a more detailed overview of lexical concept integration.

Fusion is the integrative process at the heart of semantic composition in LCCM Theory, and the second of the two constituent processes of meaning construction.[7] It results in the construction of a conception. This is achieved by recourse to two sorts of knowledge: linguistic content and conceptual content. As already noted, fusion is made up of two processes: lexical concept integration and interpretation. The first relates to the integration of linguistic content, in order to produce, informally, the "scaffolding" for the activation of conceptual content. Both sorts of information, and both types of processes, are necessary for the construction of meaning, and thus the formation of a conception.

Lexical concept integration involves the integration of lexical concepts in order to produce a composite unit: a lexical conceptual unit. The lexical

---

[7] The other process is lexical concept selection discussed in the previous chapter.

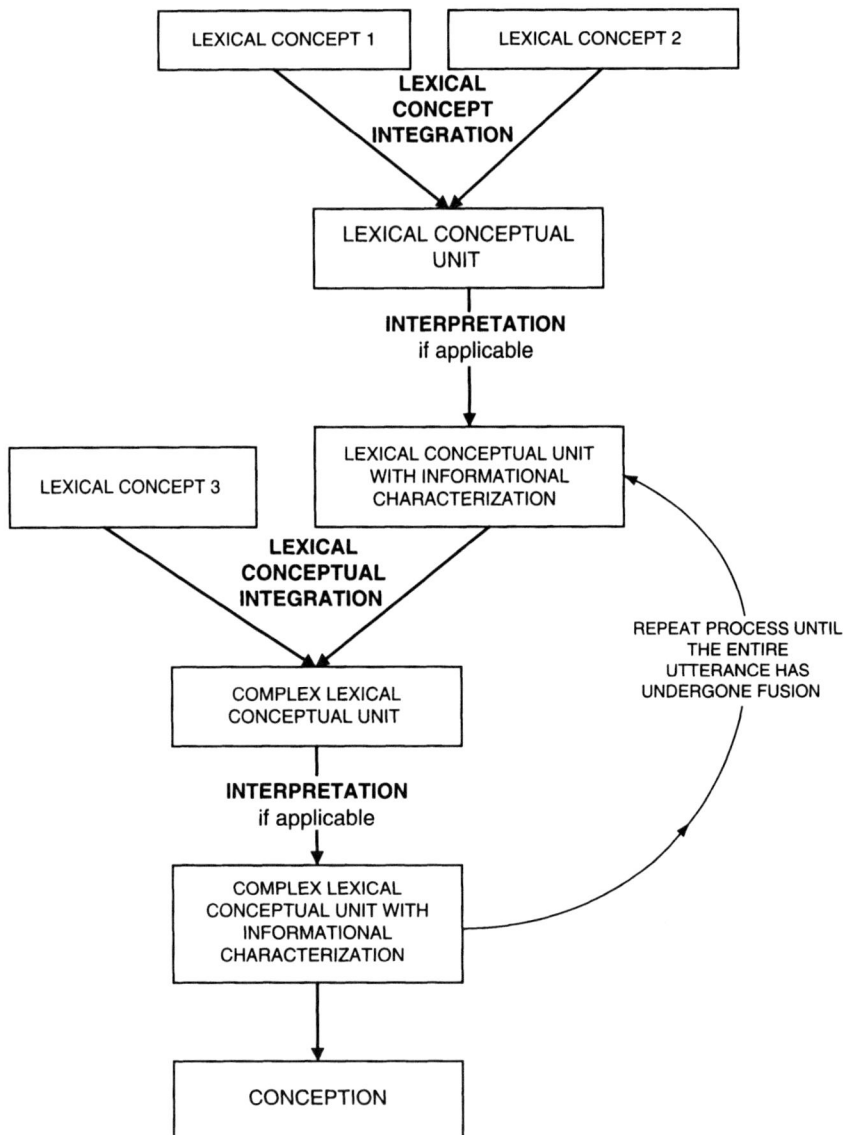

FIGURE 12.1. Stages in the process of fusion

conceptual unit then undergoes interpretation in order to produce a situated reading: an informational characterization. Once this has occurred, the lexical conceptual unit is integrated with other lexical concepts or lexical conceptual units in the utterance, which, in turn, undergo interpretation. This process is repeated until the entire utterance has undergone fusion. The complete informational characterization for the utterance represents a conception. Crucially, the process of lexical concept integration relates to the unpacking of linguistic content.

Once linguistic content has been unpacked, and hence integrated, this results in the lexical conceptual unit achieving what I term a semantic value. Once a lexical concept and/or lexical conceptual unit has achieved a semantic value it is subject to interpretation. Only open-class lexical concepts in a lexical conceptual unit undergo interpretation. The outcome of interpretation is that the lexical concept or lexical conceptual unit achieves an informational characterization. This takes place by virtue of the cognitive model profile of a given lexical concept being matched with that of another, and hence undergoing **matching**.[8] See Figure 12.1 for a diagrammatic representation of fusion.

Internally open and internally closed lexical concepts

The essential insight of lexical concept integration, and one drawn from the work on compositionality associated with Cognitive Grammar and Cognitive Construction Grammar, is the following. Some lexical concepts are more schematic than others, and hence have "slots" that can be, informally, "filled in" by less schematic lexical concepts. Schematic lexical concepts of this sort are those that I refer to as internally open lexical concepts. Integration, then, takes place by virtue of an internally open lexical concept being "filled-in" by a less schematic lexical concept—what I term an internally closed lexical concept—terms introduced in Chapter 5. Once all the slots available in an internally open lexical concept have been "filled-in," the lexical concept becomes internally closed, and integration is complete.

Before illustrating this process, it is first necessary to rehearse some key notions introduced earlier in the book, and introduce some others. Lexical concepts are conventionally paired with vehicles, a consequence of their status as the semantic pole of symbolic units. As the vehicles can be complex, made up from simpler vehicles, lexical concepts can be simpler or more complex. Moreover, just as a vehicle can be construed as having part-whole organization,[9] so too lexical concepts have part-whole organization. To illustrate, consider the following examples of symbolic units:

(3) a. vehicle   "*France*"
     b. lexical concept   [FRANCE]

(4) a. vehicle   "NP *kick*(FINITE) *the bucket*"
     b. lexical concept   [AN ANIMATE ENTITY DIES]

---

[8] The mechanisms involved in interpretation are considered in detail in the next chapter.
[9] See Croft (2002) for discussion of this point.

(5) a. vehicle   "NP1 VERB(FINITE) NP2 NP3"
     b. lexical concept   [THING X CAUSES THING Y TO RECEIVE THING Z][10]

In the example in (3), the vehicle relates to the lexical item *France* which is conventionally paired with the lexical concept [FRANCE]. The linguistic content is relatively impoverished, relating to a nominal entity. It is, in part, this linguistic content, in conjunction with its lexical profile, which determines the ways in which this lexical concept can be combined with other lexical concepts. That is, this lexical concept, by virtue of being lexically filled, is internally closed: it has no internal specification for the integration of further lexical concepts. However, by virtue of having a lexical profile associated with it, it is **externally open**.[11]

A class of lexical concepts which don't exhibit lexical profiles, and hence are externally closed—as discussed in Chapter 7—are greetings, such as *hello*. That is, expressions such as these, among others, constitute fully formed utterances in their own right. A similar although slightly distinct pattern is exhibited by lexical concepts which require a response of a certain kind. Such lexical concepts which require an adjacent response of a specified kind are often referred to as **adjacency pairs**. For instance, a question/answer sequence constitutes an adjacency pair. The interrogative vehicle is conventionally paired with an [INTERROGATIVE] lexical concept, which encodes linguistic content.[12] In so far then as the interrogative lexical concept signals to the interlocutor that a response is required, it can be thought of as having a lexical profile: one that it, itself, stipulates as part of its linguistic content.

The example in (4) involves the vehicle "NP *kick*FINITE *the bucket*", which relates to the [AN ANIMATE ENTITY DIES] lexical concept. Unlike the lexical concept in (3b), this lexical concept is internally open: lexical concept integration can occur internally as the lexical concept is not fully **specified**. The diagnostic as to whether a lexical concept is fully specified or not relates to whether the lexical concept is completely filled with phonetically overt vehicles: the situation I refer to as being lexically filled.[13] In terms of the lexical concept in (4b), the lexically filled components are restricted to the vehicles *kick, the,* and *bucket.* As such, this lexical concept remains internally open as its vehicle is only partially lexically filled. That is, and more precisely, the lexical concept is **partially internally open**. This actually leaves a good deal of

---

[10] Recall the formatting conventions first introduced in Chapter 5. I use italics to represent a phonetically overt form, such as *France, the bucket,* or *kick.* I use capitals to represent phonetically implicit vehicles, such as FINITE to indicate the finite vehicle, e.g. the nature of the tense involved, or NP, which stands for "noun phrase".

[11] The lexical concept [FRANCE] selects for relational lexical concepts, as evidenced by the examples in (1) in Chapter 1, and elsewhere in the book.

[12] Although the linguistic content encoded by the [INTERROGATIVE] lexical concept is highly schematic, it nevertheless does consist of semantic structure, requiring, as it does, an informational response.

[13] As discussed in Chapter 5.

flexibility in terms of other lexical concepts which can be integrated. For instance, some of the possibilities are presented below:

(6)   a. S/he kick/s/ed the bucket
      b. S/he will kick the bucket

Some lexical concepts, such as that in (5b), are **fully internally open**: all the vehicles that make up the lexical concept are phonetically implicit. The example in (5) relates to the ditransitive symbolic unit. The "ditransitive" lexical concept in (5b) is fully internally open as it is made up of simpler lexical concepts all of which are associated with vehicles which are phonetically implicit. Hence, the larger "ditransitive" lexical concept is fully internally open.

A further distinction relates to those lexical concepts that can be described as internally simple versus those that are internally complex.[14] An internally simple lexical concept is one that has no part-whole structure and hence cannot be analysed[15] in terms of more than one lexical concept. An example of such a lexical concept is [FRANCE] associated with the form *France*.

However, being internally simple is not the same as being internally closed (or open). For instance, the lexical concept [THING] is internally open being an abstract lexical concept and hence one that is associated with a vehicle which is phonetically implicit, namely the vehicle NOUN. Yet this lexical concept is internally simple.

An example of an internally complex lexical concept is, of course [THING X CAUSES THING Y TO RECEIVE THING Z] as in (5b). This follows as this lexical concept is made up of **abstract lexical concepts**: lexical concepts which are associated with phonetically implicit vehicles, specifically the vehicles NP, VERB, and FINITE.

Finally, while both complex vehicles and their associated internally complex lexical concepts each have part-whole structure, it doesn't always follow that there is an isomorphic relationship between the part-whole organization of complex vehicles and internally complex lexical concepts. A case in point is the internally complex vehicle in (4b). The **obligatory lexically filled components** that form the vehicle associated with this lexical concept, namely *kick*, *the*, and *bucket* do not have corresponding lexical concepts associated with them. Put another way, the vehicles *kick* and *the bucket* are not, in the context of the lexical concept [AN ANIMATE ENTITY DIES] associated with independent lexical concepts.

---

[14] This distinction was first introduced in Chapter 5.

[15] My claim, following Langacker (e.g., 1987, 2000), is that lexical concepts exhibit categorical relations. Hence, lexical concepts (and the symbolic units of which they are components) are modelled in terms of a network of related lexical concepts. While one type of categorical relation is semantic relatedness (which gives rise to the phenomenon of polysemy), another concerns the part-whole structure exhibited by symbolic units and hence lexical concepts. The "ditransitive" lexical concept is stored as an entrenched mental routine in the grammar, along with the categorical relations that hold between it and its component lexical concepts.

This is not to say that there aren't lexical concepts [KICK], [THE], and [BUCKET] which are associated with the vehicles *kick*, *the*, and *bucket*. For instance, consider the utterance in (7):

(7)   He kicked the bucket

The literal interpretation of (7) involves a male individual who kicks a bucket, perhaps in frustration. My claim is that this reading is sanctioned by the independently existing "active" lexical concept:[16]

(8)   [PROFILED RELATIONSHIP INVOLVING AGENT AND PATIENT VIEWED
       FROM PERSPECTIVE OF AGENT]

The lexical concept in (8), like the lexical concepts in (4b) and (5b), is also internally complex. The difference is that the lexical concept in (8), but not in (4b), for instance, has part-whole structure in which there are discrete lexical concepts associated with the vehicles *kick*, *the*, and *bucket*. Put another way, the "obligatory" vehicles *kick* and *the bucket* have no semantic structure associated with them independently of the [AN ANIMATE ENTITY DIES] lexical concept. Hence, the lexical concept in (8), which licenses the example (with the "literal" reading) in (7), has a completely different lexical profile from that associated with the lexical concept in (4b). This determines the nature of the lexical concepts (and hence vehicles) which can be integrated with each.

Principles of lexical concept integration

Lexical concept integration is governed by a number of principles, which I now address. Integration can be divided into two types: **internal lexical concept integration**, which applies to internally open lexical concepts, and is the result of a lexical concept's internal selectional tendencies.[17] The other concerns **external lexical concept integration**, which involves the integration of a lexical concept with its lexical concepts specified by its **external selectional tendencies**.[18] Both sorts are governed by the three Principles of Lexical Concept Integration, described in this section. For expository purposes I illustrate application of the Principles of Integration with internal lexical concept integration. I then deal, more briefly, with external lexical concept integration.

Internal lexical concept integration

Lexical concept integration is governed by the **Principle of Linguistic Coherence**. This is stated as follows:

---

[16] Recall the discussion of example (12) in Chapter 7.
[17] As discussed in Chapter 7.
[18] Recall the discussion of *time* and *flying* in Chapter 7.

(p1)   Principle of Linguistic Coherence:
        A lexical concept that is internally open may only be integrated with a
        lexical concept with which it shares schematic coherence in terms of
        linguistic content.

This principle in (p1) relies on a second principle, the **Principle of Schematic
Coherence:**

(p2)   Principle of Schematic Coherence:
        The content associated with entities, participants, and the relations
        holding between them must exhibit coherence in fusion operations.

The principle in (p2) entails the following. Any **fusion operation**—namely
lexical concept integration, and interpretation—must exhibit alignment in
terms of the schematic aspects associated with the lexical concepts undergoing the fusion operation.
     To illustrate how these principles serve to constrain integration, consider
the internally open lexical concept [RELATION EVOLVING THROUGH TIME]
associated with the vehicle VERB, represented, for convenience, in (9):

(9)   a. vehicle   "VERB"
      b. lexical concept   [RELATION EVOLVING THROUGH TIME]

Recall that integration proceeds by virtue of an internally open lexical concept,
for instance the lexical concept in (9b) being filled by an internally closed lexical
concept. Nevertheless, not just any internally closed lexical concept can fill just
any internally open lexical concept. For instance, the internally closed lexical
concept [FRANCE] from (3b), for instance, cannot be integrated with the lexical
concept in (9b). This follows given the Principle of Linguistic Coherence in
conjunction with the Principle of Schematic Coherence. Recall that the Principle
of Linguistic Coherence requires that the lexical concepts being integrated share
schematic coherence at the level of linguistic content. In terms of linguistic
content, the lexical concept [FRANCE] is a nominal lexical concept and as such
relates to a thing, rather than a relation that evolves through time. In terms of
linguistic content, there is no schematic coherence then between [FRANCE] and
[RELATION THAT EVOLVES THROUGH TIME] as [FRANCE] encodes thing-like
content rather than content which is relation-like. As such, the principle in
(p1) prohibits integration between [FRANCE] and [RELATION].
     In contrast, however, [FRANCE] can be integrated with the internally open
lexical concept [THING] encoded by the vehicle NOUN:

(10)   a. vehicle   "NOUN"
       b. lexical concept   [THING]

This follows as both lexical concepts share schematic coherence at the level of
linguistic content.

Now let's consider contexts in which [FRANCE] and [THING] might undergo such lexical concept integration. Such a context might involve the fully internally open lexical concept [THING X CAUSES THING Y TO RECEIVE THING Z], which relates to the semantic pole of the ditransitive vehicle, as represented in (5) above. In the "ditransitive" lexical concept in (5b), [FRANCE] can potentially be integrated with any of the [THING] lexical concepts which make up the larger lexical concept. That is, the lexical concept in (5b) is internally complex and is comprised of three distinct [THING] lexical concepts: [THING X], [THING Y], and [THING Z]. To better illustrate how integration occurs, consider the utterance below which relates to abstract transfer:

(11)   The 1940 armistice gave Germany France

In the example in (11), [FRANCE] is integrated with [THING Z]. By virtue of being integrated with this lexical concept, [FRANCE] receives a particular semantic value: namely, an entity which is subject to being transferred to [THING Y]. In other words, while interpretation—discussed in the next chapter—is necessary in order to understand that the entity designated by the vehicle *France* relates to a European nation state with all the complex knowledge a language user may be able to draw upon relating to this particular nation, in the context of the utterance in (11), the semantic value associated with the use of *France* relates to an entity which is the object of abstract transfer.

It is also important to note that the Principle of Linguistic Coherence can occur recursively. This principle applies until all internally open lexical concepts have undergone lexical concept integration such that they have achieved integration with a lexical concept associated with a phonetically overt vehicle. As such they become internally closed, and thus cannot, by definition, undergo further internal lexical concept integration.

The Principle of Linguistic Coherence does not proceed in a random fashion. Rather it proceeds in an ordered way, occurring in internally simpler lexical concepts prior to taking place in more internally complex lexical concepts. This is guaranteed by the **Principle of Ordered Integration in Internally Open Lexical Concepts**:

(p3)   Principle of Ordered Integration in Internally Open Lexical Concepts: Lexical concept integration takes place by applying to internally simpler lexical concepts before applying to internally more complex lexical concepts.

What this principle does is ensure that linguistic content is integrated and hence unpacked "outwards," applying to internally simpler lexical concepts first. For instance, in the utterance in (11), the principle in (p3) ensures that individual lexical concepts are integrated in a way that preserves the part-whole structure of internally complex lexical concepts. That is, the lexical concepts which collectively comprise the "ditransitive" lexical concept in (5b) are integrated as follows. The simplest internally open lexical concepts undergo integration first until they become closed. For instance, the vehicle in (5a) consists of three NPs, associated with the highly abstract lexical concept [SPECIFIED THING]:

(12) a. vehicle   "NP"
      b. lexical concept   [SPECIFIED THING]

Yet the lexical concept in (12) is itself extremely abstract, and can be filled by a range of more specific lexical concepts. One such lexical concept is provided, together with its vehicle, in (13):

(13) a. vehicle   "DETERMINER MODIFIER NOUN"
      b. lexical concept   [SPECIFIED THING WITH A PARTICULAR ATTRIBUTE]

The lexical concept in (13) is itself internally complex, consisting of three more specific lexical concepts associated with distinct vehicles. Hence, the internally complex and abstract lexical concept in (13b) is associated with internally simpler but still abstract lexical concepts given in (14):

(14) a. i.   vehicle   DETERMINER
          ii. lexical concept   [SPECIFICATION]
      b. i.   vehicle   MODIFIER
          ii. lexical concept   [ATTRIBUTE]
      c. i.   vehicle   NOUN
          ii. lexical concept   [THING]

In turn, each of these lexical concepts, and symbolic units, can be integrated with a range of other lexical concepts. For instance, given the utterance in (11) the lexical concepts associated with the vehicles: *the*, *1940*, and *armistice* are integrated, respectively, with the lexical concepts [SPECIFICATION], [ATTRIBUTE], and [THING].[19]

Once this has taken place, the principle in (p3) stipulates that the linguistic content associated with each of these now internally closed lexical concepts can be integrated with the more complex lexical concept of which these are constituents, namely the lexical concept given in (12), [SPECIFIED THING], which has the form NP. The consequence of this is that once the linguistic content associated with each of these lexical concepts has been unpacked, the result of the principle in (p1), the individual lexical concepts are related to one

---

[19] Note that the lexical concept associated with the vehicle *1940* typically relates to a temporal entity. However, by virtue of undergoing integration with the internally open [ATTRIBUTE] lexical concept which forms part of the larger lexical concept given in (13), the semantic value that results from unpacking is of an entity which is an attribute of some sort. Put another way, an attribute semantic value is coerced for the lexical concept associated with *1940* (see Michaelis 2004 for related discussion of coercion).

another such that they form a coherent unit. Put another way, the [SPECIFIED THING] lexical concept ensures that the lexical concepts associated with the vehicles *the*, *1940*, and *armistice* function as a whole, serving to provide the following schematic content: that there is a specific thing in question, and that it has a particular quality associated with it—although the details of the thing and the nature of the particular quality are not specified until the application of interpretation.

Once this process has taken place for each of the lexical concepts that make up the internally complex [THING X CAUSES THING Y TO RECEIVE THING Z] lexical concept given in (5b), then the lexical concepts which make up the larger lexical concept are integrated in the way determined by the linguistic content associated with the most complex lexical concept. In other words, each [SPECIFIED THING] lexical concept receives a semantic value in relation to how it is integrated with the most complex, and hence, the most encompassing lexical concept, in keeping with the ordering principle given (p3).

It follows then, given the example in (11), that the semantic value associated with the expression *the 1940 armistice* will be that of "causer," the semantic value associated with the expression *Germany* is that of "recipient," and the semantic value associated with the expression *France* will be that of "entity transferred." This is the consequence of unpacking, in which linguistic content from the simpler lexical concepts are integrated with linguistic content encoded by the most complex lexical concept, as given in (5b). In sum, internal lexical concept integration results from integration of simpler lexical concepts which are "nested" in more complex, internally open lexical concepts.[20]

Finally, it is important to stress the following. In saying that a lexical concept is internally complex and possesses part-whole structure I am not claiming that its semantic structure is "built up" from atomic elements. The lexical concept [THING X CAUSES THING Y TO RECEIVE THING Z] associated with the ditransitive vehicle given in (5a) encodes linguistic content and hence has semantic structure in its own right, given the symbolic thesis discussed earlier in the book. Hence, the overall semantic structure encoded by this lexical concept exists independently of the lexical concepts which constitute it. This claim is consistent with "constructional" accounts of grammar, as presented in Cognitive Grammar and Cognitive Construction Grammar. Thus, the complex lexical concept is not the sum of its parts, as it exists independently to them.[21]

External lexical concept integration

External lexical concept integration relates to the role of internally closed lexical concepts in lexical concept integration, as they are integrated with lexical concepts sanctioned by their lexical profile, for instance the examples of *time*

---

[20] Of course, the nature of the transfer relates not to physical transfer, but abstract transfer: a "transfer" of power or control. This conception is a consequence of interpretation, discussed in the next chapter.

[21] For detailed presentation of arguments for the independent existence of the ditransitive construction, see Goldberg (1995).

and *flying* discussed in Chapter 7. Specifically, external lexical concept integration involves integration of the following:

- an internally closed lexical concept, or
- an internally open lexical concept that has become closed, due to internal lexical concept integration.

As with the process of internal lexical concept integration, external lexical concept integration results in the formation of a lexical conceptual unit, which is then subject to the process of interpretation. To illustrate, consider the lexical concept [FRANCE] associated with the vehicle *France* in the following exchange:

(15)   a. Do you know which country its inhabitants refer to as the hexagon?
       b. France!

In this exchange, the lexical concept [FRANCE] does not undergo integration of any sort. This follows as it is a response to a prior question, and, in the light of this, achieves an informational characterization—an interpretation—without requiring further lexical concept integration. Hence, the exclamation: *France!* constitutes a complete utterance in its own right.

However, now consider the following:

(16)   France is a geographical region

In this example, from the perspective of the lexical concept [FRANCE], this undergoes external lexical concept integration. That is, [FRANCE] is integrated with the internally complex nominal lexical concept associated with the predicate nominative lexical concept. This utterance involves an encompassing internally complex lexical concept. The highly schematic lexical concept, which I gloss as in (17b) serves to equate some quality, property, or other distinction to a given entity.

(17)   a. vehicle   "DEFINITE-NP, *be*FINITE INDEFINITE-NP"
       b. lexical concept   [ATTRIBUTION OF A QUALITY TO AN ENTITY]

In terms of deriving a conception for (16), [FRANCE] is integrated with the lexical concept: [UNIQUE SPECIFIED THING], which is associated with the vehicle provided in (18a) rather than the entire [ATTRIBUTION OF A QUALITY TO AN ENTITY] lexical concept in (17b).

(18)   a. vehicle   "DEFINITE-NP"
       b. lexical concept   [UNIQUE SPECIFIED THING]

It is by virtue of the integration of [FRANCE] with the [SPECIFIED THING] lexical concept which forms part of the "predicate nominative" lexical concept, that [FRANCE] receives its status as Theme or Subject of a predicating expression. Put another way, just as the [THING] lexical concepts that form part of the larger "ditransitive" lexical concept in (5b) encode differential linguistic content, ensuring that each [THING] slot is distinct, so too, by virtue of [FRANCE] occupying the NP slot it does in (16), it achieves a distinct semantic value, vis-à-vis the semantic value achieved by the lexical concept [GEOGRAPHICAL REGION] in the same utterance.

Now let's consider a slightly more complex example of external lexical concept integration. This concerns the integration of an internally open lexical concept which, via internal lexical concept integration, has become internally closed. The example involves the "ditransitive" lexical concept given in (5b) above.

To illustrate, consider the following utterance:

(19)   John gave Mary a bracelet and he gave Jane a necklace.

In this example two "ditransitive" lexical concepts are being coordinated by the [CONJUNCTION WITH Z BY ADDITION OF Y] lexical concept associated with the vehicle *and*:

(20)   a. vehicle   *"and"*
        b. lexical concept   [CONJUNCTION WITH Z BY ADDITION OF Y]

The utterance in (19) illustrates what I refer to as a **complex conceptual lexical unit**. Internal lexical concept integration gives rise to two internally closed "ditransitive" lexical concepts. By virtue of having undergone internal lexical concept integration this gives rise to two conceptual lexical units. Each of these lexical conceptual units is further integrated by virtue of being integrated with the lexical concept in (20b). This gives rise to a more complex integrated unit.

Summary

This chapter has presented an overview of lexical concept integration, or integration for short, which is one of the two constituent processes of fusion. Integration involves the integration of the linguistic content encoded by the various lexical concepts that make up an utterance. Integration takes place by unpacking the linguistic content associated with each lexical concept and integrating internally open—informally, more abstract—lexical concepts with internally closed—informally, more concrete—lexical concepts. The diagnostic for an abstract lexical concept is that it is conventionally paired with a vehicle that is phonetically implicit. Two types of integration were distinguished. The first, internal lexical concept integration, applies to internally open lexical concepts, while the second, external lexical concept integration, involves the integration of an internally closed lexical concept. Integration is influenced by the lexical profile of the lexical profile associated with internally open and closed lexical concepts. Both sorts of integration are governed by Principles of Lexical Concept Integration, of which three were presented in the chapter. Finally, as lexical concept integration involves integration of linguistic content, it is primarily concerned with utterance context.

13

Interpretation

This chapter addresses the mechanism of interpretation, the last of the compositional operations at the heart of LCCM Theory. Interpretation provides the compositional interface between semantic structure and conceptual structure, facilitating the deployment of conceptual content in service of linguistically mediated meaning construction. The essential insight is that interpretation involves a process I refer to as matching—briefly introduced in the previous chapter. Matching takes place between the cognitive model profiles of the open-class lexical concepts which have undergone integration, and hence which result in a lexical conceptual unit. That is, interpretation involves lexical concepts within the same lexical conceptual unit. As the formation of lexical conceptual units takes place recursively, serving to integrate internally simpler lexical concepts first, so too interpretation takes place recursively, applying to each lexical conceptual unit once it has undergone integration. Hence, interpretation is guided by linguistic context—the outcome of lexical concept integration. In addition, interpretation is guided by inferential processes relating to extra-linguistic context. Moreover, as with integration, interpretation is constrained by various principles, which will also be introduced and discussed.

In more general terms, the mechanism of interpretation represents an attempt to formalize the way in which what previous researchers have referred to as encyclopaedic knowledge "gets into" language. In fact, from the perspective of LCCM Theory, it is not so much that encyclopaedic knowledge "gets into" language. Rather, language provides the means—by way of instructions of specific kinds—for the conceptual system to produce complex simulations. The outcome, then, of language understanding, involves the activation of non-linguistic representations, which arise due to prompts of the kind provided by lexical concept selection and integration, as described in the previous two chapters.

Before proceeding with the description of interpretation below, I reiterate the following. Once lexical concept integration has taken place, each lexical concept receives a semantic value as part of an integrated lexical conceptual unit. Interpretation proceeds by subjecting each open-class lexical concept in a given lexical conceptual unit to the operation known as matching: the cognitive model profiles of two (or more) open-class lexical concepts undergo matching. The result is that each lexical conceptual unit receives an informational characterization. Once all the lexical conceptual units in an utterance have achieved an informational characterization the utterance as a whole thereby receives its utterance-level informational characterization: a conception, which is to say, meaning.

An illustration

Interpretation involves the activation of cognitive models belonging to distinct cognitive model profiles which are matched. The matching process gives rise to an informational characterization. In this way, the lexical concepts subject to matching result in a "unified" interpretation: a linguistically mediated simulation. This linguistically mediated simulation (the informational characterization) can then be matched with other lexical concepts that facilitate access to their unique cognitive model profile, until each open-class lexical concept in an utterance has undergone interpretation.

To provide an immediate illustration of how interpretation proceeds, let's consider a straightforward example. Consider the expressions in (1) and (2) in the light of the partial primary cognitive model profiles for [FRANCE] in Figure 13.1, for [REGION] in Figure 13.2, and for [NATION] in Figure 13.3.

(1)   France, the landmass

(2)   France, the nation

In each of these examples *France* receives a distinct informational characterization. In (1) France relates to a geographical area, while in (2) it relates to a political entity. My purpose here is to illustrate how it is that each of these instances of *France* receives distinct interpretations.

As we have seen in previous chapters, the lexical concept [FRANCE]—see Figure 13.1—affords access to conceptual content relating, at the very least, to France as a geographical region, as a political entity—including knowledge relating to the French political system, the French people and their social customs and practices, their history and language and the national sports engaged in, and so forth—and to France as a holiday destination, with,

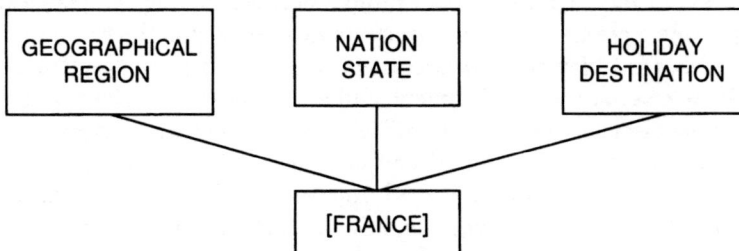

FIGURE 13.1. Partial primary cognitive model profile for [FRANCE]

```
  ┌──────────────┐          ┌──────────────┐
  │   PHYSICAL   │          │ GEOGRAPHICAL │
  │   TERRAIN    │          │    REGION    │
  └──────────────┘          └──────────────┘
              \              /
               \            /
              ┌──────────────┐
              │  [LANDMASS]  │
              └──────────────┘
```

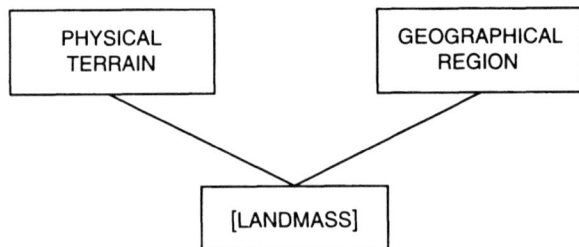

FIGURE 13.2. Partial primary cognitive model profile for [LANDMASS]

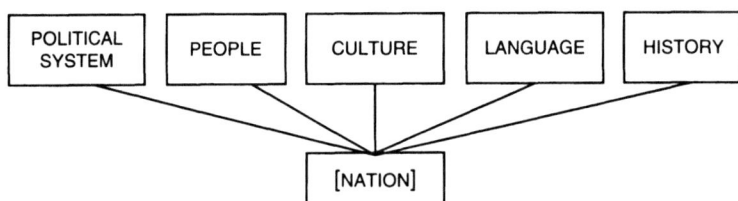

```
┌──────────┐ ┌────────┐ ┌─────────┐ ┌──────────┐ ┌─────────┐
│POLITICAL │ │ PEOPLE │ │ CULTURE │ │ LANGUAGE │ │ HISTORY │
│ SYSTEM   │ │        │ │         │ │          │ │         │
└──────────┘ └────────┘ └─────────┘ └──────────┘ └─────────┘
        \        \          │         /         /
                  ┌──────────────┐
                  │   [NATION]   │
                  └──────────────┘
```

FIGURE 13.3. Partial primary cognitive model profile for [NATION]

perhaps, knowledge relating to the sorts of holiday activities it is possible (or typical) to engage in, in France, such as skiing (in the Alps), seaside holidays (on the Mediterranean coast), and so on.

The lexical concept [LANDMASS]—see Figure 13.2—facilitates access, at the very least, to primary cognitive models that relate to a physical terrain—a landmass can be hilly, mountainous, may consist of plains, woodland, and so on—or to a geographical area.

Figure 13.3 relates to a very partial primary cognitive model profile for [NATION]. This lexical concept, at the very least, facilitates access to cognitive models having to do with a political entity and nation state, and hence a particular political system, a people (with common customs, traditions, cuisine, and so on), and language (and/or languages), and a common (often complex) history.

Interpretation works by virtue of the process of matching, which takes place between the cognitive model profiles accessed by the relevant lexical concepts which are subject to matching. As we have seen in the previous part of the book, the "relevant" lexical concepts are those that are specialized for affording access to conceptual content, and hence, those which have a semantic potential associated with them, namely open-class lexical concepts.[1]

In terms of the examples in (1) and (2), the relevant lexical concepts are [FRANCE], [LANDMASS], and [NATION]. Interpretation involves establishing a match between one (or more) cognitive models in the cognitive model

---

[1] One consequence of this is that LCCM Theory predicts that the process of semantic bleaching (or attenuation) in grammaticalization involves the loss of access to a cognitive model profile.

profiles associated with the relevant lexical concepts. This process serves to **activate** the matched cognitive models. For instance, in the example in (1), a match is established between the primary cognitive model profile associated with [LANDMASS], and one of the cognitive models to which [FRANCE] affords access. This of course is the cognitive model GEOGRAPHICAL REGION which becomes activated. In the second example, the match takes place between the primary cognitive model profile to which [NATION] affords access and the NATION STATE cognitive model to which [FRANCE] affords access. Hence, the reason for different readings of [FRANCE] in (1) and (2) is because the lexical concept in each utterance receives a distinct informational characterization. In (1) interpretation results in an informational characterization for [FRANCE] relating to France as geographical landmass. In (2) interpretation results in an informational characterization of a political entity: France the nation state.

Governing Principles of Interpretation

The analysis presented for the interpretation of [FRANCE] in the previous section exhibited an asymmetry in the process of matching: While all the primary cognitive models listed for [LANDMASS] and [NATION] are activated in the interpretations presented to account for the semantic variation exhibited by *France*, the primary cognitive models to which [FRANCE] affords access undergo **selective activation**—although as we will see below the situation is slightly more complex than this. That is, the claim made by LCCM Theory is that interpretation of [FRANCE] in (1) results in the GEOGRAPHICAL REGION cognitive model being activated while in (2) a different cognitive model receives what I refer to as **primary activation**, namely the NATION STATE cognitive model. Simply put, not all of the primary cognitive models presented in Figure 13.1 which are accessed by [FRANCE] receive primary activation. In informal terms, this follows as the referent identified by *France* is the Theme or Subject of the expression: the purpose of the expression, which, more technically, is appositive in nature, is to identify which aspect of the referent of *France* we are concerned with. But how then does the process of matching "know" which referent is the subject of the expression, and hence which cognitive model profile is to receive selective activation? The answer is due to the output of lexical concept integration: the lexical conceptual unit. In other words, by virtue of the lexical concepts undergoing integration, the expression serves as an instruction to derive an interpretation which treats the referent of *France* as the Subject of the expression: the entity that the expression is about.

In LCCM Theory this asymmetric application of matching, in keeping with the output of integration, is governed by the overarching principle of interpretation referred to as the **Principle of Guided Matching**. This can be stated as follows:

(p4)   Principle of Guided Matching
       Matching of cognitive models in interpretation proceeds in a way that
       is compatible with the output of lexical concept integration.

This principle has two implications. Firstly, interpretation proceeds in the
order determined by the order in which lexical concepts undergo lexical
concept integration, as determined, in particular, by the principle given in
(p3) in the previous chapter. That is, lexical concept integration proceeds by
integrating lexical concepts in "bottom-up" fashion, applying to internally
simpler lexical concepts before integrating more internally complex lexical
concepts. The Principle of Guided Matching ensures, accordingly, that the
matching process central to interpretation proceeds by virtue of interpreting
relevant lexical concepts in the order in which they undergo lexical concept
integration. To make this point clear, consider the following example:

(3)   France is a beautiful country

Without further (extra-linguistic) context, the example in (3) is likely to give rise
to what I will term a "geographical area" conception: France, in this utterance, is
understood as referring to a specific geographical region of marked physical
beauty. The principle in (p4) guarantees that interpretation takes place in
conjunction with lexical concept integration. That is, in (3), for instance,
[BEAUTIFUL] and [COUNTRY] undergo lexical concept integration to provide
an unpacked [SPECIFIED THING WITH A PARTICULAR ATTRIBUTE] lexical concept associated with the vehicle DETERMINER MODIFIER NOUN (i.e., an
NP), prior to being integrated with the more complex lexical concept associated
with the predicate nominative vehicle which comprises the entire utterance.
    The relevant lexical concepts for interpretation in (3) are [FRANCE], [BEAUTI-
FUL], and [COUNTRY].[2] The principle in (p4) ensures, then, that [BEAUTIFUL] and
[COUNTRY] are subject to matching in order to build an informational characterization, prior to interpretation, and hence matching, involving [FRANCE]. It is
only once an informational characterization of the lexical conceptual unit "beautiful country" has been achieved that it is subject to matching with [FRANCE]
giving rise to a complex informational characterization.
    Very partial primary cognitive model profiles accessed via [BEAUTIFUL] and
[COUNTRY] are provided in Figures 13.4 and 13.5 respectively. Primary cognitive models that are accessed by [BEAUTIFUL] range from assessments relating
to the receipt or awareness of physical pleasure, particularly physical appear-
ances, often of a sexual nature, to the awareness of non-visual but physical
pleasure, such as aural pleasure, as in the appreciation of music, or pleasure
derived from touch, for instance. The lexical concept [BEAUTIFUL] also
affords access to a cognitive model having to do with non-physical pleasure,

---

    [2] Note that the vehicle *country* also has a [COUNTRYSIDE] lexical concept associated with it which is
not selected for in this utterance.

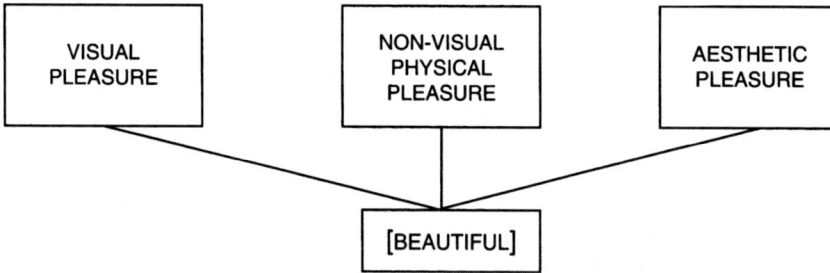

FIGURE 13.4. Partial primary cognitive model profile for [BEAUTIFUL]

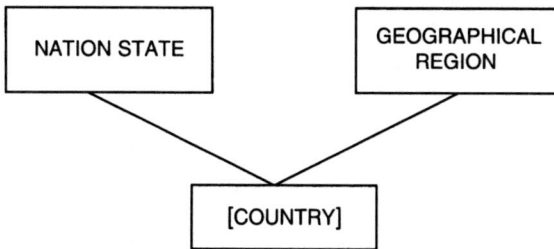

FIGURE 13.5. Partial primary cognitive model profile for [COUNTRY]

which I gloss as AESTHETIC PLEASURE. This relates to the appreciation of pleasure that is non-physical in nature, such as the appreciation of literature, or culture, or a particular language, and so forth. In contrast, the lexical concept [COUNTRY] facilitates, at the very least, access to cognitive models relating to knowledge concerning what it means to be a NATION STATE, and a cognitive model relating to a GEOGRAPHICAL AREA.

The matching process proceeds as follows. A search is established in the cognitive model profiles accessed by the lexical concepts subject to matching. The initial cognitive model profiles undergoing interpretation are those accessed by [BEAUTIFUL] and [COUNTRY]. The search serves to identify one (or more) cognitive model(s) in the respective (primary) cognitive model profiles which match—as constrained by a number of other principles discussed below. The informational characterization associated with "beautiful country" arises due to matching between the visual pleasure (and perhaps also the non-visual physical pleasure) cognitive model(s) accessed via [BEAUTIFUL] and the GEOGRAPHICAL AREA cognitive model accessed via the [COUNTRY] lexical concept. Once the "beautiful country" informational characterization has been constructed, this is subject to matching with the lexical concept as determined by the next level of complexity emerging from lexical concept integration. In terms of the utterance in (3), and the relevant lexical concepts—those that have access sites to a cognitive model profile—the next level of lexical concept complexity involves the entire utterance, and the "predicate nominative" lexical concept. This entails that the informational characterization "beautiful country" is matched with the cognitive model profile to which the lexical concept [FRANCE] facilitates access.

I now turn to the second implication of the Principle of Guided Matching. This is as follows. The way in which matching takes place is guided by the linguistic content associated with the lexical conceptual units, and the larger utterance, in question. To illustrate, reconsider the examples in (1) and (2). Each of these constitutes an appositive vehicle, associated with what I gloss as the [SPECIFICATION OF THING X] lexical concept. The semantic function of this lexical concept is to specify in greater detail a particular entity, represented by "x." That is, the internally closed lexical concept that is integrated with the internally open lexical concept [THING X], which occupies the "x" slot in the larger lexical concept, constitutes the entity which is being specified. The consequence of lexical concept integration is that in (1) and (2) it is [FRANCE] which is the lexical concept being specified, rather than [LAND-MASS] or [NATION].

The Principle of Guiding Matching, then, ensures that interpretation proceeds in a way which is compatible with the output of this unpacking process. In terms of the specific utterances in (1) and (2), it follows that matching occurs as a means of specifying the conceptual content associated with [FRANCE], rather than with [LANDMASS] or [NATION]. Hence, the cognitive model profiles accessed by [LANDMASS] and [NATION] are employed in order to activate compatible cognitive models in the cognitive model profile associated with [FRANCE] rather than the other way round. It is for this reason that in the examples in (1) and (2) there is selective activation of one cognitive model in the cognitive model profile to which [FRANCE] affords access, as evidenced by the variation in meaning evident: it is [FRANCE] whose semantic contribution is being specified, rather than that of [LANDMASS] or [NATION].

The matching operation central to interpretation is constrained by the **Principle of Conceptual Coherence**. This can be stated as follows:

(p5)   Principle of Conceptual Coherence
       Matching occurs between one or more cognitive models/informational characterizations, belonging to distinct cognitive model profiles/lexical conceptual units, which share schematic coherence in terms of conceptual content.

This principle in (p5) mirrors the Principle of Linguistic Coherence (p1), central to lexical concept integration, discussed in the previous chapter. In particular, this principle (p5) relies on the Principle of Schematic Coherence (p2) also introduced in the previous chapter, which I reproduce below:

(p2)   Principle of Schematic Coherence
       The content associated with entities, participants and the relations holding between them must exhibit coherence in fusion operations.

What the two principles do, in (p5) and (p2), is to guarantee that matching takes place only when the cognitive model profiles or informational characterizations that are subject to the matching process (i) belong to different cognitive model profiles or lexical conceptual units as relevant, and hence are accessed by different lexical concepts, and (ii) exhibit coherence.

To illustrate consider the example in (4), which minimally contrasts with the example in (3).

(4)   France is a beautiful nation

While the example in (3) related to what I termed a "geographical area" conception, the example in (4) provides what I will term a "nation state" conception. A common conception arising from (4), without a further specifying extra-linguistic context, might relate to an understanding of France as a nation state whose culture, language, cuisine, art forms (e.g., literature), and so on are held to be aesthetically pleasing. This takes place by virtue of [BEAUTIFUL] and [NATION] undergoing matching, giving rise to an informational characterization, before being matched with the cognitive model profile accessed via [FRANCE], as determined by the principle in (p5).

The Principle of Conceptual Coherence determines how the matching process(es) are constrained and hence how, in general terms, the cognitive model(s) across cognitive model profiles or informational characterizations to be matched are selected. In the example in (4) the first step in interpretation is the matching that takes place between the cognitive model profiles accessed via [BEAUTIFUL] and [NATION] which form part of an internally simpler lexical concept than the one also involving [FRANCE].[3] Recall the partial primary cognitive model profiles for [BEAUTIFUL] and [NATION] provided in Figures 13.4 and 13.3 respectively.

The Principle of Schematic Coherence ensures that in the matching process only cognitive models that are schematically coherent can be matched. In terms of the cognitive models to which [BEAUTIFUL] and [NATION] afford access, those that achieve schematic coherence across the two partial primary cognitive model profiles are the AESTHETIC PLEASURE cognitive model associated with the cognitive model profile for [BEAUTIFUL] and the CULTURE and LANGUAGE cognitive models associated with the cognitive model profile accessed via [NATION]. The AESTHETIC PLEASURE, CULTURE, and LANGUAGE cognitive models achieve schematic coherence as CULTURE and LANGUAGE relate to bodies of knowledge concerning entities which may exhibit properties relating to knowledge concerning AESTHETIC PLEASURE.

Once matching has occurred, the resulting informational characterization is then subject to matching with the cognitive model profile accessed via the [FRANCE] lexical concept. The "beautiful nation" informational characterization

---

[3] The lexical concepts [BEAUTIFUL] and [NATION] make up the [SPECIFIED THING] lexical concept which is a simpler lexical concept than the more encompassing "predicate nominative" lexical concept.

is matched with the NATION STATE cognitive model from the primary cognitive model accessed via [FRANCE]. This follows as the NATION STATE cognitive model relates to knowledge of entities such as the people and their national identity, including culture and language. Hence, this kind of knowledge relates to entities which are coherent with knowledge arising from the "beautiful nation" informational characterization.

Before proceeding, it is worth noting that the utterance in (4) can readily give rise to an alternative conception subject to an appropriate extra-linguistic context, one which involves understanding the French people as being physically attractive: what might be glossed as the "beautiful people" conception. This involves constructing an informational characterization for [BEAUTIFUL] and [NATION] by virtue of matching the VISUAL PLEASURE cognitive model from the primary cognitive model profile accessed via [BEAUTIFUL] and the PEOPLE cognitive model from the primary cognitive model accessed via [NATION]. This informational characterization is then matched with the NATION STATE cognitive model associated with the cognitive model profile accessed via [FRANCE]. This results in the "beautiful people" conception. This example illustrates, then, that different interpretations, and hence conceptions, can be accounted for by LCCM Theory, and arise precisely because of the diverse ways in which matching can occur, as constrained by the principles of interpretation, and as made more (or less) salient by virtue of the salience associated with particular interpretations, and as guided by extra-linguistic context.

I now turn to a related issue, and hence the need for further principles which serve to constrain interpretation. In discussing the example in (3) above, I argued that this utterance gives rise to a "geographical area" conception. Yet, what I have just indicated regarding the possibility of multiple interpretations, due to the diverse ways in which matching can occur, suggests that this example should, in principle, be capable of more than one conception. Indeed, it should be equally possible, based on what I have posited thus far, for a "beautiful nation" conception to be derivable from (3). That is, just as matching may serve to construct an informational characterization in which VISUAL PLEASURE and GEOGRAPHICAL AREA cognitive models are matched, giving rise to the "geographical area" conception, it should also be possible for the AESTHETIC PLEASURE and NATION STATE cognitive models to undergo matching, giving rise to a conception in which the products of a nation state, language, culture, and so on, are conceived of as being aesthetically pleasing. However, and based on intuitions from a large number of native speakers, this is not a conception that native speakers of English readily derive for (3), without further specifying extra-linguistic context.

Based on the principles thus far presented, this finding is not predicted. Hence, we require a further principle, the **Principle of Schematic Salience in Matching**. This principle can be stated as follows:

(p6)   Principle of Schematic Salience in Matching
       Matching across cognitive model profiles/informational characteriza-
       tions achieves greater schematic salience when relatively more cognitive
       models are matched than matches involving fewer cognitive models.

The principle provided in (p6) accounts for the fact that without additional
linguistic or extra-linguistic context, certain utterances give rise to what may
be considered to be a canonical or what I term a **default conception**. For
instance, in (3), the "geographical area" conception represents a default
conception: it emerges automatically for most native speakers of standard
modern English, unless there is further specifying context. That is, while
a "beautiful nation" conception should, in principle, be possible, this doesn't
emerge unless, for instance, the utterance features additional context:

(5)   France is a beautiful country, according to a recent survey of the
      aesthetic contribution of a range of European cultural traditions.

   Applied to an example such as (3), the principle in (p6) guarantees that the
"geographical area" conception emerges at the expense of other possible
conceptions. This principle applies as follows. As we saw above, due to the
Principles of Interpretation already introduced, the first lexical concepts
to undergo interpretation are [BEAUTIFUL] and [COUNTRY]. The Principle
of Conceptual Coherence serves to establish two matches between the cognitive model profiles of [BEAUTIFUL] and [COUNTRY]. The "geographical area"
match emerges due to a match between the VISUAL PLEASURE and NON-
VISUAL PHYSICAL PLEASURE cognitive models of the cognitive model profile
accessed by [BEAUTIFUL] and the GEOGRAPHICAL REGION cognitive model
from the cognitive mode profile accessed via the [COUNTRY] lexical concept.
The "beautiful nation" match emerges due a match between the AESTHETIC
PLEASURE cognitive model of the cognitive model profile accessed by [BEAU-
TIFUL] and the NATION STATE cognitive model from the cognitive model
profile accessed via the [COUNTRY] lexical concept. Once these two distinct
matches have been derived, the Principle of Schematic Salience in Matching identifies the "geographical area" match as involving matching across
a larger number of cognitive models, and hence as involving (i) a broader
base and (ii) a greater quantity of matched information. This serves to
establish this match as the default. Hence, and in the light of there being
no additional context, the other match is discarded, with the "geographical
area" match being established as the informational characterization which
proceeds to the next stage of interpretation: to be matched with the cognitive
model profile accessed via the [FRANCE] cognitive model. In short, the
principle in (p6) accounts for the insight that certain conceptions arise
automatically, and can be considered typical, canonical, or what I refer to as
default conceptions.

Of course, default conceptions can be overridden by further context, as illustrated by the example in (5) above, where additional utterance context, notably the complex NP: "a recent survey of the aesthetic contribution of a range of European cultural traditions" serves to ensure that, at least for some native speakers, a "beautiful nation" interpretation for [FRANCE] emerges. This arises due to the construction of a "beautiful nation" informational character-ization following matching between the cognitive model profiles associated with [BEAUTIFUL] and [COUNTRY]. This takes place by virtue of a process I refer to as **co-activation** due to the context provided by the complex NP which forms part of the comment clause introduced by "according to". That is, the informational characterization associated with the complex NP is subject to matching with the cognitive model profiles associated with [BEAUTIFUL] and [COUNTRY] simultaneously, giving rise to a co-activation of cognitive models AESTHETIC PLEASURE derived from the cognitive model profile for [BEAUTIFUL], and the NATION STATE cognitive model accessed via [COUNTRY] together with the informational characterization associated with the complex NP.

The reason that matching with the informational characterization of the complex NP involves simultaneous activation across two cognitive model profiles follows from application of the overarching Principle of Interpret-ation: the Principle of Guided Matching. As the lexical concepts [BEAUTIFUL] and [COUNTRY] form part of a lexical conceptual unit, given that they comprise part of a complex lexical concept, and given the nature of lexical concept integration, these two lexical concepts are matched with the informational characterization of the complex NP, in tandem. Once the informational characterization of "beautiful nation" is derived for the lexical conceptual unit associated with the expression *beautiful country*, this informational char-acterization is matched, in turn, with the cognitive model profile accessed via [FRANCE]. This results in an interpretation of [FRANCE] in which a "nation state" informational characterization is derived. Together these various infor-mational characterizations result in the conception associated with the entire utterance which can be paraphrased as follows: "According to a survey exam-ining attitudes towards the aesthetic pleasure resulting from products of distinctive European cultures, the nation of France is found to have a culture that is ranked as being high, in terms of the aesthetic pleasure it provides".

The finding that the cognitive model profiles accessed via [BEAUTIFUL] and [COUNTRY] are matched simultaneously with a distinct informational char-acterization is predicted by the **Principle of Simultaneous Matching**, which can be stated as follows:

(p 7)   Principle of Simultaneous Matching
        When matching takes place between an informational characterization
        and a complex lexical concept, matching may occur simultaneously
        across cognitive model profiles of the lexical concepts that form part of
        the complex lexical concept.

In essence, the Principle of Simultaneous Matching ensures that when an informational characterization, such as that associated with the complex NP in the clause introduced by the complex preposition *according to* in (5), is matched with the complex lexical concept associated with the expression *beautiful country*, the cognitive model profiles which constitute the simpler lexical concepts: [BEAUTIFUL] and [COUNTRY] respectively, undergo matching simultaneously with the informational characterization with which they are being matched. In this particular example then, LCCM Theory is able to distinguish between the distinct interpretations associated with *beautiful country* in (5) and the default interpretation which is associated with this expression in the utterance given in (3), and in so doing, account for the distinct interpretations associated with [FRANCE] in each example.[4]

I now turn to a further principle of interpretation, which is termed the **Principle of Primary Activation**. In the discussion thus far I have repeatedly talked about matching in terms of activation of cognitive models. Moreover, I earlier introduced the term primary activation. Activation has to do with the resonance of the conceptual (i.e., multimodal) content associated with cognitive models (or informational characterizations) that form part of the cognitive model profiles accessed via distinct lexical concepts. The Principle of Primary Activation can be stated as follows:

(p8)   Principle of Primary Activation
        Matched cognitive model(s) are subject to primary activation.

What this principle does is to guarantee that cognitive models which are subject to matching achieve a high degree of resonance. Hence, in an utterance such as (3), the reason for the emergence of the "beautiful geographical area" conception is due to the high level of resonance (primary activation) of the cognitive models NATION STATE, VISUAL PLEASURE, and GEOGRAPHICAL REGION accessed, respectively, by the lexical concepts [FRANCE], [BEAUTIFUL], and [COUNTRY]. As we shall see below, some cognitive models can receive a relatively attenuated form of resonance which I refer to as **secondary activation**.

Thus far in the discussion of interpretation, I have been assuming, for the most part, that a match is always possible in the primary cognitive model profiles of lexical concepts which are subject to interpretation. However, sometimes, there is a **clash**. To illustrate, consider the following examples:

---

[4] It is worth considering what LCCM Theory predicts, from a processing perspective, which is to say, as the utterance in (5) unfolds. After processing of the first clause in the utterance: *France is a beautiful country*, LCCM Theory predicts that following standard Principles of Interpretation, (p4) to (p7) inclusive, a default interpretation arises in which a "beautiful country" interpretation emerges. However, with the advent of the second clause, this conception is revised, and a new matching process takes place, in which a new informational characterization emerges for *beautiful country*. This in turn serves to revise the interpretation which emerges for [FRANCE]. Hence, LCCM Theory predicts that conceptions emerge dynamically, and can be revised during processing as further linguistic context emerges in order to produce new matches which "overwrite" previously established conceptions during the process of language understanding.

(6)   a. ?John, the landmass
    b. ?John, the nation

The utterances in (6) are not straightforwardly interpretable, signalled by the question marks, precisely because an informational characterization is not possible for [LANDMASS] or [NATION] when matched with the primary cognitive model profile associated with the lexical concept [INDIVIDUAL NAMED JOHN]. This is due to a clash in the primary cognitive model profiles associated with the [INDIVIDUAL NAMED JOHN] lexical concept on the one hand and [LANDMASS] and [NATION] on the other. This is not to say, of course, that matching is impossible, thereby avoiding a clash. However, **clash resolution** requires recourse to what in Chapter 10 I referred to as the level of secondary cognitive models: activation at this level is the hallmark of figurative language, as we shall see in detail in the next chapter.

If, then, a match is not possible in the primary cognitive model profile of a lexical concept, then clash resolution proceeds by virtue of the establishment of a **search region** in the secondary cognitive model profile of one (or more) of the lexical concepts in question. For instance, in terms of the example in (6a), this involves the lexical concepts [INDIVIDUAL NAMED JOHN] and [LANDMASS] whose cognitive model profiles are subject to matching. A very partial cognitive model profile for [INDIVIDUAL NAMED JOHN] is provided in Figure 13.6.

The [INDIVIDUAL NAMED JOHN] lexical concept facilitates access to a number of primary cognitive models which include, at the very least, BODY, SOCIAL IDENTITY, and IDIOSYNCRATIC COGNITIVE TRAITS, which is to say personality. However, when these are subject to matching with the primary cognitive model profile associated with [LANDMASS] there is a match failure, which is to say a clash. This follows due to application of the Principle of Conceptual Coherence (p5) as applied to the default search region: the primary cognitive

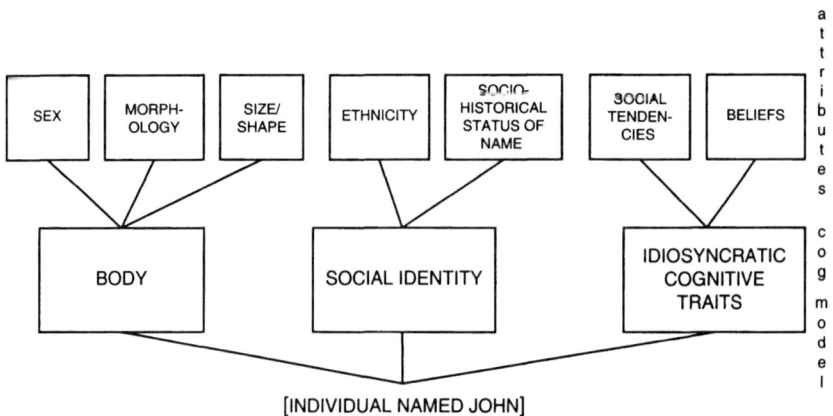

FIGURE 13.6. A partial primary cognitive model profile with attributes for the lexical concept [INDIVIDUAL NAMED JOHN]

model profiles. That is, there is no schematic coherence readily apparent in the primary cognitive model profiles accessed via the [LANDMASS] and [INDIVID-UAL NAMED JOHN] lexical concepts. The consequence of this is that a search region must be established in the secondary cognitive model profile of one or more of the relevant lexical concepts. This follows from the **Principle of Ordered Search**, which can be stated as follows:

(p9)   Principle of Ordered Search
Matching takes place in the primary cognitive model profile, which is the default search region for that subset of lexical concepts that facilitate access to a cognitive model profile. If matching is unsuccessful in the default search domain, which is to say, a clash occurs, then a new search domain is established in the secondary cognitive model profile. The search proceeds in an ordered fashion, proceeding on the basis of secondary cognitive models that are conceptually more coherent with respect to the primary cognitive models (and hence modelled as being "closer" in the cognitive model profile) prior to searching cognitive models that exhibit successively less conceptual coherence.

In essence, the Principle of Ordered Search ensures the following. When there is a clash in the primary cognitive model profiles of the lexical concepts or informational characterization(s) in question, a larger search region is established which includes cognitive models in relevant secondary cognitive model profile(s). Indeed, and as we shall see in more detail in the next chapter, a clash in one or more primary cognitive model profiles necessitating access to secondary cognitive models is the hallmark of figurative language. The principle in (p9) thus serves to facilitate clash resolution by virtue of facilitating a search region beyond the default search region.

In terms of the example in (6a), application of principle (p4) ensures that interpretation, and hence the matching process, proceeds by respecting the output of lexical concept interpretation. With respect to (6a) then, from this it follows that interpretation seeks to establish a match in a way in which the second NP in the utterance, *the landmass*, serves to specify the subject element, the lexical concept [INDIVIDUAL NAMED JOHN]. This is a consequence of the unpacking of linguistic content, and the integration of the complex and internally open lexical concept paired with the appositive vehicle.[5]

The consequence, then, of linguistic unpacking is that interpretation results in a search being established in the secondary cognitive model profile of [LANDMASS] in order to establish a match with one (or more) of the primary cognitive models of [INDIVIDUAL NAMED JOHN] lexical concept. As [LAND-MASS] is "about" the subject which it serves to specify, and as the primary

---

[5] The principle (p4) ensures that matching takes place in a way in which the cognitive model(s) accessed via the [LANDMASS] lexical concept specify the quality associated with [INDIVIDUAL NAMED JOHN], in terms of a match in schematic coherence.

cognitive model profile accessed via [LANDMASS] cannot actually (i.e., literally) match with the primary cognitive model profile of [INDIVIDUAL NAMED JOHN] the lexical concept it is about, a search region is established in the secondary cognitive model profile accessed via [LANDMASS] in order to establish a match.

The Principle of Ordered Search further ensures that the search domain is progressively enlarged, beginning with secondary cognitive models, which are searched based on their relative conceptual coherence with those cognitive models that populate the primary cognitive model profile. This ensures that cognitive models which are, in relative terms, conceptually "closer" to the access site that is represented by the lexical concept, are searched prior to those cognitive models which are less close. This captures the intuition that knowledge which is likely to be more "central" to what we might think of, informally, as constituting "word meaning" is searched before knowledge that, in relative terms, is more "peripheral." In LCCM Theory, the central-peripheral distinction, as we saw in Chapter 10, is modelled in terms of a hierarchical cognitive model profile, with those cognitive models deemed to be more peripheral represented diagrammatically as further away.

The application of the Principle of Ordered Search serves to ensure that due to the failure to establish a match between the primary cognitive model profile of [LANDMASS] and [INDIVIDUAL NAMED JOHN] a search region is established in the secondary cognitive model profile to which [LANDMASS] facilitates access. The secondary model that achieves primary activation in the cognitive model of [LANDMASS] is that of being significantly larger than other geographical features. This secondary cognitive model we might gloss as OVERSIZE. This is matched with the primary cognitive model of BODY associated with [INDIVIDUAL NAMED JOHN], providing an informational characterization of an "excessively large individual named John".

The final Principle of Interpretation I consider in this chapter is the **Principle of Secondary Activation**. This can be stated as follows:

(p10)   Principle of Secondary Activation
All primary cognitive models, and all secondary cognitive models on the route of access which do not achieve primary activation, achieve secondary activation.

I mentioned above that cognitive models which are matched achieve a high level of resonance and give rise to the meaning-construction process. This I referred to as primary activation. In addition, other cognitive models which form part of the search region achieve a more diffuse level of activation. This is guaranteed by the principle in (p10). This more diffuse level of activation is what I refer to as secondary activation. The rationale for positing two levels of activation comes from the view that a search region will necessarily entail a minimal level of activation in order to establish whether a match is available. Hence, this level of activation may make the searched cognitive models more

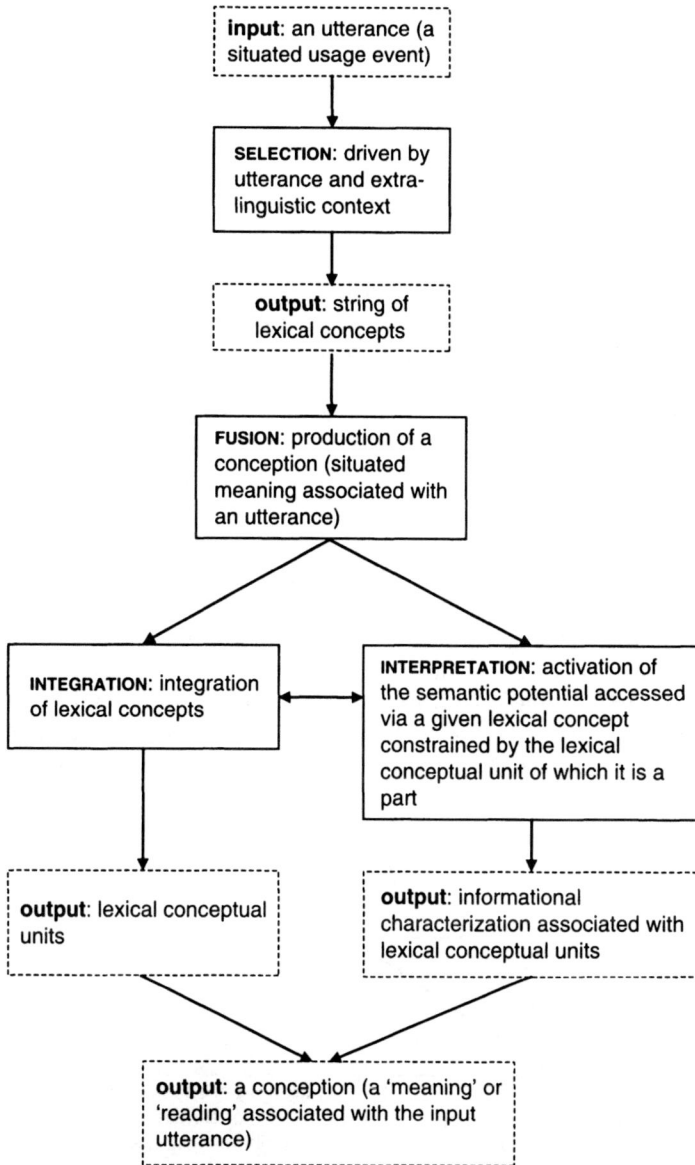

FIGURE 13.7. Meaning construction in LCCM Theory

readily accessible, and hence they achieve a diffuse level of activation which, in part, informs the informational characterization of the lexical concept in question. As the primary cognitive model profile is the default search region, then all the primary cognitive models necessarily achieve secondary activation. In addition, all secondary cognitive models on the access route in a secondary cognitive model profile achieve secondary activation. This is discussed in more detail in the next section.

By virtue of concluding this section on the Principles of Interpretation, I present a summary, in Figure 13.7, of meaning construction in LCCM Theory.

Types of activation

As we have seen thus far in our discussion of interpretation, the result of matching—the process at the heart of interpretation—is activation. In this section I present a taxonomy of the types of activation that take place in interpretation. In general terms there are two types:

- **activation of an access route**: this serves to facilitate both primary and secondary activation of cognitive models.
- **highlighting** of a cognitive model: this serves to activate part of a cognitive model.

In broad terms, the key distinction between activation of an access route, and highlighting, is that access route activation takes place over more than one cognitive model, while highlighting involves activation within a single cognitive model. The hallmark of activation of an access route is that while one (or more) cognitive model(s) undergoes primary activation, the majority of activated cognitive models undergo the lesser form of resonance that I refer to as secondary activation. The distinction in activation types is presented in Figure 13.8.

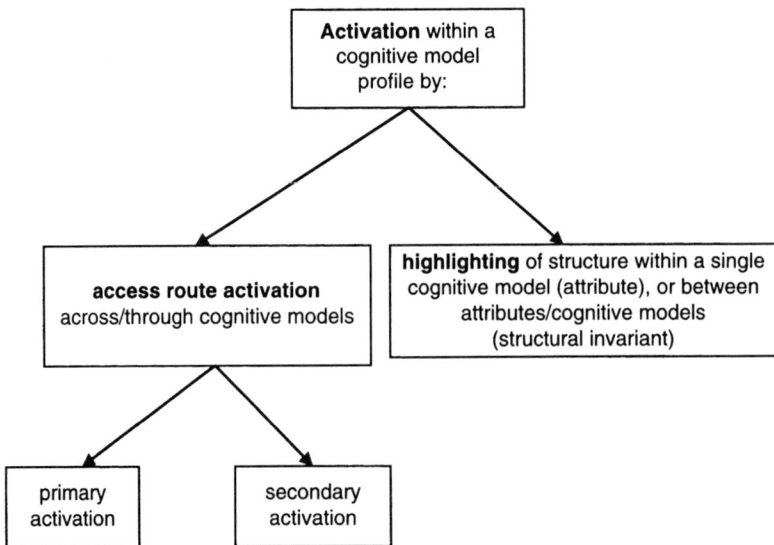

FIGURE 13.8. Activation types within a cognitive model profile

Access route activation

To illustrate the first type of activation, access route activation, reconsider the following example discussed in earlier chapters:

(7)   France voted against the EU constitution in the 2005 referendum

The conception which arises for the example in (7) involves primary activation of the ELECTORATE cognitive model, a secondary cognitive model to which the lexical concept [FRANCE] affords access. Yet, in addition, the cognitive models in the primary cognitive model profile achieve secondary activation, as do other secondary cognitive models which comprise the access route to the cognitive model which achieves primary activation. The access route constitutes all those cognitive models which intervene between the **access point**—the point at which the lexical concept affords access to the cognitive model profile—and the cognitive model which receives primary activation. In an informational characterization which is restricted to the default search domain, this involves all the cognitive models in the primary cognitive model profile: the access site. However, in an informational characterization involving a search region in the secondary cognitive model profile, this includes other cognitive models, as is the case in the example in (7). The access route for the informational characterization for [FRANCE] based on (7) is captured in Figure 13.9. In this figure, all those

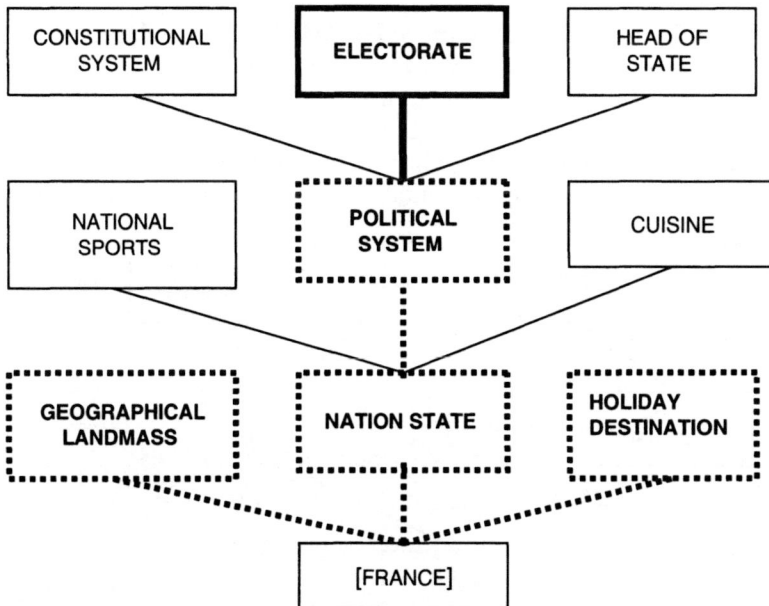

FIGURE 13.9. Access route established by the interpretation of [FRANCE] in the utterance *France voted against the EU constitution in the 2005 referendum*

cognitive models which achieve secondary activation are represented with dashed boldface. The cognitive model which achieves primary activation is marked with undashed boldface.

Before concluding this discussion of access routes, it is important to point to an important consequence. LCCM Theory predicts that there is a correlation between **access route length** and figurativity. That is, the "longer" the access route the more likely it is that language users will judge a particular utterance as being figurative, with greater length correlating with assessments of greater figurativity.

Highlighting

I now turn to the phenomenon of highlighting. This results from differential activation of attributes internal to a given cognitive model, as we will see in the discussion of the examples in (8) and (9) below, which relate to the lexical concept [BOOK]. A partial cognitive model profile for this lexical concept is provided in Figure 13.10.

(8) a. That's a heavy book
     b. That antiquarian book is illegible

(9) a. That's a long book
     b. That's an interesting book

Let's consider the cognitive models accessed via [BOOK]. As illustrated in the partial cognitive model profile given in Figure 13.10, the knowledge accessed by [BOOK] includes, at the very least, that a book is a physical entity and is interacted with via a process of reading. These two distinct sorts of knowledge— knowledge relating to an artefact, and the process of reading—are captured in Figure 13.10 by the two cognitive models (BOOK) PHYSICAL STRUCTURE and

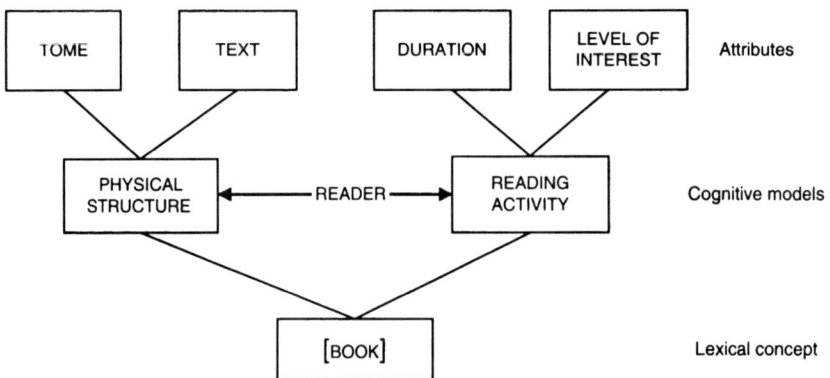

FIGURE 13.10. The relationship between lexical concepts, cognitive models, and attributes

READING ACTIVITY respectively. The two cognitive models are related by virtue of a READER—the structural invariant—who interacts with the physical artefact by virtue of reading the printed text. This relation holds between cognitive models and/or attributes, as discussed in Chapter 10. I capture the structural invariant in Figure 13.10 by a double-headed arrow, and the specific relation involved is signalled by the mnemonic READER. In addition, cognitive models consist of a large, detailed, but structured, body of knowledge. Figure 13.10 provides two attributes for each of the cognitive models which [BOOK] provides access to. The cognitive model PHYSICAL STRUCTURE relates to the physical artefact, consisting of, at the very least, knowledge as to the physical structure and organization of a given book. This includes detailed knowledge concerning the material aspects of the artefact, including its dimensions, weight, binding (paper or cloth), and so forth. This aspect of our knowledge about books I refer to as the TOME attribute. In addition to the physical organization and construction of a book, books consist of text which is interacted with through the process of reading. This I refer to as the TEXT attribute.

The READING ACTIVITY cognitive model relates to the process involved in interacting with books, especially the nature of the interaction with the text itself. One consequence of this interaction is that reading takes up a period of time, which I refer to as the DURATION attribute. That is, depending on the amount of text involved, reading can take lesser or greater amounts of time. Another consequence of interaction with books is the level of interest that a given book holds for the reader. This I refer to as the LEVEL OF INTEREST attribute. That is, while the reader might judge the book to be interesting, another might be judged to be boring, and so on.

Now let's return to the issue of highlighting. Each of the utterances in (8) and (9) involves a distinct informational characterization for the [BOOK] lexical concept. This is achieved by virtue of each instance of [BOOK] being interpreted in a way consistent with the utterance context such that a slightly different access route is established through the cognitive model profile accessed via [BOOK].

For instance, the conceptions that result from (8) have to do with primary activation of the PHYSICAL STRUCTURE cognitive model. However, each conception involves differential activation of attributes associated with this cognitive model—the process of highlighting. While the informational characterization associated with [BOOK] in (8a) involves highlighting of the TOME attribute, the informational characterization associated with [BOOK] in (8b) involves highlighting of the TEXT attribute.

In contrast, the conceptions that result from the utterances in (9) have to do with primary activation of the READING EVENT cognitive model accessed via [BOOK]. The informational characterization associated with [BOOK] in (9a) results from highlighting of the DURATION attribute. The informational characterization associated with [BOOK] in (9b) results from highlighting the LEVEL OF INTEREST attribute.

Types of matching

I now turn to a consideration of the process of matching. Matching is the central mechanism in interpretation, and involves simultaneous primary activation of cognitive models accessed via, or arising from, distinct lexical concepts and/or lexical conceptual units in order to produce a complex informational characterization.

Matching takes two distinct forms. This is a consequence of the broad distinction which holds between nominal versus relational lexical concepts first discussed in Chapter 6, and hence, the sorts of cognitive model profiles that, in broad terms, these two types of lexical concepts facilitate access to. Put another way, not only is there a distinction in the nature of the linguistic content that nominal, e.g., [EXPLOSION], versus relational, e.g., [(TO) EX-PLODE] lexical concepts encode, but as each lexical concept has a unique access site, the cognitive models accessed via each lexical concept will be slightly distinct. With respect to matching, the claim in LCCM Theory is that the distinctive nature of these classes of lexical concept—and hence their associated cognitive model profiles—entails a differential contribution to the construction of a complex informational characterization—the interpretation that arises from integration of a lexical conceptual unit—due to differences in the way matching applies to the two distinct sorts of cognitive models in question.

Specifically, I assume that the cognitive model profile associated with a relational lexical concept typically does not contribute determinate properties to the complex informational characterization, but contributes a set of qualities, or characteristics that are **adjusted** in response to the cognitive model profile of the nominal lexical concept. In contrast, the cognitive model profile of the nominal lexical concept has a range of determinate properties which are selected in conjunction with the relational lexical concept. This serves to **perspectivize** the properties associated with the cognitive model profile accessed via the nominal lexical concept. Hence, the interpretation of a relational lexical concept involves a matching process I refer to as **adjustment** whereas the matching process as it applies to the cognitive profile accessed via the nominal lexical concept is referred to as **perspectivization**.

To illustrate this distinction consider the following expressions:

(10)   a. a good man
       b. a good meal

In these expressions, the contribution of [GOOD] in each example is slightly different. Moreover, the contribution of [GOOD] is qualitatively distinct across the two expressions from the respective contributions of the nominal lexical concepts [MAN] and [MEAL]. That is, because [GOOD] facilitates access to conceptual content which is relational in nature, the nature of the matching

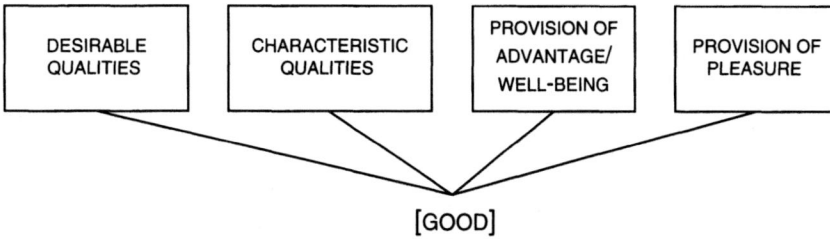

FIGURE 13.11. Partial cognitive model profile for [GOOD]

process as it applies to the cognitive model profile accessed via [GOOD] is of a distinct kind. To illustrate consider the partial cognitive model profile for [GOOD] as presented in Figure 13.11.

The complex informational characterization associated with "good man", for instance, might relate to notions such as physical beauty, honour, being morally upstanding, providing for one's family, and so on, depending upon the relevant utterance and/or extra-linguistic context. Such notions relate to bodies of knowledge having to do with desirable qualities, characteristic qualities, provision of advantage and provision of pleasure, as they relate to the ways in which being a man affects such issues.

In contrast, while a "good meal" also concerns the same bodies of knowledge, the complex informational characterization associated with "good meal" has to do with the size of the portions, how tasty the food is, that it consists of wholesome ingredients, and so on. Thus, while both complex informational characterizations involve the same cognitive models associated with [GOOD], the knowledge is adjusted in a way that corresponds to the cognitive models perspectivized by the nominal lexical concept, [MAN] versus [MEAL].

An even clearer example is provided by the following examples:

(11)   a. a small galaxy
       b. a small elephant
       c. a small mouse

The metric properties that *small* provides in these examples are wholly different, by several orders of magnitude. However, this is not due to [SMALL] facilitating access to a distinct cognitive model profile on each instance of access. Rather, the scale at which [SMALL] applies is adjusted, depending on the cognitive model(s) it is being matched with.

In contrast, in building **complex informational characterizations**—informational characterizations of more than one lexical concept within the same lexical conceptual unit—matching as applied to nominal lexical concepts involves not adjusting of cognitive models, but the activation of distinct cognitive models—the phenomenon of perspectivization. To illustrate, consider the distinction in the following:

(12)   a. a good man
        b. a small man

The complex informational characterizations that result from the expressions
in (12) involve activation of distinct cognitive models accessed via [MAN].
While (12a) involves activation of behavioural characteristics, the example in
(12b) involves the activation of knowledge relating to body structure. That is,
matching as it applies to nominal lexical concepts involves activation of a
different cognitive model—the phenomenon of perspectivization—as opposed to adjusting scalar properties of the same cognitive model—the phenomenon of adjustment.

Semanticality

In this section I briefly address the semantic well-formedness of conceptions.
Conceptions are, by definition, semantically coherent. We will see that this is
the case by considering situations in which conceptions fail to materialize.

The term **semanticality**, as introduced into linguistics by Pustejovsky
(1995), related to the semantic well-formedness of a sentence. In LCCM
Theory, semanticality relates to well-formed utterances, which is to say
those that give rise to conceptions. Utterances that fail in this regard are
semantically anomalous. The reason for failing to achieve semanticality is due
either to a failure to conform to the Principles of Lexical Concept Integration
(principles p1-p3), or a failure to conform to the Principles of Interpretation
(principles p4-p10), or a failure to conform to both. In other words, **semanticality failure** is a consequence of failure to successfully undergo fusion,
thereby resulting in a string of vehicles, but no conception.

To consider this phenomenon consider some examples involving the verbal
vehicle *began*:

(13)   a. He began the book
        b. ?He began the dictionary
        c. ??He began the rock

On the face of it, while the first example evidences a semantically well-formed
conception, the utterance in (13b) is not well-formed. This follows as dictionaries are not something we "begin", as their function relates to reference and
look-up. Thus, there is a clash between the cognitive model profiles as
accessed by the lexical concepts in this utterance.

However, in certain situations extra-linguistic context can help, as pointed
out by Pustejovsky (1995). For instance, Malcolm X, the African American civil
rights activist who promoted violent struggle in the 1950s and 1960s, is famously
known to have read a dictionary whilst in prison "like a book". As the only book

available to him was a dictionary he began at the letter A and read through to Z. In such a situation, the example in (13b) becomes semantically acceptable.

The example in (13c), on the face of it, is also semantically anomalous as a rock is not an entity that has internal structure that is subject to a sequential process that can be construed as having a starting point. Thus, while a dictionary is a book that can, under certain novel contexts, be construed as an entity that can be read sequentially, (13b) is less semantically anomalous than (13c). However, if the context relates to the act of beginning a sculpture, then interpretation can successfully apply and a conception for (13c) emerges. Hence, semanticality is a function of both linguistic and extra-linguistic context.

Above the utterance: discourse models

As noted in Chapter 3, LCCM Theory is a theory of what I refer to as frontstage cognition. That is, it is concerned with the way in which conceptions emerge, and is focused on the interaction between linguistic content, conceptual content and extra-linguistic context at the level of the utterance.

However, a full account of meaning construction requires understanding the compositional processes "above" the level of the utterance. This involves building what I will refer to as a **discourse model**.[6] That is, utterances do not occur in isolation: they form part of ongoing discourse. Moreover, utterances themselves are not delivered and interpreted in isolation from other forms of symbolic representation. For instance, the following attested utterance appeared on the back of a red double-decker eco-friendly bus in Brighton:

(14)   Red is green!

In order to form a conception, extra-linguistic knowledge is required relating to the recently introduced fleet of eco-friendly buses in the city of Brighton, visual information relating the colour of the bus, and background knowledge relating to the notion of the colour green as a symbolic representation of environmental "friendliness." That is, language understanding involves a lot more than semantic composition, but integration with visual cues, and access to and integration of knowledge relating to other sorts of stored information, both propositional and visual.

In addition, utterances must be related and integrated with knowledge derived from other utterances and the model that is being constructed during ongoing discourse. As is now known from the language and cognitive sciences, meaning results from complex inferential processes (Sperber and Wilson 1995), the interactional nature of the exchanges during ongoing discourse, including the range of roles that speakers adopt and negotiate with respect to one another

---

[6] See Zwaan and Radvansky (1998), Zwaan and Madden (2004) for discussion of the related notion of a "situation model."

during ongoing discourse (Goffman 1981; Schiffrin 1994), the range of context-ualization cues employed (Gumperz 1982), the goal-directed nature of language as use in interaction with others (Clark 1996), the extensive use of gesture that is co-timed with language (McNeill 1992; Kendon 2004), the proliferation of mental spaces, and the spreading of information across a lattice of intercon-nected mental spaces (Fauconnier 1994, 1997), the integration of knowledge from multimodal sources in the construction of mental spaces by virtue of the compression of what is referred to as **vital relations** (Fauconnier and Turner 2002), the deployment of cross-domain conceptual metaphors that are neurally instantiated (Lakoff and Johnson 1999), and the triggering of motor and sensory resonances in the process of language understanding (Zwaan 2004). All of these issues operate at or above the level of the utterance, and are in various ways beyond the scope of LCCM Theory. A full account of meaning construction then, must, at the very least, be able to be integrated with the full panoply of ways in which language users deploy language, in part, in service of expressing and understanding situated communicative intentions.

In short, many of the mechanisms just described are crucial to the construc-tion of a discourse model. A discourse model is related to what psycholinguists have referred to as a **mental model** (Johnson-Laird 1983) or a **situation model** (van Dijk and Kintsch 1983; see Zwaan and Radvansky 1998 for a review). A discourse model can be described as "a mental representation of the described situation" resulting from situated language understanding (Zwaan and Rad-vansky 1998: 162). It represents a dynamic mental model constructed during ongoing discourse, to which information is continually added. As such it is in a continual state of modification, drawing upon the language user's "background knowledge," and the "common ground" established by interlocutors by virtue of the negotiation and realization of interactional goals, as discussed in Chapter 11.[7] A discourse model constitutes shared (or public) knowledge that emerges from discourse and other modalities, and concerns states of affairs, knowledge relat-ing to interlocutors, their interactional goals, and so forth. A discourse model, then, relates to information that is stored in memory and hence can be described and reported on later.

From the present perspective then, LCCM Theory, a theory of frontstage cognition is not primarily concerned with the meaning construction pro-cesses involved in this level of representation. Rather this is the function of backstage cognition. I distinguish frontstage and backstage cognition as follows, in so far as they relate to meaning construction:

- **Frontstage cognition**

    - involves the relationship between phonological vehicles (lexical forms) and semantic structure, including access to encyclopaedic/conceptual knowledge (=semantic potential)

---

[7] See in particular Clark (1996); see also Chafe (1994).

   - involves principles of semantic composition that serve to narrow the semantic potential accessed in a given utterance, as constrained by (extra-linguistic) context

- **Backstage cognition**

   - involves non-linguistic principles that facilitate construction of a discourse model
   - must involve extra-linguistic context, background knowledge, e.g., pattern completion, recognition of situated communicative intention of language user, and so forth.

LCCM Theory attempts to provide a sound basis for the role of linguistic knowledge, its interface with conceptual knowledge and the linguistic compositional processes involved at the level of the utterance. It seeks to do so in a way which is cognitively realistic, i.e., consistent with the guiding principles of cognitive linguistics—as discussed in Chapter 3—and in a way which builds on many of the theoretical advances made by cognitive linguists and others such as cognitive psychologists. However, a full account of meaning construction requires the integration of such an account with an account that addresses the construction of a discourse model, in the sense sketched above.

Summary

This chapter has addressed interpretation. Interpretation involves access to conceptual content encoded by cognitive models, in service of linguistically mediated meaning construction. Interpretation applies to lexical concepts within a given lexical conceptual unit, resulting in an informational characterization, which, in effect, is a linguistically mediated simulation. Matching occurs recursively, operating on additional cognitive model profiles and/or informational characterizations. Once the entire utterance has undergone interpretation, the result is the formation of an utterance-level informational characterization, which is to say a conception: a complex simulation, involving multimodal knowledge guided by language use. The central process in interpretation is referred to as matching. Matching takes place between the cognitive model profiles of the open-class lexical concepts which have undergone integration, and hence which result in a lexical conceptual unit. Hence, interpretation involves lexical concepts within the same lexical conceptual unit. Matching involves activation of cognitive models that achieve schematic alignment across the cognitive model profiles accessed via the lexical concepts and/or informational characterizations undergoing interpretation. Interpretation is constrained by a number of Principles of Interpretation. The overarching principle of interpretation is the Principle of Guided Matching. This ensures that the matching of cognitive models in interpretation proceeds in a way that is compatible with the output of lexical concept integration. The chapter also discussed activation across cognitive models resulting in an access route, as well as activation within a cognitive model, known as highlighting.

Part IV

Figurative Language and Thought

This part of the book represents an application of LCCM Theory to figurative language and thought. Part IV consists of two chapters. The first, Chapter 14, addresses the phenomena of metaphor and metonymy, and provides an LCCM account of figurative language understanding which, it is argued, complements the major insights provided by Conceptual Metaphor Theory. The second, Chapter 15, provides an LCCM account of the semantics of Time, presenting an analysis of a subset of lexical concepts from English for this domain. The purpose is to provide an application to one area of figurative language to demonstrate how LCCM Theory might be applied to specific domains.

14

Metaphor and metonymy

One of the major successes of cognitive linguistics has been to model the complexity and richness of the human imagination. Until relatively recently in linguistics and in cognitive science more generally, it was assumed either that the human imagination was peripheral to cognition or that it could not be systematically studied—see representative papers in Ortony (1993) which assume exactly this, and references and discussion in Gibbs (1994). The cognitive linguistics enterprise has provided an approach to studying human imagination, and has been influential in arguing that language reveals systematic processes at work. Cognitive linguists have argued that such processes are central to the way we think.

The role of imagination in human thought has been approached, in cognitive linguistics, by way of positing relatively stable knowledge structures which are held to inhere in long-term memory. These knowledge structures are termed conceptual metaphors (Lakoff and Johnson 1980, 1999) and are claimed to have psychological reality. In addition, conceptual metaphors are held to be manipulated by an inclusive dynamic meaning-construction process known as conceptual blending (Fauconnier and Turner 1998, 2002; Grady 2005). The way in which these structures and processes have been studied has predominantly been to examine systematicities in figurative language, particularly in the study of conceptual metaphors. George Lakoff and Mark Johnson, the proponents of the study of conceptual metaphor and the architects of Conceptual Metaphor Theory, argue that figurative language is a consequence of the existence of a universal set of pre-linguistic primary metaphors (Lakoff and Johnson 1999; see also Grady 1997), and a language-specific set of conceptual metaphors, both of which map structure from more concrete domains of conceptual structure, referred to as source domains, onto less easily apprehended aspects of conceptual structure, referred to as target domains. Together these knowledge structures are held to give rise both to the productive use of figurative language, as well as to more creative aspects, such as poetic metaphor, for instance (see Lakoff and Turner 1989). More recently, it has been argued that conceptual metaphors have a neural instantiation (see discussion in Feldman 2006; Gallese and Lakoff 2005; Lakoff and Johnson 1999).

While the success of both Conceptual Metaphor Theory and Conceptual Blending Theory provides the backdrop for the discussion in this chapter, the analyses presented here are orthogonal to, and, I argue, complement the approaches developed by these theories. For instance, Conceptual Metaphor Theory is not primarily (if at all) a theory *about* metaphor understanding in language. Rather, Conceptual Metaphor Theory has traditionally been concerned with the nature and the level of the various cognitive representations—cognitive models in present terms—that serve to structure target domains in terms of source domains. That is, Conceptual Metaphor Theory is a theory concerned with backstage cognition. What is required, in addition, is a theory of how language deploys and interfaces with these non-linguistic knowledge structures— the conceptual metaphors—in service of figurative language understanding. That is, we require a theory that addresses frontstage cognition. In this chapter, I attempt to provide such an account from the perspective of LCCM Theory.[1]

Phenomena in need of explanation

In order to be able to provide an LCCM account of figurative language understanding, we must first identify the phenomena to be addressed. In particular I address the following:

- the distinction between literal and figurative language,
- the distinction between metaphor and metonymy.

I elaborate below on some of the issues at stake in accounting for these distinctions.

Literal versus figurative language

While Gibbs (1994) warns against the possibility of making a principled distinction between the two, pointing to the range of often contradictory ways in which linguists, philosophers, and cognitive scientists have defined these notions, I will assume for now that there are reasonable grounds for supposing that there is some basis for the intuition that there is a distinction between literal and figurative language, even if drawing a hard and fast line between the two may not be straightforward. To make this point clear, consider the expression *went up*, and examples of the following kind:

(1)   The rocket *went up* (in the sky)

(2)   The student's grades *went up* (during the course of the semester)

Without a specific utterance context, native speakers of English informally define *went up* as relating to veridical (i.e., actual) motion in an upwards direction along the vertical axis. In terms of LCCM Theory, we can say that the vehicle *went up* is conventionally associated with a lexical concept which, given

---

[1] I shall examine the relationship between conceptual metaphors and knowledge representation, as assumed by LCCM Theory, in the next chapter.

the linguistic content encoded and the cognitive model profile to which it affords access, might be glossed as [UPWARD VERTICAL MOTION BEFORE NOW].

In (1) the expression in italics, *went up*, relates to an entity which can undergo veridical (i.e., actual) motion. Hence, the lexical concept sanctions an interpretation in which *went up* relates to upward motion on the vertical axis. In the second example in (2) the expression *went up* relates to the student's grades. As *the student's grades* refers to a non-physical entity which thus cannot undergo veridical motion, the expression *went up* would appear not to apply in the same way as it does in (1). In (2) *went up* refers to an improvement in the student's grades. Given that *went up* is not being used in its spatial sense, we might informally describe its usage as being non-literal or figurative in nature. Hence, one of the challenges in this chapter is to present an LCCM account of figurative meaning construction which captures the different conceptions associated with the two utterances in (1) and (2), and doing so while accounting for the quite different contributions of the same expression: *went up*.

Metaphor versus metonymy

Secondly, we need to be able to account for the intuition that metaphor and metonymy, the two forms of figurative language which have received most attention in cognitive linguistics, and cognitive science more generally, are distinct phenomena, with, presumably, distinct sorts of linguistic and perhaps conceptual operations giving rise to them. An important objective in the present chapter is to develop an LCCM account of the meaning-construction processes responsible for the figurative language phenomena often described as constituting metaphor and metonymy. These are exemplified by expressions of the following kind:

Metaphor
(3) a. My boss is *a pussycat*
     b. The student's grades *went up*

Metonymy
(4) a. *France* rejected the EU constitution
     b. The *ham sandwich* has asked for the bill

In modern linguistics, metaphor is often understood as involving the interpretation (or conceptualization) of one entity in terms of something else, as in *my boss* in terms of a *pussycat*, or an improvement in student's grades in terms of an object in motion. Metonymy on the other hand is often taken to relate to a referent other than the one literally designated. For instance, in (4a), *France* refers to the portion of the French electorate that voted against endorsing a European Union constitution in a 2005 referendum held by the French government. Similarly, given a restaurant scenario, and two waiting staff talking about a particular customer, *ham sandwich* refers to the customer who ordered the ham sandwich rather than to the sandwich.

Traditionally, metaphor has been thought of as an implicit comparison.[2] Examples such as those in (3a) making use of the predicate nominative vehicle of which I shall have more to say below are the kinds of examples that are usually employed to support this perspective. Lakoff and Johnson in their development of the theoretical construct of the conceptual metaphor have subsumed a wider range of examples as relating to metaphor, to include examples of the following sort:

(5)   Things are *going smoothly* in the operating theatre

(6)   He was *in* a state of shock after the election result

(7)   The economy *is going from* bad *to* worse

As Lakoff and Johnson (1980) first observed, examples such as these are representative of ordinary, everyday ways of talking about events such as medical operations, emotional or psychological states, and changes in the economy. However, each utterance makes use of language that, on the face of it, relates to motion, physical location, or change in location in order to describe non-physical entities. Hence, Lakoff and Johnson use the term metaphor more inclusively than has traditionally been the case. This follows as they argue that linguistic metaphors are surface manifestations of underlying cognitive associations, which presumably inhere in long-term memory, relating often diverse bodies or domains of conceptual knowledge. That is, linguistic behaviour that is metaphoric is a consequence of sets of stable cross-domain conceptual mappings, conceptual metaphors, which license the patterns evident in language use. From this perspective, then, the sorts of linguistic data which Lakoff and Johnson provide in order to evidence the existence of conceptual metaphors, such as the examples in (5) to (7) inclusive, are not claimed to be motivated by comparison.

In contrast to metaphor, metonymy has typically been identified as having a distinct discourse function, which, for a number of scholars reflects a conceptual distinction vis-à-vis metaphor.[3] Metonymy is often held to be referential in nature, highlighting a particular referent by virtue of activating a contextually salient entity closely associated with the referent in question (this is sometimes expressed in terms of conceptual contiguity). For instance, in (4b) above, given a restaurant scenario, the food item ordered by a given customer is likely, among waiting staff, to be particularly salient, and thus an effective means of identifying a specific referent, in this instance, a particular customer. As this example demonstrates, linguistic metonymy is referential in nature: it relates to the use of expressions to "pinpoint" entities in order to talk about them. This shows that

---

[2] See Evans and Green (2006) for a review.
[3] See the collection of papers in Barcelona (2000) for instance.

metonymy functions differently from metaphor. Hence, while we might informally gloss metonymy as the relation in which "X stands for Y," by the same
token, metaphor is the relation "X understood in terms of Y."

Assumptions

Before proceeding with an LCCM account of the phenomena introduced above,
I first, briefly, present my assumptions. A consequence of the LCCM perspective
is that literal and figurative language are seen as arising from the same processes
of meaning construction. In other words, they can be seen as points lying along a
continuum of meaning construction, rather than being due to wholly different
mechanisms. Analogously, metaphor and metonymy, as two particular exemplars of figurative language use can be seen, from this perspective, as arising from
similar meaning-construction processes, differing in terms of the way meaning
construction occurs. The key assumptions associated with the LCCM approach
to figurative language can be summarized as follows:

- the meanings associated with figurative utterances are guided by context—both linguistic and extra-linguistic—in the same way as literal
  utterances
- there is continuity between figurative and literal language
- there is continuity between metaphor and metonymy
- figurative language understanding is a consequence of the nature of
  semantic representation and semantic composition, which is to say, the
  same structures and processes as described for literal language in Parts II
  and III of the book.

Literal versus figurative language understanding

The distinction between what I will refer to as a **literal conception**—the
meaning associated with a literal utterance—on the one hand, and a **figurative conception**—the meaning associated with a figurative utterance—on the
other, relates to that part of the semantic potential which is activated during
the process of interpretation during the construction of a conception. While a
literal conception canonically results in an interpretation which activates a
cognitive model, or cognitive models, within the default, which is to say,
primary, cognitive model profile, a figurative conception arises when cognitive models are activated in the secondary cognitive model profile. Moreover,
the greater the access route length, in the sense defined in Chapter 13, the more
figurative the conception is likely to feel.

The basic distinction between literal versus figurative conceptions, in terms
of the mechanisms of meaning construction posited by LCCM Theory,
relates, as we began to see in the previous chapter, to a clash in one of the

primary cognitive model profiles of the lexical concepts in the same lexical conceptual unit undergoing matching in interpretation. As we shall see below, the distinction between metaphor and metonymy, from the perspective of LCCM Theory, concerns the respective discourse function of each type of figurative language understanding, and hence, the way in which clash resolution functions in terms of the conception being constructed. In order to get a sense of how the language understanding process results in literal and figurative conceptions, consider Figure 14.1.

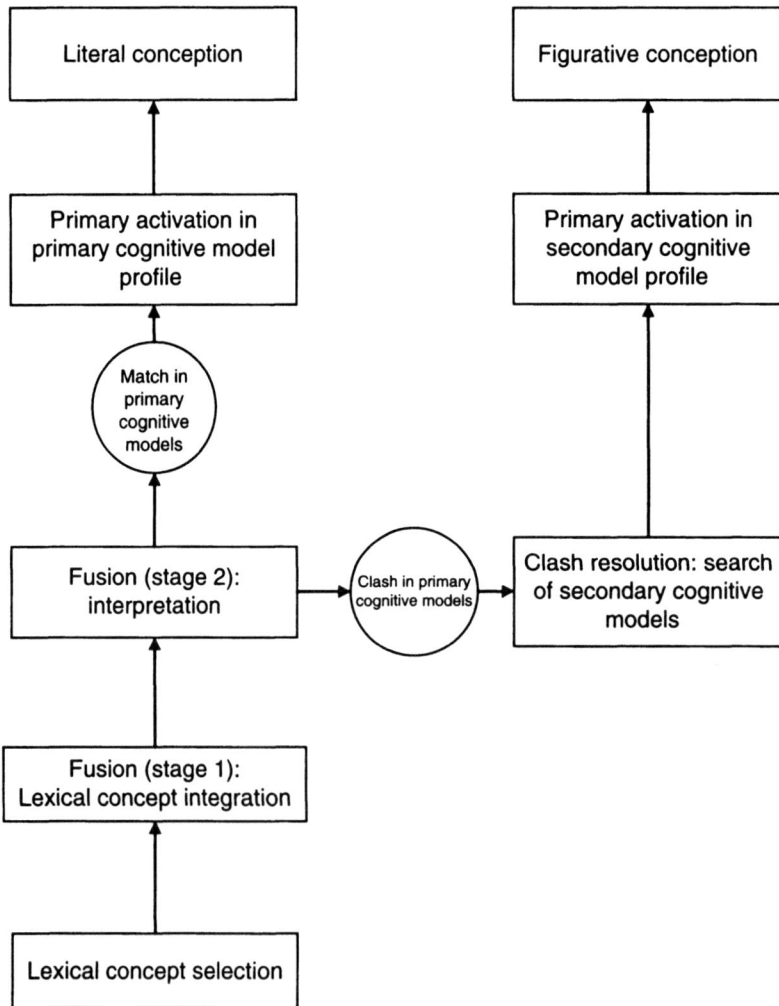

FIGURE 14.1. Meaning-construction processes in LCCM Theory leading to literal versus figurative conceptions

Figure 14.1 illustrates the following. At interpretation, the primary cognitive model profiles for lexical concepts which afford access to conceptual content and are in the same lexical conceptual unit undergo matching. The Principle of Conceptual Coherence requires that a clash in the cognitive model profiles of the two (or more) lexical concepts undergoing interpretation is avoided. The Principle of Ordered Search ensures that primary cognitive models undergo matching first. If there is a match, primary activation of one or more primary cognitive models occurs. If there is no match then there is a clash in the primary cognitive model profiles of the relevant lexical concepts. In order to avoid a clash, a search is initiated in the secondary cognitive model profile.

As we saw in Chapter 10, the secondary cognitive model profile relates to knowledge that is not directly associated with a given lexical concept, as it does not form part of a lexical concept's access site. As such, the secondary cognitive model profile constitutes a very large semantic potential available for search. The Principle of Ordered Search serves to ensure that the search in the secondary cognitive model profile proceeds in a coherent way. That is, the secondary cognitive models are searched to facilitate a match based on their conceptual coherence with the primary cognitive models which form part of the lexical concept's access site. Put another way, this principle also ensures that secondary cognitive models are searched in the order of their relative "distance" from the point of lexical access. Hence, secondary activation continues "upwards" through the secondary cognitive model profile until a match is achieved, giving rise to primary activation of one or more secondary cognitive models.

In order to illustrate, I consider by now familiar examples relating to the lexical concept [FRANCE]. A literal conception arises from the utterance in (8) while a figurative conception arises for the utterance in (9). By way of reminder, the partial cognitive model profile for [FRANCE] presented in previous chapters is given here as Figure 14.2.

Literal conception
(8)   France has a beautiful landscape

Figurative conception
(9)   France rejected the EU constitution

A literal conception arises for the first example by virtue of a match occurring between the informational characterization of [BEAUTIFUL LANDSCAPE] and the primary cognitive model profile to which [FRANCE] affords access. As interpretation relates, in the utterance in (8), to a lexical concept [FRANCE] and an informational characterization associated with [BEAUTIFUL LANDSCAPE], these being the only elements in this utterance which are associated with conceptual content, a search takes place in the cognitive model profile associated

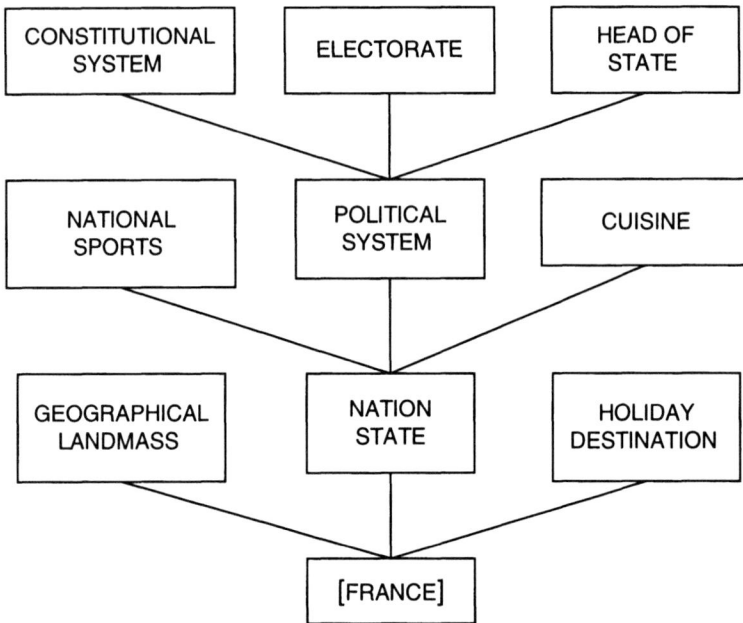

FIGURE 14.2. Partial cognitive model profile for [FRANCE]

with [FRANCE], as the lexical concepts [BEAUTIFUL] and [LANDSCAPE] having undergone interpretation have formed an informational characterization. Hence, their cognitive model profiles are no longer available as search domains. Hence, a search occurs in the primary cognitive model profile for [FRANCE]. The Principles of Conceptual Coherence and Ordered Search serve to ensure a match for (8) in the primary cognitive model profile of [FRANCE].

In terms of primary activation in (8), the Principle of Conceptual Coherence ensures that the GEOGRAPHICAL LANDMASS cognitive model for [FRANCE] receives primary activation. That is, this cognitive model matches the informational characterization associated with "beautiful landscape". This follows as there is a clash between the informational characterization and the other cognitive models in the primary cognitive model profile for [FRANCE]: NATION STATE, and HOLIDAY DESTINATION. Hence, the conception which arises for (8) is literal as activation occurs solely in the primary cognitive model profile.

In contrast, in (9) there is a clash between all the cognitive models in the primary cognitive model profile associated with [FRANCE] and the informational characterization associated with "EU constitution". Due to application of the Principles of Conceptual Coherence and Ordered Search, this gives rise to a search region being established. A secondary cognitive model is identified which achieves schematic coherence thereby avoiding a clash, and thus achieving a match. The cognitive model which achieves this, and thereby achieves primary activation, is the ELECTORATE cognitive model. Hence, in (9), following interpretation, the informational characterization associated with [FRANCE] is that of "electorate", and specifically due to highlighting, that "portion of the French electorate which voted 'non' in the 2005 EU constitution referendum". As the ELECTORATE cognitive model is a secondary cognitive model, this means that the conception is figurative in nature.

In sum, the defining feature of a literal conception is that matching occurs in the primary cognitive model profiles of the relevant lexical concepts. The defining feature of a figurative conception is a clash in the primary cognitive model profiles of the relevant lexical concepts necessitating clash avoidance, and hence primary activation in the secondary cognitive model profile of one (or more) of the relevant lexical concepts.

Metaphor

Having just illustrated the distinction between literal and figurative conceptions, I now provide a sketch of the meaning-construction processes that give rise to metaphoric conceptions. I first of all consider metaphoric conceptions employing the predicate nominative (i.e., the "X is a Y") vehicle. This has traditionally been the kind of linguistic form *par excellence* that has been studied under the heading of metaphor. Examples of this kind are illustrated in (3a) reproduced below. I will also examine how LCCM Theory accounts for the sort of metaphoric conceptions that Conceptual Metaphor Theory has been concerned with, as exemplified in the example in (3b)[4] also reproduced below:

(3) a. My boss is a pussycat
     b. The student's grades went up

My boss is a pussycat

What is strikingly figurative about the example in (3a) is that the entity designated by *my boss* is not normally taken as being a member of the class of pussycats. However, the predicate nominative vehicle is normally taken as having a class-inclusion function associated with it:

(10)   My boss is a pianist

---

[4] However, and as we shall briefly see in the next chapter, the analysis of metaphor presented here is orthogonal to the account provided by Conceptual Metaphor Theory. In particular, while conceptual metaphors are hypothesized to structure primary cognitive models, in terms of language understanding figurative language conceptions involve a clash in the primary cognitive model profile(s) of the lexical concepts undergoing fusion. The relationship between conceptual metaphors—which structure abstract concepts and hence concern knowledge representation—and figurative language conceptions—which involve the compositional mechanisms central to linguistically mediated meaning construction—is the subject of ongoing and future research within the framework of LCCM Theory.

This vehicle exemplified by the utterance in (10) involves the copular or "linking" verb *be* which combines with a nominal, e.g., "a pianist". The nominal functions as the essential part of the clausal predicate: "is a pianist". The function of the lexical concept conventionally paired with BE in this symbolic unit is to signal a stative relation (Langacker 1991*a*). Namely, "my boss is a member of the class of pianists", a situation which persists through time.

The same cannot hold for the example in (3a) as, in the normal course of events, someone's boss cannot literally be a pussycat. That is, the person designated by the expression *my boss* is not normally taken to be a member of the class of pussycats. The metaphoric conception which this utterance gives rise to is derived from a property which is usually associated with pussycats, namely that they are extremely docile and often affectionate, and thus not frightening or intimidating in any way. In this utterance, we are being asked to understand the boss not in terms of being a pussycat, but in terms of exhibiting some of the properties and behaviours often associated with pussycats as manifested towards their human owners, such as being docile, extremely friendly, and thus non-forbidding and perhaps easy to manipulate. Such a conception might be contrasted with the conception which might derive from an utterance such as:

(11)   My boss is an ogre

The metaphoric conception derived from (11) involves understanding the boss in terms of extreme ferocity, a property associated with the mythical creature referred to as an ogre.

Yet how does the metaphoric conception associated with (3a) arise? The LCCM approach to figurative meaning construction allows us to see the similarities and differences between metaphor and the literal predicate nominative examples such as (10). An important point of similarity relates to the process of fusion crucial for meaning construction, involving both integration and interpretation. As noted in the previous section, figurative language, of which metaphor is a subtype, diverges from literal language use in terms of the sorts of access routes it provides, and specifically primary activation in the secondary cognitive model profiles of the lexical concept which is undergoing clash resolution.

In an utterance such as "My boss is a pianist", the two relevant lexical concepts for interpretation are [BOSS] and [PIANIST]. This follows as these are the only two lexical concepts in the utterance which have access sites and thus provide direct access to conceptual content. Interpretation proceeds by attempting to match cognitive models in the primary cognitive model profiles associated with each of these lexical concepts as guided by the Principle of Conceptual Coherence and application of the Principle of Ordered Search. A match is achieved in the primary cognitive model profiles of each lexical concept. That is, it is semantically acceptable to state that *My boss is a pianist* because the referent of *my boss* is a human and humans can be pianists. The reason, then, why the conception associated with (10) intuitively feels literal is that the access route is relatively short, limited to the primary cognitive model profiles to which both [BOSS] and [PIANIST] afford access.

Now let's consider how the metaphoric conception arises. In the example in (3a), the process of interpretation leads to a clash in the primary cognitive model profiles of [BOSS] and [PUSSYCAT]. This is where metaphor differs from literal class-inclusion statements. A partial primary cognitive model profile for [BOSS] is provided in Figure 14.3.

The primary cognitive model profile for [BOSS] includes, at the very least, cognitive models relating to the fact that a boss is, typically, a human being, and the complex body of knowledge we each possess concerning what is involved in being a human being, that a boss has particular pastoral responsibilities with respect to those for whom he or she is line-manager, as well as managerial responsibilities and duties, both with respect to those the boss manages, the subordinate(s), and the particular company or organization for whom the "boss" works. In addition, there are an extremely large number of secondary cognitive models associated with each of these, only a few of which are represented in Figure 14.3. In particular, by virtue of being a human being, a boss has a particular personality and exhibits behaviour of various sorts, in part a function of his/her personality, in various contexts and situations. In addition, each boss exhibits a particular managerial style, which includes interpersonal strategies and behaviours with respect to those the boss manages. The boss can, for instance, be aggressive or docile with respect to the subordinate. Moreover, there is a clichéd cultural model of a ferocious and aggressive boss, who seeks to keep employees "on their toes" by virtue of aggressive and bullying interpersonal behaviour. By contrast, a boss who is relatively placid and can thus be treated as a colleague rather than a superior may be somewhat salient with respect to the stereotype.[5]

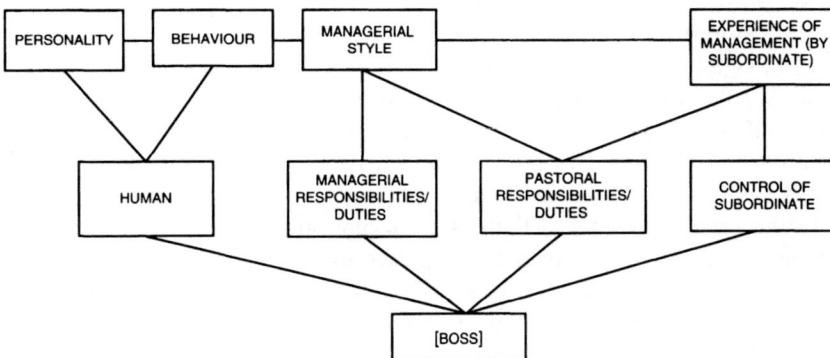

FIGURE 14.3. Partial primary cognitive model profile for [BOSS]

---

[5] See Lakoff's (1987) discussion of the way ICMs can metonymically give rise to prototype effects, by serving as "cognitive reference points."

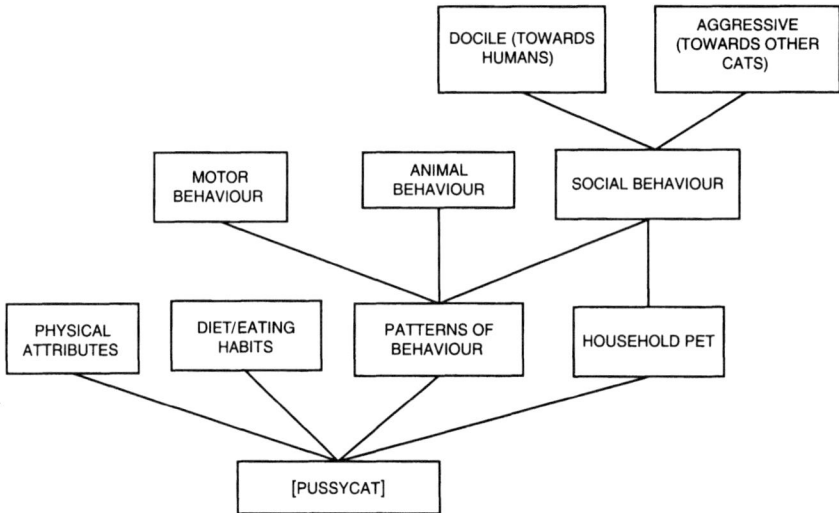

FIGURE 14.4. Partial cognitive model profile for [PUSSYCAT]

Just as the lexical concept for [BOSS] has a sophisticated cognitive model profile to which the lexical concept potentially affords access, so too the [PUSSYCAT] lexical concept provides access to a wide range of knowledge structures. A very partial cognitive model profile is provided in Figure 14.4.

The lexical concept [PUSSYCAT] relates to cognitive models having to do with, at least, knowledge concerning physical attributes, including body shape and size, diet and eating habits, patterns of behaviour, and a pussycat's status, in Western culture, as the household pet of choice for many people. In terms of secondary cognitive models, there are a number that relate to our knowledge associated with the sorts of behaviours pussycats exhibit. For instance, pussycats exhibit motor behaviour of certain kinds including the particular manner of motion pussycats engage in. Pussycats also exhibit animal behaviours of certain kinds including hunting, reproduction and so forth. Finally, pussycats also exhibit social behaviour, including behaviour towards other conspecifics, and behaviour towards humans. Hence, social behaviour is a cognitive model related to at least two primary cognitive models: those of PATTERNS OF BEHAVIOUR and HOUSEHOLD PET.

In the example in (3a), a figurative conception arises due to a failure to establish a match in the primary cognitive model profiles associated with [BOSS] and [PUSSYCAT], the two lexical concepts relevant for interpretation. Hence, a clash occurs leading to a search in a secondary cognitive model profile. In LCCM Theory, the particular lexical concept selected for clash resolution, and hence, for primary activation in the secondary cognitive model profile, is contextually determined. This is formalized as the **Principle of Context-induced Clash Resolution**. This states the following:

(p11)   Principle of Context-induced Clash Resolution
In cases where clash resolution is required, the lexical concept whose secondary cognitive model profile is searched to resolve the clash is determined by context. This is achieved by establishing a **figurative target** and a **figurative vehicle**, on the basis of context. The lexical concept that is established as the figurative vehicle is subject to clash resolution.

In the utterance in (3a) I am assuming a discourse context in which the speaker has been discussing their boss. In such a context, the figurative target (or target for short) is the boss, as this is the topic or theme of the utterance. Informally, the point of the utterance is to say something "about" the boss. From this it follows that the figurative vehicle (or vehicle for short[6]), is the pussycat. Crucially, it is the secondary cognitive model profile of the vehicle, here [PUSSYCAT], rather than the target, which undergoes search in order to facilitate clash resolution. In other words, the principle in (p11) serves to determine which of the lexical concepts' secondary cognitive model profiles is subject to search.

Before concluding the discussion of the example in (3a), consider a context in which the speaker, in making the utterance provided in (3a) is actually talking about their pussycat and bemoaning the fact that, due to an extremely fussy and awkward pet, the speaker's life is, in certain respects, constrained by the "demands" of their cat for food, affection, attention, and so on. In such a scenario, the cat owner might say: *My boss is a pussycat.* This interpretation, which I refer to as the "bossy cat" interpretation is also accounted for by the Principle of Context-induced Clash Resolution. In this case, it is the [BOSS] rather than the [PUSSYCAT] lexical concept which becomes the figurative vehicle, and hence whose secondary cognitive model profile is subject to search and hence clash resolution. Moreover, the [PUSSYCAT] lexical concept becomes the figurative target as the interpretation represents an attempt to ascribe some quality *to* the "pussycat".

The interpretation arises as follows. There is a clash between the primary cognitive model profiles associated with [BOSS] and [PUSSYCAT] as in the canonical interpretation described earlier. With the "bossy cat" interpretation, the difference arises due to context: the speaker is describing their pet hence, the utterance is "about" their pet rather than their boss. The principle given in (p11) ensures that the [BOSS] lexical concept is treated as the figurative vehicle. That is, [BOSS] receives an informational characterization that relates not to an adult human in a workplace scenario, but rather any organism that exhibits behaviour that serves to constrain and thus restrict a given human's freedom in certain respects. This is achieved by conducting a search in the secondary cognitive model profile for [BOSS] in order to provide

---

[6] The figurative vehicle is the lexical expression which is being deployed in a non-literal way, and is not to be confused with the notion of a (phonological) vehicle.

primary activation of a cognitive model relating to restrictive behaviour and practice.

The student's grades went up

Now let's consider the kind of metaphoric conception associated with an intransitive motion vehicle: *The student's grades went up*. The metaphoric conception typically associated with this utterance relates to an improvement in the student's grades. As with the "pussycat" example, interpretation involves matching which is guided by application of the Principle of Conceptual Coherence to ensure a match is achieved. The Principle of Ordered Search ensures that attempts are made to match in the primary cognitive model profiles before proceeding to the secondary cognitive model profiles. Due to the Principle of Context-induced Clash Resolution, given that the communicative intention is to ascribe some quality to the student's grades, it is the lexical concept [WENT UP] which is designated as the figurative vehicle in the meaning construction process, and hence which undergoes the search operation in its secondary cognitive model profile. A partial cognitive model profile for *went up* is provided below in Figure 14.5.

As we see, [WENT UP] affords access to knowledge relating to a physical entity that is capable of motion, and the motion is directed against gravity on the vertical axis. These represent at least three of the primary cognitive models

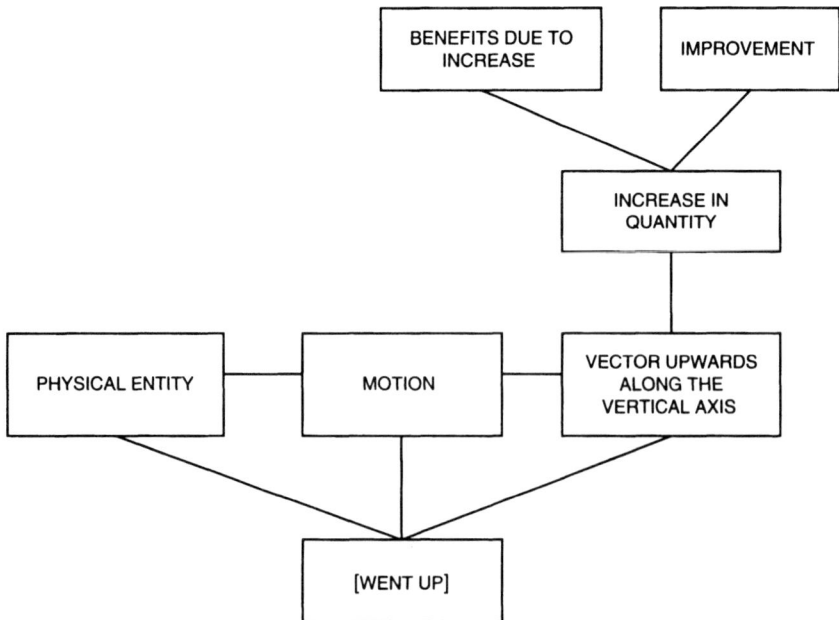

FIGURE 14.5. Partial cognitive model profile for [WENT UP]

to which [WENT UP] affords access. There are, additionally, a small number of secondary cognitive models illustrated in Figure 14.5. The first relates to INCREASE IN QUANTITY. In many cases in everyday interaction with our environment, being located further up on the vertical axis correlates with an increase in quantity—for instance, the higher the level of water in a glass, the more there is. In each of these cases, an increase in height correlates with an increase in quantity. A further secondary cognitive model concerns the benefits that naturally accrue by virtue of greater quantity. For instance, a higher pile of oranges correlates with more oranges, which correlates with more food and thus greater opportunity for nourishment. The greater the amount of liquid in a glass relates to greater ability to receive refreshment, and so forth. In addition, there is also a secondary cognitive model of IMPROVEMENT which derives from an increase in quantity. Improvement relates to a change evaluated as positive, in this instance an increase in amount, over time, i.e., an amount at one point in time measured against an increased amount at a later point.

Clash resolution is achieved by virtue of the secondary cognitive model of improvement achieving primary activation. This provides a match between the informational characterization associated with [STUDENT'S GRADES] and the secondary cognitive profile to which [WENT UP] affords access. This example provides a figurative conception, as it involves clash resolution in a secondary cognitive model profile.

Metonymy

I now turn, briefly, to the LCCM account of metonymic conceptions. Earlier in this chapter I presented the following examples as instances of metonymy:

(4)   a. *France* rejected the EU constitution
      b. The *ham sandwich* has asked for the bill

I provided an LCCM analysis of the example in (4a) earlier in order to illustrate the distinction between the meaning-construction processes involved in deriving literal and figurative conceptions associated with utterances. In this section I will consider the example in (4b), *The ham sandwich has asked for the bill*, in order to illustrate the way metonymic conceptions are derived.

As we saw with the earlier analysis of the example in (4a) and the analysis of metaphoric conceptions, what is common to both metaphor and metonymy in the LCCM account is that meaning construction involves primary activation of cognitive models in the secondary cognitive model profile of a particular lexical concept. Hence, clash resolution is required, which is the distinguishing feature of figurative as opposed to literal meaning construction. In order to illustrate the distinction between a metonymic conception and metaphoric conceptions discussed earlier, let's consider the example in (4b).

The Ham Sandwich Has Asked for the Bill

In an utterance of this kind the relevant elements that afford access to conceptual content are the lexical concept [HAM SANDWICH] and the lexical concepts [ASK FOR] and [BILL]. As [ASK FOR] and [BILL] form a simpler lexical conceptual unit than the entire utterance, by virtue of the principles of integration, these lexical concepts undergo interpretation, giving rise to an informational characterization. The lexical concept [HAM SANDWICH] then undergoes interpretation in conjunction with the informational characterization "asked for the bill". However, there is a clash between the informational characterization, and the primary cognitive model profile of [HAM SAND-WICH]. After all, a ham sandwich is not, normally, conceived of as an animate entity that can ask for the bill.

Due to the Principle of Context-induced Clash Resolution, the customer who ordered the ham sandwich is identified as the figurative target, and the ham sandwich is identified as the figurative vehicle. Accordingly, it is the cognitive model profile associated with the lexical concept [HAM SANDWICH] which becomes the site for clash resolution. Following the Principle of Ordered Search, the search region for clash resolution is expanded to take in secondary cognitive models associated with [HAM SANDWICH]. A partial cognitive model profile for [ham sandwich] is provided in Figure 14.6.

In this example, clash resolution is achieved by virtue of a search occurring in the secondary cognitive model profile of [HAM SANDWICH]. The cognitive model which achieves primary activation is that of RESTAURANT CUSTOMER.

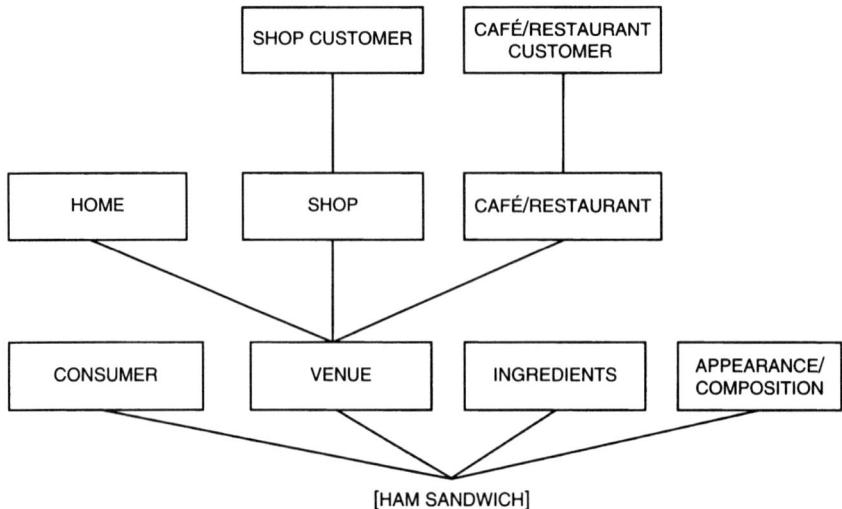

FIGURE 14.6. Partial cognitive model profile for [HAM SANDWICH]

Metaphor versus metonymy

As observed earlier, it has often been pointed out that metonymy, but not metaphor, has a **referential function**—one entity serves to stand for, or identify, another, as in a "ham sandwich" serving to identify the particular customer who ordered the ham sandwich. In contrast, previous scholars have variously argued that metaphor serves to frame a particular target in terms of novel categories, e.g., *My job is a jail* (e.g., Glucksberg and Keysar 1990; Carston 2002), or analogy, e.g., *Juliet is the sun* (e.g., Gentner *et al.*, 2001). That is, metaphor has what we might *very* loosely refer to as a **predicative function**.[7]

From the perspective of LCCM Theory the distinction between metaphor and metonymy relates to whether the figurative target and figurative vehicle exhibit **alignment**, and hence whether the **clash resolution site** corresponds to the figurative target. To illustrate, let's reconsider the canonical metaphoric "docile boss" interpretation of *My boss is a pussycat*. In this example the figurative target is [BOSS] and the figurative vehicle is [PUSSYCAT]. Following the Principle of Context-induced Clash Resolution, the cognitive model profile for [PUSSYCAT], the figurative vehicle, is the clash resolution site: primary activation of a secondary cognitive model takes place here.

This situation differs with respect to metonymy. In the "ham sandwich" example, the "customer" corresponds to the figurative target, as determined by the Principle of Context-induced Clash Resolution, and the figurative vehicle corresponds to the "ham sandwich". However, both contextually salient elements are accessed via the cognitive model profile associated with a single lexical concept: [HAM SANDWICH]. In other words, there is alignment, in a single cognitive model profile of the figurative target and vehicle. Hence, the site of clash resolution corresponds to the access route for the figurative target: "customer".

In sum, LCCM Theory reveals a divergence in metaphor and metonymy, which emerges as an outcome of the application of regular meaning construction mechanisms. Figurative conceptions which are labelled as "metonymic" arise due to the figurative vehicle facilitating direct access to the figurative target due to alignment of the figurative vehicle and target in the same lexical concept and cognitive model profile. In contrast, "metaphoric" conceptions arise due to a divergence between figurative vehicles and targets across two distinct lexical concepts.

Based on this discussion, we see that the "bossy pussycat" interpretation of *My boss is a pussycat* discussed earlier is metaphor-like, in the sense that there is non-alignment of the figurative target and vehicle. After all, in that interpretation, the lexical concept [BOSS] is the figurative vehicle and hence the site of clash resolution, while [PUSSYCAT] is the figurative target. Yet, the "bossy pussycat" interpretation doesn't intuitively feel metaphoric. While this interpretation does

---

[7] Note that the class of cross-domain mappings ("conceptual metaphors"), of the type studied by Lakoff and Johnson, as exemplified by the examples in (3b) and (5)–(7) appear to be of a different kind than those studied by scholars such as Carston, Glucksberg, and Gentner.

constitute a figurative conception, given the way figurativity is operationalized in LCCM Theory, involving, as it is does, primary activation of a secondary cognitive model in one of the cognitive model profiles undergoing matching, the interpretation is somewhat atypical, from the perspective of the canonical discourse function associated with metaphor. As we have seen, metaphor normally has a predicative function: it says something "about" a Subject or Theme. Yet, in the "bossy pussycat" interpretation, the predicative interpretation is at odds with the organization of the linguistic content as it emerges following integration. That is, while at the level of linguistic content lexical concept integration leads to the [BOSS] lexical concept having the semantic value of Subject, interpretation leads to a conception in which the utterance serves to attribute the quality of bossiness to the "pussycat", the figurative target in this interpretation, rather than the "boss". For this reason, there is what we might think of as a **mismatch** between the output of lexical concept integration on one hand, and interpretation on the other. The net result is that such an interpretation is unlikely to feel metaphoric, although the utterance *is* figurative, in present terms.

In the final analysis, metaphor and metonymy, rather than being neatly identifiable types of figurative language, are terms that have been applied by different scholars to a range of overlapping and sometimes complementary figurative language phenomena. What emerges from the LCCM account is that the intuitions that lie behind the use of these terms for data of particular kinds are a function of a small set of compositional mechanisms that are guided by various sorts of constraints (the principles identified in this and earlier chapters). Moreover, the application of these mechanisms and principles gives rise to a range of figurative conceptions which, in terms of discourse functions, are continuous in nature. That is, from the perspective of language understanding, while there are what might be thought of as symptoms of metaphor and metonymy, there is not always a neat distinction that can be made that serves to identify where metaphor ends and metonymy begins.

What is not figurative language

In some accounts of figurative language phenomena,[8] examples such as the italicized lexical items in each of the following examples are taken to be metaphoric in nature:

(12) a. That is a *loud* shirt
      b. They have a *close* relationship
      c. She is *in* love
      d. That took a *long* time

---

[8] For instance, see the metaphor identification criteria as developed by the Pragglejaz Group (2007). See also discussion in papers in Barcelona (2000).

In these examples, the use of *loud* refers to a brightly coloured shirt, *close* relates to emotional "closeness", *in* relates to an emotional state while *long* relates to extended duration.

From the perspective of LCCM Theory, such usages relate to distinct lexical concepts rather than being due, for instance, to figurative language conceptions. For instance, *long* has at least two conventionally established lexical concepts associated with the vehicle *long*: [EXTENDED IN HORIZONTAL SPACE] and [EXTENDED DURATION]. During lexical concept selection the [EXTENDED DURATION] lexical concept is selected, thereby avoiding a clash in the primary cognitive model profiles associated with [EXTENDED DURATION] and [TIME].

Evidence that *long* has (at least) two distinct lexical concepts conventionally associated with it comes from examples such as the following:

(13) a. A long kiss
      b. A long book

"Long" in "long kiss" relates to extended duration, not to physical length—a kiss cannot, obviously, be extended in space. Similarly in (13b), we are not, or at least not typically, dealing with an oversize book, but rather with an extended reading time. Understanding the form *long* as relating to [EXTENDED DURATION] relates to the process of lexical concept selection, as discussed in Chapter 11. During language understanding we select the [EXTENDED DURATION] lexical concept in conjunction with the lexical concept [BOOK] as facilitating provision of most coherent conception, as guided by context. Of course, we are helped by the frequency with which these two forms collocate and are associated with this very conception. Collocations of this kind which provide a pre-assembled conception I refer to as **concept collocations**. In the same way, *long time* represents a concept collocation.

In view of the LCCM Theory account, concept collocations such as "long time" are not, then, appropriately thought of as involving "metaphor," in the sense that they do not result from the online process of clash resolution, as described above. This view of highly conventional "lexical metaphors" is consonant with the approach developed in the **Career of Metaphor Hypothesis** (Bowdle and Gentner 2005), which builds on the **Structure Mapping Approach** to metaphor developed by Dedre Gentner (e.g., 1988; Gentner *et al.* 2001). In that approach, highly conventionalized "metaphors" are treated as being polysemous sense units which are conventionally associated with the "base" term, here, *long*, and which are accessed via a "lexical look-up" process, rather than by establishing structural alignments and inference projections (mappings) between a base and target. This aspect of the LCCM perspective is also consonant with the work of Rachel Giora (2003). In her work, Giora demonstrates that certain examples of "figurative" meanings associated with lexical items appear to be stored in memory and can be more salient than so-called "literal" meanings.

From the LCCM perspective, the interesting question in such cases is how an [EXTENDED DURATION] lexical concept became conventionally associated with the form *long*. Recent work on semantic change pioneered by Elizabeth Closs Traugott (e.g., Traugott and Dasher 2004) has argued that situated implicatures (or invited inferences) can become "detached" from their contexts of use and reanalysed as being distinct sense-units—lexical concepts in present terms—which are associated with a given vehicle. Intuitions, by some scholars, that these examples are figurative are based, I suggest, on **interference** of contextually irrelevant lexical concepts, in the case of our example the lexical concept [EXTENDED IN HORIZONTAL SPACE]. I assume that such interference can occur when the temporal restrictions on language processing are relaxed, as is the case in the theoretical practice of language scientists who often appear to analyse such expressions without taking (any) account of their usage context(s).[9] In actual conversation, I would argue, talk of a "long time" is hardly ever felt to be figurative.[10]

The [EXTENDED DURATION] lexical concept associated with *long* might be historically derived from contexts of communication in which reference to length can be understood as reference to duration without harming expression of the communicative intention, as in communication about "long journeys". Through repeated use of this form, with the inferred meaning, in such bridging contexts (Evans and Wilkins 2000),[11] it is plausible that *long* developed an [EXTENDED DURATION] lexical concept by virtue of **decontextualization** (Langacker 1987).

Summary

This chapter has been concerned with an LCCM account of figurative language understanding. In particular, the chapter addressed the distinction between a literal conception—the meaning associated with a literal utterance—on one hand, and a figurative conception—the meaning associated with a figurative utterance—on the other. While a literal conception canonically results in an interpretation which activates a cognitive model, or cognitive models, within the default, which is to say primary, cognitive model profile, a figurative conception arises when cognitive models are activated in the secondary cognitive model profile. This takes place when there is a clash in one of the primary cognitive models involved in interpretation. A clash results in enlargement of the search domain, such that matching takes place in the secondary cognitive model profile associated with one of the relevant lexical concepts. In some cases, context serves to determine which

---

[9] See Leezenberg (2001) and Stern (2000) for discussion of the importance of context in metaphor understanding.
[10] See Bowdle and Gentner (2005) for a related perspective (cf. the Graded Salience Hypothesis of Giora, e.g., 1997).
[11] Recall the discussion in Chapter 8.

lexical concept is the site for clash resolution, captured by the Principle of Context-induced Clash Resolution, introduced in this chapter. A further distinction made was the distinction in discourse function associated with figurative conceptions referred to as metaphor and metonymy. It was argued that the distinction is due to whether there is alignment or not between what was referred to as figurative target and figurative vehicle. While the hallmark of metaphor is that there is divergence between the two, the symptom of metonymy is that there is alignment. In general terms, LCCM Theory predicts that the same set of compositional mechanisms are responsible for literal and figurative language understanding. Hence, figurative language does not involve a distinct module or set of processes. Rather, it is continuous with literal language understanding.

15

The semantics of Time

In this chapter I apply LCCM Theory to a single domain: the domain of Time. As Time is often taken to be an instance of an abstract domain, *par excellence*, structured in terms of content from more concrete domains such as Space, it provides an arena for investigating the relationship between linguistic representations (e.g., lexical concepts) and conceptual representations (cognitive models) from the perspective of a single domain. Hence, my strategy in this chapter is to explore a specific domain (Time), structured figuratively, rather than a type of figurative phenomenon (e.g., metaphor). I do so in order to investigate semantic representation, rather than meaning-construction processes as in the previous chapter.

A further reason for selecting Time is that this chapter also addresses the role of conceptual metaphors in LCCM Theory. Recall that LCCM Theory represents, in part, a self-conscious attempt to integrate and synthesize a number of extant theories and perspectives within cognitive linguistics in order to provide a joined-up account of (i) lexical representation and (ii) meaning construction. Hence, as part of this general goal, it is important to situate Conceptual Metaphor Theory with respect to LCCM Theory—Conceptual Metaphor Theory has exerted a profound influence not only in terms of accounts and analysis of figurative language and thought, but in many other aspects of cognitive linguistic theory, including linguistic semantics and grammar. My overall argument is that LCCM Theory is orthogonal to and complements Conceptual Metaphor Theory, with conceptual metaphors providing an important level of knowledge structure which is accessed by the temporal lexical concepts detailed in this chapter. I argue then that conceptual metaphors relate to, in the sense of structure, cognitive models, rather than lexical concepts. As such, conceptual metaphors are not central to the meaning-construction mechanisms that work on lexical concepts. Rather, conceptual metaphors provide an enhanced layer of knowledge at the conceptual level which figurative (as well as literal) conceptions rely on in service of linguistically mediated meaning construction.

The discussion, below, on the relationship between temporal lexical concepts (in the linguistic system), and space-to-time conceptual metaphors (in the conceptual system) also bears on a crucial methodological issue. That branch of cognitive linguistics known as cognitive semantics[1] is predicated on the assumption that language can be employed to investigate the conceptual system. For Langacker (1987), for instance, language is *equated* with conceptual structure. For Lakoff (1987), language *reflects* conceptual structure. In LCCM Theory, linguistic representations provide a means of interacting with the conceptual system, but are not equated with them (in the sense of Langacker), and do not directly reflect them either. This follows as the linguistic content encoded by lexical concepts is highly schematic, and takes an attenuated form, in the shape of parameterization, with respect to the rich conceptual content encoded by cognitive models. LCCM Theory posits distinct roles for semantic structure and conceptual structure in the formation of conceptions, hence it is to be expected that the parameters encoded by semantic structure are but a pale reflection of conceptual structure. As we shall see, the nature of the linguistic content encoded by temporal lexical concepts is quite distinct from the rich spatial content provided by the level of conceptual metaphors, associated with conceptual structure.

Before proceeding with the LCCM analysis of Time, I begin, in the next two sections by providing some of the context for the study presented in this chapter. The first of these two sections briefly reviews the linguistic evidence for the widely held view that Time is asymmetrically structured in terms of Space. The second section takes issue with the view adopted by Lakoff and Johnson, based primarily on the linguistic evidence, that Time is primarily structured in terms of motion events, and possesses little (if any) inherent structure of its own. Indeed, I argue that, on the contrary, an important aspect of our conceptual representation of Time is inherently temporal.[2] The subsequent section provides an overview of some of the temporal lexical concepts encoded in English. The final two sections provide details of how temporal lexical concepts interface with temporal cognitive models, which are structured, in part, by virtue of conceptual metaphors.

The spatialization of Time

One of the key findings in cognitive linguistics and cognitive psychology is that Time, a putatively abstract domain, appears to recruit conceptual structure from the more concrete domains of motion and three-dimensional space. Evidence for this recruitment most often arises on the basis of language data (e.g., Alverson 1994; Bender *et al.* 2005; Clark 1973; Evans 2004a, 2004b, 2005; Fauconnier and Turner 2008; Fleischman 1982; Gentner *et al.* 2002; Grady 1997; Lakoff and Johnson 1980, 1999; Lakoff 1990, 1993; Moore 2000,

---

[1] Recall the discussion in Chapter 3.

[2] This is a position, incidentally, that is also assumed by more recent work on the semantics of Time within the conceptual metaphor tradition (e.g., Moore 2006).

2006; Núñez and Sweetser 2006; Shinohara 1999; Radden 2003; Traugott 1978; Yu 1998; Zinken forthcoming), as exemplified by the following:

(1)   a. She arrived on Saturday
      b. a short time
      c. Christmas is approaching

The putative spatial words are underlined. Indeed, while Time often has spatial ideas ascribed to it—and we may find it difficult to conceptualize and lexicalize Time without recourse to spatial notions—the reverse tends not to be the case. That is, we are far less inclined to invoke temporal notions to understand Space. In other words, the structuring of Time in terms of Space is asymmetric.[3]

A particularly influential account of the asymmetric structuring of Time in terms of Space is that provided by Conceptual Metaphor Theory (e.g., Lakoff and Johnson 1980, 1999). Moreover, recent behavioural studies have provided empirical evidence for the psychological reality of conceptual metaphors for Time: the position that space is indeed recruited to structure time in asymmetric fashion (e.g., Boroditsky 2000; Gentner et al. 2002; Núñez et al. 2006). More recently, it has additionally been established that this recruitment is involuntary (Casasanto and Boroditsky 2008). Further converging evidence for the conceptual metaphor account comes from gestural studies (e.g., Núñez and Sweetser 2006) and from signed languages (e.g., Engberg-Pederson 1993).

Various reasons have been posited for the asymmetric structuring of the domain of Time in terms of Space. Some scholars have argued for shared neurological resources. For instance, Walsh (2003) argues that a common magnitude system underpins spatial and temporal processing. While a drawback of Walsh's account is that it fails to account for the asymmetric structuring of Time in terms of Space, other accounts have argued, in various ways, that the recruitment of Space to structure Time is a consequence of exaptation: the re-use, in evolutionary terms, of pre-existing mechanisms for new purposes. Somewhat different accounts along these lines have been argued for by, for example, Jackendoff (1983) and O'Keefe (1996). See also the discussion in Casasanto (forthcoming).

The explanation provided by Conceptual Metaphor Theory emphasizes the role of embodiment in ontogenetic development, rather than an evolutionary motivation. Lakoff and Johnson (1999), influenced by the ground-breaking

---

[3] It is sometimes possible to express spatial notions in terms of temporal ideas, as in the following exchange:

A. How far is Bangor from London?
B. Three and a half hours by train.

However, this is by no means productive. That is, the structuring is not symmetric. Yet, the fact that Time can be deployed to structure Space argues against the position that the structuring is unidirectional. Hence, the relationship appears to be asymmetric.

work of Grady (1997), argue that conceptual metaphors arise as an inevitable consequence of humans acting in the world, such that tight correlations in pre-linguistic experience serve to establish connections between concepts that have, what Grady refers to as, **image content**, i.e., source concepts, and those concepts which have **response content**, i.e., target concepts. Grady posits what he terms **primary scenes**: recurrent humanly relevant scenarios in which the relevant experiences co-occur. These primary scenes, he argues, facilitate the establishment of conceptual metaphors (see Grady and Johnson 2000).[4] Lakoff and Johnson (1999) couch Grady's notion of experiential correlation and primary scenes in neurological terms. Lakoff (personal communication) argues, for instance, that the consequence of tight and recurring correlations in experience types, gives rise to the notion of Hebbian neurological learning: "what fires together wires together."

The temporal nature of Time

Despite the success of Conceptual Metaphor Theory in highlighting the asymmetric structuring of domains such as Time in terms of Space, one of the consequences, and I argue, drawbacks, has been to neglect the study of the inherent temporal structure that is part and parcel of our conceptual system for Time.[5] Part of the reason for this has been that Lakoff and Johnson have, for the most part, successfully focused the study of Time on the nature of spatial structure that is recruited. Indeed, they have explicitly argued that very little of our understanding of Time is purely temporal. They suggest, in fact, that most of our understanding of time is a metaphorical version of our understanding of motion in space. The premise from which the Lakoff and Johnson account of Time proceeds is that we cannot observe time, if it even exists as a thing unto itself. Rather, what can be observed are events of various kinds, including motion events such as objects in motion. Moreover, events can be compared. Hence, for Lakoff and Johnson our conceptualization of Time is grounded in our direct experience of events. That is, the properties associated with Time arise from understanding Time in terms of events which, unlike Time, are directly perceived. In particular:

- Time is directional and irreversible, because events are. In other words, events cannot "unhappen."
- Time is ongoing because events are experienced as being ongoing.
- Time is divisible because we perceive events as having beginnings and end points.
- Time can be measured because instances of event types can be counted.

---

[4] See Moore's (2006) related notion of a **Grounding Scenario**.
[5] For a critique of the conceptual metaphor approach to Time see Evans (2004a).

Nevertheless, while it is incontrovertible that structure recruited from non-temporal domains, such as Space, form part of the conceptual content encoded by temporal cognitive models, it is increasingly clear that a significant portion of conceptual structure in the domain of Time is inherently temporal, rather than spatial. In particular, there are two general criticisms that can be levelled against the perspective that Time is primarily (or solely) constituted of non-temporal content, what I will dub the **Time-Is-Space perspective**. These relate to the following two issues, which I outline here and elaborate on further below:

- *The Inherent Structure Issue*:
  Lakoff and Johnson (e.g., 1999) sometimes appear to assume that Time has limited, if any, inherent structure of its own. On this Time-Is-Space account, the function of conceptual metaphor is to structure the target domain, Time, in terms of structure derived from the source domain, Space. That is, Time obtains structure *by virtue of* the metaphoric mappings. In a telling passage, Lakoff and Johnson put things as follows:

  What is literal and inherent about the conceptual domain of time is that it is characterized by the comparison of events.... [This means] that our experience of time is dependent on our embodied conceptualization of time in terms of events...Experience does not always come prior to conceptualization, because conceptualization is embodied.

  (*ibid.* 138–9)

- *The complexity issue*:
  The Time-Is-Space perspective assumes that conceptual metaphors relate to entire domains: Space and Time. The difficulty here is that this leads to the position that Time, and indeed Space, are undifferentiated internally homogenous bodies of knowledge—a criticism also made by Moore (e.g., 2006) in his analysis of space-to-time metaphors.

i. The inherent structure issue
There are two objections that can and have been levelled at the view of inherent structure for Time, often attributed to Lakoff and Johnson. The first relates to the kind of general criticism presented in Murphy (1996). Murphy argues that if abstract domains such as Time have little or no inherent structure of their own, thereby requiring conceptual projection from source domains to provide structure, then it is not clear what motivates the projection in the first place. That is, it is not clear what motivates the structuring of Time in terms of domains such as Motion and Space rather than something else. Indeed, this is a criticism that other researchers in the conceptual metaphor tradition have been alive to. For instance, Joseph Grady (1997) in his work on primary metaphors argued that Time must have literal

and inherent structure independently of the metaphoric structuring. This is also the position adopted in the revised account of space-to-time metaphors developed by Kevin Moore (2000, 2006).

The second objection is as follows. There are specific neurobiological mechanisms and structures which are implicated in temporal processing. Moreover, time can be directly perceived and experienced in the absence of motion events. Accordingly, there is no reason to assume that Time has no inherent structure of its own (see Evans 2004a for a review of some of these points).

For instance, research in neurobiology reveals that there are many different sorts of temporal processes which are essential for regulating bodily function, such as the various circadian rhythms, including the wake–sleep cycle, which are controlled by chemical processes, and the range of temporal mechanisms that guide perceptual processing. The latter range from processing intervals of a fraction of a second up to an outer limit of around three seconds. This three-second range may correspond to what James ([1890]/1950) referred to as the specious present: "the prototype of all conceived times...the short duration of which we are immediately and incessantly sensible" (*ibid.* 1950: 631), and what is more commonly known as the **perceptual moment** (see Evans 2004a).

Research on temporal processing reveals that there are sophisticated timing mechanisms in the brain that are key to behaviours including speech (Chafe 1994), music and poetry (Davies 2006; Turner and Pöppel 1983), as well as the phenomenologically real experience of perceiving the present: our experience of now (Pöppel 1994). The specific brain structures implicated in temporal processing include the parietal cortex, which may be involved in quantifying time and hence facilitating assessments of temporal magnitude (Walsh 2003), as well as the basal ganglia and cerebellum for fundamental timekeeping operations such as coordinating motor control (Harrington *et al.* 1998, but see Ivry and Spencer 2004). Other neuroscentists have argued that temporal processing is widely distributed across brain structures being intrinsic to neural function (Mauk and Buonomano 2004).

In addition, research on the perception of time by psychologists reveals that we do indeed directly perceive time. That is, temporal experience is phenomenologically real, and, moreover, humans experience time in the absence of specific externally perceived events (e.g., Flaherty 1999). For instance, a person placed in solitary confinement, in a darkened, sound-proofed cell and hence severely restricted in terms of the sensory stimuli they are exposed to, would nevertheless still perceive the elapse of time. That is, we do not have to first perceive events in order to conceptualize and thus experience time—contra the Time-Is-Space perspective. Indeed, the fact there are a range of neurological mechanisms for processing time, some of which appear to be central for perception in general, suggests that rather than the perception of events being the precursor of temporal experience, temporal experience is necessary in order to perceive events in the first place.

A range of behavioural studies conducted by psychologists reveal that time is directly experienced by human subjects, and moreover, the nature of our experience of time is often independent of the nature of events in question. For instance, Ornstein ([1969]/1997) found that our perception of duration is a function of stimulus complexity, while familiarity with a particularly complex stimulus array can impact on our perception of duration. Zachay and Block (1997) found that temporal perception was influenced by how interesting subjects found a particular activity to be, while Flaherty (1999) found that perception of duration is a function of how much we attend to a particular stimulus array, and how familiar with particular activities and events we are. In short, a range of studies reveal that our experience of duration, rather than being a function of event comparison, as assumed by the Time-Is-Space perspective, is a consequence of subjective evaluations of stimuli types, and of how we process particular types of stimuli on particular occasions. Evidence of this sort makes a persuasive case for thinking that temporal experience is internal rather than external in origin, constituting a subjectively-driven response to events, rather than emerging from events themselves, an abstract mental achievement.

Other research reveals that the human ability to judge temporal magnitude (i.e., duration) is a function of physiological mechanisms, and varies in predictable ways. For instance, if vital functions are accelerated, for instance by the consumption of coffee or stimulants such as amphetamines, this results in overestimation of time (Fraisse 1963). This is known as protracted duration and constitutes the phenomenologically real experience whereby subjects perceive standard units of duration as being of greater magnitude: the perception that time is proceeding more "slowly" than usual and hence there is more of it. Overestimation of duration also occurs when the body temperature is raised, for instance when suffering from fever (see Wearden and Penton-Voak 1995 for a review). In contrast, nitrous oxide and other anaesthetic gases which slow down the body's vital functions have the opposite effect, giving rise to an underestimation of time, the phenomenologically real experience that there is less time, known as temporal compression.[6] Baddeley (1966) showed that exposing the body to low temperatures also gives rise to an underestimation of time.[7]

---

[6] The notions of protracted duration and temporal compression were introduced earlier in the book—recall the discussion in Chapter 7, for instance.

[7] This was achieved by exposing scuba divers to cold water (4°C). The divers estimated time by counting from 1 to 60 at what they presumed to be the rate of 1 numeral per second. The counting took place before the dive, and immediately following the dive once the divers' body temperatures had been lowered.

ii. The complexity issue:

As with the inherent structure issue, there are two objections that can be levelled against the view of Time as an undifferentiated domain. The first holds that temporal experience is highly differentiated. That is, it is far more complex than Lakoff and Johnson appear to acknowledge. For instance, Pöppel (1978) has pointed to what he terms "elementary time experiences." These constitute distinct yet fundamental types of temporal experience. There are a number of elementary time experiences that we can point to, all of which are fundamental to a range of human behaviours, including perception and successful (inter)action in the world. These include: (i) the ability to perceive an elapse of duration, (ii) the ability to perceive simultaneity, (iii) the ability to perceive non-simultaneity, (iv) the ability to perceive order (or succession), (v) past and present, and (vi) change.

The second objection relates to the way in which language encodes temporal experience. In previous work based on a detailed examination of a single vehicle, *time*, in a single language, I found that there are a range of distinct temporal lexical concepts (Evans 2004a)—see also the discussion of *time* in Chapter 7 and below. Thus, both phenomenological experience and language suggest that Time is a highly differentiated domain (or domains), more internally complex than allowed by Lakoff and Johnson.

In more recent work, Kevin Moore (2000, 2006) has developed a revised conceptual metaphor account of Time by addressing exactly these criticisms. Moore (2006) makes the following two assumptions. Firstly, he assumes that Time has inherent structure independently of the metaphors that serve to structure it. Secondly, he posits that, in analysing space-to-time mappings, we are not dealing with distinct and homogenous domains such as Space and Time, but with a complex array of experience types. Moore's general assumptions are consonant with the ones being adopted here.

Conceptual metaphors for time in LCCM Theory: a first look

In view of the above, what then is the status of conceptual metaphor in LCCM Theory? Conceptual metaphors provide a means of structuring cognitive models in terms of structure recruited from cognitive models associated with other domains of experience. That is, conceptual metaphors serve to provide one of (probably) many types of links which connect cognitive models, allowing them to inherit structure. Conceptual metaphors provide stable, long-term links which allow the automatic and unconscious recruitment of structure in asymmetric fashion. They serve to structure, in part, attributes and values, providing massive redundancy across concepts within the conceptual system. Conceptual metaphors arise when stable links are established between cognitive models encoding experience that is sensorimotor in nature, and cognitive models which encode conceptual content that is subjective in nature. In terms of the semantics of Time this amounts to the following. Much of the structure associated with temporal representation is inherently temporal. However, conceptual metaphors facilitate the recruitment of structure from cognitive models derived from the domain of Space. Nevertheless, this structure is but one way in which temporal knowledge is organized and understood.

I return to the relationship between conceptual metaphors and knowledge representation later in the chapter once we have discussed temporal lexical concepts in more detail.

Temporal lexical concepts

I now turn to an overview of some of the main types of temporal lexical concepts. I illustrate with examples from English. The challenge for future research is to identify the nature and range of the temporal lexical concepts for other languages. Indeed, preliminary findings suggest that the range of lexical concepts available to a language such as English may vary quite considerably in other languages.[8] I suggest that the methodology for identifying lexical concepts, introduced earlier in the book, may provide a systematic and insightful way of cataloguing the range of lexical concepts within and across specific languages in a range of domains including Time.

The overview below is meant to be illustrative rather than exhaustive. I divide the discussion into the following types of lexical concepts:

- Lexical concepts for temporal relations
- Lexical concepts that encode aspect
- Nominal lexical concepts
- Lexical concepts that encode temporal frames of reference (TFoRs)

Lexical concepts for temporal relations

One way in which temporal experience is encoded in language relates to closed-class lexical concepts that encode what I will refer to as **temporal relations**. In a language such as English, these lexical concepts are associated with an adverbial vehicle introduced, typically, by prepositions, as the examples below illustrate.

(2)   a. in March
       b. on Saturday
       c. at 2 pm

---

[8] Findings presented in Silva Sinha *et al.* (forthcoming) on the temporal representation for Time in the Amondawa language—until relatively recently an isolated community of around 150 speakers in Amazonia—provides evidence of a language which encodes Time in a startlingly different way from a language such as English. The challenge that awaits linguists is to describe the semantics of Time in some of the less well-studied languages of the world about which, at present, virtually nothing is known.

The symbolic unit—vehicle and lexical concept—which sanctions expressions such as those in (2) is provided in (3):

(3) a. vehicle   "PREP NP"
     b. lexical concept   [X SITUATED WITH RESPECT TO TIME PERIOD]

The lexical concept glossed in (3b) encodes a highly schematic temporal relation, in which a particular entity such as an event, glossed as X, occurs with respect to a particular time period, as exemplified by the expression in (3):

(4) The exam took place in March

The lexical concept in (3b) is internally open, and in (4) is integrated with internally closed lexical concepts. The specific lexical concepts which are integrated are derived by virtue of lexical concept selection, as described in Chapter 11. For instance, there are a great many lexical concepts conventionally associated with the vehicle *in*. These include a spatial lexical concept such as [ENCLOSURE], the range of "state" lexical concepts described in Chapter 8, and several distinct "temporal" lexical concepts, evidenced in (5):

(5) a. He completed the exam in March   [PERIOD OF TEMPORAL
                                             ENCLOSURE FOR X]
     b. He completed the exam in one hour   [PERIOD OF CONTINUOUS
                                             DURATION OF X]
     c. He will take the exam in one hour   [PERIOD AFTER WHICH
                                             X OCCURS]

In each of these examples, a distinct lexical concept associated with *in* is in evidence. In (5a) the lexical concept glossed as [PERIOD OF TEMPORAL ENCLOSURE FOR X] mediates a temporal relation between a particular event, the exam, and the period of time, March, at some point in which the event occurs. In (5b), the lexical concept I gloss as [PERIOD OF CONTINUOUS DURATION OF X] mediates a temporal relation between a particular event, the exam, and the temporal period for which the exam continues. Finally, in (5c), the lexical concept [PERIOD AFTER WHICH X OCCURS] mediates a temporal relation between an event, the exam, and the period after which the exam takes place. In other words, the distinct conceptions associated with the utterances in (5) are a consequence, in part, of distinct lexical concepts for *in* being selected. We are also now in a position to see that the conception which arises as a result of the utterance in (4) is a consequence of the [PERIOD OF TEMPORAL ENCLOSURE FOR X] for *in* being selected and integrated with the internally open lexical concept given in (3b).

Lexical concepts that encode aspect

Another way in which temporal experience gets encoded in terms of linguistic content relates to the range of linguistic phenomena often referred to, variously, as aspect. In general terms, aspect relates to the highly schematic encoding of the distribution of action through time. Nevertheless, aspect is not a homogenous category, and even an individual language (such as English, for instance), has a range of ways in which aspectual phenomena are encoded. Two examples of aspectual categories encoded by English are given below:

Category: Boundedness
(6)   a. He is drinking the beer   [UNBOUNDED EVENT]
      b. He has drunk the beer   [BOUNDED EVENT]

These examples relate, respectively, to what is traditionally referred to as imperfective aspect (6a) and perfective aspect (6b). What I gloss as the [UNBOUNDED EVENT] lexical concept is associated with the vehicle provided in (7a), and is conventionally associated with the vehicle "BE + VERB*ing*", and works in conjunction with lexical concepts for Time-reference (i.e., the tense system). The [BOUNDED EVENT] lexical concept is conventionally associated with the vehicle "HAVE + VERB PAST PARTICIPLE". The [UN-BOUNDED EVENT] lexical concept encodes highly schematic content which can be paraphrased as follows: the event in question is/was in progress at the time reference indicated by the time-reference lexical concepts (i.e., the tense system). The [BOUNDED EVENT] lexical concept encodes the following schematic content: the event in question occurred (or was initiated) at an earlier point and is complete, but still relevant, at the more recent time reference, as indicated by the time-reference lexical concepts.

Hence, the conception which typically arises as a consequence of the utterance in (6a) is that the drinking of the beer is ongoing at time of speaking. That is, the [UNBOUNDED EVENT] lexical concept contributes the following content: in terms of the time period covered by the utterance, the drinking event is unbounded. The conception associated with the utterance in (6b) is that the drinking of the beer was initiated at an earlier point in time, and was completed prior to, or at the moment of speaking. That is, the [BOUNDED EVENT] lexical concept encodes the following: in the time period covered by the utterance, the drinking event is bounded.

As I have observed earlier in the book, linguistic content is typically bundled in a single lexical concept. For example, in the examples in (6a), the lexical concept paired with the vehicle "*is drinking*" bundles the Un-bounded parameter from the temporal category Boundedness, with the Non-past parameter from the temporal category Time reference.[9]

---

[9] Recall the discussion of Time reference in Chapter 6.

Another aspectual category that is often bundled with parameters from other categories relates to what I refer to as Event Contour. The glosses for the relevant parameters, provided below in (7), are drawn from Talmy (2000):

Category: Event Contour

		Vehicle:	Parameter:	Lexical concept gloss:
(7)	a.	(to) die	One-way non-resettable	[(TO) DIE]
	b.	(to) fall	One-way resettable	[(TO) FALL]
	c.	(to) flash	Full cycle	[(TO) FLASH]
	d.	(to) breathe	Multiplex	[(TO) BREATHE]
	e.	(to) sleep	Steady state	[(TO) SLEEP]

While the examples in (7) relate to open-class lexical concepts which facilitate access to the conceptual content encoded by the cognitive models that are associated with the lexical concept, the temporal experience directly encoded by the lexical concepts as linguistic content is highly schematic. This relates to schematic aspects of the distribution of action during the course of the event in question. The nature of this schematic content I refer to as an Event Contour. This category of linguistic content has a number of parameters, bundled with other aspects of linguistic content as part of the various lexical concepts, whose glosses are also provided.

For instance, [(TO) DIE] encodes schematic content relating to an event that one can do only once, at least under normal circumstances. Hence, it encodes the parameter which, following Talmy, I term One-way non-resettable. In contrast, [(TO) FALL] encodes content which is resettable: you can do it more than once. However, it is one-way, like [(TO) DIE]: it involves a beginning and an end. Hence, [(TO) FALL] encodes the parameter One-way resettable. In contrast, [(TO) FLASH] encodes the parameter: Full cycle. That is, it encodes the following schematic content: the event involves a return to its initial state. The lexical concept [(TO) BREATHE] encodes the schematic content that the event involves a series of actions and hence constitutes a multiplex event, while [(TO) SLEEP] encodes content relating to an action that is ongoing, and thus encodes the parameter which I gloss as Steady state.

Nominal lexical concepts

Another type of temporal lexical concept relates to what I refer to as nominal temporal lexical concepts. These are temporal lexical concepts associated with noun vehicles, or nominal vehicles, as exemplified by the following: *time, tomorrow, yesterday, aeon, era, century, hour, minute, second, past, future, now, present, moment, January, December, week, summer,* and so forth. The lexical concepts conventionally paired with these vehicles are each associated with a unique access site, facilitating access to rich knowledge relating to distinct sorts of temporal elapses.

As with other temporal lexical concepts, nominal lexical concepts may also exhibit polysemy.[10] As we saw in Chapter 7, the vehicle *time* exhibits polysemy, having a number of distinct lexical concepts associated with it. Moreover, lexical concepts paired with the same vehicle can be distinguished based on identifying distinct lexical profiles by examining usage data. In other words, divergences in the lexical profile is a symptom of polysemy. Utterances involving distinct temporal lexical concepts associated with *time* are provided below:

(8)   Time drags when you're bored   [PROTRACTED DURATION]

(9)   Time flies when you're having fun   [TEMPORAL COMPRESSION]

(10)   Time flows on forever   [TEMPORAL MATRIX]

(11)   The time for a decision has arrived   [TEMPORAL MOMENT]

While each of these lexical concepts encodes linguistic content, the gloss provided refers to the nature of the conceptual content to which these lexical concepts facilitate access. For instance, the [PROTRACTED DURATION] lexical concept facilitates access to conceptual content relating to the phenomenologically real experience of protracted duration—the experience of having more time than usual, and hence the experience of time proceeding more "slowly" than usual. The lexical concept illustrated in (9) facilitates access to the phenomenologically real experience of temporal compression—the experience of having less time than usual, and hence the experience of time proceeding more "quickly" than usual. The lexical concept in evidence in (10) facilitates access to the conceptualization of time as the event which encompasses all others, which I gloss as the Matrix conceptualization—time as the manifold in which all other events takes place. Finally, the lexical concept which sanctions the use of *time* in (11) relates to conceptual content concerning time as a temporal moment or point without regard for its duration.

Lexical concepts which encode temporal frames of reference (TFoRs)

The final kind of temporal lexical concept that I consider are those that encode what I refer to as **temporal frames of reference, or TFoRs** for short. Akin to spatial frames of reference (e.g., Levinson 2003; see also Talmy 2000), TFoRs are complex symbolic units, involving a vehicle and an internally open closed-class lexical concept. The lexical concept serves to encode highly schematic aspects of temporal reference. Yet, and as we shall see below, TFoR lexical concepts are integrated with open-class nominal lexical concepts

---

[10] Recall that in LCCM Theory polysemy arises due to the same phonological vehicle being conventionally paired with distinct lexical concepts, and hence potentially distinct access sites.

which facilitate access to temporal cognitive models, including purely temporal content as well as rich spatial content recruited by virtue of conceptual metaphors, in the sense discussed above, and in more detail below.

In order to contextualize the notion of a TFoR, consider the related notion of a spatial frame of reference (SFoR). In a SFoR, a figure (F) is located by virtue of employing a reference object (RO) which serves to establish a search region for locating the figure. Consider the following example:

(12)   The bike is in front of the church

In (12) *the bike* constitutes the F, the entity whose location is established by virtue of employing a RO. The RO thereby serves to narrow down the search region in which the F can be located.

In analogous fashion, TFoRs employ a reference point in order to "locate" a given event in time. I will employ English as the language of illustration. Although other languages differ, often quite radically, from English, there is reasonably robust evidence that English is not alone in possessing lexical concepts that encode TFoRs (see Alverson 1994; Bender *et al.* 2005; Moore 2000; Núñez and Sweetser 2006). Nevertheless, work by Silva Sinha *et al.* (forthcoming) reveals that TFoRs may not be cross-linguistically universal.

Before proceeding with a discussion of specific TFoR lexical concepts, a caveat is in order. In Conceptual Metaphor Theory it has been common to assume that the type of linguistic expressions I discuss below are a consequence of conceptual metaphors—cross-domain associations that underlie language usage. From the LCCM perspective, conceptual metaphors apply at the level of the cognitive model, and hence, at the conceptual level, rather than at the level of linguistic encoding in language. In other words, lexical concepts provide a schematic type of knowledge that is unique to language. They also provide a form of temporal content upon which the process of interpretation, which draws on conceptual structure, can function. That is, language carries a set of symbolic resources independent of conceptual metaphors for time, which both complement and are necessary for the deployment of the sort of conceptual content provided by temporal conceptual metaphors in linguistically mediated communication. We will see how this works later on in the chapter, once I have sketched the nature of TFoR lexical concepts.

English, along with other languages, exhibits in broad terms, two sorts of TFoR lexical concepts. The first can be characterized as being experiencer-based, encoding a schematic relation with respect to an experiencing consciousness. In other words, experiencer-based TFoR lexical concepts encode a schematic relation holding between a temporal event and the present or "now," thereby serving to locate an event *in* time. As such a schematic future/past relation is encoded. The second type is event-based, and encodes a schematic relation between two events, serving to encode a schematic earlier/later relation. Both types are illustrated with specific utterances below:

(13)   Christmas is approaching (us)   (Experiencer-based)

(14)   Christmas precedes New Year   (Event-based)

As with spatial frames of reference, temporal reference encodes a reference point which serves to "locate" a particular event in time. In the example in (13), the notion of "now" associated with the location of an experiencing consciousness—the "Experiencer"—serves as the reference point. With respect to this Experiencer, an event can be understood in terms of its **imminence**—the degree to which it is "located" in the future with respect to the Experiencer—or its **occurrence**—the degree to which it is "located" in the past with respect to the Experiencer. Hence, the example in (13) is licensed by an Experiencer-based TFoR lexical concept and the open-class lexical concepts which are integrated with it. Together these give rise to a conception in which a past/future relation holds between the event, Christmas, and the reference point, "now," associated with the Experiencer.

In contrast, the example in (14) employs a given event as the reference point, rather than the notion of "now." In (14), it is New Year, a temporal event which serves as the reference point in order to establish the relative "location" in time of another event, here Christmas. Hence, the utterance in (14) is licensed by an Event-based TFoR lexical concept and the open-class lexical concepts that are integrated with it. Together these give rise to a conception in which there is an earlier/later relation holding between the event, Christmas, and the reference point, New Year. The distinction between the linguistic content encoded by these two TFoR lexical concepts is summarized in Table 15.1.

The two broad types of TFoR lexical concept are manifested in terms of a number of specific TFoR lexical concepts. Below I briefly describe some of the most common types.

TABLE 15.1.   Linguistic content encoded by two types of TFoR lexical concept

Type of Temporal Frame of Reference (TFoR) lexical concept	Experiencer-based e.g., *Christmas is approaching*	Event-based e.g., *Christmas precedes New Year*
Reference point (RP) encoded	Human experience of "now" ("Experiencer")	Temporal event
Relation encoded	Relative location in time (i.e., past/future) of event with respect to RP	Relative sequence (i.e., earlier/later) of event with respect to another event

Experiencer-based TFoR lexical concepts

While there are a large number, I will illustrate by considering just two TFoR lexical concepts of this type:

- [LOCATION OF EVENT IN TIME, FROM PERSPECTIVE OF EVENT]
  e.g., *Christmas is approaching (us)*
- [LOCATION OF EVENT IN TIME, FROM PERSPECTIVE OF EXPERIENCER]
  e.g., *We are approaching Christmas*

As with all TFoR lexical concepts, these are complex closed-class lexical concepts which consist of phonetically overt as well as phonetically implicit vehicles. Hence, they constitute partially internally open lexical concepts, which can be integrated with other closed-class as well as open-class lexical concepts.

I begin by considering the first of the two experiencer-based TFoR lexical concepts. The symbolic unit is given in (15):

(15) a. vehicle   "NP1 VERBAL COMPLEX OF DIRECTED MOTION (NP2)"
      b. lexical concept   [LOCATION OF EVENT IN TIME, FROM PERSPECTIVE OF EVENT]

The lexical concept in (15b) encodes the following. There is an event (E) which is located in time with respect to an experiencer which serves as the reference point (RP). Additionally, the temporal location is viewed from the perspective point (PP) of the event. This can be represented diagrammatically as in Figure 15.1.

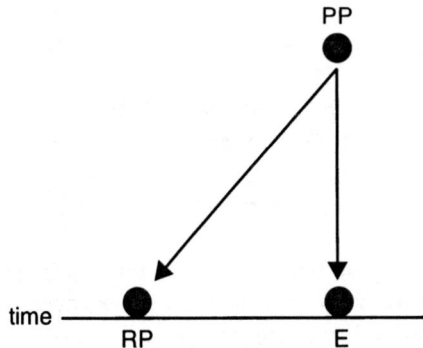

FIGURE 15.1. Representation of the linguistic content encoded by [LOCATION OF EVENT IN TIME, FROM PERSPECTIVE OF EVENT]

The linguistic content encoded by the lexical concept illustrated in Figure 15.1 is highly schematic in nature. It does not relate to the phenomenological experience of what it "feels" like, for instance, to experience the passage of time. Nor does it encode phenomenologically rich notions relating to the experience of pastness or futurity. That is, this lexical concept simply encodes a relation holding between an event and the RP: the present. In other words, what "gets into" language, so to speak, in terms of linguistic content, is a highly paramaterized version of temporal experience. It says nothing about whether the event is located in the future or the past with respect to the RP. This rich inference emerges following interpretation, once open-class lexical concepts have been integrated with the TFoR lexical concept, as discussed later. For this reason, the time line in Figure 15.1 has no directionality.

In addition to this schematic content, the lexical concept also encodes a lexical profile. As this TFoR lexical concept is internally open, the lexical profile encodes internal formal and semantic selectional tendencies. This includes the following: NP1 must be a temporal event of some kind, and the optional NP2 (signalled by the parentheses in (15a)) must be an experiencer of some kind. The verbal complex of directed motion must relate to motion events that can be construed as facilitating arrival at the experiencer. These include verbs of deictic motion, such as *come*, verbs of terminal motion, such as *approach*, verbal complexes involving increase in proximity, such as *get/move closer*, or verbs of motion which are manner-neutral, such as *move*, but which are paired with a path satellite of directed motion, such as *up on*, to give the verbal complex *move up on*. Examples of utterances licensed by this lexical concept are given below:

(16)   a. Christmas is moving towards us
       b. Christmas is approaching (us)
       c. Christmas is getting closer (to us)
       d. Christmas is coming
       e. Christmas is whizzing towards us

The second experiencer-based TFoR symbolic unit can be stated as follows:

(17)   a. vehicle   "NP1 VERBAL COMPLEX OF DIRECTED
                            MOTION NP2"
       b. lexical concept [LOCATION OF EVENT IN TIME, FROM
                            PERSPECTIVE OF EXPERIENCER]

The lexical concept in (17b) encodes the following. There is an event (E) which is located in time with respect to an experiencer which serves as the reference point (RP), and that the temporal location is viewed from the perspective point (PP) of the experiencer. This can be represented diagrammatically as in Figure 15.2.

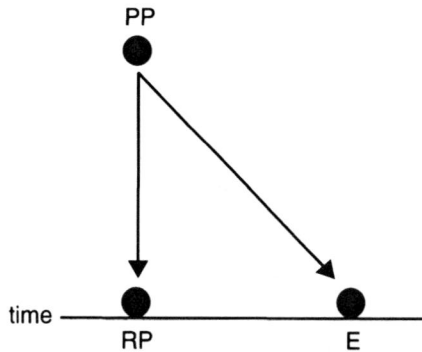

FIGURE 15.2. Representation of the linguistic content encoded by [LOCATION OF EVENT IN TIME, FROM PERSPECTIVE OF EXPERIENCER]

The lexical profile for this lexical concept stipulates that NP1 must be an experiencer of some sort, and that NP2 must be a temporal event of some kind. The verbal complex of directed motion must relate to motion events that involve directed motion with respect to the event. Illustrative examples are provided below:

(18)   a. We are moving towards Christmas
       b. We are approaching Christmas
       c. We are getting close to Christmas

Event-based TFoR lexical concepts

As with experiencer-based TFoR lexical concepts, there are a number of distinct kinds of event-based TFoR lexical concepts. In this section I exemplify just two. Recall that the essential difference between experiencer-based and event-based TFoR lexical concepts is the RP encoded, and hence the schematic relation encoded. While experiencer-based TFoR lexical concepts encode an event that is located in time with respect to the experiencer, event-based TFoR lexical concepts encode the relation of an event with respect to another event, and hence encode a sequential (i.e., an earlier/later), rather than a temporal (i.e., past/future) relation. To illustrate, consider the symbolic unit provided in (19):

(19)   a. vehicle   "NP1 COME *before* NP2"
       b. lexical concept [X IS SEQUENCED EARLIER THAN Y]

In this example, the lexical concept in (19b) encodes a schematic relation in which one temporal event is sequenced earlier than another. That is, there is one event, event E, which is sequenced prior to a second event, which serves as the reference point (RP). Moreover, as the relation is one of being earlier, the perspective point (PP) is fixed at the earlier event. Hence, this TFoR lexical concept encodes what I refer to as a **prospective relation**. It says nothing about the nature of the temporal event in question, nor about the degree of temporal proximity of the two events nor about phenomenological aspects of temporal experience. In short, the content encoded is linguistic in nature and hence highly schematic. The phenomenologically rich details are derived from interpretation of the open-class lexical concepts which are integrated with the closed-class internally open lexical concept in (19b). The symbolic unit in (19) sanctions an example such as (20):

(20)   In France, cheese comes before dessert

The typical conception that arises from (20) is that in France, cheese is sequenced prior to dessert in a four-course meal—which happens to contrast with the convention in the United Kingdom where cheese follows dessert. The TFoR lexical concept described here can be diagrammed as in Figure 15.3.

In Figure 15.3, Time is represented by the directed arrow, so as to signify the earlier/later relation. The black circles labelled E and RP represent the two events (X and Y), while the circle labelled PP signals which event is the perspective point. The arrows leading from the PP to the two events (E and RP) signal the prospective relation. The lexical profile associated with this lexical concept stipulates the following. NP1 and NP2 must be temporal events, there is a finite form of *come*, and an obligatory element, *before*.

The second event-based TFoR lexical concept I consider is given below as part of the symbolic unit of which it is a component:

(21)   a. vehicle   "NP1 COME *after* NP2"
       b. lexical concept   [X IS SEQUENCED LATER THAN Y]

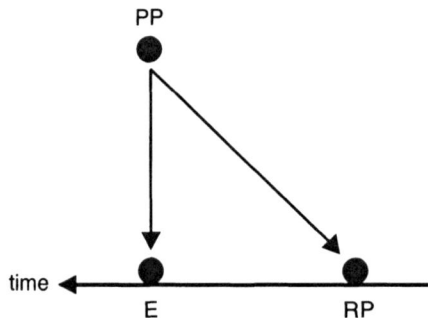

FIGURE 15.3. Prospective relation encoded by the TFoR lexical concept: [X IS SE-QUENCED EARLIER THAN Y]

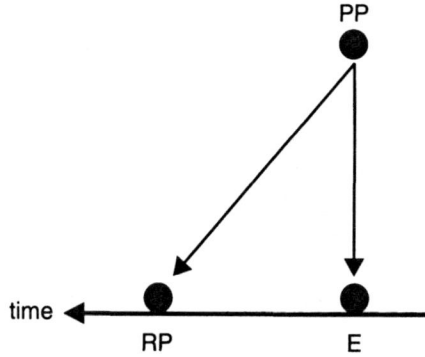

FIGURE 15.4. Retrospective relation encoded by the TFoR lexical concept: [EVENT X IS SEQUENCED LATER THAN EVENT Y]

In this example, the lexical concept in (21b) encodes a schematic relation in which one temporal event is sequenced later than another. That is, there is one event, event E, which is sequenced subsequent to a second event, and the second event serves as the reference point (RP). Moreover, as the relation is one of being later, the perspective point (PP) is fixed at the later event. Hence, this TFoR lexical concept encodes what I refer to as a **retrospective relation**. As before, it says nothing about the nature of the temporal event in question, nor about the degree of temporal proximity of the two events nor about phenomenological aspects of temporal experience. The content encoded is linguistic in nature and hence highly schematic. The symbolic unit in (21) sanctions an example such as (22):

(22)   In France, dessert comes after cheese

In Figure 15.4, Time is represented by the directed arrow, so as to signify the earlier/later relation. The black circles labelled E and RP represent the two events (X and Y), while the circle labelled PP signals which event is the perspective point. The arrows leading from the PP to the two events (E and RP) signal the retrospective relation. The lexical profile associated with this lexical concept stipulates the following. NP1 and NP2 must be temporal events, there is a finite form of *come*, and an obligatory element, *after*.

The role of temporal linguistic content and temporal conceptual content in meaning construction

Providing an account of the level of schematic linguistic content associated with TFoR lexical concepts is only part of the story, however. Temporal conceptions also involve the integration of open-class temporal lexical concepts with the closed-class TFoR lexical concepts, and hence access to cognitive model profiles and so structure recruited via conceptual metaphor. That is, we need to consider the way in which linguistic and conceptual content interact in giving rise to temporal conceptions, the subject of this section. To do this, I consider an example relating to the first of the experiencer-based TFoRs discussed: the lexical concept provided in (15b), which sanctions the following example:

(23)   Christmas is approaching

On the face of it, the utterance in (23) is distinctly odd if taken literally. After all, Christmas is a temporal event, which usually lasts for a determined period, and as such cannot undergo veridical motion of the sort indicated by the expression *approaching*. Yet, this utterance is straightforwardly understood by native speakers of English as relating, not to a motion event, but to a temporal event. Moreover, there are two further inferences that arise. Firstly, Christmas is located in the future with respect to the present, as encoded by the utterance, and secondly, the event of Christmas, while located in the future, is relatively imminent. To see that this is so, we can contrast the utterance in (23) with that in (24):

(24)   Christmas is approaching, but is still a long way off

In (24), while Christmas is also located in the future, it is not imminent.

Accordingly, there are three specific issues that need to be accounted for in terms of explaining how LCCM Theory models the conception which arises for the utterance in (23). These are summarized below:

- *Issue 1*: The utterance in (23) is interpreted as relating to a temporal scene rather than a spatial scene. That is, the utterance is interpreted as concerning a temporal scenario rather than one involving veridical motion.
- *Issue 2*: The temporal event of Christmas is located in the future with respect to our understanding of the present which is implicit, although not explicitly mentioned, in the utterance in (23).
- *Issue 3*: The future event of Christmas is interpreted as being relatively imminent with respect to the present.

Before accounting for these issues, I first consider the way in which spatial conceptual content is recruited, via conceptual metaphor, to structure temporal cognitive models. I do so by considering the cognitive model profile accessed via the lexical concept [CHRISTMAS].

The cognitive model profile for [CHRISTMAS]

I assume in LCCM Theory, in keeping with Lakoff and Johnson (1999), that conceptual metaphors facilitate the automatic and unconscious recruitment of conceptual content from cognitive models from distinct domains, in the case of Time, from Space. This thereby facilitates the recruitment of spatial conceptual content which serves to structure temporal cognitive models. That is, conceptual metaphors, in effect, provide the primary cognitive models to which, for instance, [CHRISTMAS] affords access, with additional structure. To illustrate, consider a partial cognitive model profile for [CHRISTMAS], provided in Figure 15.5.

The lexical concept [CHRISTMAS] facilitates access to a number of primary cognitive models. These include knowledge relating to Christmas as a CUL-TURAL FESTIVAL, including the exchange of gifts and other cultural practice, including food consumed, activities engaged in, the coming together of family, and so forth. The second type of knowledge relates to Christmas as a TEMPORAL EVENT. This includes a whole host of temporal knowledge, as illustrated by the attributes and values associated with the TEMPORAL EVENT cognitive model. For instance, part of our knowledge relating to a temporal event is that it can be situated in the PAST, PRESENT, and FUTURE. A further

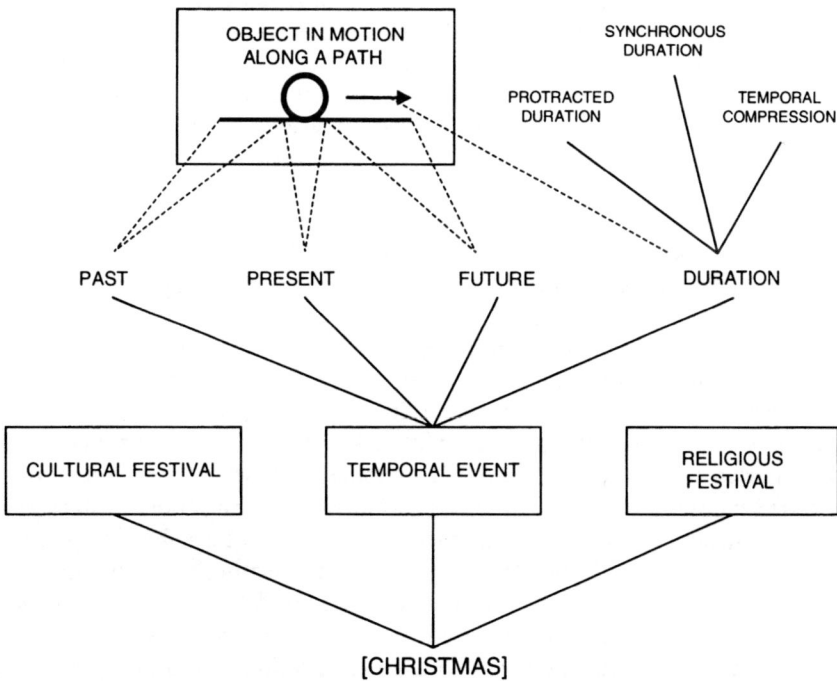

FIGURE 15.5. Partial primary cognitive model profile for [CHRISTMAS]

attribute relates to the nature of the durational elapse associated with the event, which is to say its DURATION. This attribute has a number of values associated with it. Moving from right to left, the first is TEMPORAL COMPRES-SION—the underestimation of time, which is to say, the experience that time is proceeding more "quickly" than usual. The second is SYNCHRONOUS DUR-ATION—the normative estimation of time, which is to say, the experience of time unfolding at its standard or equable rate. The final value is PROTRACTED DURATION. This relates to an overestimation of duration, which is to say the felt experience that time is proceeding more "slowly" than usual.

The sorts of experiences that give rise to the range of different attributes and values represented in the conceptual system in the domain of Time are of myriad kinds. For instance, we experience the past in terms of the range of measures we deploy to record temporal "distance" from now, such as time lines, calendars, diaries, and so on. We also experience the past in terms of biological ageing, photographic records of past events, narrative and story which recount past happenings, as well as personal and autobiographical memory, and so on. The present is experienced by virtue of direct perceptual processing, the phenomenologically real perceptual moment briefly described above.[11] The future is apprehended in terms of our experiences of intention-ality and the realization of intentions, as well as our experience of waiting and the subsequent occurrence of events. Moreover, it is apprehended in terms of our experience and interaction with the recording mechanisms that we deploy in order to gauge the relative imminence of future events such as calendars, timetables, schedules, time plans, and time-reckoning systems and devices on a daily basis. Finally, we also have detailed knowledge of the range of phe-nomenologically real aspects of duration which we experience throughout our lives.

The final primary cognitive model diagrammed in Figure 15.5 is that of Christmas as a RELIGIOUS FESTIVAL. This relates to knowledge concerning the nature and status of Christmas as a Christian event, and the way in which this festival is enacted and celebrated.

In addition, the primary cognitive models for [CHRISTMAS] recruit struc-ture from other cognitive models via conceptual metaphor. That is, as oper-ationalized in LCCM Theory, a conceptual metaphor provides a stable link that allows aspects of conceptual content encoded by one cognitive model to be imported so as to form part of the permanent knowledge representation encoded by another. For instance, the primary cognitive model TEMPORAL EVENT is structured via conceptual metaphor in terms of a stable, long-term link holding between it and the cognitive model relating to an OBJECT IN MOTION ALONG A PATH. As such, the cognitive model, OBJECT IN MOTION ALONG A PATH, which is represented, in Figure 15.5, by virtue of a circle located on a path, with the arrow indicating direction of motion, provides

---

[11] See Evans (2004a) for further details.

the TEMPORAL EVENT cognitive model with inferential structure relating to our knowledge of objects undergoing motion along a path. The conceptual content recruited via conceptual metaphor is indicated by the dashed lines. Specifically, inferential structure from this cognitive model is inherited by the PAST, PRESENT, and FUTURE attributes, such that content relating to the region of the path behind the object serves to structure, in part, our experience of pastness, conceptual content relating to the object's present location serves to structure, in part, our experience of the present, and content relating to that portion of the path in front of the object serves to structure our experience of futurity. This is indicated by the dashed lines which map the relevant portions of the path of motion from the OBJECT IN MOTION ALONG A PATH cognitive model onto the relevant attributes: FUTURE, PRESENT, PAST. In addition, content relating to the nature of motion is inherited by the DURATION attribute. Again this is captured by the dashed arrow, which links the arrow—signifying motion—with the DURATION attribute.

In Chapter 10, I discussed chaining within the conceptual system—the phenomenon whereby links and associations are established such that a web of connections serves to relate cognitive models. Hence, cognitive models are related to one another, facilitating activation of knowledge as it is required, for instance, by linguistically mediated communication. In LCCM Theory, conceptual metaphors provide one of the ways in which cognitive models from other regions of the conceptual system can become linked with cognitive models belonging to the access site of a given lexical concept. By virtue of humans acting in the world, tight reoccurring correlations serve to establish connections between cognitive models associated with distinct domains in the conceptual systems of human infants prior to the onset of language (see Lakoff and Johnson 1999). The establishing of these links provides a powerful organizational device that facilitates the deployment and re-use of multi-modal knowledge in order to structure other (less easily apprehended) domains of experience.[12]

From the perspective of LCCM Theory then, as conceptual metaphors serve to establish stable links between specific cognitive models that may belong to the access sites of many lexical concepts—for example, *Easter, Spring, the concert, his prime*, and so forth—this leads to massive redundancy of spatial conceptual content subserving temporal concepts. That is, conceptual metaphors provide a fundamental structuring mechanism of the human conceptual system.

---

[12] It is important to note that conceptual metaphor—the establishment of linked cognitive models which derive from unrelated domains of experience—is but one way in which cognitive models inherit structure. Others include the phenomenon of transcendence, as well as attribute systematicities, discussed in Chapter 10. These phenomena also serve to establish links between cognitive models.

Meaning construction in Christmas is approaching

I now return to a consideration of how the various interpretations (issues 1–3 discussed above), associated with (23), arise.

Issue 1

Firstly, how is it that the utterance in (23) is interpreted as relating to a temporal scenario rather than a spatial one? The answer is as follows. The TFoR lexical concept that sanctions the utterance as a whole serves as a frame for interpreting the open-class lexical concepts—those associated with the vehicles *Christmas* and *approaching*—allowing them to achieve an informational characterization relating to a **temporal scene.** That is, the linguistic content encoded by this TFoR lexical concept, as described above, ensures that the interpretations that arise for the lexical concepts paired with *Christmas* and *approaching* are a consequence of these lexical concepts undergoing integration in the context of schematic temporal, as opposed to spatial, content. Put another way, as the overarching internally open TFoR lexical concept relates to a temporal scene, this provides a schematic framework which constrains the process of interpretation, as it applies to the open-class lexical concepts that populate the larger TFoR lexical concept.

Issue 2

Secondly, how is it that the utterance is understood as relating to a temporal event which is "located" in the future? After all, as we saw above the experiencer-based TFoR lexical concept which licenses the utterance as a whole does not encode whether a given temporal event is situated in the past or future. The answer, I suggest, relates to a special kind of matching that involves the spatial content recruited via conceptual metaphor, which structures the cognitive model profile of [CHRISTMAS] and the primary cognitive model profile accessed via [APPROACHING]. This type of matching I refer to as conceptual metaphor matching, which is constrained by the **Principle of Conceptual Metaphor Matching**, summarized below:

(p12)   Principle of Conceptual Metaphor Matching
        During interpretation, (an) open-class lexical concept(s) structured in terms of conceptual metaphor(s) are subject to matching, whenever possible, in the primary cognitive model profile of relevant lexical concepts in the same lexical conceptual unit. Conceptual metaphor matching does not preclude regular matching.

This principle does two things. Firstly, it ensures that in the case of (23) the spatial content to which [CHRISTMAS] has access in its primary cognitive model profile by virtue of recruitment via conceptual metaphor is matched with relevant cognitive model(s) in the primary cognitive model profile of [APPROACHING]. Secondly, this matching operation does not interfere with, and hence does not prevent regular matching, matching that takes place on conceptual content which is not recruited via conceptual metaphor.

In terms of the utterance in (23), the spatial content to which [CHRISTMAS] facilitates access has to do with inferential structure derived from the motion scenario involving an object in motion. This is matched with the kind of terminal motion accessed via [APPROACHING]. The cognitive model profile associated with [APPROACHING] involves motion towards an entity, and hence, the object in motion is in front of the entity with respect to which it is "approaching". As the FUTURE attribute of the TEMPORAL EVENT cognitive model accessed via [CHRISTMAS] is structured in terms of that part of the motion trajectory that is in front, the resulting match involves an interpretation in which the temporal event of Christmas is "located" in the future. In other words, this particular interpretation is a consequence of the special type of matching I refer to as conceptual metaphor matching.

Issue 3

The final issue relates to the interpretation that the temporal event of Christmas in (23) is interpreted as being relatively imminent. This interpretation arises, I argue, due to the regular process of matching as described in earlier chapters. Matching, as guided by the previously introduced Principles of Interpretation, attempts to build an informational characterization for [CHRISTMAS] and [APPROACHING] by first searching the primary cognitive models of both these open-class lexical concepts. As Christmas is a temporal, cultural, and religious event, and hence something that cannot undergo the sort of veridical motion implicated by the primary cognitive model profile associated with [APPROACHING], a clash arises. This necessitates clash resolution. Due to the Principle of Context-induced Clash Resolution, introduced in the previous chapter, [CHRISTMAS] is designated as the figurative target, and [APPROACHING] the figurative vehicle. This follows as the utterance is "about" Christmas, and specifically serves to "locate" Christmas "in" time. The consequence of the foregoing is that a search is established in the secondary cognitive model profile of [APPROACHING]. A very partial cognitive model for [APPROACHING] is provided in Figure 15.6.

The cognitive model profile for [APPROACHING] includes primary cognitive models for a TARGET LOCATION, the DIRECTED MOTION OF AN ENTITY, and the IMMINENCE OF ARRIVAL OF AN ENTITY. A consequence of the relative imminence of arrival of an entity is the IMMINENCE OF OCCURRENCE OF EVENT, which is a secondary cognitive model. As a temporal event such as Christmas can occur, but not (literally) arrive,

```
                                        ┌─────────────────┐
                                        │  IMMINENCE OF   │
                                        │  OCCURRENCE OF  │
                                        │     EVENT       │
                                        └─────────────────┘
                                                 │
                                                 │
┌─────────────┐   ┌─────────────┐   ┌─────────────────┐
│   TARGET    │   │  DIRECTED   │   │  IMMINENCE OF   │
│  LOCATION   │   │ MOTION OF AN│   │  ARRIVAL OF     │
│             │   │   ENTITY    │   │    ENTITY       │
└─────────────┘   └─────────────┘   └─────────────────┘
          \              │               /
           \             │              /
            \────────────┼─────────────/
                   [APPROACHING]
```

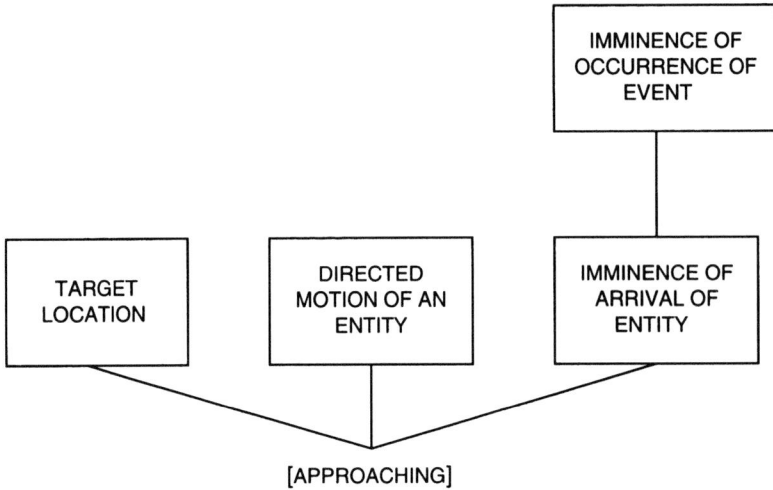

FIGURE 15.6. Partial cognitive model profile for [APPROACHING]

there is a match between the secondary cognitive model IMMINENCE OF
OCCURRENCE OF EVENT and the primary cognitive model profile of
[CHRISTMAS]. Hence, the interpretation of the imminence of the occurrence of Christmas is due to a metaphoric conception arising, along the
lines discussed in more detail in the previous chapter.

The status of conceptual metaphors in LCCM Theory

I conclude this chapter by considering the status of conceptual metaphors in
LCCM Theory. I do so by asking, and attempting to answer, four questions:

- What is the status of conceptual metaphors in LCCM Theory?
- What is the distinctive role of lexical concepts and cognitive models?
- What is the motivation for TFoR lexical concepts to deploy vehicles
  relating to literal spatial language?
- What does this show about the utility of using semantic structure in
  language as a lens for investigating conceptual structure?

i.   What is the status of conceptual metaphors?

Conceptual metaphors, in LCCM Theory, provide a means of structuring
cognitive models in terms of conceptual content recruited from cognitive
models associated with other domains of experience. That is, conceptual
metaphors serve to provide one of (probably) many types of links which
connect cognitive models, allowing them to inherit structure. Conceptual

metaphors provide stable, long-term links which allow the automatic and unconscious recruitment of conceptual content in asymmetric fashion. They serve to structure, in part, attributes and values, providing massive redundancy across concepts within the conceptual system. Conceptual metaphors arise when stable links are established between cognitive models encoding perceptual experience that is sensorimotor in nature, and cognitive models which encode conceptual content that is subjective in nature.

ii.   What is the distinctive role of lexical concepts, cognitive models, and conceptual metaphors in figurative meaning construction for time?

Based on the guiding premise of LCCM Theory, the conception that arises from the situated usage of a given utterance is a consequence of two distinct sorts of representations: purely linguistic content encoded by lexical concepts, and purely conceptual content encoded by the cognitive model profile to which lexical concepts facilitate access. For instance, the TFoR lexical concepts, considered briefly above, encode schematic temporal content, as well as information about the nature of the sorts of internally closed lexical concepts, and vehicles that make up these internally complex lexical concepts. The result of linguistic unpacking is a schematic level of temporal representation. However, this level provides a prompt for interpretation: the deployment of conceptual content associated with conceptual structure, resulting in an utterance-level simulation, which is to say a conception, and hence meaning. Interpretation makes use of the cognitive model profile associated with a lexical concept, and in figurative language understanding, this involves primary activation of secondary cognitive models. In other words, temporal conceptions are the result both of linguistic content and conceptual content.

As we saw earlier in the discussion of the interpretations which arise from the utterance, *Christmas is approaching*, temporal language understanding involves activating conceptual content inherited from other cognitive models, via conceptual metaphor—in the sense defined in this chapter—and also involves activation of secondary cognitive models, which are not due to conceptual metaphor. In this sense, conceptual metaphors are features of conceptual structure, rather than mechanisms that facilitate dynamic meaning construction per se. The interpretation that a particular event is located in the future is a consequence of inferential structure drawn from motion through space, a consequence of conceptual metaphor. However, the interpretation regarding the relative imminence of the occurrence is a consequence of a secondary cognitive model associated with the cognitive model profile for [APPROACHING] being matched with the primary cognitive model profile of [CHRISTMAS], as discussed above. In other words, figurative language understanding does not inevitably result from the existence of conceptual metaphors.

iii.   What is the motivation for TFoR lexical concepts to deploy vehicles relating to literal spatial language?

This issue relates to the fact that TFoR lexical concepts are associated with vehicles that literally relate to motion through space, and yet, I argue, encode a schematic temporal relation independently of the conceptual metaphors that structure Time in terms of Space at the conceptual level. The question then is why? As semantic representation in language (semantic structure) reflects conceptual structure, albeit indirectly (see discussion below), the linguistic content encoded by lexical concepts, and the vehicles employed, reflect—again indirectly—the nature of the simulations that they serve as partial prompts for constructing. In other words, symbolic units (lexical concepts and phonological vehicles) are conventionalized prompts for building complex simulations (conceptions). As thinking and communicating about temporal relationships is central to the way we coordinate our actions with one another and with our sociophysical environment, and hence the sorts of complex simulations we (seek to) evoke, it is (perhaps) natural that the nature and make-up of TFoR lexical concepts should reflect aspects of conceptual structure that they serve, in part, to evoke.

iv.   What does this show about the utility of using semantic structure in language as a lens for investigating conceptual structure?

At the outset of the chapter I alluded to the assumption made by cognitive linguistics that language can be deployed in order to investigate conceptual structure as, in some sense, language reflects conceptual structure—although different authors take different views on the precise way in which language reflects conceptual organization. From the perspective of LCCM Theory, semantic structure is a pale reflection of conceptual structure. After all, linguistic content encodes highly schematic representations, which stand in stark contrast to the perceptually and phenomenologically rich representations encoded as cognitive models. This does not mean, of course, that semantic structure cannot be deployed in order to investigate conceptual structure. In point of fact, the central argument of LCCM Theory is that as lexical concepts facilitate access to conceptual structure, semantic structure can be deployed as a means of, albeit indirectly, investigating conceptual structure.

Summary

This chapter has provided a reasonably detailed examination of a range of lexical concepts for Time, and a selection of the cognitive models which populate the domain of Time at the level of conceptual structure. In particular, I have examined the way in which the theoretical construct of conceptual metaphor is incorporated into LCCM Theory, in the domain of Time. The central argument of the chapter is that temporal representation has reflexes in terms of direct encoding in language, temporal lexical concepts, which encode highly schematic parameterizations of temporal experience, and perceptually and phenomenologically rich temporal cognitive models. The temporal cognitive models include much that is purely temporal in nature. For instance, phenomenologically rich temporal experiences relate to notions such as sequentiality, simultaneity, temporal compression, protracted duration, our experience of pastness, futurity, the present, and so on. In addition, such notions are systematically structured in terms of structure recruited from cognitive models which relate to non-temporal aspects of perceptual experience such as motion through space. This is achieved via conceptual metaphors, which serve to provide an unconscious and automatic level of access to non-temporal knowledge allowing inferential structure from cognitive models associated with the domain of Space to form part of our conceptual representations for temporal concepts. In terms of linguistically mediated simulations, this can lead to conceptions which are not figurative, in the canonical sense, as defined in Chapter 14. However, canonically figurative temporal conceptions are also possible in tandem, as in the case of the example: *Christmas is approaching*.

Part V

Conclusion

This final part of the book consists of one chapter. The chapter situates LCCM Theory with respect to the various theories within cognitive linguistics which it synthesizes and builds upon. As such, this final part serves to contextualize the development of LCCM Theory.

16

LCCM Theory in context

This short chapter considers the status of LCCM Theory as a "theory." In certain respects, of course, LCCM Theory is not a new theory at all. After all, it examines well-studied phenomena that countless scholars of every conceivable theoretical persuasion have examined before me. It also incorporates seminal ideas developed by others, in both cognitive linguistics and cognitive psychology, and incorporates and synthesizes many of the core insights developed in the best-known approaches to linguistic semantics and grammar developed by other cognitive linguists.

My aim, in the preceding pages, has not been to add yet another theory to the mix, so to speak, simply for the sake of doing so. Nevertheless, there are three aspects of LCCM Theory, as presented in the preceding pages, which I believe are noteworthy, and, which provide a new and, I hope, elegant account of the range of linguistic phenomena discussed during the course of the book. I also believe that the cognitive linguistics movement has reached a point in its development where it requires (something like) LCCM Theory. The three notable aspects are detailed below.

i. LCCM Theory provides a self-conscious attempt to synthesize key developments relating to cognitive lexical semantics, and cognitive approaches to grammar from across a number of distinct theories and approaches within cognitive linguistics thereby providing a single joined-up theory of linguistic semantics.

One of the hallmarks of cognitive linguistics is that it constitutes an approach to the study of language and the relationship between language, the mind, and sociophysical experience. Hence, it comprises a number of distinct, complementary and sometimes competing theoretical frameworks and approaches, which often address overlapping phenomena. From this perspective, one challenge for cognitive linguists is to integrate the range of perspectives and frameworks on offer in order to provide a more focused attempt to account for the object of analysis, whatever that happens to be. As I noted earlier, cognitive linguistics can be notionally divided into two sub-branches: cognitive semantics and cognitive approaches to grammar. One concern within cognitive semantics has been to study lexical representation from a cognitively realistic framework. This work has assumed that semantic structure reflects cognitive organization, particularly the embodied nature of the human conceptual system, as enshrined in the thesis of embodied cognition (Lakoff 1987; Johnson 1987; see Evans and Green 2006 for an overview), as well as other organizing principles of human cognition such as categorization and attentional mechanisms. In addition, cognitive semantic accounts have made significant strides in modelling lexical representation, as is evident in exemplars such as Lakoff (1987), Geeraerts (1994), Tyler and Evans (2003), and the collection of papers in Cuyckens *et al.* (2003). Some of the notions apparent in cognitive semantics have also been important in the development of cognitive approaches to grammar, especially as evidenced in the work of Talmy and Langacker. For instance, both these scholars have underlined the importance of the embodied (or conceptual) basis of linguistic structure, with emphasis on humanly relevant aspects of experience, such as attention, time, space, force dynamics, and motion. The experiential influence of linguistic organization is also evident in the theory of Cognitive Construction Grammar developed by Goldberg, (e.g., 1995, 2006). This is evidenced, for instance, by Goldberg's scene-encoding hypothesis, which predicts that sentence-level argument-structure constructions serve to encode ubiquitous humanly relevant scenes.

However, what is apparent is that there is not a common set of vocabulary. And, moreover, distinct approaches have emerged within both cognitive semantics and cognitive approaches to grammar which partially replicate (and are partially distinct from) other related cognitive linguistic theories. While this may have advantages, it sometimes leads to confusion and can thus be a disadvantage.

For instance, Talmy (e.g., 2000) and Langacker (e.g., 1987, 2008) use distinct sets of terms for covering some—arguably much—of the same conceptual territory. Moreover, Langacker (e.g., 1987) and Goldberg (e.g., 1995) differ quite significantly in how they define the term "construction," a fundamental theoretical construct in their respective theories. Thus, not only is there replication, but when there is overlap different theorists use the same terms, on occasion, in markedly different ways. Moreover, different cognitive linguistic approaches to linguistic organization while ostensibly grounded in cognitive semantics, base their accounts of lexical and conceptual representation on different semantic theories. For instance, Goldberg bases her account on Frame Semantics (Fillmore 1982), while Langacker bases his account on his own version of what he dubs "conceptual semantics" (e.g., Langacker 2008). Indeed, what Langacker refers to as a domain is not quite the same as Fillmore's notion of a semantic frame. Moreover, both are different from what Lakoff and Johnson refer to, in Conceptual Metaphor Theory (e.g., 1980, 1999), as a domain, which is different again from what Lakoff (1987) refers to as an Idealized Cognitive Model (ICM). The plethora of theoretical constructs can, on occasion, be contradictory. For instance, while Langacker includes Time and Emotion as basic, but not abstract, domains, for Lakoff and Johnson both are abstract domains. This lack of a unified vocabulary can also undermine a concerted focus on a delimited set of agreed-upon phenomena. As such, this state of affairs is potentially confusing to the analyst who seeks to apply and deploy the various theories on offer, and moreover, can make it difficult to compare (and contrast) the distinct theoretical positions, their main claims and objectives. The divergences also, potentially, undermine the claim that cognitive linguistics represents a coherent enterprise that offers scholars from other disciplines (e.g., cognitive psychologists, literary analysts, and so on) a toolkit for use in examining phenomena that fall under the purview of study in their respective disciplines.

One of the aims of LCCM Theory has been to unify many of the objectives of cognitive semantics and cognitive approaches to grammar. This is achieved by attempting to clarify the key contributions of each, and incorporating them into a single framework. Both cognitive semanticists and cognitive grammarians assume that meaning is fundamental. Cognitive lexical semanticists are concerned with lexical representation, while cognitive grammarians have often distinct albeit related aims. At base, these approaches are united in a common attempt to uncover the semantic basis for linguistic organization. From cognitive semantics, LCCM Theory has taken recent advances in lexical representation. Recent work has demonstrated the complexity associated with lexical items, and that word senses are relatively granular in terms of their storage in long-term semantic memory. From cognitive approaches to grammar, LCCM Theory has taken two essential insights.

Firstly, cognitively oriented grammarians have argued that grammar is meaningful, a position that until relatively recently was a marginal view in mainstream linguistics. In particular, scholars such as Talmy and Langacker have successfully demonstrated that although grammatical meaning is highly schematic in nature, when compared to the relatively rich meaning associated with open-class forms such as nouns and verbs, it is, nevertheless, meaningful. This finding is incorporated in LCCM Theory and provided the basis for elaborating the construct of the lexical concept.

Secondly, cognitive approaches to grammar, particularly those that take a constructional perspective, notably Langacker's Cognitive Grammar and Goldberg's version of Construction Grammar, place compositionality at the heart of grammatical mechanisms. For instance, the Cognitive Construction Grammar framework of Goldberg building on the seminal ideas of Fillmore and Kay (e.g., Fillmore et al. 1988; Kay and Fillmore 1999), and Lakoff (1987), explicitly addresses the way in which grammatical constructions fuse with one another thereby facilitating the integration of verbs and nouns with more schematic sentence-level constructions such as the ditransitive construction. Langacker, using different terminology, develops a related idea. For Langacker semantic compositionality is at the heart of Cognitive Grammar, although this is not the term he uses. He conceives of grammatical operations involving the assembling of phrase, clause, and sentence-level structures as involving the integration of conceptually dependent with conceptually autonomous symbolic units. For Langacker conceptually dependent entities encode schematic trajectors and/or landmarks which can be filled in—Langacker uses the terms "elaboration." As a consequence, in a phrase such as: *under the sofa, the sofa* serves to elaborate the schematic landmark encoded as part of the semantic representation of the relational predication *under*. As we have seen, LCCM Theory is influenced by both these accounts of integration involving grammatical units, and develops a principle-driven account of semantic compositionality which owes much to the pioneering work of Langacker, Goldberg, and indeed, other researchers in cognitive linguistics.

In essence, LCCM Theory represents a self-conscious attempt to draw out the major insights and successes with respect to lexical representation and semantic composition apparent in the various theoretical frameworks that populate cognitive semantics and cognitive approaches to grammar. It has sought to develop a framework which is both cognitive semantic in spirit, while also constituting a semantically informed model of grammar. In so doing, it aspires to be able to account for the complete range of semantic variation evident in language use. While such an ambitious goal may or may not be within reach of the current version of the theory, as presented in this book, the theoretical apparatus developed here will, it is hoped, provide a programmatic framework that may facilitate this long-term goal.

This all said, in attempting to integrate ideas and constructs from specific theories, LCCM Theory does not seek to replace the theories it draws upon. After all, Cognitive Grammar and Cognitive Construction Grammar, for instance, are well-established (sets of) theories that have specific goals and objects of study, which LCCM Theory complements, rather than directly replicating. Yet, pulling together some of the strands from other theories that are concerned with linguistic semantics and meaning construction into a single framework, as I have attempted to do, is, I suggest, a worthwhile endeavour.

ii. LCCM Theory gives back to cognitive linguists the importance of language in meaning-construction processes.

One of the outstanding successes of cognitive semantics, as a sub-branch of cognitive linguistics, has been to emphasize the role of embodiment in cognitive function and in language. Another has been to demonstrate the importance of imagination in meaning construction. However, one of the consequences of this move has been to downplay the significance of language itself in meaning construction. This is apparent in perhaps the two cognitive linguistic theories that have the highest profiles beyond the confines of cognitive linguistics itself. These are Conceptual Metaphor Theory, pioneered by George Lakoff and Mark Johnson, and Conceptual Blending Theory, developed by Gilles Fauconnier and Mark Turner. This is not to say, of course, that either of these theories ignores language, or explicitly attempts to reduce its significance in meaning construction. The issue is more one of focus.

For its part, Conceptual Metaphor Theory is primarily a theory of knowledge representation. Although it has traditionally relied on language to provide evidence for conceptual metaphors, and seeks to account for a subset of semantic composition exhibited by figurative language, it is not a theory of language understanding nor of metaphor comprehension. I have assumed in this book that Conceptual Metaphor Theory is correct *en grandes lignes*. That is, there is compelling evidence from behavioural studies demonstrating, for instance, that knowledge representation is structured in terms of conceptual substrate taken from other domains of conceptual representation, in the sense predicted by Conceptual Metaphor Theory. However, I believe that Conceptual Metaphor Theory needs to be supplemented in two ways.

Firstly, Conceptual Metaphor Theory has traditionally been concerned with sensory-motor experience and how this gives rise to abstract concepts. For instance, Lakoff and Johnson have emphasized that notions such as Anger, Time, and Quantity are, in some sense, subjective and hence, in certain respects abstract notions. Much of the impetus behind Conceptual Metaphor Theory has been to show how these more abstract notions are structured in terms of what have been referred to as concrete dimensions of experience, for instance, Time in terms of Motion through space, Anger in terms of Heat, Quantity in terms of Vertical elevation, and so forth.

However, this focus has sometimes given rise to the impression that Conceptual Metaphor Theory views abstract domains, such as Time, as lacking any inherent structure of their own. Such a position—if indeed this is a view held by Lakoff and Johnson—is clearly untenable, as pointed out by a number of authors (e.g., Murphy 1996; Barsalou 1999; Barsalou and Wiemar-Hastings 2005). In my own work on Time (e.g., Evans 2004a), I make the point that Time relates to a complex and diverse set of experiences—rather than consisting solely of mappings derived from the concrete realm of space—and is real and directly experienced, a point I also made in the previous chapter. That is, abstract concepts, such as Time, do consist of, in part, content which is purely temporal, and hence subjective in nature. Thus, Conceptual Metaphor Theory, which focuses primarily on the sensory-motor substrate associated with abstract concepts and domains, must be supplemented with approaches that also address the subjective content associated with abstract concepts. One such an approach, I have argued in this book, is Barsalou's Perceptual Symbol Systems perspective, which incorporates sensory-motor information as well as subjective (or in his terms, introspective) aspects of experience in the make-up of (abstract) concepts.

Secondly, and as already noted, Conceptual Metaphor Theory is not an approach to language, as such. As was seen in Part IV of the book, while conceptual metaphors constrain the symbolic resources available in language, a given language is a unique semiotic system, which represents conceptual resources in a form independent of non-linguistic conceptual structure. Indeed, the notion of a lexical concept represents a language-specific bundle of knowledge. Hence, what is required is an account of lexical representation and semantic composition which complements the perspective on knowledge representation provided by Conceptual Metaphor Theory. Yet, such an account must also remain mindful of the unique contribution of language to meaning construction. This is what LCCM Theory attempts to do.

Turning now to Conceptual Blending Theory, while this overlaps in certain respects with Conceptual Metaphor Theory, its primary impulse is somewhat different. Unlike Conceptual Metaphor Theory which is primarily concerned with a subset of knowledge representation—accounting for the relatively stable aspects of the structuring of abstract domains—Blending Theory is concerned with a wider range of domains, and is primarily exercised by the desire to account for dynamic aspects of meaning construction. Like Conceptual Metaphor Theory, however, Blending Theory is not concerned with language per se. Indeed, the architects of the theory emphasize the overriding importance of non-linguistic processes which are, they argue, conceptual rather than linguistic in nature. It is these processes, operating "behind the scenes" which guide meaning construction (Fauconnier 1997; Fauconnier and Turner 2002). My purpose in this book has not been to dispute this claim. Indeed, as with Conceptual Metaphor Theory, I assume that Blending Theory is, in general terms, correct. Rather, LCCM Theory represents an attempt to redress the balance. It seeks to do so by demonstrating the complexity associated with lexical concepts—the prompts for the conceptual processes operating behind the scenes—and to show that language does in fact make a significant contribution to meaning construction, involving a range of highly complex meaning construction mechanisms. Indeed, this is an assertion with which Fauconnier and Turner would no doubt agree.

In essence, I conceive of LCCM Theory as complementing, rather than competing with, the theories of Conceptual Metaphor and Blending. It provides, I suggest, the missing link in meaning construction which is essential for a complete understanding of how language interfaces with conceptual structure. That is, while Conceptual Metaphor and Blending Theories address the role of conceptual processes in meaning construction, LCCM Theory is concerned with the role of language and linguistically mediated access to knowledge representation. Hence, while Conceptual Metaphor and Blending Theories constitute theories of, what Fauconnier (1997) has termed backstage cognition, LCCM Theory constitutes a theory of what I have called frontstage cognition.

iii. LCCM Theory reanalyses and thereby reinterprets the encyclopaedic approach to linguistic semantics developed in cognitive linguistics.

The encyclopaedic approach to semantics developed in cognitive linguistics is, in no small measure, due to the work of Ronald Langacker in his development of a conceptual semantics which is part and parcel of his theory of Cognitive Grammar. While the encyclopaedic semantics perspective equates semantic structure with conceptual structure, LCCM Theory seeks to nuance and so revise this perspective. This is achieved by making a principled distinction between semantic structure and conceptual structure, which is to say a distinction between linguistic knowledge—as encoded by lexical concepts—and non-linguistic conceptual knowledge—modelled in terms of the theoretical construct of the cognitive model. This distinction provides, in certain respects, a somewhat different take on what an encyclopaedic account of semantic representation looks like, and so diverges from the standard account in cognitive linguistics. Part of the argument I have made in this book has been that language provides a level of representation, linguistic content, which is unique to language. This level of knowledge is, in certain respects, coarse-grained. As I argued in Part II of the book, linguistic content relates to a highly schematic level of information which abstracts away from much of the richness available at the level of cognitive models. In essence, I claimed that the primary function of the emergence of language is to facilitate access to and control of the representations which inhere in the pre-existing (in evolutionarily terms) conceptual system. I suggested that linguistic content takes a completely different representational form from conceptual representations—the advantage of linguistic access to the conceptual system is the ability to evoke simulations, which developed for non-linguistic functions such as perception and action (Barsalou 2005; Barsalou *et al.* forthcoming). In view of this, the separation of semantic representation into lexical concepts (linguistic content) and cognitive models (conceptual content) serves to provide a somewhat nuanced perspective on encyclopaedic semantics.

In the final analysis, what I have provided in these pages is a programmatic framework that seeks to provide an account for how words mean. Much remains to be done, not least to provide experimental psychologists with a framework that offers specific proposals that can be empirically verified. Nevertheless, these are exciting times in language science.

Glossary

Below is a listing of technical terms, along with brief definitions, that are either novel to LCCM Theory or which assume a special interpretation in the context of LCCM Theory. For a listing of page references for the technical terms listed, please see the index. Terms preceded by an asterisk within definitions have their own entry.

Access   The phenomenon whereby lexical concepts serve to activate *conceptual content. There are two types of access: *primary access and *secondary access.

Access point   The point where a *lexical concept interfaces with the *conceptual system in a given *cognitive model profile.

Access route   The path of *activation through a *cognitive model profile afforded by a *lexical concept given the particular linguistic and extra-linguistic context in which it is embedded.

Access route length   The number of cognitive models activated in a given *cognitive model profile: the greater the number of cognitive models activated, the greater the access route length.

Access site   The range of (typically) many *association areas that a lexical concept potentially affords access to. Due to the precise nature and make-up of association areas, an access site is unique to each *lexical concept.

Activation   The process whereby part of the *semantic potential to which a lexical concept provides access achieves resonance. This can be facilitated by *primary access or *secondary access.

Adjustment   The type of *matching that takes place with respect to the *cognitive model profile accessed by a *relational lexical concept. This contrasts with *perspectivization.

Alignment   Relates to the distinction between *metaphor and *metonymy. A *figurative conception that is judged as being metonymic (as opposed to metaphoric) exhibits alignment. That is, in cases of metonymy the *cognitive model profile associated with the *figurative target and *figurative vehicle is one and the same and hence exhibits alignment. The consequence is that in cases of metonymy, but not metaphor, the cognitive model profile for the figurative target and figurative vehicle serves simultaneously as the *clash resolution site.

Association area   A region in the *conceptual system—typically one, or more than one, *cognitive model—where a *lexical concept facilitates *primary access. An *access site typically consists of countless association areas.

Attribute   See *Attribute-value sets.

Attribute frame   Attributes within a *frame that are associated with their own frame, providing an embedded form of framing.

Attribute systematicity   The property associated with certain attributes which form the core of a *frame, due to frequency of occurrence across a range of distinct contexts.

Attribute taxonomy   Attribute-value sets form taxonomies whereby a given value, while subordinate to a superordinate attribute, can in turn serve as an attribute, and hence be superordinate, to more specific values.

Attribute-value sets   The set of attributes—superordinate concepts—and values— subordinate concepts—that together with a related kind of concept—*structural invariants—make up a *frame.

Bipartite structure   The idea that lexical concepts both encode information that can be directly encoded in and externalized via language and (a subset, namely *open-class lexical concepts) provide an *access site to representational knowledge structures which are non-linguistic in nature: the *cognitive model. Information that is directly encoded by lexical concepts is referred to as *linguistic content. Information encoded by cognitive models is referred to as *conceptual content.

Bridging context   The context of use in which a new *lexical concept emerges as a situated (or invited) inference. In such a context, lexical concept A, associated with *vehicle a, is used such that the invited inference b is also apparent. Through a process known as *pragmatic strengthening, inference b is instantiated as a distinct lexical concept B, conventionally associated with form a. A polysemous relationship thereby holds between the extant lexical concept A, and the derived lexical concept B.

Broad selection   Selection of a distinct *lexical concept from among a number of possible lexical concepts conventionally associated with a particular *vehicle. There are two main types of broad selection, namely *single selection and *multiple selection. Broad selection contrasts with *narrow selection.

Chaining   The phenomenon whereby cognitive models are linked in a web of interconnections of diverse sorts. The consequence of this, in terms of linguistic interaction, is that each *access site associated with an *open-class lexical concept provide a deep *semantic potential for purposes of linguistically mediated communication.

Clash   The phenomenon when a *match is not achieved across the *primary cognitive model profile and/or *informational characterization undergoing *matching.

Clash resolution   The process in which a *search region is established in the *secondary cognitive model profile of one of the cognitive model profiles undergoing *matching, in order to facilitate a *match.

Clash resolution site   The *secondary cognitive model profile that serves as the *search region in facilitating *clash resolution.

Closed-class lexical concept   That subset of lexical concepts that are conventionally paired with *closed-class vehicles. Lexical concepts of this kind do not facilitate *access to *conceptual structure, and hence do not have an *access site nor do they have a *cognitive model profile.

Closed-class vehicles   The subset of *phonological vehicles conventionally paired with *closed-class lexical concepts.

Cognitive model   A coherent body of multimodal knowledge of any kind to which a *lexical concept can facilitate access and which can give rise to a *simulation. Cognitive models are comprised of one or more *frames, and can be classified based on the way in which they relate to *individuals, *types, *episodic situations, or *generic situations.

Cognitive model profile   The range of cognitive models to which a given lexical concept potentially facilitates *access. The cognitive model profile constitutes a lexical concept's *semantic potential. A cognitive model profile is made up of a *primary cognitive model profile and a *secondary cognitive model profile.

Common ground   Constitutes the shared knowledge between participants that is built up incrementally during the course of a *joint activity. Joint activities proceed in incremental steps which are cumulative in nature. These incremental steps serve to accumulate the common ground.

Conception   A complex *simulation resulting from processes of *semantic composition, involving an interaction between representations in the *linguistic system and the *conceptual system. A conception is thus an utterance-level unit of meaning. Conceptions emerge dynamically and can be revised during processing as further linguistic context emerges thereby resulting in new *matches which "overwrite" previously established conceptions during the process of language understanding.

Conceptual content   The knowledge represented in the *conceptual system. Conceptual content coheres in terms of a conceptual unit referred to as a *cognitive model, and is multimodal in nature (cf. *linguistic content).

Conceptual polysemy   The phenomenon whereby a single *phonological vehicle is conventionally associated with distinct lexical concepts which are semantically related. Semantic relatedness is a matter of degree and is determined by the *bipartite structure of lexical concepts. For instance, lexical concepts can be related by virtue of shared or overlapping *linguistic content, for instance in terms of shared *parameters. The second way concerns the nature of the *conceptual structure that *open-class lexical concepts afford potential *access to. For instance, there may be significant overlap between parts of the *cognitive model profile accessed via open-class lexical concepts associated with the same vehicle.

Conceptual structure   The non-linguistic knowledge representations that words tap into and can draw upon in situated language use. In LCCM Theory, conceptual structure is modelled in terms of the construct of the *cognitive model.

Conceptual system   The repository of concepts—mental representations—available to a human being. The conceptual system is populated by cognitive models, and each *cognitive model encodes *conceptual content. Conceptual content is what is activated during *simulation.

Conceptually autonomous   A characteristic property of *nominal lexical concepts. Lexical concepts of this kind relate to entities which are independently identifiable, such as "chair", or "shoe". The notion of being conceptually autonomous contrasts with that of being *conceptually dependent.

Conceptually dependent   A characteristic property of *relational lexical concepts. Lexical concepts of this kind constitute a relation holding between other entities, and are thus "dependent" on those other entities in order to fully determine the nature of the relationship. The notion of being conceptually dependent contrasts with that of being *conceptually autonomous.

Constraints   A type of relation that holds within *attribute-value sets in a *frame. There are two types of constraints: *global constraints and *local constraints.

Contextual factors   *Factors that relate to *attribute–value sets. Concerns the way in which context influences the interaction between values associated with related attributes within a frame.

Counterfactual situations   A *situation that hasn't and/or won't occur. These are often alternatives to *episodic situations that have occurred or are likely to occur. The difference is that in the counterfactual situation, the *individuals and/or *types, their states, and the actions they perform vary with respect to the episodic situation.

Default conception   The canonical *interpretation that arises for certain utterances, in the absence of a further novel or qualifying context.

Default search region   The *primary cognitive model profile, for purposes of *interpretation.

Discourse representation   A type of mental representation of the discourse event which is maintained by participants during a *joint activity. It is by virtue of the maintenance of a discourse representation that *common ground accumulates. The discourse representation consists of two other sorts of representation, a *textual representation and a *situational representation.

Embodied cognition   The view that mental representation is grounded in the multi-modal experiences constructed from the interaction between the human body (in the world) and the brain. As such, mental representation is grounded in multi-modal brain states that arise from sensory-motor, proprioceptive, as well as subjective experience. One consequence of this view is that knowledge representation is variable, a consequence of both species-specific embodiment and, indeed, the unique embodiment of each member of any given species.

Encapsulation The illusion that words have semantic unity, by virtue of open-class lexical concepts providing an *access site of conceptual knowledge which is often complex and informationally diffuse. Encapsulation is a function of two distinct systems being related such that the *linguistic system provides a means of interfacing at specific points, known as an *access point, with the *conceptual system.

Episodic situations A type of *cognitive model in which a mental representation is established for a unique situation that is actually experienced. Episodic situations contrast with *generic situations.

Experiencer-based temporal frame of reference (TFoR) A *temporal frame of reference which takes as its reference point an experiencing consciousness, referred to as the experiencer. Such TFoRs encode relative location in time (e.g., past, present, and future).

External lexical concept integration An *integration process whereby *internally closed lexical concepts are integrated with lexical concepts sanctioned by their *lexical profile. This process contrasts with *internal lexical concept integration.

Event-based temporal frame of reference (TFoR) A *temporal frame of reference which takes as its reference point an event. Such TFoRs encode relative sequence in time (e.g., earlier versus later).

Events A type of *cognitive model that is comprised of *situations. Events have three features. They involve a series of two or more situations, the situations are related in a coherent manner, and they lead to a significant outcome.

Factors A type of relation that holds within *attribute-value sets in a *frame. There are two types of factors: *contextual factors and *goal factors.

Figurative conception The type of *conception that arises when cognitive models are activated in the *secondary cognitive model profile of the *figurative vehicle. A figurative conception contrasts with a *literal conception.

Figurative target The *open-class lexical concept which is established as the focus or topic of an *utterance in a *figurative conception.

Figurative vehicle The *open-class lexical concept whose *secondary cognitive model profile is established as the *clash resolution site in a *figurative conception.

Formal selectional tendencies Concerns the (range of) *phonological vehicles with which a given *lexical concept co-occurs, or in which it can be embedded. Formal selectional tendencies contrast with *semantic selectional tendencies.

Frame A coherent body of *conceptual content that makes up a *cognitive model. Frames exhibit organization in terms of *attribute-value sets and *structural invariants.

Fully internally open lexical concept   A type of *internally open lexical concept which is wholly comprised of *phonetically implicit vehicles.

Functional category   A salient humanly relevant consequence of acting and interacting in the spatio-physical environment, which leads to the emergence of a new *lexical concept by virtue of *pragmatic strengthening.

Functionally detached   A property of a *cognitive model that exhibits *transcendence. A functionally detached cognitive model is one that becomes abstracted from the context of which it is part. This gives rise to a decontextualized representation.

Fusion   One of the two processes of *semantic composition central to *LCCM Theory, the other being *selection. Fusion works on the output of selection and is the mechanism whereby lexical concepts are integrated. Fusion consists of two constituent processes: *lexical concept integration and *interpretation.

Fusion operation   The two constituent processes of *fusion: *lexical concept integration and *interpretation.

Generic situations   A type of *cognitive model in which a mental representation is established for a type of situation that is actually experienced. Hence, an episodic situation is abstracted from across commonalities found in *episodic situations, with which it contrasts.

Global constraints   One of two *constraints that relate to *attribute-value sets. Global constraints constrain attribute values globally. This means that a modification in one value entails a proportional modification in a related value.

Goal factors   One of two *factors that relate to *attribute-value sets. Concerns the way in which an agent's goal(s) influences the interaction between values associated with related attributes within a frame.

Grounded cognition   See *embodied cognition.

Highlighting   Activation that takes place within a single *cognitive model. This can involve activation of specific *attribute-value sets and/or *structural invariants.

Images   A conceptual representation that is a component of *situations. There are four characteristic features of images. They are made up of a set of discrete perceptual features, they can represent *individuals and/or *types, they do so in a static spatial configuration, which is viewed from a particular perspective.

Imminence   The degree to which an event is "located" in the future with respect to the experiencer in an experiencer-based *temporal frame of reference.

Individuals   A type of frame that relates to animate and inanimate entities that are held to persist continuously in a given environment, whether real or imagined. Individuals provide relatively stable information about a given entity: information that is both stable over time, as well as incorporating episodic information.

Informational characterization   The *simulation associated with a linguistic unit such as a *conceptual lexical unit or an *utterance following *interpretation. An *utterance-level informational characterization is known as a *conception.

Integration   See *Lexical concept integration.

Internal lexical concept integration   The type of lexical concept integration that applies to internally open lexical concepts.

Internally closed lexical concept   A lexical concept which doesn't have "slots" that can be "filled in" by other lexical concepts. An internally closed lexical concept is associated with a *phonetically overt vehicle.

Internally complex lexical concept   A lexical concept made up of simpler constituent lexical concepts. A *lexical concept of this kind contrasts with an *internally simple lexical concept.

Internally open lexical concept   A schematic lexical concept which has "slots" that can be "filled in" by less schematic lexical concepts. Internally open lexical concepts are associated with *phonetically implicit vehicles. This contrasts with an *internally closed lexical concept.

Internally simple lexical concept   A lexical concept that is not made up of simpler constituent lexical concepts. A *lexical concept of this kind contrasts with an *internally complex lexical concept.

Interpretation   One of the two constituent processes of *fusion. Interpretation involves the *access to and *activation of *conceptual content associated with the access sites of *open-class lexical concepts. Interpretation takes place once *lexical concept integration has occurred, and involves a process of *matching that takes place between two or more distinct cognitive model profiles or informational characterizations. Interpretation is constrained by the operation of a number of principles. These include: *Principle of guided matching, *Principle of conceptual coherence, *Principle of schematic salience in matching, *Principle of simultaneous matching, *Principle of primary activation, *Principle of ordered search, *Principle of secondary activation, *Principle of context-induced clash resolution, and *Principle of conceptual metaphor matching.

Joint activities   A culturally recognized activity engaged in by two or more participants, in order to achieve some mutually understood goal. Language use arises in joint activities, which are typically impossible without language.

LCCM Theory   The Theory of Lexical Concepts and Cognitive Models (LCCM), which takes its name from the two theoretical constructs at the heart of the theory: the *lexical concept and *cognitive model.

Lexical concept   A bundle of various types of schematic knowledge conventionally associated with a unique *phonological vehicle in a *symbolic unit. Lexical concepts are stored in the *linguistic system and can facilitate *access to *conceptual structure. There are two types of lexical concept: the *open-class lexical concept and the *closed-class lexical concept.

Lexical concept integration   One of the two constituent processes of *fusion. Lexical concept integration involves the integration of linguistic content associated with the lexical concepts which are subject to integration. This is achieved by the linguistic content encoded by the lexical concepts involved undergoing an operation termed *unpacking. Lexical concept integration is constrained by the operation of three principles: *Principle of linguistic coherence, *Principle of schematic coherence, and *Principle of ordered integration in internally open lexical concepts.

Lexical concept potential   The range of lexical concepts conventionally associated with a given *phonological vehicle.

Lexical concept selection   The first of the two processes of *semantic composition central to *LCCM Theory, the other being *fusion. Selection is the process whereby the most appropriate lexical concepts are associated with the phonological vehicles which populate a given *utterance. There are two main types of selection: *broad selection and *narrow selection.

Lexical conceptual unit   An integrated unit of *linguistic content which is the result of *lexical concept integration.

Lexical profile   The selectional tendencies which form part of the linguistic content encoded by a lexical concept, and which is unique to any given lexical concept. Two distinct types of selectional tendencies are distinguished: *semantic selectional tendencies and *formal selectional tendencies.

Lexical representation   The primary substrate in linguistically mediated meaning construction. Lexical representation is made up of *symbolic units and *cognitive models.

Linguistic content   Knowledge which is represented in the linguistic system. Knowledge of this kind is highly schematic in nature (cf. *conceptual content), and is encoded as a bundle of distinct types of schematic knowledge referred to as a *lexical concept.

Linguistic system   The repository of lexical concepts—units of *semantic structure—specific to a given language. A language user may have knowledge of more than one language or linguistic variety, and hence can be said to possess more than one linguistic system.

Literal conception   The type of *conception that arises when there is no *clash in the primary cognitive models of the *default search region during *interpretation. A literal conception contrasts with a *figurative conception.

Local constraints   One of two *constraints that relate to *attribute-value sets. Local constraints constrain attribute values locally. That is, the presence of a given value entails the presence of a related value, while the absence of one entails the absence of another.

Match The end result of successful *interpretation. A match is achieved when one or more cognitive models in two or more cognitive model profiles receive *primary activation.

Matching The process whereby *search regions are established in *cognitive model profiles subject to *interpretation. Matching attempts to establish conceptual coherence between two (or more) cognitive models which belong to separate cognitive model profiles.

Metaphor A type of *figurative conception in which the *figurative target and *figurative vehicle do not exhibit *alignment in *clash resolution.

Metonymy A type of *figurative conception in which the *figurative target and *figurative vehicle do exhibit *alignment in *clash resolution.

Multiple instance multiple selection A type of *multiple selection. Arises when a single *vehicle occurs or is implicated multiple times in a single *utterance giving rise to distinct lexical concepts on each instance of use.

Multiple selection The *selection of more than one *lexical concept for a single *vehicle. There are two types of multiple selection: *single instance multiple selection and *multiple instance multiple selection.

Narrow selection Concerns *selection within a *lexical concept. This is achieved by selecting from among the *parameters encoded by a given lexical concept.

Nominal lexical concept A lexical concept which relates to an entity which is independently identifiable, and hence independent of any relation in which it stands. This contrasts with a *relational lexical concept.

Non-restricted selectional tendencies The lack of a specification of narrow restrictions which otherwise impose severe limits on the nature of the *selectional tendencies encoded by a lexical concept. This contrasts with *restricted selectional tendencies.

Occurrence The degree to which an event is "located" in the past with respect to the experiencer with respect to an *event-based temporal frame of reference.

Open-class lexical concept That subset of lexical concepts that are conventionally paired with an *open-class vehicle. Lexical concepts of this kind, in addition to encoding *linguistic content, additionally facilitate access to *conceptual structure.

Parameter One aspect of the bundle of *linguistic content encoded by a *lexical concept. A parameter represents a highly schematic compression across rich multi-modal brain states for purposes of direct representation in language.

Parameterization The phenomenon whereby a multimodal brain state is encoded as a *parameter for purposes of encoding in a form amenable to representation in the *linguistic system.

Perceptual moment   A neurobiologically instantiated temporal processing interval with an outer limit of about three seconds. This three-second range may correspond to our experience of the present.

Perspectivization   The type of *matching that takes place with respect to the *cognitive model profile accessed by a *nominal lexical concept. This contrasts with *adjustment.

Phonetic potential   The property associated with a *phonetically implicit vehicle. Such vehicles encode schematic phonetic potential such that they can be lexically filled by vehicles that correspond to their schematic phonetic potential.

Phonetically implicit vehicle   A *phonological vehicle that is not lexically filled and hence exhibits *phonetic potential. This contrasts with a *phonetically overt vehicle.

Phonetically overt vehicle   A *phonological vehicle that is lexically filled and hence does not exhibit *phonetic potential. This contrasts with a *phonetically implicit vehicle.

Phonological vehicle   The formal component of a *symbolic unit, and conventionally paired with a lexical concept. Phonological vehicles can be of two kinds: a *phonetically overt vehicle, or a *phonetically implicit vehicle.

Polysemy   See *conceptual polysemy.

Pragmatic point   The schematic aspects of extra-linguistic dimensions that are encoded as *linguistic content by a given *lexical concept. Pragmatic point relates to two extra-linguistic dimensions: (i) schematic aspects of the contexts of use in which a given lexical concept is conventionally employed, including settings and participants, and (ii) some aspects of the communicative purpose for which a lexical concept is employed.

Pragmatic strengthening   The process whereby an invited inference that emerges in a *bridging context is reanalysed as a distinct *lexical concept such that *vehicle A comes to have a distinct lexical concept B associated with it in addition to the extant lexical concept A.

Predicative function   The communicative function of *metaphor, namely to say something about the subject or theme of an utterance.

Primary access   The establishment of a *search region in the *primary cognitive model profile of an *open-class lexical concept, which is to say in the *default search region. This contrasts with *secondary access.

Primary activation   Activation of one or more cognitive models in the *primary cognitive model profile of an *open-class lexical concept. This contrasts with *secondary activation.

Primary cognitive model   A *cognitive model that is included in the *access site of an *open-class lexical concept. This contrasts with *secondary cognitive model.

Primary cognitive model profile   The set of cognitive models included in the *access site of an *open-class lexical concept and hence, the set to which the lexical concept facilitates direct *access. This contrasts with *secondary cognitive model profile.

Principle of conceptual coherence (p5)   One of the principles that constrain *interpretation. This holds that *matching occurs between one or more cognitive models/informational characterizations, belonging to distinct cognitive model profiles/lexical conceptual units, which share schematic coherence in terms of *conceptual content.

Principle of conceptual metaphor matching (p12)   One of the principles that constrains *interpretation. This holds that conceptual metaphors are subject to *matching in the *primary cognitive model profile(s) of relevant lexical concepts.

Principle of context induced clash resolution (p11)   One of the principles that constrain *interpretation. This holds that in cases where *clash resolution is required, the *lexical concept whose *secondary cognitive model profile is searched to resolve the *clash is determined by context. This is achieved by establishing a *figurative target and a *figurative vehicle, on the basis of context. The lexical concept that is established as the figurative vehicle is subject to clash resolution.

Principle of guided matching (p4)   One of the principles that constrain *interpretation. This holds that the *matching of cognitive models in interpretation proceeds in a way that is compatible with the output of *lexical concept integration.

Principle of linguistic coherence (p1)   One of the principles that govern *lexical concept integration. This states that a *lexical concept that is internally open may only be integrated with a lexical concept with which it shares schematic coherence in terms of *linguistic content.

Principle of ordered integration in internally open lexical concepts (p3)   One of the principles that govern *lexical concept integration. This holds that lexical concept integration takes place by applying to internally simpler lexical concepts before applying to internally more complex lexical concepts.

Principle of ordered search (p9)   A principle that constrains *interpretation. This holds that *matching takes place in the *default search region for that subset of lexical concepts that facilitate *access to a *cognitive model profile. If matching is unsuccessful in the default search region, a new search region is established in the *secondary cognitive model profile. The search proceeds in an ordered fashion, proceeding on the basis of secondary cognitive models that are conceptually more coherent with respect to the primary cognitive models prior to searching cognitive models that exhibit successively less conceptual coherence.

Principle of primary activation (p8)   One of the principles that constrain *interpretation. This holds that matched cognitive model(s) are subject to *primary activation.

Principle of schematic coherence (p2)   A principle that governs both *lexical concept integration and *interpretation. This states that the content associated with entities, participants, and the relations holding between them must exhibit coherence in *fusion operations.

Principle of schematic salience in matching (p6)   A principle associated with *interpretation. This states that *matching across cognitive model profiles/informational characterizations achieves greater schematic salience when relatively more cognitive models are matched than matches involving fewer cognitive models.

Principle of secondary activation (p10)   One of the constraining principles of *interpretation. This states that all primary cognitive models, and all secondary cognitive models on the *access route which do not achieve *primary activation, achieve *secondary activation.

Principle of simultaneous matching (p7)   One of the principles that constrain *interpretation. This states that when *matching takes place between an *informational characterization and an *internally complex lexical concept, matching may occur simultaneously across cognitive model profiles of the lexical concepts that form part of the complex lexical concept.

Prospective relation   The schematic temporal relation encoded by an *event-based temporal frame of reference lexical concept. A prospective relation is one in which one temporal event is sequenced earlier than another, such that the reference point is the earlier temporal event.

Protracted duration   The phenomenologically real experience whereby subjects perceive standard units of duration as being of greater magnitude: the perception that time is proceeding more "slowly" than usual and hence there is "more" of it. This results in an overestimation of temporal magnitude, and contrasts with *temporal compression.

Referential function   The communicative function of *metonymy, in which the *figurative vehicle serves to identify the *figurative target by virtue of *alignment of the figurative vehicle and target.

Relational lexical concept   A *lexical concept which concerns a relation, and which is not identifiable independently of the entities that it relates. This contrasts with a *nominal lexical concept.

Restricted selectional tendencies   The specification of restrictions of some kind which impose relatively severe limits with respect to the nature of the *selectional tendencies encoded by a lexical concept. This contrasts with *non-restricted selection tendencies.

Retrospective relation   The schematic temporal relation encoded by an *event-based temporal frame of reference lexical concept. A retrospective relation is one in which one temporal event is sequenced later than another, such that the reference point is the later temporal event.

Search region   The region of a cognitive model profile in which *matching takes place. A specific type of search region is the *default search region.

Secondary access   The establishment of a *search region in the *secondary cognitive model profile of an *open-class lexical concept. This contrasts with *primary access.

Secondary activation   Activation of one or more cognitive models in the *secondary cognitive model profile of an *open-class lexical concept. This contrasts with *primary activation.

Secondary cognitive model   A *cognitive model that is not included in the *access site of an *open-class lexical concept, but which is connected to a *cognitive model that is in the *access site via *chaining. This contrasts with a *primary cognitive model.

Secondary cognitive model profile   The set of cognitive models not included in the *access site of an *open-class lexical concept, but which are connected to those that are via *chaining. Hence, these *secondary cognitive models are not subject to direct *access by the *lexical concept. This contrasts with the *primary cognitive model profile.

Selection   See *Lexical concept selection.

Selection revision   A type of *selection. The revision of which *lexical concept is selected for a given *vehicle during ongoing *semantic composition.

Selectional tendencies   Usage patterns conventionally associated with a lexical concept and hence stored as part of the linguistic content encoded by a lexical concept. The stored selectional tendencies are referred to as a *lexical profile. Two types of selectional tendencies can be distinguished: *semantic selectional tendencies and *formal selectional tendencies.

Selective activation   The distinction between *primary activation and *secondary activation. During *activation one or more cognitive models are selected for primary activation at the expense of others, an outcome of *matching.

Semantic composition   The process of meaning construction whereby an *utterance-level *simulation, a *conception, is constructed by virtue of interaction between the *linguistic system and the *conceptual system during linguistically mediated communication. Semantic composition arises by virtue of two compositional processes: *selection and *fusion.

Semantic potential   The entire set of cognitive models to which an *open-class lexical concept potentially facilitates *access. This includes both primary cognitive models and secondary cognitive models. A lexical concept's semantic potential is modelled, in *LCCM Theory, in terms of the construct of the *cognitive model profile.

Semantic representation   The semantic dimension of *lexical representation. This involves an interaction between *cognitive models and *lexical concepts.

Semantic selectional tendencies   Concerns the (range of) lexical concepts with which a lexical concept co-occurs and in which it can be embedded. Semantic selectional tendencies contrast with *formal selectional tendencies.

Semantic structure   Schematic dimensions of *semantic representation which are directly encoded in language. Semantic structure is modelled, in *LCCM Theory, in terms of the construct of the *lexical concept.

Semantic value   The value associated with a *lexical concept once it has undergone *lexical concept integration and prior to *interpretation.

Semanticality   The property associated with a *conception; informally, this can be thought of as the semantic well-formedness of an *utterance, and relates to its success in communicating a specific intention given a particular context.

Semanticality failure   The failure of a *conception to emerge, due to a failure in *matching.

Simulation   A general-purpose computation performed by the brain which reactivates multimodal brain states. Such brain states include those relating to diverse experience types including sensory-motor experience, proprioceptive experience, and subjective experience. Simulations arise during language understanding, due to the interaction between representations in the *linguistic system and *conceptual system.

Simulator   A *cognitive model, which is constituted by one or more frames, which are subject to *simulation.

Single instance multiple selection   A type of *multiple selection. Arises when there is a single instance of a *vehicle which selects more than one *lexical concept.

Situational representation   Part of the representation that participants maintain in service of *discourse representation. The situational representation comprises the participants, the time, venue, and physical environment, the referents of the linguistic expressions deployed, and the social commitments implied by the participants' utterances, in carrying out a *joint activity. In addition, participants also maintain a *textual representation.

Spatial scene   A scene involving a spatial relation holding between a figure, a reference object, and, optionally, a secondary reference object encoded via language.

Structural invariant   A type of concept, along with *attribute-value sets, that makes up a *frame. A structural invariant is a relational knowledge structure that holds between distinct attribute-value sets.

Symbolic unit   A conventional assembly involving a *phonological vehicle and a semantic unit. The semantic unit is modelled, in *LCCM Theory, in terms of the construct of the *lexical concept.

Temporal compression   The phenomenologically real experience whereby subjects perceive standard units of duration as being of lesser magnitude: the perception that time is proceeding more "quickly" than usual and hence there is "less" of it. This results in an underestimation of temporal magnitude, and contrasts with *protracted duration.

Temporal frame of reference (TFoR)   Akin to spatial frames of reference, TFoRs are complex symbolic units, involving a *vehicle and an internally open *closed-class lexical concept. The TFoR lexical concept serves to encode highly schematic aspects of temporal reference.

Textual representation   Part of the representation that participants maintain in the service of *discourse representation. During a *joint activity, participants keep track of all the utterances issued and other signals, such as accompanying gestures, prosody, and so on. This constitutes the textual representation. In addition, participants maintain a *situational representation.

Transcendence   Concerns the number and range of locations at which and when *individuals, *types, *episodic situations, and *generic situations are represented in our mental representation of the world. The greater the number and range of locations, the more transcendent the *cognitive model in question. Transcendence can lead to a cognitive model becoming *functionally detached.

Types   A kind of *cognitive model. Types are mental representations based on abstracting across particular *individuals in order to leave points of similarity. A type is thus a generic representation based on a set of related individuals.

Unpacking   The process, central to *lexical concept integration, whereby linguistic content encoded by lexical concepts in an utterance is integrated in the way constrained by the three principles of integration.

Utterance   A somewhat discrete entity that has unit-like status in that it represents the expression of a single coherent idea, making (at least partial) use of the norms and conventions of linguistic behaviour in a particular linguistic community. An utterance represents a specific, contextualized, and unique instance of language use, performed by a language user in service of signalling a particular communicative intention. Hence, an utterance constitutes a discrete usage event.

Value   See *Attribute-value sets.

Vehicle   See *Phonological vehicle.

References

Aitchison, Jean. (1996). *Words in the Mind.* Oxford: Blackwell.

Allport, D. A. (1985). Distributed memory, modular subsystems and dysphasia. In S. K. Newman and R. Epstein (eds), *Current Perspectives in Dysphasia*, 207–44. Edinburgh: Churchill Livingstone.

Allwood, Jens. (2003). Meaning potentials and context: Some consequences for the analysis of variation in meaning. In H. Cuyckens, R. Dirven, and J. Taylor (eds), *Cognitive Approaches to Lexical Semantics*, 29–66. Berlin: Mouton de Gruyter.

Alverson, Hoyt. (1994). *Semantics and Experience: Universal Metaphors for Time in English, Mandarin, Hindi and Sesotho.* Baltimore, MA: Johns Hopkins University Press.

Atkins, B. T. S. (1987). Semantic-ID tags: corpus evidence for dictionary senses. In *The Uses of Large Text Databases: Proceedings of the Third Annual Conference of the New OED Centre*, 17–36. Canada: University of Waterloo.

Bach, Kent. (1997). The semantics-pragmatics distinction: What it is and why it matters. *Linguistiche Berichte* 8, Special Issue on Pragmatics, 33–50.

Baddeley, Alan D. (1966). Time estimation at reduced body temperature. *American Journal of Psychology*, 79 (3): 475–9.

Barcelona, Antonio. (2000). *Metaphor and Metonymy at the Crossroads.* Berlin: Mouton de Gruyter.

Barsalou, Lawrence. (1991). Deriving categories to achieve goals. In G. H. Bower (ed.), *The Psychology of Learning and Motivation: Advances in Research and Theory*, vol. 27, 1–64. San Diego, CA: Academic Press.

—— (1992a). Frames, concepts, and conceptual fields. In A. Lehrer and E. F. Kittay (eds), *Frames, Fields, and Contrasts: New Essays in Lexical and Semantic Organization*, 21–74. Hillsdale, NJ: Lawrence Erlbaum.

—— (1992b). *Cognitive Psychology: An Overview for Cognitive Scientists.* Hillsdale, NJ: Lawrence Erlbaum.

—— (1999). Perceptual symbol systems. *Behavioral and Brain Sciences*, 22: 577–660.

—— (2003). Situated simulation in the human conceptual system. *Language and Cognitive Processes*, 18: 513–62.

—— (2005). Continuity of the conceptual system across species. *Trends in Cognitive Sciences*, 9: 309–11.

—— (2008). Grounded cognition. *Annual Review of Psychology*, 59: 617–45.

—— and Billman, Dorrit. (1989). Systematicity and semantic ambiguity. In D. Gorfein (ed.), *Resolving Semantic Ambiguity*, 146–203. New York: Springer-Verlag.

—— Santos, Ava, Simmons, Kyle, and Wilson, C. D. (forthcoming). Language and simulation in conceptual processing. In M. De Vega, A. Glenberg, and A. Graesser (eds), *Symbols, Embodiment, and Meaning*. Oxford: Oxford University Press.

Barsalou, Lawrence. and Wiemer-Hastings, Katja. (2005). Situating abstract concepts. In D. Pecher and R. Zwaan (eds), *Grounding Cognition: The Role of Perception and Action in Memory, Language, and Thought*, 129–63. New York: Cambridge University Press.

—— Yeh, Wenchi, Luka, Barbara, Olseth, Karen, Mix Kelly, and Wu, Ling-Ling. (1993). Concepts and meaning. In K. Beals, G. Cooke, D. Kathman, K. E. McCullough, S. Kita, and D. Testen (eds), *Chicago Linguistics Society 9: Papers from the Parasessions on Conceptual Representations*, vol. 2, 23–61. Chicago Linguistics Society.

Bender, Andrea, Bennardo, Giovanni, and Beller, Sieghard. (2005). Spatial frames of reference for temporal relations: A conceptual analysis in English, German, and Tongan. In B. G. Bara, L. Barsalou, and M. Bucciarelli (eds), *Proceedings of the Twenty-Seventh Annual Conference of the Cognitive Science Society*, 220–5. Mahwah, NJ: Lawrence Erlbaum.

Bennett, David. (1975). *Spatial and Temporal Uses of English Prepositions*. London: Longman.

Bergen, Benjamin K. and Chang, Nancy. (2005). Embodied construction grammar in simulation-based language understanding. In J.-O. Östman and M. Fried (eds), *Construction Grammars: Cognitive Grounding and Theoretical Extensions*, 147–90. Amsterdam: John Benjamins.

—— Polley, Carl, and Wheeler, Kathryn. (forthcoming). Language and inner space. In V. Evans and P. Chilton (eds), *Language, Cognition and Space: The State of the Art and New Directions*. London: Equinox Publishing.

Boroditsky, Lera. (2000). Metaphoric structuring: Understanding time through spatial metaphors. *Cognition*, 75 (1): 1–28.

—— (2001). Does language shape thought? Mandarin and English speakers' conceptions of time. *Cognitive Psychology*, 43: 1–22.

—— and Prinz, Jesse. (forthcoming). What thoughts are made of. In G. Semin and E. Smith (eds), *Embodied Grounding: Social, Cognitive, Affective, and Neuroscientific Approaches*. Cambridge: Cambridge University Press.

Bowdle, Brian and Gentner, Dedre. (2005). The career of metaphor. *Psychological Review*, 112: 193–216.

Bowerman, Melissa and Choi, Soonja. (2003). Space under construction: Language-specific spatial categorization in first language acquisition. In D. Gentner and S. Goldin-Meadow (eds), *Language in Mind: Advances in the Study of Language and Thought*, 387–428. Cambridge, MA: MIT Press.

Brenier, Jason M. and Michaelis, Laura A. (2005). Optimization via syntactic amalgam: Syntax-prosody mismatch and copula doubling. *Corpus Linguistics and Linguistic Theory*, 1: 45–88.

Brugman, Claudia. (1988). *The Story of "over": Polysemy, Semantics and the Structure of the Lexicon*. New York: Garland.

—— and Lakoff, George. (1988). Cognitive topology and lexical networks. In S. Small, G. Cottrell, and M. Tannenhaus (eds), *Lexical Ambiguity Resolution*, 477–507. San Mateo, CA: Morgan Kaufman.

Burling, Robbins. (2007). *The Naked Ape: How Language Evolved*. Oxford: Oxford University Press.

Cann, Ronnie (1993). *Formal Semantics*. Cambridge: Cambridge University Press.

Carston, Robyn. (2002). *Thoughts and Utterances: The Pragmatics of Explicit Communication*. Oxford: Blackwell.

Casasanto, Daniel. (forthcoming). Space for thinking. In V. Evans and P. Chilton (eds), *Language, Cognition and Space: The State of the Art and New Directions*. London: Equinox Publishing.

—— and Boroditsky, Lera. (2008). Time in the mind: Using space to think about time. *Cognition*, 106: 579–93.

Chafe, Wallace. (1994). *Discourse, Consciousness, and Time: The Flow and Displacement of Conscious Experience in Speaking and Writing*. Chicago: University of Chicago Press.

Choi, Soonja and Bowerman, Melissa. (1991). Learning to express motion events in English and Korean: The influence of language-specific lexicalization patterns. *Cognition*, 41: 83–121.

Chomsky, Noam. (1957). *Syntactic Structures*. The Hague: Mouton.

—— (1965). *Aspects of the Theory of Syntax*. Cambridge, MA: MIT Press.

—— (1981). *Lectures on Government and Binding*. Dordrecht: Foris.

—— (1991). Some notes on economy of derivation and representation. In R. Freidin (ed.), *Principles and Parameters in Comparative Grammar*, 417–54. Cambridge, MA: MIT Press.

—— (1995). *The Minimalist Program*. Cambridge, MA: MIT Press.

Christiansen, Morten H. and Kirby, Simon. (2003). *Language Evolution*. Oxford: Oxford University Press.

Clark, Andy. (1998). *Being There: Putting Brain, Body and World Together Again*. Cambridge, MA: MIT Press.

Clark, Herbert. (1973). Space, time, semantics, and the child. In T. Moore (ed.), *Cognitive Development and the Acquisition of Language*, 27–63. New York: Academic Press.

—— (1983). Making sense of nonce sense. In G. Flores D'Arcais and R. J. Jarvella (eds), *The Process of Language Understanding*, 297–332. Chichester: John Wiley.

—— (1996). *Using Language*. Cambridge: Cambridge University Press.

Corballis, Michael. (2003). *From Hand to Mouth: The Origins of Language*. Princeton: Princeton University Press.

Coulson, Seana. (2000). *Semantic Leaps*. Cambridge: Cambridge University Press.

Coventry, Kenny and Garrod, Simon. (2004). *Saying, Seeing and Acting: The Psychological Semantics of Spatial Prepositions*. Hove: Psychology Press.

Croft, William. (1993). The role of domains in the interpretation of metaphors and metonymies. *Cognitive Linguistics*, 4: 335–70.

—— (1998). Mental representations. *Cognitive Linguistics*, 9 (2): 151–74.

—— (2000). *Explaining Language Change: An Evolutionary Approach*. London: Longman.

—— (2002). *Radical Construction Grammar: Syntactic Theory in Typological Perspective*. Oxford: Oxford University Press.

—— (2007). The origins of grammar in the verbalization of experience. *Cognitive Linguistics*, 18 (3): 339–82.

Croft, William and Cruse, D. Alan. (2004). *Cognitive Linguistics*. Cambridge: Cambridge University Press.

Cruse, D. Alan. (2002). Aspects of the micro-structure of word meanings. In Y. Ravin and C. Leacock (eds), *Polysemy: Theoretical and Computational Approaches*, 30–51. Oxford: Oxford University Press.

Cuyckens, Hubert, Dirven, René, and Taylor, John (2003). *Cognitive Approaches to Lexical Semantics*. Berlin: Mouton de Gruyter.

—— Sandra, Dominiek, and Rice, Sally. (1997). Towards an empirical lexical semantics. In B. Smieja and M. Tasch (eds), *Human Contact through Language and Linguistics*, 35–54. Frankfurt: Peter Lang.

Dąbrowska, Ewa. (2009). Words as constructions. In V. Evans and S. Pourcel (eds), *New Directions in Cognitive Linguistics*, 201–24. Amsterdam: John Benjamins.

Damasio, Antonio. (1989). Time-locked multiregional retroactivation: A systems-level proposal for the neural substrates of recall and recognition. *Cognition*, 33: 25–62.

—— (1994). *Descartes' Error: Emotion, Reason and the Human Brain*. London: Vintage.

Dancygier, Barbara and Sweetser, Eve. (2005). *Mental Spaces in Grammar: Conditional Constructions*. Cambridge: Cambridge University Press.

Davies, Paul. (2006). *About Time: Einstein's Unfinished Revolution*. London: Penguin.

Deacon, Terrence. (1997). *The Symbolic Species: The Co-evolution of Language and the Brain*. New York, NY: W. W. Norton and Co.

Deane, Paul. (2005). Multimodal spatial representation: On the semantic unity of "over." In B. Hampe (ed.), *From Perception to Meaning: Image Schemas in Cognitive Linguistics*, 235–82. Berlin: Mouton de Gruyter.

Dijk, Teun van and Kintsch, Walter. (1983). *Strategies of Discourse Comprehension*. New York, NY: Academic Press.

Donald, Merlin. (1991). *Origins of the Modern Mind: Three Stages in the Evolution of Culture and Cognition*. Harvard: Harvard University Press.

Dunbar, Robin. (1996). *Grooming, Gossip and the Evolution of Language*. London: Faber & Faber.

Engberg-Pederson, Elisabeth. (1993). *Space in Danish Sign Language: The Meaning and Morphosyntactic Use of Space in a Visual Language*. Hamburg: Signum-Verlag.

Evans, Nicholas and Wilkins, David. (2000). In the mind's ear: The semantic extensions of perception verbs in Australian languages. *Language*, 76 (3): 546–92.

Evans, Vyvyan. (2004a). *The Structure of Time: Language, Meaning and Cognition*. Amsterdam: John Benjamins.

—— (2004b). How we conceptualise time. *Essays in Arts and Sciences*, 33 (2): 13–44.

—— (2005). The meaning of "time": Polysemy, the lexicon and conceptual structure. *Journal of Linguistics*, 41 (1): 33–75.

—— (2006). Lexical concepts, cognitive models and meaning-construction. *Cognitive Linguistics* 17 (4): 491–534.

—— (forthcoming a). From the spatial to the non-spatial: The "state" lexical concepts of *in*, *on* and *at*. In V. Evans and P. Chilton (eds), *Language*,

Cognition and Space: The State of the Art and New Directions. London: Equinox Publishing.

Evans, Vyvyan. (forthcoming *b*). The perceptual basis of spatial representation. In V. Evans and P. Chilton (eds), *Language, Cognition and Space: The State of the Art and New Directions.* London: Equinox Publishing.

—— and Chilton, Paul (eds). (forthcoming). *Language, Cognition and Space: The State of the Art and New Directions.* London: Equinox Publishing.

—— and Green, Melanie. (2006). *Cognitive Linguistics: An Introduction.* Edinburgh: Edinburgh University Press.

—— and Tyler, Andrea. (2004). Rethinking English "prepositions of movement": The case of *to* and *through*. In H. Cuyckens, W. De Mulder, and T. Mortelmans (eds), *Adpositions of Movement. Belgian Journal of Linguistics,* 18: 245–70. Amsterdam: John Benjamins.

Fauconnier, Gilles. (1994). *Mental Spaces.* Cambridge: Cambridge University Press.

—— (1997). *Mappings in Thought and Language.* Cambridge: Cambridge University Press.

—— and Turner, Mark. (1998). Conceptual integration networks. *Cognitive Science,* 22 (2): 33–187.

—— —— (2002). *The Way we Think: Conceptual Blending and the Mind's Hidden Complexities.* New York: Basic Books.

—— —— (2008). Rethinking metaphor. In R. W. Gibbs (ed.), *The Cambridge Handbook of Metaphor and Thought.* Cambridge: Cambridge University Press.

Feist, Michele. (forthcoming). Inside *in* and *on*: Typological and psycholinguistic perspectives. In V. Evans and P. Chilton (eds), *Language, Cognition and Space: The State of the Art and New Directions.* London: Equinox Publishing.

Feldman, Jerome. (2006). *From Molecule to Metaphor: A Neural Theory of Language.* Cambridge, MA: MIT Press.

—— and Narayanan, Srini. (2004). Embodied meaning in a neural theory of language. *Brain and Language,* 89: 385–92.

Fillmore, Charles. (1975). An alternative to checklist theories of meaning. *Proceedings of the First Annual Meeting of the Berkeley Linguistics Society,* 123–31.

—— (1982). Frame semantics. In *Linguistics in the Morning Calm,* 111–37. Seoul: Hanshin Publishing Company.

—— (1985). Frames and the semantics of understanding. *Quaderni di Semantica,* 6: 222–54.

—— (1997). *Lectures on Deixis.* Stanford: CA: CSLI.

—— Kay, Paul, and O'Connor, Mary Catherine. (1988). Regularity and idiomaticity in grammatical constructions: The case of *let alone. Language,* 64: 501–38.

Finke, Ronald A. (1989). *Principles of Mental Imagery.* Cambridge, MA: MIT Press.

Flaherty, Michael. (1999). *A Watched Pot: How We Experience Time.* New York, NY: New York University Press.

Fleischman, Suzanne. (1982). The past and the future: Are they coming or going? *Berkeley Linguistics Society,* 8: 322–34.

Fodor, Jerry A. (1983). *The Modularity of Mind.* Cambridge, MA: MIT Press.

Fraisse, Paul. (1963). *The Psychology of Time.* New York: Harper and Row.

Gainotti, Guido, Silveri, Maria Caterina, Daniele, Antonio, and Giustolisi, Laura. (1995). Neuroanatomical correlates of category-specific semantic disorders: A critical survey. *Memory,* 3: 247–64.

Gallagher, Shaun. (2006). *How the Body Shapes the Mind.* Oxford: Oxford University Press.

Gallese, Vittorio and Lakoff, George. (2005). The brain's concepts: The role of the sensory-motor system in reason and language. *Cognitive Neuropsychology,* 22: 455–79.

Garner, W. R. (1978). Selective attention to attributes and to stimuli. *Journal of Experimental Psychology: General,* 107 (3): 287–308.

Geeraerts, Dirk. (1994). *Diachronic Prototype Semantics.* Oxford: Oxford University Press.

Gentner, Dedre. (1982). Why nouns are learned before verbs: Linguistic relativity versus natural partitioning. In S. A. Kuczaj (ed.), *Language Development: Vol. 2. Language, Thought and Culture,* 301–34. Hillsdale, NJ: Lawrence Erlbaum.

—— (1988). Metaphor as structure mapping: The relational shift. *Child Development,* 59: 47–59.

—— and Boroditsky, Lera. (2001). Individuation, relational relativity and early word learning. In M. Bowerman and S. Levinson (eds), *Language Acquisition and Conceptual Development,* 215–56. Cambridge: Cambridge University Press.

—— Bowdle, Brian, Wolff, Phillip, and Boronat, Consuelo. (2001). Metaphor is like analogy. In D. Gentner, K. J. Holyoak, and B. N. Kokinov (eds), *The Analogical Mind: Perspectives from Cognitive Science,* 199–253. Cambridge, MA: MIT Press.

—— and Goldin-Meadow, Susan. (2003). *Language in Mind: Advances in the Study of Language and Thought.* Cambridge, MA: MIT Press.

—— Imai, Mutsumi, and Boroditsky, Lera. (2002). As time goes by: Evidence for two systems in processing space time metaphors. *Language and Cognitive Processes,* 17 (5): 537–65.

Gibbs, Raymond W. (1994). *The Poetics of Mind.* Cambridge: Cambridge University Press.

—— (2006). *Embodiment and Cognitive Science.* Cambridge: Cambridge University Press.

Giora, Rachel. (1997). Understanding figurative and literal language: The graded salience hypothesis. *Cognitive Linguistics,* 8 (3): 183–206.

—— (2003). *On our Mind: Salience, Context, and Figurative Language.* New York: Oxford University Press.

Glenberg, Arthur. (1997). What memory is for. *Behavioral and Brain Sciences,* 20: 1–55.

—— and Kaschak, Michael. (2002). Grounding language in action. *Psychonomic Bulletin and Review,* 9: 558–65.

Glucksberg, Sam. (2001). *Understanding Figurative Language.* New York: Oxford University Press.

—— (2003). The psycholinguistics of metaphor. *Trends in Cognitive Science,* 7: 92–6.

—— and Keysar, Boaz. (1990). Understanding metaphorical comparisons: Beyond similarity. *Psychological Review,* 97: 3–18.

Goffman, Erving. (1981). *Forms of Talk*. Philadelphia: University of Pennsylvania Press.

Goldberg, Adele. (1995). *Constructions. A Construction Grammar Approach to Argument Structure*. Chicago: University of Chicago Press.

—— (2006). *Constructions at Work: The Nature of Generalization in Language*. Oxford: Oxford University Press.

Gonzalez-Marquez, Monica, Mittelberg, Irene, Coulson, Seana, and Spivey, Michael J. (2007). *Methods in Cognitive Linguistics*. Amsterdam: John Benjamins.

Grady, Joseph E. (1997). Foundations of meaning: Primary metaphors and primary scenes. Unpublished doctoral thesis, Linguistics Dept., UC Berkeley.

—— (2005). Primary metaphors as inputs to conceptual integration. *Journal of Pragmatics*, 37–10: 1595–614.

—— and Johnson, Christopher. (2000). Converging evidence for the notions of "subscene" and "primary scene". *Proceedings of the 23rd Annual Meeting of the Berkeley Linguistics Society*, 123–36. Berkeley, CA: Berkeley Linguistics Society.

Grice, Paul H. (1989). *Studies in the Way of Words*. Cambridge, MA: Harvard University Press.

Gries, Stefan Th. (2006). Corpus-based methods and cognitive semantics: The many meanings of "to run." In S. Th. Gries and A. Stefanowitsch (eds), *Corpora in Cognitive Linguistics: Corpus-based Approaches to Syntax and Lexis*, 57–99. Berlin: Mouton de Gruyter.

—— and Divjak, Dagmar. (2009). Behavioral profiles: A corpus-based approach to cognitive semantic analysis. In V. Evans and S. Pourcel (eds), *New Directions in Cognitive Linguistics*, 57–76. Amsterdam: John Benjamins.

Gumperz, John. (1982). *Discourse Strategies*. Cambridge: Cambridge University Press.

—— and Levinson, Stephen. (1996). *Rethinking Linguistic Relativity*. Cambridge: Cambridge University Press.

Haiman, John (1980). Dictionaries and encyclopedias. *Lingua*, 50: 329–57.

Hanks, Patrick. (1996). Contextual dependency and lexical sets. *International Journal of Corpus Linguistics*, 1 (1): 75–98.

Harder, Peter. (2009). Meaning as input: The instructional perspective. In V. Evans and S. Pourcel (eds), *New Directions in Cognitive Linguistics*, 15–26. Amsterdam: Johns Benjamins.

Harley, Trevor. (2008). *The Psychology of Language: From Data to Theory*, 3rd edition. Hove: Psychology Press.

Harrington, Deborah L., Haaland, Kathleen Y., and Knight, Robert T. (1998). Cortical networks underlying mechanisms of time perception. *Journal of Neuroscience*, 18 (3): 1085–95.

Heine, Bernd and Kuteva, Tania. (2007). *The Genesis of Grammar: A Reconstruction*. Oxford: Oxford University Press.

Herskovits, Annette. (1986). *Language and Spatial Cognition*. Cambridge: Cambridge University Press.

—— (1988). Spatial expressions and the plasticity of meaning. In B. Rudzka-Ostyn (ed.), *Topics in Cognitive Linguistics*, 271–98. Amsterdam: John Benjamins.

Hopper, Paul and Traugott, Elizabeth Closs. (2003). *Grammaticalization*, 2nd edition. Cambridge: Cambridge University Press.

Hurford, James. (2007). *Origins of Meaning*. Oxford: Oxford University Press.

Ivry, Richard B. and Spencer, Rebecca M. C. (2004). The neural representation of time. *Current Opinion in Neurobiology*, 14 (2): 225–32.

Jackendoff, Ray. (1983). *Semantics and Cognition*. Cambridge, MA: MIT Press.

—— (1990). *Semantic Structures*. Cambridge, MA: MIT Press.

—— (1992). *Languages of the Mind: Essays on Mental Representation*. Cambridge, MA: MIT Press.

—— (2002). *Foundations of Language: Brain, Meaning, Grammar, Evolution*. Oxford and New York: Oxford University Press.

Jaeger, Jeri and Ohala, John. (1984). On the structure of phonetic categories. *Proceedings of the 10th Annual Meeting of the Berkeley Linguistics Society*, 15–26. Berkeley, CA: Berkeley Linguistics Society.

James, William. ([1890] 1950). *The Principles of Psychology*. New York: Dover.

January, David and Kako, Edward. (2007). Re-evaluating evidence for the linguistic relativity hypothesis: Response to Boroditsky (2001). *Cognition*, 104: 417–26.

Jasmin, Kyle. (2008). *Declaring Genius at Customs*. Unpublished MA term paper, University of Brighton.

Johansson, Sverker. (2005). *Origins of Language: Constraints on Hypotheses*. Amsterdam: Benjamins.

Johnson, Mark. (1987). *The Body in the Mind: The Bodily Basis of Meaning, Imagination and Reason*. Chicago: University of Chicago Press.

—— (2007). *The Meaning of the Body: Aesthetics of Human Understanding*. Chicago: University of Chicago Press.

Johnson-Laird, Philip N. (1983). *Mental Models*. Cambridge, MA: Harvard University Press.

Jorg-Schmid, Hans. (2000). *English Abstract Nouns as Conceptual Shells: From Corpus to Cognition*. Berlin: Mouton de Gruyter.

Kaschak, Michael and Glenberg, Arthur. (2000). Constructing meaning: The role of affordances and grammatical constructions in sentence comprehension. *Journal of Memory and Language*, 43: 508–29.

Katz, Jerrold J. (1972). *Semantic Theory*. New York, NY: Harper and Row.

—— and Fodor, Jerry A. (1963). The structure of a semantic theory. *Language*, 39: 170–210.

—— and Postal, Paul M. (1964). *An Integrated Theory of Linguistic Descriptions*. Cambridge, MA: MIT Press.

Kay, Paul and Fillmore, Charles. (1999). Grammatical constructions and linguistic generalizations: The *What's X doing Y* construction. *Language*, 75: 1–34.

—— and McDaniel, Chad. (1978). The linguistic significance of the meanings of basic color terms. *Language*, 54–3: 610–46.

—— and Michaelis, Laura A. (forthcoming). Constructional meaning and compositionality. In C. Maienborn, K. von Heusinger, and P. Portner (eds), *Semantics: An International Handbook of Natural Language Meaning*. Berlin: Mouton de Gruyter.

Kemmerer, David and Tranel, Daniel. (2000). A double dissociation between linguistic and perceptual representations of spatial relationships. *Cognitive Neuropsychology*, 17: 393–414.

Kendon, Adam. (2004). *Gesture: Visible Action as Utterance*. Cambridge: Cambridge University Press.

Kövecses, Zoltán and Radden, Günter. (1998). Metonymy: Developing a cognitive linguistic view. *Cognitive Linguistics*, 9–1: 37–77.

Kreitzer, Anatol. (1997). Multiple levels of schematization: A study in the conceptualization of space. *Cognitive Linguistics*, 8–4: 291–325.

Lakoff, George. (1987). *Women, Fire and Dangerous Things: What Categories Reveal about the Mind*. Chicago: Chicago University Press.

—— (1990). The invariance hypothesis: Is abstract reason based on image-schemas? *Cognitive Linguistics*, 1 (1): 39–74.

—— (1993). The contemporary theory of metaphor. In A. Ortony (ed.), *Metaphor and Thought*, 2nd edition, 202–51. Cambridge: Cambridge University Press.

—— (1996). *Moral Politics: How Liberals and Conservatives Think*. Chicago: University of Chicago Press.

—— (2006). *Don't Think of an Elephant: Know your Values and Frame the Debate*. Vermont: Chelsea Green Publishing.

—— and Johnson, Mark. (1980). *Metaphors We Live By*. Chicago: University of Chicago Press.

—— —— (1999). *Philosophy in the Flesh*. New York: Basic Books.

—— and Thompson, Henry. (1975). Introduction to cognitive grammar. *Proceedings of the 1st Annual Meeting of the Berkeley Linguistics Society*, 295–313. Berkeley, CA: Berkeley Linguistics Society.

—— and Turner, Mark. (1989). *More than Cool Reason: A Field Guide to Poetic Metaphor*. Chicago: University of Chicago Press.

Landau, Barbara, Dessalegn, Banchiamlack, and Goldberg, Ariel Micah. (forthcoming). Language and space: Momentary interactions. In V. Evans and P. Chilton (eds), *Language, Cognition and Space: The State of the Art and New Directions*. London: Equinox Publishing.

Langacker, Ronald W. (1987). *Foundations of Cognitive Grammar: Volume I Theoretical Prerequisites*. Stanford: Stanford University Press.

—— (1991a). *Foundations of Cognitive Grammar: Volume II Theoretical Prerequisites*. Stanford: Stanford University Press.

—— (1991b). *Concept, Image, Symbol: The Cognitive Basis of Grammar*. Berlin: Mouton de Gruyter.

—— (1999). *Grammar and Conceptualization*. Berlin: Mouton de Gruyter.

—— (2000). A dynamic usage-based model. In M. Barlow and S. Kemmer (eds), *Usage-based Models of Language*, 1–64. Stanford, CA: CSLI Publications.

—— (2008). *Cognitive Grammar: A Basic Introduction*. Oxford: Oxford University Press.

Leezenberg, Michiel. (2001). *Contexts of Metaphor*. Oxford: Elsevier Science.

Levinson, Stephen. (1983). *Pragmatics*. Cambridge: Cambridge University Press.

—— (2000). *Presumptive Meanings: The Theory of Generalized Conversational Implicature*. Cambridge, MA: MIT Press.

Levinson, Stephen. (2003). *Space in Language and Cognition: Explorations in Linguistic Diversity.* Cambridge: Cambridge University Press.

Livingstone, Margaret and Hubel, David. (1988). Segregation of form, color, movement and depth: Anatomy, physiology and perception. *Science,* 240: 740–9.

Lucy, John. (1982). *Language Diversity and Thought: A Reformulation of the Linguistic Relativity Hypothesis.* Cambridge: Cambridge University Press.

Martin, Alex. (2001). Functional neuroimaging of semantic memory. In R. Cabeza and A. Kingstone (eds), *Handbook of Functional Neuroimaging of Cognition,* 153–86. Cambridge, MA: MIT Press.

—— (2007). The representation of object concepts in the brain. *Annual Review of Psychology,* 58: 25–45.

Mauk, Michael D. and Buonomano, Dean V. (2004). The neural basis of temporal processing. *The Annual Review of Neuroscience,* 27: 307–40.

McNeill, David. (1992). *Hand and Mind: What Gestures Reveal about Thought.* Chicago: University of Chicago Press.

Michaelis, Laura. A. (2003). Word meaning, sentence meaning, and syntactic meaning. In H. Cuyckens, R. Dirven, and J. Taylor (eds), *Cognitive Approaches to Lexical Semantics,* 163–210. Berlin: Mouton de Gruyter.

—— (2004). Type shifting in construction grammar: An integrated approach to aspectual coercion. *Cognitive Linguistics,* 15: 1–67.

—— and Lambrecht, Knud. (1996). Toward a construction-based model of language function: The case of nominal extraposition. *Language,* 72: 215–47.

Miller, George and Johnson-Laird, Philip. (1976). *Language and Perception.* Harvard: Harvard University Press.

Mithen, Steven. (1996). *The Prehistory of the Mind: A Search for the Origins of Art, Religion and Science.* London: Orion Books.

Moore, Kevin Ezra. (2000). Spatial experience and temporal metaphors in Wolof: Point of view, conceptual mapping and linguistic practice. Unpublished doctoral thesis, University of California, Berkeley.

—— (2006). Space-to-time mappings and temporal concepts. *Cognitive Linguistics,* 17–2: 199–244.

Munnich, Edward, Landau, Barbara, and Dosher, Barbara Anne. (2001). Spatial language and spatial representation: A cross-linguistic comparison. *Cognition,* 81 (3): 171–207.

Murphy, Gregory. (1991). Meaning and concepts. In P. J. Schwanenflugel (ed.), *The Psychology of Word Meanings,* 11–35. Hillsdale, NJ: Lawrence Erlbaum.

—— (1996). On metaphoric representation. *Cognition,* 60, 173–204.

Nerlich, Brigitte and Clarke, David D. (2007). Cognitive linguistics and the history of linguistics. In D. Geeraerts and H. Cuyckens (eds), *Handbook of Cognitive Linguistics,* 589–607. Oxford: Oxford University Press.

Núñez, Rafael, Motz, Benjamin, and Teuscher, Ursina. (2006). Time after time: The psychological reality of the Ego- and Time-Reference-Point distinction in metaphorical construals of time. *Metaphor and Symbol,* 21: 133–46.

—— and Sweetser, Eve. (2006). With the future behind them: convergent evidence from Aymara language and gesture in the crosslinguistic comparison of spatial construals of time. *Cognitive Science,* 30: 401–50.

O'Keefe, John. (1996). The spatial prepositions in English, vector grammar, and the cognitive map theory. In P. Bloom, M. A. Peterson, L. Nadel, and M. F. Garrett (eds), *Language and Space*, 277–316. Cambridge, MA: MIT Press.

Ornstein, Robert. ([1969]/1997). On the experience of time. Boulder, CO: Westview Press.

Ortony, Andrew. (1993). *Metaphor and Thought*, 2nd edition. Cambridge: Cambridge University Press.

Paivio, Allan. (1979). *Imagery and Verbal Processes*. New York: Holt, Rinehart and Winston.

—— (1986). *Mental Representations: A Dual Coding Approach*. Oxford: Oxford University Press.

Pöppel, Ernst. (1994). Temporal mechanisms in perception. In O. Sporns and G. Tononi (eds), *Selectionism and the Brain: International Review of Neurobiology*, 37: 185–201.

—— (1978). Time Perception. In R. Held, H. W. Leibowitz, and H.-L. Teuber (eds), *Handbook of Sensory Physiology*, 713–29. Heidelberg: Springer.

Pragglejaz Group. (2007). MIP: A method for identifying metaphorically used words in discourse. *Metaphor and Symbol*, 22 (1): 1–39.

Prinz, Jesse. (2002). *Furnishing the Mind: Concepts and their Perceptual Basis*. Cambridge, MA: MIT Press.

Pulvermüller, Friedemann. (1999). Words in the brain's language. *Behavioral and Brain Sciences*, 22: 253–336.

—— (2003). *The Neuroscience of Language: On Brain Circuits of Words and Serial Order*. Cambridge: Cambridge University Press.

Pustejovsky, James (1995). *The Generative Lexicon*. Cambridge, MA: MIT Press.

Radden, Günter. (2003). The metaphor TIME AS SPACE across languages. In N. Baumgarten, C. Böttger, M. Motz, and J. Probst (eds), *Übersetzen, Interkulturelle Kommunikation, Spracherwerb und Sprach-vermittlung—das Leben mit mehreren Sprachen. Festschrift für Juliane House zum 60 Geburtstag. Zeitschrift für Interkulturellen Fremdsprachenunterricht* [online], 8 (2/3): 1–14.

Recanati, François. (2004). *Literal Language*. Cambridge: Cambridge University Press.

Renfrew, Colin. (2007). *Prehistory: The Making of the Human Mind*. London: Weidenfield and Nicolson.

Rosch, Eleanor. (1978). Principles of categorization. In B. Lloyd and E. Rosch (eds), *Cognition and Categorization*, 27–48. Hillsdale, NJ: Erlbaum. Reprinted in E. Margolis and S. Laurence (eds), (1999), *Concepts: Core Readings*, 189–206. Cambridge, MA: MIT Press.

Ruhl, Charles. (1989). *On Monosemy: A Study in Linguistic Semantics*. New York, NY: State University of New York Press.

Sacks, Harvey, Schegloff, Emanuel, and Jefferson, Gail. (1974). A simplest systematics for the organisation of turn-taking for conversation. *Language*, 50: 696–735.

Sag, Ivan. (2007). *Sign-based Construction Grammar. An Informal Synopsis*. Unpublished manuscript. Available online at: <http://lingo.stanford.edu/sag/papers/theo-syno.pdf>.

Sandra, Dominiek. (1998). What linguists can and can't tell you about the human mind: A reply to Croft. *Cognitive Linguistics*, 9 (4): 361–478.

Schank, Roger. (1975). *Conceptual Information Processing*. New York: Elsevier.

—— (1982). *Dynamic Memory: A Theory of Reminding and Learning in Computers and People*. Cambridge: Cambridge University Press.

—— and Abelson, Robert. (1977). *Scripts, Plans, Goals, and Understanding: An Inquiry into Human Knowledge Structures*. Hillsdale, NJ: Lawrence Erlbaum.

—— and Kass, Alex. (1988). Knowledge representation in people and machines. In U. Eco, M. Santambrogio, and P. Violi (eds), *Meaning and Mental Representations*, 181–200. Bloomington, IN: Indiana University Press.

Schiffrin, Deborah. (1994). *Approaches to Discourse: Language as Social Interaction*. Oxford: Blackwell.

Searle, John. (1969). *Speech Acts: An Essay in the Philosophy of Language*. Cambridge: Cambridge University Press.

—— (1983). *Intentionality*. Cambridge: Cambridge University Press.

—— ([1979] 1993). Metaphor. In A. Ortony (ed.), *Metaphor and Thought*, 2nd edition, 83–111. Cambridge: Cambridge University Press.

Shepard, Roger N. and Cooper, Lynn A. (1982). *Mental Images and their Transformations*. Cambridge: Cambridge University Press.

Shinohara, Kazuko. (1999). *Epistemology of Space and Time*. Kwansei, Japan: Gakuin University Press.

Silva Sinha, Vera da, Sinha, Chris, Zinken, Jörg, and Sampaio, Wany. (forthcoming). When Time is not Space: The social and linguistic construction of time intervals in an Amazonian culture. *Journal of Pragmatics*.

Sinha, Chris and Kuteva, Tania. (1995). Distributed spatial semantics. *Nordic Journal of Linguistics*, 18: 167–99.

Sperber, Dan and Wilson, Deidre. (1995). *Relevance: Communication and Cognition*, 2nd edition. Oxford: Blackwell.

Stalnaker, Richard. (1978). Assertion. In P. Cole (ed.), *Syntax and Semantics 9: Pragmatics*, 315–32. New York: Academic Press.

Stern, Josef. (2000). *Metaphor in Context*. Cambridge, MA: MIT Press.

Sweetser, Eve. (1999). Compositionality and blending: Semantic composition, in a cognitively realistic framework. In T. Janssen and G. Redeker (eds), *Cognitive Linguistics: Foundations, Scope and Methodology*, 129–62. Berlin: Mouton de Gruyter.

Talmy, Leonard. (2000). *Toward a Cognitive Semantics* (2 volumes). Cambridge, MA: MIT Press.

Taylor, John. (2002). *Cognitive Grammar*. Oxford: Oxford University Press.

—— (2003). *Linguistic Categorization*, 3rd edition. Oxford: Oxford University Press.

Taylor, Lawrence J. and Zwaan, Rolf A. (2009). Action in cognition: The case of language. *Language and Cognition*, 1 (1): 45–58.

Thompson, Sandra A. (2002). "Object complements" and conversation. *Studies in Language* 26 (1): 125–64.

Thompson-Schill, Sharon. (2003). Neuroimaging studies of semantic memory: Inferring "how" from "where". *Neuropsychologia*, 41: 280–92.

Tomasello, Michael. (1999). *The Cultural Origins of Human Cognition*. Harvard: Harvard University Press.

—— (2003). *Constructing a Language: A Usage-based Theory of Language Acquisition*. Harvard: Harvard University Press.

Tranel, Daniel and Kemmerer, David. (2004). Neuroanatomical correlates of locative prepositions. *Cognitive Neuropsychology*, 21: 719–49.

Traugott, Elizabeth Closs. (1978). On the expression of spatio-temporal relations in language. In J. Greenberg (ed.), *Universals of Human Language*, 369–400. Stanford, CA: Stanford University Press.

—— and Dasher, Richard. (2004). *Regularity in Semantic Change*. Cambridge: Cambridge University Press.

Turner, Frederick and Pöppel, Ernst. (1983). The neural lyre: Poetic meter, the brain and time. *Poetry*, 142 (5): 277–309.

Turner, Mark. (1991). *Reading Minds: The Study of English in the Age of Cognitive Science*. Princeton, NJ: Princeton University Press.

Tyler, Andrea and Evans, Vyvyan. (2001). Reconsidering prepositional polysemy networks: The case of *over*. *Language*, 77 (4): 724–65.

—— —— (2003). *The Semantics of English Prepositions: Spatial Scenes, Embodied Meaning and Cognition*. Cambridge: Cambridge University Press.

Vandeloise, Claude. (1990). Representation, prototypes, and centrality. In S. Tsohatzidis (ed.), *Meanings and Prototypes: Studies in Linguistic Categorization*, 403–37. London: Routledge.

—— (1991). *Spatial Prepositions: A Case Study from French* (trans. Anna R. K. Bosch). Chicago: University of Chicago Press.

—— (1994). Methodology and analyses of the preposition *in*. *Cognitive Linguistics*, 5 (2): 157–84.

Varela, Francisco, Thompson, Evan, and Rosch, Eleanor. (1991). *The Embodied Mind: Cognitive Science and Human Experience*. Cambridge, MA: MIT Press.

Vigliocco, Gabriella, Meteyard, Lotte, Andrews, Mark, and Kousta, Stavroula. (2009). Toward a theory of semantic representation. *Language and Cognition*, 1 (2).

Walsh, Vincent. (2003). A theory of magnitude: Common cortical metrics of time, space and quantity. TRENDS in Cognitive Science, 7 (11): 483–8.

Wearden, John and Penton-Voak, Ian. (1995). Feeling the heat: Body temperature and the rate of subjective time, revisited. *Quarterly Journal of Experimental Psychology*, 48B: 129–41.

Whitney, Paul. (1998). *The Psychology of Language*. Boston, MA: Houghton Mifflin.

Wierzbicka, Anna. (1988). *The Semantics of Grammar*. Amsterdam: John Benjamins.

—— (1996). *Semantics: Primes and Universals*. Oxford: Oxford University Press.

Wilson, Margaret. (2002). Six views of embodied cognition. *Psychonomic Bulletin and Review*, 9 (4): 625–36.

Yu, Ning. (1998). *The Contemporary Theory of Metaphor: A Perspective from Chinese*. Amsterdam: John Benjamins.

Zakay, Dan and Block, Richard A. (1997). Temporal cognition. *Current Directions in Psychological Science*, 6: 12–16.

Zeki Semir (1992). The visual image in mind and brain. *Scientific American*, 267 (3): 68–76.

—— and Shipp, Stewart. (1988). The functional logic of cortical connections. *Nature*, 335: 311–17.

Ziemke, Tom. (2003). What's that thing called embodiment? In *Proceedings of the 25th Annual Meeting of the Cognitive Science Society*, 1134–9. Mahwah, NJ: Lawrence Erlbaum.

Zinken, Jörg. (forthcoming). Temporal frames of reference. In V. Evans and P. Chilton (eds), *Language, Cognition and Space: The State of the Art and New Directions*. London: Equinox Publishing.

Zlatev, Jordan. (1997). *Situated embodiment: Studies in the Emergence of Spatial Meaning*. Stockholm: Gotab.

—— (2003). Polysemy or generality? Mu. In H. Cuyckens, R. Dirven, and J. Taylor (eds), *Cognitive Approaches to Lexical Semantics*, 447–94. Berlin: Mouton de Gruyter.

Zwaan, Rolf A. (1999). Embodied cognition, perceptual symbols, and situation models. *Discourse Processes*, 28: 81–8.

—— (2004). The immersed experiencer: toward an embodied theory of language comprehension. In B. H. Ross (ed.) *The Psychology of Learning and Motivation*, 35–62). New York, NY: Academic Press.

—— and Kaschak, Michael P. (2008). Language in the brain, body and world. In P. Robbins and M. Aydede (eds), *The Cambridge Handbook of Situated Cognition*, 368–81. Cambridge: Cambridge University Press.

—— and Madden, Carol. (2004). Updating situation models. *Journal of Experimental Psychology: Learning, Memory, and Cognition*, 30: 283–8.

—— and Radvansky, Gabriel A. (1998). Situation models in language and memory. *Psychological Bulletin*, 123: 162–85.

Index

Lightning Source UK Ltd.
Milton Keynes UK
02 August 2010

157671UK00003B/3/P